POLITICS OF RIGHTFUL KILLING

Politics of
[RIGHTFUL KILLING]

Civil Society, Gender, and Sexuality in Weblogistan

SIMA SHAKHSARI

DUKE UNIVERSITY PRESS *Durham and London* 2020

© 2020 Duke University Press
All rights reserved

Designed by Matthew Tauch
Typeset in Minion by Westchester Publishing Services

Library of Congress Cataloging-in-Publication Data
Names: Shakhsari, Sima, [date] author.
Title: Politics of rightful killing : civil society, gender, and
  sexuality in Weblogistan / Sima Shakhsari.
Description: Durham : Duke University Press, 2020. | Includes
  bibliographical references and index.
Identifiers: LCCN 2019015470 (print) | LCCN 2019981093 (ebook)
ISBN 9781478006657 (paperback)
ISBN 9781478005964 (hardcover)
ISBN 9781478007333 (ebook)
Subjects: LCSH: Blogs—Social aspects—Iran. | Blogs—Political
  aspects—Iran. | Civil society—Iran. | Political participation—
  Iran—Computer network resources. | Cyberspace—Social
  aspects—Iran. | Cyberspace—Political aspects—Iran.
Classification: LCC HM851 .S535 2020 (print) | LCC HM851
  (ebook) | DDC 306.20955—dc23
LC record available at https://lccn.loc.gov/2019015470
LC ebook record available at https://lccn.loc.gov/2019981093

Cover art: Kree Arvanitas, *Twitter Revolution in Heaven*,
2011. Courtesy of the artist.

[Contents]

vii		ACKNOWLEDGMENTS
xiii		PROLOGUE
1		Introduction
32	CHAPTER 1	Weblogistan and the Iranian Diaspora: Nation and Its Re-territorializations in Cyberspace
72	CHAPTER 2	Civil Society (*jaame'e-ye madani*), Soccer, and Gendered Politics in Weblogistan: The 2005 Presidential Election
112	CHAPTER 3	Whores, Homos, and Feminists: Weblogistan's Anti-modern Others
145	CHAPTER 4	Weblogistan and Its Homosexual Problem
169	CHAPTER 5	The War Machine, Neoliberal *Homo Œconomicus*, and the Experts
195	CODA	Revolutionary Ends: Weblogistan's Afterlife

207	APPENDIX
209	NOTES
257	REFERENCES
277	INDEX

[Acknowledgments]

This book has been "touched" by so many people who, in one way or another, have been a part of its lengthy and ongoing process of becoming. There are no words to describe the paralyzing grief that comes with the tyranny of geography—the cruelty of mourning one's beloveds from afar twice in one year. During the writing of this book, I lost two of my dearest, mother and my *paareye jaan*, Farideh Mirzapour, and my *noor-e cheshm* sister, Monir Mojgan Shakhsari. This book is for them and for my gentle, hardworking, and generous father, Karim Shakhsari, who left us not too long after the end of the Iran–Iraq war, on a day when "black rain" poured on Tehran.

In 2010, soon after I finished the writing of what was then my doctoral dissertation, I contacted Courtney Berger at Duke University Press. Since then, Courtney has been the calm and patient dream editor who allowed time for self-care and grief, without making the process feel like a soulless assembly. I cannot thank her enough for her graceful guidance and her support. Sandra Korn, Susan Albury, the editorial board, and other staff at Duke University made the multiple stages of the process into a pleasant experience. My sincere gratitude to three anonymous readers who provided invaluable and generous feedback. I am indebted to Sandy Soto for meticulously editing several chapters of this book and for her insightful comments. Many thanks to Harshit Rathi for his help with indexing and permissions.

It is rare that one's undergraduate professor becomes a lifelong mentor and friend. Minoo Moallem is that rare being whose "Women in the Muslim and Arab World" course in the early 1990s at San Francisco State University attracted me and many other young queer Middle Eastern students. Since then, Minoo has mentored me as my master's thesis advisor, dissertation committee member, and friend. Her fierceness, wisdom, and genuine care have helped me navigate and survive the ups and downs and the toxicity of the neoliberal academic business. Inderpal Grewal, who "converted" me to the cult of women and gender studies when I was a premedical undergraduate student at San Francisco State University, continues to be a significant inspiration. Taking my first women's studies course with Inderpal in early 1990s at SFSU motivated me to focus my course work on gender and sexuality, and led me to antiviolence activist work in San Francisco after graduation. Eight years later, I found myself again in the classroom at SFSU's women's studies MA program, learning from Inderpal and Minoo, both of whom convinced me to pursue a PhD in anthropology at a time when doctoral programs in women and gender studies that offered a postcolonial and transnational feminist approach were rare. While I take responsibility for all the shortcomings of this book, I owe my intellectual trajectories and my transnational feminist practice to Minoo and Inderpal. Even though I was never "officially" Caren Kaplan's student, I consider her my mentor. Caren helped me with the first draft of my book proposal and gave me excellent advice about the book. If there is such a thing as teaching someone to "stay out of trouble," Minoo, Inderpal, and Caren, with their wealth of experience and knowledge, have done exactly that for me, while teaching me to "trouble" the untroubled.

Many thanks to the faculty in the Department of Anthropology at Stanford University, from whom I learned immensely during my graduate studies. In particular, my advisors, Miyako Inoue and Purnima Mankekar, and professors Akhil Gupta, Barbara Voss, James Ferguson, Paula Ebron, and Renato Rosaldo were instrumental in my intellectual growth. I benefited from the mentorship of Afsaneh Najmabadi and Leila Ahmed during my exchange-scholar semester at Harvard University. Fellow Stanford graduate students, among them Aisha Beliso de Jesus, Chiarra De Cessari, Erica Williams, Lalaie Ameeriar, Rania Kassab Sweis, Jocelyn Lim Chua, Fernando Armstrong-Furero, Angel Roque, Kristin Monroe, Nikhil Anand, Elif Babul, Robert Samet, Ramah McKay, Tania Ahmad, Zhanara Nauruzbayeva, Nina Hazleton, Bryn Williams, Aisha Ghani, Tomas Matza, and Marcia Ochoa, provided good conversations and much-needed moral support during graduate school. Neha Vora at UC Irvine, Niki Akhavan at UC Santa Cruz, and Mana Kia and Alireza Doostdar at Harvard were fellow graduate students whose friendship made graduate school much more fulfilling.

My gratitude to Elizabeth Gregory, Guillermo de los Reyes, Dina Alsowayel, Gabriela Baeza, Jennifer Wingard, and Hosam Aboul Ela, colleagues at the University of Houston, where I was a postdoctoral fellow between 2010 and 2012. Elora Shehubbudin, Rosemary Hennessy, Jennifer Tyburczy, and Brian Riedel at Rice University were amazing collaborators and colleagues. Yasmine Ramadan, Lamia Balafrej, and Catia Confortini at Wellesley College provided laughter and camaraderie in a "dry town" where liberal racism abounds. My students at Wellesley and the Wellesley Students for Justice in Palestine inspired me with their determination. The "sex fellows" and faculty at the University of Pennsylvania's Humanities Forum, in particular Kadji Amin, Tan Hoang Nguyen, Zeb Tortorici, Durba Mitra, Hsiao-Wen Cheng, Heather Love, and James English, provided stimulating conversations and rigorous critique.

I am thankful to Richa Nagar, David Valentine, Eden Torres, Karen Ho, and Kevin Murphy, whose mentorship and support have been humbling. Richa is her own category and I cannot thank her enough for her integrity and unmatched and ethical commitment to junior faculty. I have benefited from conversations with the faculty at the Gender, Women and Sexuality Studies Department, Interdisciplinary Center for Global Change (ICGC), Race, Indigeneity, Gender and Sexuality Studies Initiative (RIGS), and colleagues in the Middle East, North Africa and Islamic Studies (MENAIS) Collective at the University of Minnesota (UMN). Many of my UMN colleagues, in particular Roozbeh Shirazi, Serra Hakyemez, Zozan Pehlivan, Joseph Farag, Sonali Pahwa, Jennifer Row, and Aisha Ghani have been writing buddies and/or provided good conversations over cocktails and hookah. My thanks to members of the UMN Bodies and Borders research cluster, MENAIS writing group, and the audience at the UMN Geography Coffee Hour for their invaluable feedback. UMN undergraduate and graduate students and Teaching Assistants continue to amaze me. Among them, Qais Munhazim, Simi Kang, Nithya Rajan, Emina Buzinkic, Samira Musleh, Katayoun Amjadi, Hae Seo Kim, Khoi Nguyen, Demiliza Sagaral Saramosing, Naimah Petigny, Beaudelaine Pierre, Joanna Núñez, Jose Meño Santillana, Ariana Yang, Kathryn Savage, John Kendall, Mary Marchan, Sara Musaifer, Kai Pyle, Sayan Bhattacharya, Ilana Turner, Nina Medvedeva, AK Wright, Tankut Atuk, and Miray Philips have challenged me to think in new ways with their insights.

I greatly benefited from the feedback I received at different universities where I presented parts of this work. Among these are UC Berkeley's Center for Middle East Studies; Yale's Women, Gender, and Sexuality Studies Program; Cultural Studies at UC Davis; Women's Studies, Center for Persian Studies, and Center for Ethnography at UC Irvine; Rice University's Department of Anthropology; the Center for the Study of Women, Gender, and Sexuality at Rice University; Feminist and Gender Studies at Colorado Springs College; Women and Gender Studies at the University of Toronto; the Center for American Studies and Research at the American University of Beirut; the Department of Social and Cultural Analysis at New York University; the Department of Anthropology at Texas A&M; and the Middle East Studies Program at Tufts University. I am thankful to colleagues at these universities, in particular Minoo Moallem, Inderpal Grewal, Caren Kaplan, Jennifer Terry, Rosemary Hennessy, Elora Shehabuddin, Nadia Guessous, Victoria Tahmasebi, Jasbir Puar, Lisa Duggan, Neha Vora, Vanita Reddy, and Thomas Abowd. I am especially grateful to Nadje Al-Ali and Lizzie Thynne for featuring "Weblogistan Goes to War" (an early version of chapter 5) in the special launch of the *Feminist Review* at Sussex University, and to Gholam Khiabany for his response to the article.

Many colleagues and friends in different universities have provided unwavering support and intellectual engagement, in particular Nadine Naber, Elham Mireshghi, Orkideh Behrouzan, Simona Sharoni, Rabab Abdulhadi, Kehaulani Kauanui, Mimi Nguyen, Wazhmah Osman, Deborah Cohler, Dima Ayoub, Paola Bacchetta, Maya Mikdashi, Asli Zengin, Adi Kuntsman, Abigail Boggs, Anjali Arondekar, Laleh Khalili, Frances Hasso, Sherene Seikaly, and Zainab Saleh. I am grateful to Jasbir Puar for her valuable feedback and response to the book at UMN in spring 2019, and to the participants whose insights have helped me think about what might come in the future after this book.

There are no words that can possibly express my gratitude to Mahsa Nirui, my chosen kin whose unconditional friendship has kept me sane during the hardest times of my life in the past two decades. My sister, Flor Shakhsari, and my nieces and nephew, Sahar, Baharak, and Ali Majidinejad, have cried and laughed with me from afar over memories of our departed beloveds. My Bay Area fam, Setareh Sarrafan, Luella Penserga, Julia La Chica, Alma Alfie, Simin Yahaghi, Angelica Patrick, and Sorraya Shahin, have given me love, food, and laughter when I most needed these. Some bloggers call blogs their digital homes. I am indebted to Iranian bloggers and blog readers from all over the world, especially those in Toronto, Washington, DC, and Amsterdam, for opening their physical and digital homes to me. I am grateful for the friendships that emerged, the food that was shared, the tears that were shed, and the fights that made Weblogistan Weblogistan. I am thankful to all my friends in northern and southern California, Wellesley, Northampton, Toronto, Houston, Philadelphia, Denizli, Istanbul, Kayseri, and the Twin Cities and to my online community of friends whose support during the long process of research and writing I cannot take for granted. In particular, I am indebted to Nazli Kamvari, Sanam Dolatshahi, Farahnaz Kamvari, Behnam Kamvari, Aida Ahadiyani, Afra Pourdad, Kaveh Khojasteh, Negar Khalvati, Azar Saneei, Farnaz Seifi, Esha Momeni, Sussan Tahmasebi, Fataneh Kianersi, Leili Behbahani, Parisa Parnian, Ali Eslami, Anahita Forati, Barra Cohen, Samantha Lee, Nasreen Mohammad, Maryam Houshyar, Niloufar Hedjazi, Layli Shirani, Tomas Turrubiate (and the house of Russells), Stalina Villarreal, Nelia Jafroodi, Bahareh Jalali, Alireza Hariri, Ali Taj, Ari Ariel, Loana Valencia, Nadereh Fanaeian, Gol Hoghooghi, Ana Ghoreishian, Dima Ayoub, Bashezo Nicole Boyd, Genevieve Rodriguez, Maxwell Dickson, and Basak Durgun. I am so grateful to Kree Arvanitas for allowing me to use her beautiful art and to Matthew Tauch for designing the cover of this book.

As strange as it feels to thank institutions, especially in the age of corporate personhood, I must acknowledge Stanford University, University of Houston, Wellesley College, University of Pennsylvania, and University of Minnesota. Without the support of these institutions during my graduate student career, postdoctoral fellowships, and tenure track employment, this book would have not been possible in its current form.

And last but not least, my cats, Googoosh, Pashmak, and Shazdeh, kept me company, gave me gentle love, and snored away through multiple revisions. They have their paw marks all over this manuscript.

[Prologue]

Mapping the house and housing the map, the peddler who carried the shahr-e farang *box on his back walked through the familiar spaces of my childhood alleys, where my ambivalent female body, not marked by a deviant desire yet, deviated from school to the world of sightseeing.* "Shahr shahr-e farangeh bia-o tamasha kon, Az hameh rangeh bia—o tamasha kon!" *(This city is a foreign city, come and look, it is from all colors, come and look!) This rap along with the melody of its narrator's voice drew my seven-year-old body to the pleasures of scopophilia, and the shahr-e farang (foreign city), the house-shaped box that he carried on his back as he traveled through my then familiar, and now unfamiliar city, Tehran, drew the porous frontiers of my traveling imagination. Putting my ten-rial coin in his scabbed hands, I would wait for the peddler to ground the mobile house and open the round window to the liminal space of this house that contained the world. My left eye, which connected my body to the peephole, would not blink, letting my imagination travel through time and space with the narrator's voice as I tightly framed foreign cities, housed in the four-legged box, with my young, eager hands that not too many years from then would turn into fists and write anti-imperialist slogans on the walls of the revolted city. In another ten years, those hands would be laid on a cold table in the house of immigration to be mapped for their marked foreignness. Having changed their status of alienation, my hands would be summoned to be fingerprinted in the home they had inhabited—but not considered to be habituated—for years. And with a permit to dwell and travel, the same hands would increasingly be under surveillance for the possible "threat" they pose to homeland security:* "inee keh mibini Taj-e mahal tu Hindustaneeee.... In mojassameye azadiye o inja Amrikaaast...."

("This that you see is Taj Mahaaaaaaal in Hindustan. . . . This one is the Statue of Libertyyyyyyy, and here is Americaaaaaa."). That rhythmic voice and the box of pictures that housed my dwelling and motion are all distant memories now. Liberty remains nothing but a statue.[1]

...

This was the first entry on my English blog, *Farangopolis*. I made up the word *Farangopolis* by combining the Persian word *farang*[2] (foreign) and the Greek term *polis* (city-state) to reflect my liminal position and my frequent use of Pinglish/Finglish, a combination of Persian/Farsi and English that is often used by diaspora Iranians in the United States. Neither here nor there, *Farangopolis*[3] was an ironic replacement for the *shahr-e farang* of my childhood. *Shahr-e farang* (foreign city), the house-shaped picture box that contained images of foreign lands, and *shahr-e farangi*, a man who walked the picture box in Tehran's alleys and told stories of *farang*, disappeared by late 1970s. Over two decades later, it was *Farangopolis* that granted me the luxury of traveling virtually, without the anxieties of crossing borders with my Iranian passport. In this virtual *Shahr-e Farang*, I was both the spectator and the *shahr-e-farangi*, the flaneur who walked through the alleys of Weblogistan, a virtual homeland for Iranian bloggers across the world (see figure P.1). I joined the "netizens" of Weblogistan, an assemblage of Persian blogs—home pages banded together in virtual re-territorializations, where homeland politics were discussed passionately, where flame wars were ferociously fought, and where the politics of citizenship and belonging surfaced violently. I visited the virtual homes of bloggers who were strangers to me and received the visits of strangers in mine, a daily habitual practice that Doostdar (2004) has aptly compared to the Iranian practice of *deed-o-baazdeed* (to see and see again).

While the sudden popularization of blogs and the proliferation of discourses of freedom through blogging in the mainstream international media were what initially piqued my academic interest in Weblogistan, I became attached to it and passionately participated in debates about Iranian politics for reasons beyond the purpose of my research. As I read blogs written by Iranians from Iran and its diaspora, I felt a sense of belonging to a community of Iranians inside and outside of Iran. Even though there was no uniform "we" in Weblogistan, a sense of community among different blogging circles connected bloggers in Iran and its diaspora. As David Morley (2000) argues, while the desire for belonging is often equated with politically regressive and

FIGURE P.1 The author's blog (*Farangopolis*), one-year anniversary post, December 15, 2005, http://farangeopolis.blogspot.com/2005/12/blog-post_15.html. The *Shahr-e farang* images on the headboard are from Mahmoud Pakzad's Old Tehran Series, which are found on Iranian.com.

reactionary nostalgia, one needs to come to terms with this desire and account for affective attachments that cannot be reduced to nationalistic nostalgia. Morley quotes Wheeler's suggestion that one needs to articulate "a politics capable of constituting a 'we' which is not essentialist, fixed, separatist, decisive, defensive or exclusive" (Wheeler quoted in Morley, 247). This was the kind of politics that I hoped to cultivate through blogging. My longing for community and home, albeit multiple, was fraught with contradictions. I shared the desire to belong through a phantasmic movement with many diaspora and "resident" Iranian bloggers whose connection to other Iranians was maintained through their weblogs. It was the movement in spaces of dwelling and haptic dynamic, "a fantasmic structure of lived space and habitable narrative" (Bruno 2002, 6), that linked my diasporic body to other Iranian bloggers in Weblogistan.

Yet my desire to belong to an online community of Iranians was soon transformed into a constant (and at times violent) shuttling between inclusions and exclusions that marked the bounds of normative Iranianness in Weblogistan.[4] It was through my online and offline participation in the world of Persian blogging and my affective attachments to it that I realized how conflict and violence are erased in the celebratory mainstream representations of Weblogistan. My online interactions in Weblogistan repeatedly proved that online bodies were subjected to the rules and regulations of the "offline" life. Whether it was violence in the name of nationalism, liberation, secularism, democracy, religion, class, heteronormative family, or racial purity, Weblogistan was a battleground where contestations over a desired future that has not yet come culminated in a valorized notion of civil society.

A Note on Methods

Before I launched the "physical" ethnographic part of my research on Weblogistan, I had no models of a combined online and offline ethnography.[5] I often wondered about strategies to observe bloggers, who for the most part blog in the privacy of their homes, in cafés, or at work. I started the online participant-observation research before I arrived in the physical field. As the first step in my online ethnography, I launched *Farangopolis* in Persian and English in December 2004. Hoder, the "godfather of Persian blogging," had published instructions on his blog about "how to make your own weblog." However, his instructions were no longer applicable to the new Blogger template. I asked a software engineer friend and a blog reader in the San Francisco Bay Area to change the HTML code of an English template so that I could start my blog in Persian. Eventually I learned basic codes needed for changing the appearance of my blog. Shortly after I moved to Toronto for fieldwork, the writer of the weblog *Hapali*, a recent immigrant and a doctoral student at the time, and another Toronto-based blog reader (also a recent immigrant and a software engineer) volunteered to give my blog a makeover so that it would be more pleasing to the eye.

In the first post in my Persian blog, I introduced myself as a graduate student at Stanford University's Cultural and Social Anthropology Department and explained that my research was about the gendered and sexed performances of Iranianness among diasporic bloggers in Weblogistan. I also wrote a short description about my research project in the "About Me" section and posted it as a permanent feature of my blog in the sidebar. A popular blogger immediately linked to my Persian blog and welcomed me to Weblogistan by writing a post about my blog. The number of visitors to my newly launched blog increased after Iranian.com, a popular Iranian website in English, linked to my blog. Soon the news about my blog made it to *Damasanj*, a tool that ranked the events of Weblogistan, based on the number of links that a blog received. In January 2005, when talks about a possible attack on Iran escalated in the news, a group of us (four Iranian graduate students at the time) launched the English-language blog *No War on Iran*. Around the same time, one of the first Iranian women bloggers to write a popular blog approached me to start an antiwar blog with a group of Iranian bloggers who had differing political inclinations. Consequently, I participated in *Iranians for Peace*, the group blog that included a network of Iranian bloggers in Iran and its diaspora. My participation in these two group blogs introduced me to more bloggers and blog readers. Eventually, my blog became relatively popular and received between six hundred and a thousand hits per day. I became a "resident" of Weblogistan and forged several online friendships in different locations. I "exited" both offline and online fields completely in 2007, in order to be able to reflect and write about my observations about this fast-changing field.

After my blog became well known in Weblogistan, I started the offline part of my ethnography. In 2005 and 2006, concomitant to my online ethnography, I conducted offline ethnography in Toronto and Washington. While Persian-language blogs are written in numerous locations, for feasibility purposes I limited the offline part of my project to these two physical locations. Looking at field as *habitus* rather than as a physical place (Clifford 1997, 54), I conceptualize Weblogistan as an embodied field site that comprises a myriad of online and offline locations that are connected discursively and transnationally. Thus, I approach these locations not as comparative sites of analysis but as sites that are constituted in relation to one another and necessarily connected through transnational movement of information, capital, and people. I chose Toronto because some of the most popular Persian-language bloggers who wrote about homeland politics lived and work there. I spent twelve months among Iranian bloggers in Toronto, met with them on a regular basis, conducted three focus groups, and conducted semiformal in-depth interviews with fifteen bloggers and blog readers. Because I had already developed online blogging relationships with bloggers in Toronto, it did not take me long after I moved there to meet them in person and to attend social gatherings in which bloggers and their friends talked about a range of issues, from Iran's politics to life in Toronto, and gossiped about the "hot" topics and sex scandals in Weblogistan.

I chose blogs through "snowball sampling" (reading blogs that are linked in "link dumps" and "blogrolls" of other bloggers who wrote about homeland politics), traced blogging circles (who reads who and who links to whom), and paid attention to online interactions between bloggers. Like the online part of my research, the offline part was also based on "snowball sampling," with bloggers introducing me to others in social settings. I regularly attended social events and parties where other bloggers and blog readers were present, and where discussions about blogs made it into offline spaces.

For the first two weeks, I stayed with a popular and controversial Toronto blogger who generously offered to share her student housing apartment with me. She and another blogger introduced me to many Toronto bloggers and blog readers, and helped me find an apartment near the housing complex where many Iranian student bloggers lived. For the most part, nonstudent bloggers lived in the North York area of Toronto, where a high concentration of Iranians resided. A few months after moving to Toronto, with the help of Agora, the Iranian group at the University of Toronto, I organized three focus groups and invited bloggers and blog readers to discuss reasons for blogging, censorship, gender and sexuality, and ongoing debates about practicing democracy in Weblogistan. These focus groups enabled bloggers—many of whom knew about one another's blogs but had not met offline—to meet in person and form offline friendships. On one occasion after a focus group meeting, for example, I accompanied several women bloggers and blog readers to a café, where we continued our discussion about Weblogistan in an informal setting. It didn't take long before the serious debate about the politics of blogging ended in a humorous conversation about body hair, waxing, threading, and gossip about the misogynistic men in Weblogistan. A few days later, the women bloggers gathered at my apartment, where we cooked Iranian food, compared recipes, and discussed a range of issues from women's rights and electoral politics in Iran to immigrant life in Toronto.

Even though most of my offline fieldwork took place in Toronto, I spent four months in Washington, DC. While the number of Washington-area bloggers is not comparable to that of Toronto, Washington hosts many Iranian nonprofit political lobbying groups. In Washington I socialized with bloggers and blog readers, interviewed bloggers and people who worked with think tanks and nonprofit organizations, conducted three focus groups, and attended different Iranian social and cultural events. I also spent a month in Amsterdam to visit Radio Zamaneh, "the radio of Weblogistan," in order to conduct interviews with staff of that radio. Even though my stay was just a month long, I spent long hours in the studio observing the production process and socialized with the Zamaneh staff after work, talking to them about Weblogistan. After my physical fieldwork, I followed up with bloggers over the phone.

When reviewing my interviews for the writing of this book, it was often difficult to determine how much potentially identifying information to include. This was particularly a dilemma if the data involved bloggers who were later arrested in Iran or bloggers who had been hired by U.S. Department of State–funded media and other entities and think tanks that were interested in a regime change in Iran.[6] I had to navigate how much to divulge about my offline interactions with these individuals and how much to disguise the identities of bloggers. I did not want to jeopardize their credibility among other bloggers and/or pose safety concerns for them. I also wanted to be mindful in relation to bloggers' private lives, which included spousal relationships, non-hetero-normative sexual desires, and family issues. I came to terms with the fact that the point of my ethnography was not to "expose" people or to "unveil" some hidden truth about Weblogistan but to analyze the way that Weblogistan as a site of subject formation and as a lived space was implicated in the geopolitics, necropolitics, and biopolitics of the "war on terror." Most of what I have included here is what was public knowledge, either in blogs or in offline interactions. After years of contemplation, for the sake of readability and consistency, I use the real names of bloggers in some parts of this book and use pseudonyms in other parts. When discussing blog content and other material that were publicly available at the time of this research, I use the names of blogs and bloggers.[7] I also use the real names of bloggers when discussing offline observations in a public setting such as public lectures. In all other cases such as one-on-one interviews, I use pseudonyms. Where I use an individual's real name during an interview, it is with the interviewee's consent.

My participation in the world of Persian blogging was not only an emotionally taxing experience but also one that was formed by affective intensities that characterize homeland politics and the violence of freedom in times of war. I forged many friendships in Weblogistan that extended outside the virtual world of blogging, and I also made many enemies in violent exchanges in a virtual setting that claimed to be a medium for practicing democracy. Because the production of knowledge about Iran is intertwined with the geopolitics of the Middle East, taking the position of the "native ethnographer" was fraught with concerns and fears that haunted me as a graduate student at the time. The production of expertise about Iran in think tanks, such as the Iran Democracy Project at the Hoover Institute at Stanford University, the institution where I was a doctoral student, brought these concerns and fears close to home. Like many Middle Eastern researchers, my research and writing were (and still are) inevitably permeated by apprehensions about surveillance, scrutiny, and appropriation by the knowledge-production and security industries that are closely connected with academia and serve militaristic agendas under the guise of democracy projects. At times, my vulnerability as a graduate student who wrote against a lucrative knowledge-production industry was overwhelming.

With the increased surveillance and harassment of Middle Eastern and Muslim immigrants in the United States and Canada, there was a well-founded fear of deportation for many Iranians. Several students who held student visas or had conditional residency were concerned about openly criticizing the U.S. state or the Canadian state. Some of my interlocutors were suspicious of my project, fearing that I worked for the intelligence services of the "home" or the "host" state. Considering the history of U.S. intervention in Iran and the political context of the time of my fieldwork, these fears were quite understandable. During the "war on terror," when jobs for Persian-speaking immigrants were mainly in the intelligence and security industries (see chapter 5), several neoconservative think tanks and state surveillance agencies hired diasporic Iranians as "experts" or employed them in the security industry. On the other hand, the Iranian state's crackdown on Iranian activists under the rhetoric of national security (a reaction to the "democratization projects" of the United States and Europe) raised alarm among bloggers who feared that their public political positions could jeopardize their safety if they visited Iran. As a result, some bloggers approached interviews with understandable skepticism. But this culture of fear also created a hostile environment in Weblogistan, where accusations were thrown around like confetti. On a few occasions, anonymous readers and internet trolls accused me and several other bloggers of spying for either the United States or Iran.

Geopolitical concerns aside, my research in Weblogistan was fraught with other difficulties that had to do with my sexuality. While I never "came out" as queer in my blog, the offline interactions with certain homophobic informants generated rumors about my masculine appearance and sexuality, which in turn created tensions in offline and online interactions. A few homophobic men undermined my research by reducing me to my sexuality, which they considered to be un-Iranian and despicable. As I will show in chapter 4, one blogger, who blamed queers for "promoting deviant sexualities" and inciting hate and resentment in heterosexual couples' relationships, made specific references to my research. To this man, a self-proclaimed intellectual and an advocate of democracy, homosexuality was irrelevant to Iran. Several regular readers of my blog, who could not imagine that an academic could be queer, reproached me for taking *roshanfekri* (being an intellectual) to the extreme by defending "homosexuals." Some bloggers, who eventually realized that I was queer, made hostile comments on my blog or in their own blog posts.

A blog called *Laatland* (Thugland), written by anonymous characters,[8] labeled a group of Iranian women bloggers as the citizens of *"Feministrood"* ("Feminist Creek"). The authors of *Laatland* either ridiculed feminist bloggers or made sexually suggestive comments about them in their posts. After I wrote a post in response to a Toronto blogger who had claimed that feminists are angry women whose lack of sexual satisfaction has pushed them into becoming social workers or lesbians, *Laatland* authors took a screenshot of my blog and made it into a sexually explicit image that they then posted on their blog (see figure P.2). In this image my blog is turned into a naked woman's body, complete with a tree gnarl resembling a vagina. A spider is spinning a web over the vagina, connoting sexual deprivation. The tree-gnarl image was taken from a photograph that Mohammad Ali Abtahi, the reformist chief of staff under President Khatami, had posted on his own blog. Abtahi's post had become a laughingstock among some male bloggers, especially those who looked for an opportunity to ridicule and criticize the reformists. I and a few women in Weblogistan had questioned the juvenile and sexist attitude of bloggers who used the vulva-looking gnarl to question the reformist cleric's credentials as a politician. *Laatland*'s manipulation of my blog image to include Abtahi's image of the vulva-looking gnarl covered by spiderwebs was a reference to my posts in response to sexist bloggers. This was one among many examples in which, as a female-bodied and gender-nonconforming political blogger/academic who was not sexually available to heterosexual men, I was objectified and dehumanized by a group of misogynist men who considered themselves to be progressive advocates of free speech.

The hostility that I received from sexist readers and bloggers was not only because of my queerness but also had to do with being read as a feminist woman academic. I was "tested" several times by cisgender heterosexual male bloggers, who regardless of their field of study (mostly engineering, mathematics, and computer sciences), saw themselves in the position of expertise in humanities and social sciences, and treated women scholars as their subordinates. Ironically, as I will argue in chapter 2, this form of sexism often came from a number of male "intellectuals" who seemed to be uncomfortable with women's participation in intellectual discussions and political conversations. For example, a blogger who wrote a homophobic and sexist post about women social workers, feminists, and lesbians was one of the first people who interrogated me when I launched my blog. His questions in my comments

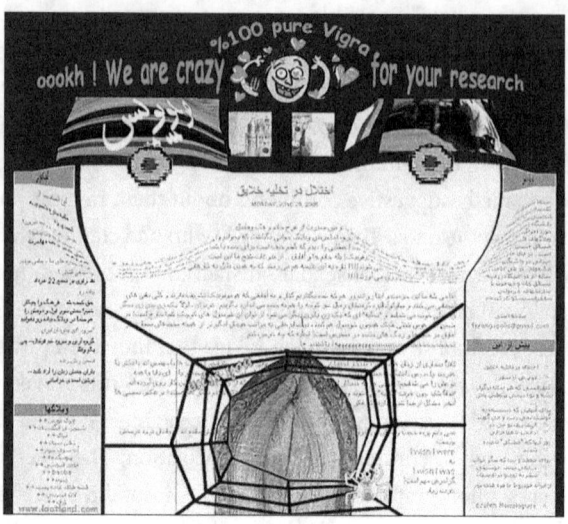

FIGURE P.2 "We are crazy for your research." The author(s) of *Laatland* deleted this image a day after it was posted.

section demanded answers to test whether I was "qualified" as a researcher. Some of these questions were very personal and involved my age, marital status, and history of immigration. I felt extremely uneasy about answering these personal questions, but as a novice blogger I found myself in a position where I wanted to accommodate my readers in order to be "accepted." After I answered his questions, he proclaimed that I had "passed" the test. Like several other male bloggers of his generation, this man used ornamental and bookish Persian language as a form of symbolic capital in Weblogistan.[9] Because English is valorized as a class marker, fluency in English often grants one social status. For some diasporic cisgender men who had experienced loss of social status as immigrants, the formal use of Persian language and the disparaging of younger bloggers (especially women) for vulgarizing Persian worked to recuperate a sense of authority. As I will discuss in chapter 3, charges of vulgarization of Persian in Weblogistan were often entangled with gendered discourses of Iranian modernity.

Female-bodied bloggers (woman-identified or not) were not the only ones who were subjected to misogynistic belittling and "mansplaining." Iranian women scholars and activists in general were targeted by misogynistic men, who, regardless of their expertise or familiarity with a topic, considered themselves (as self-proclaimed intellectuals) to be more qualified than any woman. As I will discuss in this book, throughout my fieldwork research in Weblogistan, claims of authenticity over the true understanding of democracy and civil society stood out as measures of moral aptitude. Although a wide range of bloggers shared and cultivated the desire for freedom and democracy, only heterosexual cisgender men assumed themselves to have the authority to pontificate on these concepts.[10] Contestations over the true meaning of democracy, freedom, and civil society were central in the representational and performative blogging practices among popular political bloggers who advocated "practicing democracy" in Weblogistan. For these bloggers, many of whom considered themselves to belong to an imagined community (mainly imagined as male and heterosexual) of intellectuals (*roshanfekr*), Weblogistan was figured as a microcosm of the Iranian civil society with aspirations for a democratic future. It is the fetishization and the gendered deployment of civil society and its relationship to biopolitics, ethicopolitics, necropolitics, and geopolitics that I interrogate in this book.

Introduction

Much like my now-defunct blog, this book is a product of my political and affective engagement with the Iranian diaspora, revolution, and war. My research on Weblogistan, the Iranian blogosphere, took shape during the "global war on terror," when the global was uncannily local for many who sensed belonging to multiple homes and whose gendered and sexed lives were deployed to legitimize death in the name of rights. Although far removed from the immediate material effects of war to which millions of Iraqis and Afghanis were subjected, the anxiety of a military attack on Iran preoccupied my diasporic body that had held memories of the Iran–Iraq war. Haunted by the fear of a possible war against one home while being constantly under surveillance by measures of national security in another, I combined my academic research with internet activism by participating in antiwar Persian and English blogs. With more than 100,000 Persian blogs, Weblogistan had become the spotlight of international media. The imminent threat of a military attack against Iran during the "war on terror," when Iran and Iranians were/are marked as belonging to the "axis of evil," motivated me to write a blog as a form of cyberactivism and gave me a way to feel connected to others who shared the same concerns, regardless of our multiple political positions. More than a decade later, and despite the nominal end to the "war on terror," bombs and drone attacks continue to expend lives in Yemen, Palestine, and Syria, while economic sanctions debilitate the Iranian population, subjecting Iranians to slow death.

In a resurgence of a "total war" (Khalili 2013; Terry 2017), the connective tissue among the rise of fascism, militarized white masculinity, rampant Islamophobia, antiblack violence, anti-immigrant laws in North America and Europe, and the death and debilitation of certain populations in the Middle East (Puar 2017) seems to be the conjoined technologies of security and freedom that cultivate some lives and expend others.

This book focuses on the production of democratic life in Weblogistan and its relationship to the imminent death of risky populations, in a time when (cyber) civil society and freedom exist in a "plane of immanence" (Deleuze and Guattari 1987) with geopolitics, biopolitics, and necropolitics. More specifically, this book argues that while enabling resistance and political mobilizations as elements of transnational Iranian civil society, in its heyday Weblogistan was inevitably intertwined with the *politics of rightful killing*: a form of politics that concerns not only the community of Iranian bloggers in cyberspace but also the offline lives of the Iranian population at large. The politics of rightful killing explains the contemporary political situation where those, such as the "people of Iran," whose rights and protection are presented as the raison d'être of war, are sanctioned to death and therefore live a pending death exactly because of those rights. Seen as a "window" for surveillance and data collection, and an effective venue for the dissemination of neoliberal discourses of democracy and freedom, in the first decade of the new millennium Weblogistan attracted immense attention from neoconservative think tanks and liberalizing regimes. It was in the context of internet democratization projects that Weblogistan became a site of the production and normalization of digital citizens who "practiced democracy" and imagined a desired future. Weblogistan became the virtual laboratory where the competing discourses of nationalism and neoliberalism, and the affective registers of belonging and desire, convened to produce and normalize gendered exceptional citizens in a phantasmic shuttling between a glorious, immemorial past and a democratic future. Notwithstanding the aspirations of the desiring Iranian digital citizens, I argue in this book that the possibility of exceptional citizenship is foreclosed, as risk inevitably traverses Iranian bodies inasmuch as they belong to a population that is subjected to the politics of rightful killing: the politics of death in relationship to an unstable life that is at once imbued with and stripped of liberal universal rights.

Blogging Shall Set You Free

Web gives a voice to Iranian women.
— ALFRED HERMIDA, *BBC NEWS*

On the other side of the international division of labor from socialized capital, inside and outside the circuit of the epistemic violence of imperialist law and education supplementing an earlier economic text, can the subaltern speak?
— GAYATRI CHAKRAVORTY SPIVAK, "CAN THE SUBALTERN SPEAK?"

"Take one exasperated Iranian woman. Add a computer. Hook it up to the Internet. And you have a voice in a country where it's very hard to be heard." These words appeared on CNN.com's World Section on February 19, 2004.[1] Quoting Lady Sun—a prominent Iranian woman blogger in Tehran who later immigrated to the United States and then to the United Kingdom—this article exemplifies enthusiastic news coverage about the proliferation of blogs in Iran. In these reports, the internet is often depicted as the liberating force that gives voice to Iranians, especially women, who are assumed to have been silent prior to their internet access.[2] For example, consider this excerpt from Ben Macintyre's "Mullahs versus the bloggers," which celebrates the internet as a "new species of protest" and introduces Weblogistan as the "land of free speech":

> But if Iran, under the repressive rule of the ultraconservatives, is silencing the sound of Western pop, in another area of its culture, a wild cacophony of voices has erupted.... This is the place Iranians call "Weblogistan": a land of noisy and irreverent free speech. The collision between these two sides of Iran—hardline versus online—represents the latest, and most important, battle over freedom of speech. The outcome will dictate not only the shape of Iran, but also the future of the internet as a political tool, heralding a new species of protest that is entirely irrepressible.[3]

Macintyre's narrative about the clash of "hardline versus online" is not an uncommon representation of the role of the internet in Iran. In fact, most enthusiastic scholarly and journalistic accounts about the popularity of blogs in Iran rely on a sharp distinction between the repression of freedom in Iran and liberal democratic ideals, which are assumed to exist in the "West." It is argued that Iran's lack of freedom of speech in print media has attracted younger generations, especially women, to the "democratic" world of blogging.

FIGURE I.1 "Web Gives a Voice to Iranian Women," http://news.bbc.co.uk/2/hi/sci/tech/2044802.stm.

Undoubtedly, in the first decade of the new millennium Persian-language blogging became quite popular among some educated Iranians in Iran, especially those residing in urban areas. Even though increased access to the internet in Iran was an important factor in the rise of blogging among Iranians in Iran and in its diaspora, the hypervisibility of bloggers in mainstream international media cannot be solely attributed to technological developments in Iran. Nor can this hypervisibility be reduced to the usual narrative of lack of freedom of speech in Iran and its abundance in North America and Europe. During my research, most of the high-profile Iranian bloggers lived outside of Iran, particularly in locations where "freedom of speech" is assumed to be a right granted to all citizens. In fact, some of the most famous and popular Persian blogs, including those that popularized Persian blogging and received attention from mainstream international media, were written in North America

FIGURE I.2 "Freedom in Farsi Blogs," http://www.guardian.co.uk/technology/2004/dec/20/iran.blogging.

and Europe. The freedom-of-speech narrative does not quite explain why a large number of popular Persian blogs were written in North America. This paradox, as I will show in this book, can be explained only through an examination of the role of the Iranian diaspora in the narratives of civil society, freedom of speech, bloggers' rehearsals of democracy, democratization projects during the "war on terror," and the politics of rightful killing.

Cyber-enthusiast accounts with short-term memory often overlook histories of social struggles, erasing any trace of preceding offline histories of struggle in their celebrations of "internet revolutions" in the Middle East. Ignoring the implication of cyberspace in nationalist, militaristic, and neocolonial discourses and practices, celebratory accounts of Weblogistan portray it as a stage for the rehearsal of democracy and freedom of speech, the bedrock of a revolution, and a new ground upon which the Iranian civil society flourishes.

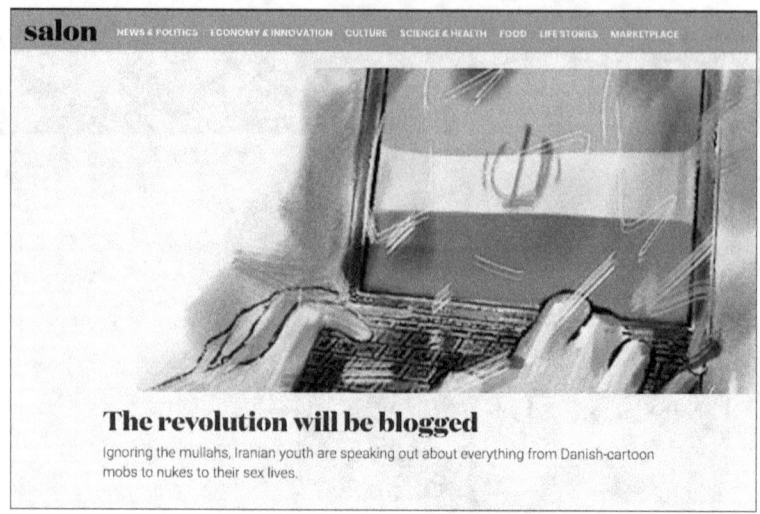

FIGURE I.3 "The Revolution Will Be Blogged," http://www.salon.com/news/feature/2006/03/06/iranian_bloggers.

FIGURE I.4 "Blogs Opening Iranian Society?," https://www.wired.com/2003/05/blogs-opening-iranian-society.

In fact, less than a decade before the 2009 Iranian Green Movement became known as the "Twitter revolution," and before Twitter and Facebook revolutions gained currency in the lexicon of the recent uprisings in the Middle East (a subject that I discuss at the end of this book), "blogging revolution," also known to some as the "turquoise revolution," named the role of the Iranian blogosphere in the language of democratization, reminiscent of the post-Soviet color revolutions that enshrined civil society.[4]

Undoubtedly, Persian blogging among Iranians in Iran and its diaspora is a historically specific phenomenon that owes its emergence to several contingent factors. As I will discuss in this book, some of these factors include the improvement of internet technologies in Iran, increased immigration of young computer-savvy Persian-speaking Iranians to North America and Europe, the desire to participate in the politics of homeland from a distance, and performances of democratic subjecthood in cyberspace. The increased emphasis on the political potentials of internet organizing in the "age of information," the opportunities for political participation, and entrepreneurial aspirations of a segment of the Iranian diaspora who provided expertise and testimonials on matters relating to Iran may also have contributed to the fast popularity of Persian blogging.

Whether the popularization of Persian blogging and the events following September 11, 2001, are coincidental or not, the fact remains that the emergence of Weblogistan was subjected to historical and political civilizational discourses and practices that gave it meaning in the context of the "global war on terror."[5] During its peak, Weblogistan was a site of production of civilizational knowledge, where Iranianness was claimed and contested through gendered and sexed performances of political intervention and where the desire for exceptional digital citizenship and democratic futurity was cultivated. As Minoo Moallem argues (2005a), in the aftermath of the 1979 revolution the print culture of modernity has gradually been replaced by mass-mediated communication. While Moallem's incisive analysis examines cinematic space after the revolution, I suggest that cyberspace plays a significant role in the formation of transnational subjectivities and the management of life and death of the Iranian population. In the post-1989 period, which marks the end of the Iran–Iraq war, the rise of the reform movement, the gradual liberalization of the Iranian economy, and the emergence of democratization projects after the fall of the Soviet Union, the increased access to internet technologies in Iran and its diaspora has made cyberspace an important venue for the articulation of gendered subjectivities and political interventions.[6] The popularization of the internet and the emergence of social media in the new millennium gave rise to neoliberal digital citizenship—a form of citizenship that assumes equal and democratic political participation in cyber civil society, is predicated on the logic of market and neoliberal entrepreneurship, justifies security in the name of freedom, demands technologies of self to normalize the population according to white heteronormative ideals of the universal human, and cultivates the desire for a "democratic" future that is imagined through the subversive capacity of civil society.

Unlike accounts that depict civil society as the mainstay of social movements and democracy, in this book I trace the ways in which Weblogistan, as a manifestation of transnational civil society, is not just a site of dialogue and resistance to the state but also a site of governmentality where normalization and the conduct of conduct operate under the rhetoric of democracy in a neoliberal and militarized world. Contrary to the accounts that celebrate Weblogistan as a unified, democratic, revolutionary, and antistate online community that epitomizes the promises of civil society, I show that it is exactly because it is—and not despite being—an element of civil society that Weblogistan is where violent conflicts take place, inequalities that exist offline are reproduced online, desiring subjects—who aspire to exceptional citizenship—are normalized according to nationalist and neoliberal discourses, and neoliberal self-entrepreneurs/experts produce and disseminate information about Iran when cyber-revolutions dominate the lexicon of democratization projects of the empire. Ultimately, I argue, Weblogistan as a part of the transnational Iranian civil society is where the desire for exceptional citizenship and democratic futurity is cultivated, while the Iranian population is simultaneously subjected to the politics of rightful killing that forecloses futurity.

Cybergovernmentality and the Fad of Civil Society

Like many Iranians of my generation, I am the product of a peculiar infatuation with civil society. Having lived through the 1979 revolution and the eight-year war between Iran and Iraq (1980–88), I left Iran in 1989.[7] That year marked the end of a decade known in postrevolutionary Iran as "*daheye shast*" (the "60's decade" according to the Iranian Solar Hijri calendar)—perhaps the most repressive period after the revolution when the exigencies of war made any form of dissent nearly impossible. The year 1989 was a significant one, not just in my personal life as a young queer immigrant facing new disciplinary measures and political sensibilities but also in the world to which I belonged. It marked the beginning of the political shifts that came after the eight-year war and the death of Ayatollah Khomeini (1902–1989), the leader of the Iranian Revolution.[8] The subsequent liberalization and relative social freedoms during the two-term presidency of Ayatollah Hashemi Rafsanjani between 1989 and 1997 and the landslide victory of President Mohammad Khatami in 1997 were closely linked to the emergence of the reform movement, the labor movement, the women's movement, and the student movement in the post-1989 period.[9] The year that I left Iran also saw a series of events in Eastern Europe that came to be known as the "1989 revolutions," "color revolutions," "the fall of communism," and the end of the cold war. A new era was under way. Democratization, civil society, and economic liberalization became buzzwords of a neoliberal rationality that replaced the logic of the cold war with a new normal: accelerated market liberalization coupled with "freedom" through seemingly "nonviolent" color revolutions, which would be followed in a decade by the militaristic violence of the "war on terror."

The post-1989 events in Eastern Europe, and the "democratization" impulse articulated through the notion of color revolutions, gave civil society a new currency. As James Ferguson (2006b) points out, unlike the Marxian notion of civil society as the arena of alienation, exploitation, and domination in capitalism, in the context of the recent history of Eastern Europe, civil society came to be valorized as the road to democracy.[10] Ferguson rightly argues that the currency of civil society in the Reagan-Thatcher neoliberal agendas to "roll back" the state, along with the postsocialist "democratization" wave, culminated in the universalization of civil society as the fad of national and transnational politics (91).

Even as the concept of civil society with all its different meanings in historical periods has been developed in the West, it has gained much currency in the "third world," where projects of democratization enshrine civil society institutions as indices of progress on the road to liberal democracy.[11] In the studies of the Middle East, as Sami Zubaida (2001, 232–49) has argued, the dominant narrative is that, as the basis of democracy, civil society is an oppositional force against totalitarian states that have controlled society and denied social autonomy. To counter this trend, the narrative goes, it is necessary to not only hold elections and form political parties but also to initiate political participation of the individual through autonomous institutions (232).

Much of the optimism about the internet in the Middle East is informed by the "fad" of civil society and the democratization impulse. But this trend is not limited to the neoliberal and neocolonial agendas of exporting democracy through military intervention. There is also enthusiasm among the left about the potentials of the internet in enabling civil society in the Middle East, where civil society is assumed to be a rarity. Whether civil society is seen as a gateway to democracy in post-Communist societies in which state bureaucracy dominated all spheres of life, as a leftist response in the West against the neoconservative capitalist atomization through the formation of nonstate associations, or as an amalgamation of new social movements with democratic aspirations, civil society is often imagined in a vertical and oppositional position in relation to the state. As Sunil Khilnani argues, regardless of their differences, the dominant views on civil society consider it to have the potential to curb the state in different domains (2001, 14). If a conservative approach sees civil society to be located in the cultural acquisitions and "inherited manners of civility" that moderate the relationships between groups and individuals, the liberal position on civil society sees the power of civil society to be residing in the economy. A more radical position places the promise of civil society to be resting in a society that is independent of economy and the state.[12]

In this book I adopt a different conceptualization of civil society, in which the state and civil society are intertwined and not defined in a static control/freedom relationship. This would entail relinquishing an imaginary that James Ferguson has called the "vertical topography of power" (2006b, 90–92). Ferguson calls into question the common top-down state-society relationship in analyses of state and civil society, where civil society is constituted of a range of institutions placed between the all-encompassing state at the top and the family at the bottom. Rather than the vertical model of state and civil society, I approach civil society as a site of governmentality in the Foucauldian sense: "the ensemble formed by the institutions, procedures, analyses and reflections, the calculations and tactics that allow the exercise of this very specific albeit complex form of power, which has as its target population, as its principal form of knowledge[,] political economy, and its essential technical means apparatuses of security" (Foucault 1988, quoted in Burchell, Gordon, and Miller 1991, 102).[13] I situate Weblogistan as a part of Iranian transnational civil society, and as such a site of governmentality. As a node of "transnational governmentality" (Ferguson and Gupta 2002), Weblogistan includes sexed and gendered strategies of regulating and disciplining that are imposed by complex international and transnational networks in neoliberal economies and are enabled by willing subjects whose desires are articulated in the language of rights, where the protection of rights legitimizes military interventions by "liberating" forces.

One of the mechanisms of liberal governmentality, Miller and Rose (1992) argue, is inscription. Writing as a normalizing technique that transmits repeatable instructions for the conduct of self can enable rule at a distance through networks and by making phenomena into calculable information that further enables the government of conduct of a population. Networks play a key role in transmitting this information (which is not neutral) for long-distance government. The government of conduct of those who are distant is aided by mechanisms of networking without appearing to impinge on their "freedom" (in fact, in the case of the internet, often conducted in the name of freedom). The "conduct of the conduct" is not limited to the law or the state power but employs forms of power that enable the government of individuals, their desires, and their bodies in the realm of civil society. Using the insights of these scholars, in this book I argue that as a part of transnational civil society, Weblogistan became an important site of *cybergovernmentality* where the condensation of nationalist and democratization discourses during the "war on terror" produced and disciplined particular sexed and gendered subjectivities that aspired to exceptional neoliberal citizenship (Grewal 2017) in online and offline encounters. I define cybergovernmentality as a significant mode of transnational governmentality (Ferguson and Gupta 2002) that operates through online and offline normalizing techniques; uses experts, diasporas, and media technologies; relies on a neoliberal economy; and employs security as its mechanism of calculation to discipline and regulate populations according to the ideals of liberal democracy.

As I will discuss in this book, the condensation of nationalist and neoliberal discourses in Weblogistan and performances of democratic Iranianness during the "war on terror" sought to normalize particular sexed and gendered subjectivities as exceptional digital Iranian citizens in online and offline encounters. As a part of the transnational Iranian civil society, Weblogistan was a new site where heated debates about Iranian politics took place among internet-savvy Iranians in Iran and its diaspora. These debates highlighted the gendered, sexed, and racial exclusions of a futurity that was imagined through rehearsals of democracy and freedom in Weblogistan. As a technology of self, "practicing democracy" became the buzzword among some Iranian internet users who assumed their blogging world to be a microcosm of the Iranian population at large. In Weblogistan, normative Iranian subjectivities were neither solely produced and regulated according to the Iranian nationalist discourses nor by an assumed unidirectional neoliberal order. Rather, hegemonic forms of Iranianness were produced (and constantly reproduced) in a complex and multidirectional discursive, affective, and economic assemblage that included Iranians in Iran, diaspora Iranians, and competing and complicit nonstate, para-state, and state entities (of several states) that operated under governmental and nongovernmental nomenclature.

The most representable (in mainstream media) Iranian bloggers as neoliberal self-entrepreneurs imagined a democratic Iranianness that drew its force from hegemonic nationalist ideals, while aspiring to an exceptional citizenship that valorized secular and liberal freedom achieved through individualism, self-interest, and participation in rehearsals of "democracy" in the realm of cyber civil society. Yet the desire for proximity to exceptional citizenship continues to be unattainable for the willing Iranian cyber-citizen, as the fear of an impending threat is inevitably attached, or to borrow from Sara Ahmed, "sticks" (2004, 4) to Middle Eastern bodies. It is in this context that many diaspora Iranians insist on highlighting their difference from Arabs and the Middle East. This distancing is not necessarily a corrective to the orientalist representations that collapse all difference in the Middle East, but a strategy of disassociation from the hypervisible figure of the "Arab terrorist" in the face of violent anti–Middle Eastern and anti-Muslim sentiments in North America and Europe. The popularity of the model-minority discourse (exemplified in television programs such as *The Shahs of Sunset*), U.S. politicians' distinctions between the "Iranian people" and the "regime," and Netanyahu's praise of Silicon Valley Iranians do not obliterate the deep anti-Iranian sentiments that exclude Iranians through immigration laws while rendering them disposable through deadly sanctions.[14] Notwithstanding the desire for proximity to whiteness, displays of market virility, and disavowal of Arabness as strategies to survive anti-Muslim and anti-Arab racism, Iranians who aspire to exceptional citizenship are constantly shuttling between rightfulness and rightlessness, as the looming fear of the Middle Eastern "terrorist" travels through contagion (to borrow from Puar), implicating all Iranians and marking them "risky citizens." In other words, the risky citizen in the digital realm is a self-responsible individual, apt for democratization through biopolitical and ethicopolitical practices that seek to normalize the (currently undemocratic) population according to the ideals of liberal democracy. However, unlike the exceptional citizen who is folded into life, this unstable figure who simultaneously maintains a desire for liberal democracy and a sense of belonging to a population that embodies a pending threat to the security of the "international community" can become disposable at any given moment. The male nationalist intellectual who desires democracy, the woman activist who desires sexual freedom, the docile homosexual who aspires to a "normal" life, and the diasporic expert/entrepreneur who produces knowledge about Iran are a few figures who exemplify risky citizens in Weblogistan. Apt for democratization and simultaneously disposable, these figures shuttle between hypervisibility and unrepresentability.[15]

Experts, Risky Business, and Security

> Homeland security is not a temporary measure just to meet one crisis. Many of the steps we have now been forced to take will become permanent in American life. They represent an understanding of the world as it is, and dangers we must guard against perhaps for decades to come. I think of it as the new normalcy.... Terrorism is a menace to the entire civilized world.
> —FORMER U.S. VICE PRESIDENT DICK CHENEY

> Iran's people are our allies. We must get behind the democrats and the dissidents in Iran and find all the ways we can to help the Iranian people.... Iranian people want freedom. The mood in the region is in favor of democratization.
> —MARK PALMER, COMMITTEE ON THE PRESENT DANGER

> There is no liberalism without a culture of danger.... Control is no longer just the necessary counterweight to freedom, as in the case of panopticism: it becomes its mainspring.
> —MICHEL FOUCAULT, *THE BIRTH OF BIOPOLITICS*

In the first decade of the new millennium, Weblogistan became the center of attention for the democratization industries and "experts" who deployed notions of international civil society, freedom, preemption, and security to ensure the geopolitical interests of the empire and global capitalism. The allocation of funding (by the U.S. Department of State and the Dutch Parliament) to the Iranian diasporic media with the purported aim of promoting democracy in Iran, the proliferation of discourse about helping "opposition groups" in Iran and its diaspora to hasten regime change in the post–9/11 era, the timely emergence of Persian blogging as a fast medium for transnational exchange of information all brought Weblogistan into the spotlight of democracy projects. It is not surprising, then, that the Committee on the Present Danger (CPD)[16] identified the Iranian blogosphere as a window through which "we" (the "international community") may monitor Iran: "Iran's regime has reason to worry. With its growing scope and reach, the Iranian 'blogosphere' can give the international community a unique window into the nature of the Islamic Republic, a damning chronicle of its repressive human rights practices, and—perhaps most importantly—insights into its intrinsic social, economic and political vulnerabilities. So, why aren't we paying attention?"[17]

The fact is that "we" were paying attention and monitoring the Iranian blogosphere in different think tanks and research centers. There was increasing interest in Persian blogs by state and nonstate institutions such as the U.S. Library of Congress, Harvard University's Berkman Center for the Internet and Society, the National Endowment for Democracy, and think tanks such as the Hoover Institute and the Washington Institute for Near East Policy. For example, Berkman Center's Internet and Democracy Project's three case studies illuminate the geopolitical motivations of research on the internet, even as the research is conducted by "civil society organizations." The research investigated "the impact of the Internet on civic engagement and democratic processes" in Iran, South Korea, and Ukraine (note the geopolitical significance of the selected case studies).[18] While the research on Ukraine explored the role of cell phones in information sharing and organizing protests during Ukraine's Orange Revolution, the Iran case study, titled "Mapping Iran's Online Public: Politics and Culture in the Persian Blogosphere," analyzed the "composition of the Iranian Blogosphere and its possible impact on political and democratic processes." The goal of these case studies, as the Berkman Center's website states, was "to draw initial conclusions about the actual impact of technology on democratic events and processes, and to identify questions for further research."[19] The report claimed that "given the repressive media environment in Iran today, blogs may represent the most open public communications platform for political discourse" (2).

These think tanks celebrated Weblogistan for its assumed democratization potentials, but their reach went beyond influencing public opinion in the United States. For example, the Committee on the Present Danger's "experts" testified in the U.S. Congress in order to shift the U.S. policy toward Iran.[20] Hard to miss in the name of this organization is the assumption of a "present" danger. This presence connotes a materiality (it is here) and a temporal urgency (it is here now). Danger, as Robert Castel (1991) has argued in the case of preventative social administration techniques in France and the United States, is a paradoxical notion. It affirms both the quality of danger immanent in a subject and a mere probability, for the proof of danger could be provided only after the fact. It is this unpredictability that conveys the idea that even if a person appears calm and harmless, they may become dangerous. Nowhere is the fear of unpredictability clearer than a statement on CPD's website, in which 1.5 billion Muslims are deemed suspect:

> The ideology of Islamist terror by itself poses a dangerous threat, capable of evil committed in the name of God. Fueled by the accelerant of state support, the threat of Islamist terror increases dramatically. But, in this case, what is proliferating are not weapons but self-anointed holy warriors. . . . Murderous ideology being nothing new, the question becomes how does this threat from radical Islamic terrorists compare to previous threats? The principal difference between this ideology and the expansionist fascist and communist regimes that preceded it in the last century is that Islamist terrorism is not a regime at all. It is the perversion of a major religion (approximately 1.5 billion members worldwide) through delusions of Muslim victimhood.[21]

The fine line between risk and danger in the rhetoric of antiterrorist experts invites a preemptive temporality wherein the risk of a disastrous future is tied to a present danger that justifies annihilation of entire populations (through war or sanctions) as an insurance measure. As a neologism of insurance, risk, as François Ewald (1991) has argued, has three characteristics: first, it is calculable; second, it is collective; and third, it is capital. Insurance technologies work through predicting and calculating the probability of the risk of a repeatable damage. In this case, the possibility of the repetition of the September 11 attacks and the threat of Islamic radicalism are both predictable risks and present dangers. Despite their differences, in the logic of CPD, "Islamic radicalism" repeats the threat of communism as the enemy of liberal democracy, while every Muslim embodies that risk. It is not surprising that in 2005, Mark Palmer the neoconservative cofounder of the National Endowment for Democracy, the former Vice Chair of Freedom House, the Reagan-era ambassador to Hungary in late 1980s, and a CPD member, authored a book titled *Breaking the Real Axis of Evil: How to Oust the World's Last Dictators by 2025*, in which he recycles the logic of "information revolution" in the former Soviet states. Similar to samizdat in the Soviet Union, Palmer advocates for the training of dissidents in places like Iran through communication technologies. Rather than fax and copy machines, this time the internet is seen as the fast vehicle for democratization. In other words, Palmer hopes to achieve the widespread regime change in Eastern Europe in the Middle East through repeating the cold war strategies, including training and funding of local dissidents by "outside democracies." These dissidents would in turn train the populace on how to blog and have street protests, à la Gene Sharp's philosophy of "nonviolence" that was used in the Eastern European "color revolutions." Following Palmer's lead and funded by the U.S. Department of State, Freedom House issued a report on internet freedom in fifteen countries (including Iran). Diaspora dissidents such as Mohsen Sazegara used the U.S. Department of State–funded Voice of America Persian and blogs to disseminate videos in which they taught Gene Sharp's "nonviolent" protests in Farsi to internet users in Iran.

The second characteristic of risk is its collectivity. While each subject is expected to act as a self-responsible individual who buys insurance (and in return expects individual compensation in the case that a disaster happens), insurance against a probable damage is not just to protect oneself but also a sign of good/exceptional citizenship in the name of the common good. As opposed to misfortunes or accidents that affect an individual, risk affects a population. Insurance against risk brings solidarity under the rhetoric of mutual interests. It is "our values" as the international civil society and "our way of life" that need to be protected from the risk of terrorism. As Castel argues, when the idea of risk is separated from danger, a systematic predetection becomes possible. Every individual must willingly submit to modalities of intervention that do not locate the danger in a subject but that instead calculate risk factors and statistics in the population. Thus, while the elimination of dangerous individuals such as Osama bin-Laden becomes necessary, that measure in itself does not eliminate the probable risk. The entire population is subjected to technologies of surveillance under the rhetoric of security. The insurance broker/expert's job is not only to calculate risk but also to produce it. Therefore, "experts" in universities, foundations, and think tanks who seek to protect the neoliberal market, coupled with ideals of liberal democracy, not only calculate the risk that terrorism poses to "the international community" but also discursively produce what constitutes terrorism. It is the probable risk that justifies the surveillance of the entire population through the logic of "security." As such, security is integral to regulatory practices that compel members of the "international civil society" to willingly ask for protection against the risk of terrorism. As Foucault has noted, the double exigency of liberalism and security, which requires state intervention, constitutes the paradox of liberalism and is at the core of the "crisis of governmentality" (2007, 384). The implementation of the U.S. National Security Agency's warrantless surveillance of email and the internet under the "terrorist surveillance program" after September 11, 2001, highlights a paradox inherent in narratives about freedom on the internet. While several civil liberties organizations challenged the U.S. surveillance acts for their unconstitutionality, the U.S. courts of appeals consistently dismissed these legal cases, upholding George W. Bush's executive order that authorized warrantless surveillance. This form of surveillance not only engaged the state apparatus but also the private telecommunication companies. After AT&T was sued in 2006 for disclosing its network records to the National Security Agency (the case was eventually dismissed), in June 2008 Congress passed legislation that warranted telecommunication firms immunity against spying lawsuits.[22] Interestingly, this form of surveillance was (and continues to be) done in the name of protecting Americans against the "terrorist threat."

The third and last characteristic of risk, according to Castel, is capital. Like Castel, Ewald argues that what is insured against risk "is not the injury that is actually lived, suffered and resented by the person it happens to, but a capital against whose loss the insurer offers a guarantee" (1991, 204). The coupling of the risk of terrorism with the risk that threatens global capitalism becomes clear in the testimony of Henry Sokolski, the executive director of the Nonproliferation Policy Education Center (NPEC). Sokolski, who testified alongside Mark Palmer—the CPD representative and the U.S. ambassador at the 2006 U.S. congressional hearings on Iran's nuclear policy—presented a study conducted by Rice University researchers titled "Getting Ready for a Nuclear-Ready Iran."[23] In his testimony, Sokolski claims that "historically, after a major terrorist attack in Saudi Arabia, markets worry, the price of oil increases, and Iran's own oil revenues, in turn, surge upward. Given that one-fifth of the world's entire oil demand flows through the Straits (as well as roughly a quarter of America's supply of oil) and no other nation that has fortified its shores near Hormuz, an Iranian threat to disrupt commerce there would have to be taken seriously by commercial concerns (e.g., insurers and commodity markets) and other nations." Sokolski's concern about the economic risks that Iran poses to commerce highlights the point that the market, which according to the neoliberal logic benefits every individual, is what needs to be insured through preemption. Thus, the insurance against terrorism is used not just to protect the "international community" but also to safeguard global capitalism, with a promise of freedom and profit for each individual as *homo œconomicus*. For the "experts" who acted as liberal democracy's insurance brokers, Weblogistan became an apt site for this business. Weblogistan's inhabitants became the risky subjects who are at once trained in democracy (to reduce the risk of terrorism) and deemed disposable (for posing the threat of terrorism).

Politics of Rightful Killing: Killing Me Softly with Your Rights

> If the power of normalization wishes to exercise the old sovereign right to kill, it must become racist. And if, conversely, a power of sovereignty, or in other words, a power that has the right of life and death, wishes to work with the instruments, mechanisms, and technology of normalization, it too must be racist.
>
> —MICHEL FOUCAULT, *SOCIETY MUST BE DEFENDED*

On July 8, 2008, toward the end of my fieldwork, an Associated Press reporter asked Senator John McCain (then a presidential candidate) why, despite sanctions against Iran, U.S. cigarette exports to Iran grew more than tenfold during President Bush's presidency. McCain responded, "Maybe that's a way of killing them."[24] Less than a year later, McCain would be paying a tribute to Neda Agha Soltan—a bystander who was shot during the protests that followed the Iranian presidential elections in Tehran in June 2009—condemning the Iranian state for repressing the Iranian people's quest for democracy, applauding Twitter and Google for making the video of Agha Soltan's death viral, and advocating U.S. support for democracy in Iran.[25] Soon after, Congress approved allocating $120 million for anti-regime broadcasting in Iran (Hivos 2011). President Obama's administration established Near East Regional Democracy (NERD) in 2009 to focus "primarily on activities that don't require an in-country presence. This included a strong focus on the support for media, technology, and Internet freedom, as well as conferences and trainings for Iranian reformers that may take place outside Iran."[26] Of the $40 million of NERD allocation in the fiscal year 2010, $10 million was specified for "internet access and freedom" (Hivos 2011). In FY2013, $8 million of the proposed $30 million was designated to "defend and promote an open internet" (McInerny 2012). The centrality of the internet in U.S. "liberation" projects was also reflected in Obama's 2012 Iranian New Year address, in which he celebrated Facebook, Twitter, and other internet social networking tools for connecting Iranians and Americans: "The United States will continue to draw attention to the electronic curtain that is cutting the Iranian people off from the world. And we hope that others will join us in advancing a basic freedom for the Iranian people: the freedom to connect with one another, and with their fellow human beings."[27]

The U.S. government's efforts to "lift the electronic curtain" in Iran while imposing the harshest sanctions in the history of sanctions on the Iranian people seems paradoxical at best. On July 1, 2010, President Obama signed into law the Comprehensive Iran Sanctions, Accountability, and Divestment Act of 2010 (CISADA) to amend the Iran Sanctions Act of 1996 (ISA).[28] CISADA added new types of restrictions that Obama proudly announced to be crippling the Iranian economy.[29] The new sanctions imposed excruciating economic pressure on the Iranian population—especially the working class—and jeopardized many people's lives by making lifesaving medicine unaffordable.[30] Ironically, the Obama administration added several provisions to make "it easier for American businesses to provide software and services into Iran that will make it easier for the Iranian people to use the internet."[31] How does one explain this aporia where the production of desire for free and democratic life is intertwined with death? What can be said about the politics of death and killing, management of life through rights, and the affective deployment of freedom in cyberspace? How do the material effects of sanctions and military intervention complicate the celebratory accounts of internet revolutions and affective mobilizations online? If mainstream representations of Weblogistan depict it as the bastion of civil society and therefore the realm of rights, what can be said about cyber civil society and rights in relation to death and disposability?

This inconsistency of the U.S. policies toward Iran delineates the position that Iran holds in a militant neoliberal order, wherein the Iranian population is seen as a desiring consumer of both commodities and liberal ideals of freedom in global capitalism, while the dispensability of Iranian lives is sanctioned in the name of security. As a trope and a fetish, "Iranian people" has been deployed by different political groups and states as a way to establish claims over legitimacy. The distinction that is often made between the "people" and the "government" is crystallized in the U.S. politicians' statements of support for the "Iranian people" who are positioned against the Islamic government. Regardless of the strategic deployment of this distinction—whether by neoconservatives for whom the production and protection of the "Iranian people" as a population in need of liberation is an excuse for military intervention, or by antiwar activists who are hopeful that through this distinction they can prevent a military attack on Iran—the fact remains that when the sovereign decides to kill, slowly with cigarettes or with sanctions, or swiftly in a manner of shock and awe, this differentiation becomes meaningless.

Given that biopolitics uses the production, management, and optimization of life of the population, the question becomes this: which populations are worth saving? Foucault defines population not as "a collection of juridical subjects in an individual or collective relationship with a sovereign will" but rather as "a set of elements in which we can note constants and regularities even in accidents, in which we can identify the universal of desire regularly producing the benefit of all, and with regard to which we can identify a number of modifiable variables on which it depends" (2007, 74). As such, the education of individual desire to produce collective interest is the organizing element of a population.[32] According to Foucault, desire is the "mainspring of action" of the population, meaning that the regulated play of individual desire will allow the production of collective interests, thus pointing to both the naturalness of population and the artificiality of its management (73).

One can expand Foucault's myopic notion of population and ask whether the universal of desire produces collective interests for all populations alike. How is the desire for freedom and democracy naturalized as one that benefits the collective interests of the "international civil society"? And if the work of governmentality is to cultivate a liberal democratic future for all, what happens to the excess of the art of governmentality—the queered nonliberal "terrorist" who poses a risk to the manufactured desire for liberal democracy and endangers the security of the "international community"? In other words, is the category of biopolitics sufficient for analyzing the "global" division of populations into those whose lives are produced and managed, sometimes under the rhetoric of "our way of life," and those whose lives become disposable, not necessarily by the juridical sovereign power of the state but by international entities and transnational market-driven actors that constitute the "international civil society"?

Achille Mbembe's concept of necropolitics, which focuses more on the significance given to death in relation to human bodies and their inscription in the order of power, is helpful in answering these questions (2003, 12). While expanding on Foucault's biopolitics, Mbembe theorizes necropolitics through a critique of the Hegelian negative relationship between death and becoming a subject. Drawing on Georges Bataille's theory of sovereignty and death,

Mbembe defines politics as the work of death and rightly points out that upholding the work of death is not the necessary prerequisite for subjecthood (2003, 14–16). Using examples of slaves in plantations and the colonized in the colonies, where the absolute lawlessness stems from the denial of humanity to the "native" and where the violence of the state of exception is exercised in the name of civilization, Mbembe (à la Agamben) argues that the state of exception and the state of siege become the normative basis of the right to kill (16). Mbembe points out that the modern colonial occupation combines the disciplinary, the biopolitical, and the necropolitical (the current example Mbembe argues is the occupation of Palestine). He argues that the "*stage of siege* is itself a military institution. It allows a modality of killing that does not distinguish between the external and the internal enemy. Entire populations are the target of the sovereign" (30).

Mbembe's analysis is an important intervention in the scope and the relevance of the biopolitical in the colonial context. His intervention expands biopolitics and points to Foucault's blind spot in theorizing the politics of life and death in the context of colonial occupation. However, neither biopolitics nor necropolitics may be sufficient to explain the work of death in relation to populations that are not stripped of rights in the state of exception (Agamben 2005) but whose deaths are sanctioned, rather, in the name of rights and in the state of normalcy. I build from biopolitics and necropolitics to suggest a form of power over the liminal state between death and life: a life that is not bare, but is instead imbued with rights. As a trope, the "people of Iran" constitute a population that is produced through the discourse of rights and for which death through sanctions and/or bombs is legitimized within the rhetoric of the "war on terror." I call the politics of death in relationship to an unstable life that is at once imbued with and stripped of liberal universal rights *the politics of rightful killing*. The politics of rightful killing explains the contemporary political situation in the "war on terror" where those, such as the "people of Iran," whose rights and protection are presented as the raison d'être of war, are sanctioned to death and therefore live a pending death exactly because of, and in the name of, those rights. Foucault argues that while "the relationship of war" ("'If you want to live, the other must die'") is not new, modern racism makes this relationship "function in a way that is completely new and that is quite compatible with the exercise of biopolitics" (2003, 255). During the "war on terror," the management and optimization of protected life (populations that are worth protecting) uphold national and international security as a justification for racism. The exercise of racism in the name of democracy entails biopolitical practices at home and abroad, as well as preemptive disposability of those who threaten "our way of life" or jeopardize the interests of the "international community." Democratization (through trainings in the realm of civil society) and protection of rights (through the work of the "international civil society") become preemptive strategies to contain the risk of terrorism in populations that are not fully redeemable and remain suspect. As such, strategies of preemption/redemption can be revamped as strategies of killing unapologetically and with no need for justification. The politics of rightful killing is also concerned with the techniques of killing of populations: the management of death on the threshold of life. How does the government of the life of one population connect to the techniques of the killing of other populations? This is not to repeat the important point that Foucault and Mbembe (drawing from Foucault) address, namely "civilized" ways of killing and disciplining. It is to address the technique of killing of different populations, different multitudes, where the sovereign kills softly with selective sanctions (cigarettes are allowed; medicine is not), or in the manner of shock and awe, all in the name of rights.

The politics of rightful killing does not replace necropolitics or biopolitics, but it exists in the same political terrain where populations are disciplined, normalized, and debilitated (Puar 2017) and where "bare life" (one that is stripped of rights in the state of exception) is subjected to death. It refers to the necessary correlate of biopolitics insofar as biopolitics encompasses the relationship of the life of one depending on the death of the other (Foucault 2003, 255). Like necropolitics, however, the politics of rightful killing addresses the insufficiency of biopolitics in accounting for contemporary configurations of politics of life and death and is concerned with the *living dead*, the population that lives on the threshold of life and death (Mbembe 2003, 40). Unlike the living dead, however, *loaned life* (*zendegiye nessiyeh*) addresses the coexistence of dreaded yet rightful life and impending death on the same plane. Neither bare life, nor the life of the shadow slave or that of the absolute enemy (as discussed by Giorgio Agamben in the death camps and Mbembe in the colonies, the plantations, and in Palestine), loaned life is killable not just in the exceptional state of emergency, state of lawlessness, or the state of siege—although it is legitimized under those states—but in the state of normalcy. Rather than being completely stripped of rights, *loaned life* is imbued with and indebted to (universal human) rights. Rather than Foucault's formulation of biopolitics ("make live, let die") or Puar's formulation of debilitation ("will not let die"), the loaned life in the politics of rightful killing encapsulates the conditional life of the population that has the potential to be democratized *and* contains the risk of terrorism. It is loaned, as it is conditional and contingent on the form of life (make live *only if* life aligns with the tenets of liberal democracy) and the temporality of rights (make live *only as long as* gifted with rights). Unlike *homo sacer*, loaned life cannot be expended by anyone except for the liberalizing states that protect the life-worthy population (even as the life-worthy population is eliminating its internal dangers through racist technologies of government). The *loaned life* holds the promise of civil society, and thus the potential of being governed transnationally, while being prone to preemptive death for the risk that it contains. In the endless state of war against the "terrorist states," a new norm is established where the loaned life becomes the target of the sovereign's right to kill in the name of rights and the protection of the "international civil society."

The analysis of Weblogistan as a site of civil society needs to be contextualized in relation to risk, danger, security, and, ultimately, the politics of rightful killing during the "war on terror." During the "war on terror," when experts produce Middle Eastern and Muslim populations as risks to the safety of the "international civil society," surveillance as well as lessons in democracy through the internet may be deployed as risk-reduction technologies. The critique of surveillance in cyberspace is often framed as the violation of individual rights and liberties, thus enshrining the sovereignty of individuals and their freedom of association in civil society. Yet the surveillance of entire populations in cyberspace is often justified in the name of security and protection of the individual. It is in this context that the Iranian population is figured as one that needs protection against censorship and human rights violations of the Iranian "regime" and is simultaneously seen as killable in the name of rights. In other words, Weblogistan is implicated in the politics of rightful killing that characterizes the paradoxical situation wherein campaigns for internet freedom exist side by side with deadly economic sanctions.

New Directions in the Studies of the Middle Eastern Cyberspace

While my ethnography in Weblogistan delves into the world of Persian blogging in order to explore the role of militarism, "democratization," and neoliberal governmentality in the Iranian cyberspace, the book's insights may be relevant to the new normative language of digital citizenship and political engagement in many parts of the world, including in Southwest Asia and North Africa (the region that for its geopolitical significance has arbitrarily been named the "Middle East"). Of course, claims about "internet revolutions" are not unique to Iran. Nor are the monetary and geopolitical investments in the internet as a vehicle for surveillance and neocolonial practices that are guised under the cloak of democratization obsolete. The internet has been deployed as the "new frontier" for liberalizing projects that in practice normalize the violence of "freedom." The transnational circulation of mediated images and online news reproduces epistemic violence and carries out the task of mobilizing affect to justify preemptive militarism. For instance, the widely circulated YouTube videos of Saddam Hussein's hanging after Iraq's "liberation" and of the sodomizing and killing of Muammar Gaddafi by NATO-supported "Libyan rebels" became violent spectacles for a networked world. These displays of "global justice" on cyber-pages were reminders that despite internet enthusiasts' claims about the disembodiment of cyberspace, the punishment and torture of the enemy are broadcast electronically with little or no delay and felt painfully by many who have bodily memories of the violence perpetuated by the U.S.-supported dictatorships and wars in the Middle East. Graphic videos of executions of despotic dictators (once allies to the executors of "justice") juxtapose the primitive apparatus of punishment with the modern technology that transmits these images in a matter of seconds across space, thus reminding *us*, the seemingly disembodied netizens of the civilized world, that *their* present and democratic future is *our* past, that liberation through military intervention is simply not enough for the barbaric brutal Muslim.[33] Lessons in democracy and freedom are necessary for the taming of the "liberated" yet backward Muslim populations. And while military presence in the name of "peacekeeping" is legitimized (because "they" are too irrational and therefore ungovernable), "teaching democracy" through the internet becomes an indispensable part of the freedom projects. The internet renders freedom viral.

It is no accident that immediately following the occupation of Iraq, Spirit of America,[34] a nonprofit/nongovernmental organization chaired by Senator McCain, created the software "Arabic Blogging Tools" to give "voice to those working for freedom and democracy in the Arab world and [to] enable them to easily connect and share ideas with their peers." The blogging tools carried out a project that its creators called "viral freedom." According to Spirit of America, "viral freedom" managed blogs that used the blogging tools in order to transmit the messages of this organization. Every blog that used the Arabic Blogging Tools included "a space that [was] under the control of organizations that we [Spirit of America] work with, such as Friends of Democracy."[35] Referred to as "real estate," this section on every blog that used the Arabic Blogging Tools was designed to promote "groups, individuals and news that, in the big picture, advance freedom, democracy and peace in the region." Not surprisingly, Spirit of America created an internet freedom and democracy project specifically designed to train Iraqi women, who were assumed to have had no experience of freedom previous to the occupation of Iraq. This liberating mission viewed the internet as a tool for democratization in Iraq and claimed that each Iraqi "who creates a blog is promoting moderate and progressive information and viewpoints in the Arab world. . . . Friends of Democracy uses the space to publicize prodemocracy groups, election information and related news. The blogs created under Friends of Democracy are ambassadors of democracy in the Arab world."[36] Shortly after the implementation of internet democracy-training projects in "postliberation" Iraq, the United States focused on internet propaganda in Iran. During the Bush administration, more than $400 million was allocated to fund covert operations and support regime change in Iran (Hivos 2011).[37] The official U.S. propaganda media, Voice of America Persian television and Radio Farda (Radio "Future"), became the main recipients of the U.S. Department of State funding. To appeal to the young Iranian population and to be "up to date," these state-funded media turned to Weblogistan for news and staffing.

In a sense, the "blogging revolution" can be seen as one of the first "internet revolutions" in a series of events that were hailed as the "Twitter revolution" or the "Facebook revolution" in Tunisia, Yemen, Egypt, and other parts of the Middle East.[38] These "internet revolutions" show that when democratic movements are hijacked and deployed by the "liberating" forces in the service of digital neocolonial projects (as I will discuss in this book), the result may very well be the suppression of these movements, not least because of the incitement of the discourse of "national security" by the so-called authoritarian regimes. It is in the online and offline wars between the "authoritarian" and "democratizing" regimes that the lives of the protesters are jeopardized and deemed disposable. Not unlike the Iranian context, the hype around "internet revolutions" in Arab countries elides the long histories of struggle while obscuring the relationship among "digital democratization," militarism, and security.[39]

While many scholars are optimistic about the role of blogging and social media in the social movements in the Middle East (Jarvis 2011; Lynch 2007; Shirky 2011; Ulrich 2009), others have argued that the uncritical celebrations of "internet revolutions" in Egypt, Yemen, Tunisia, and other locations have elided a long history of struggle that led to the protests (Alexander and Aouragh 2011, 2014; Badr 2018; Iskander 2011; Morozov 2012; Ulrich 2009). Furthermore, the utopian accounts of internet democracy and internet revolutions assume that the new media technologies' accelerated speed overcomes physical distance, bridging social, political, and economic gaps.[40] As Barnett (2004, 59) argues, "the celebration of the new technologies like the Internet as ideal for direct plebiscitary democracy, or for the proliferation of subterranean resistance networks, assumes that democracy is primarily about the expression of personal preferences or group interests outside of any context of transformative, deliberative justification." Highlighting the materiality of space and time and the role of transnational networks and resources in the emergence of publics, Barnett draws our attention to both the spaces that the uses of new media open up and the production of material infrastructure that enables technological developments.

Some of the optimistic accounts about the revolutionary potentials of the internet are informed by the hypertext theory and its use of Deleuze and Guattari's concept of rhizome as multiplicitous, nonhierarchical, heterogeneous, rapturous, and a-centered. Adopting the concepts in *A Thousand Plateaus: Capitalism and Schizophrenia* (1987), several studies of the internet in the 1990s (*The Electronic Disturbance* 1994; Landow 1994, 1997; Martin 1996; Moulthrop 1995; Snyder 1997) maintain that internet networks challenge the arborescent hierarchal structures, engendering "lines of flight" and bringing hope for liberation from structures of power.[41] Enthusiastic accounts of the internet that interpret Deleuze and Guattari's notions of war machine, nomad, and rhizome as tactics of resistance to domination see hacktivism that leaves no trace as nomadic resistance (Rosenberg 1994, 288).[42] Ignoring the U.S. military origins of the internet, in their uncritical celebration of multiplicity and lack of origins, these accounts assume the internet to have started as a "smooth space." State and capital are assumed to have only re-territorialized the rhizomatic internet later, slowly making it into a hierarchal, panoptic, and striated space. Even if the monopoly of U.S. surveillance and capital over the internet is acknowledged, some of these accounts insist that if power has become nomadic and networked, resistance must become rhizomatic and nomadic.

In their books *Empire* (2000) and *Multitude* (2004), Hardt and Negri, drawing from Foucault, as well as from Deleuze and Guattari, claim that in the age of empire, when war has become the norm, biopower—which seeks to control populations while producing life—also produces the networks that hold the possibility of democracy. Multitude, they state, as a set of rhizomatic processes, contains the possibility of absolute democracy.[43] For Hardt and Negri, multitude is the global subject of absolute democracy. As capital uses global communication technologies to exploit the labor market globally, it produces mobile and hybrid subjects, who are no longer limited to the national boundaries but constitute the new political subject: the multitude that is the force behind the self-organizing decentralized democracy.[44] Hardt and Negri remain faithful to freedom and pure resistance through the binary logic of revolution, where the constituent power contests the constituted power through exodus. Yet in their enthusiasm about the revolutionary power of multitude and their humanist belief in the power of human creativity and innovation, they ignore the fact that the multitude itself is biopolitically mediated.[45] Somehow the multitude and its desires stay pure, as if not implicated in the national and transnational networks that enable the hegemonic power of the empire. If the empire cannot be dethroned through countering global capitalism, it can be contested by the multitude through "subtraction, a flight, an exodus from sovereignty" (2004, 341).[46]

Celebrations of the internet's potential for democratizations are not limited to the analyses of rhizomatic multitude. The redistribution of political influence and "political voice" is often presented as the internet's exceptional capability for deliberative and participatory democracy. As Matthew Hindman (2009) argues, such valorizations assume political equality online, thus omitting gatekeeping and infrastructural inequalities. Hindman suggests that even if the digital divide has decreased with more internet accessibility, the internet is not eliminating exclusivity in the political realm, as gatekeeping remains a reality because of social media design and search engine algorithms (13–19). While the seemingly equal access to social media may give the impression of egalitarianism, the readership reproduces political hierarchies (16–19). Paolo Gerbaudo (2012) further challenges the valorization of the decentralized character of "networks" and the faithful optimism of "swarms" theorized by scholars such as Castells (2009, 2015) and Hardt and Negri (2000, 2004), arguing that social media have enabled the rise of "'soft' forms of leadership which exploit the interactive and participatory character of the new communication technologies" (Gerbaudo 2012, 139).[47]

I build on and contribute to critiques of digital democracy, and what Jodi Dean (2005) has aptly called "technology fetishism," by focusing on the notion of cyber civil society and its relationship to biopolitics, necropolitics, and geopolitics in internet democratization projects.[48] In other words, this book refrains from valorizing the promise and possibility of a liberal and democratic future through "internet revolutions," as this promise is contingent on the killability of those who pose a threat to the security of the "international civil society." While the "war on terror" has seemingly ended, the present moment is marked by wars and military occupations in the Middle East, the threat of a military attack on Iran, and security discourses and practices that deem the Middle East and Middle Eastern immigrants and refugees in North America and Europe as risks to national and global security (Naber 2006). Even as the internet enables political organizing, "information revolutions" through internet technologies continue the cold war logic and the U.S. interventions in the Middle East under the rhetoric of democratization. As I discussed above, the digital realm since the 1990s (with the popularization of internet-mediated social media) has become a significant site of transnational neoliberal governmentality. Whether theorized as an element of the "human security state" (Amar 2013) or a characteristic of "advanced neoliberalism" (Grewal 2017), national security has become the *sine qua non* for the state suppression of social movements. The need for expertise continues to provide online entrepreneurship opportunities for "native informants" during a time when U.S. military intervention in the Middle East is more pervasive than before. In this milieu, when populations are subjected to debilitation and disposability, the analyses of civil society, resistance, and revolution in digital realms cannot afford to ignore the geopolitical.

Needless to say, this book does not claim to provide a full account of the use of the internet among Iranians in Iran and its diaspora. Despite the fast development of internet technologies, like any ethnographic account this research is limited by its temporal and spatial specificity. While the trend in studies of the internet is to produce scholarship about the newest technological advances caused by the fast pace of internet technologies, I resist the modernist impulse and the amnesiac tempo that fixates on the "new." I hope to counter the hasty enthusiasm in technocentric accounts that is informed by a linear progressive temporality and the colonial desire for expeditions in "new frontiers." In other words, this ethnography dwells in Weblogistan in the first decade of the new millennium, when blogging by Iranians was celebrated as a tool of democratization during the "war on terror." However, considering the currency of discourses of liberation in the language of digital citizenship, this book may offer some insights for the current political atmosphere.

Chapter Summaries

In the first chapter of this book, "Weblogistan and the Iranian Diaspora: Nation and Its Re-territorializations in Cyberspace," I introduce Weblogistan by discussing conventions of Persian-language blogging, representations of Weblogistan as a liberalizing technology in Iran, and the role of diasporic bloggers in the world of Persian blogging. I show the that rehearsals of democracy and the desire for exceptional citizenship in Weblogistan were necessarily implicated in nationalist discourses that produced a heteronormative and homogenous image of Iranianness against Iran's internal and external others. Despite the nationalist displays of Iranianness through market virility and whiteness in the United States, the desire for exceptional citizenship is rendered impossible for the desiring Iranian subject, because Iranianness is overdetermined as a contagious risk.

In chapter 2, "Civil Society (*jaame'e-ye madani*), Soccer, and Gendered Politics in Weblogistan: The 2005 Presidential Election," I discuss the notion of civil society in the Iranian political context and argue that while Iranian cyberspace (including blogs) has expanded transnational Iranian civil society by enabling faster communication between a certain group of middle-class Iranians in Iran and their counterparts in diaspora, the Iranian civil society is neither new nor a gift granted by internet technologies. By considering Weblogistan as an element of transnational Iranian civil society, I do not intend to celebrate civil society as a site of consensus and debate or to glorify the internet as an emancipatory technology. On the contrary, I show that Weblogistan is where gendered inequalities surface and where women are excluded from the realm of "proper politics." The online and offline reactions to women bloggers who voted in the presidential election and the encounters among women activists/bloggers, reformist men, and secular diaspora opposition groups and individuals demonstrate how blogger women activists were often caught between discourses of liberation that legitimized imperialism and nationalist discourses that used women as markers of national pride. The figure of the woman activist in Weblogistan as para-human (Amar 2013)—a victim in need of rescue and protection, and also a menacing figure who poses a risk to national security—constitutes a risky subject (Patel 2006) whose vulnerability sanctions violence in the name of protection and whose loaned life is subjected to the politics of rightful killing.

In chapter 3, "Whores, Homos, and Feminists: Weblogistan's Anti-modern Others," I discuss Weblogistan as a site of cybergovernmentality where gendered subjects are disciplined and normalized under the rhetoric of "practicing democracy" and through the "conduct of the conduct" of others and "technologies of self." Following Aihwa Ong's assertion (2006) that the ethics of citizenship and governing of populations is increasingly concerned with individual self-management according to moral codes, I argue that the normalization of language in Weblogistan is deployed to regulate individual bloggers' conduct according to the codes of heteronormative monogamy and democratic futurity. The proper subjects of Weblogistan are those who aspire to an exceptional citizenship and a democratic futurity that purges its unwanted excess: the backward and unstable woman. Unlike the desiring subject who aspires to exceptional citizenship, the untamed Iranian woman who crosses lines of civility is the excess of the art of normalization. No longer redeemable under the rhetoric of gendered victimhood, her death is sanctioned in the name of national security and democratic futurity.

In chapter 4, "Weblogistan and Its Homosexual Problem," I show that performances of modern citizenship in Weblogistan repeat heteronormative nationalist discourses alongside the neoliberal discourses of freedom and democracy. By discussing the debates around homosexuality, I argue that despite the idealization of Weblogistan as a new platform for democratic inclusion, nationalist imaginations of Iranianness often exclude queers. At best, in a competition to envision a democratic future in the market for democratization, intellectual bloggers who strived to prove their modernity advocated tolerance (with a limit) for homosexuals. This tolerance was contingent on homonormative notions of sexual identity that reified a heterosexual and homosexual binary and reiterated heteronormative nationalism through condemning sexualities that were deemed to be unethical or inauthentic. As such, the *chic of queer* in Weblogistan stemmed from the desire for a particular Iranian modernity and exceptional citizenship that valorized freedom and democracy and produced universalized sexual and homogenous national identities, while simultaneously emphasizing sexual and racial difference. Through discussing representations of queer death, I show that while white queers are folded into life as exceptional citizens who die heroic deaths, others become representable in life or death only as victims of Islamic homophobia. Even as some Iranian queers desire exceptional citizenship through proximity to whiteness, neoliberal entrepreneurship, embodiment of sanitized homosexuality, and the rejection of Islam, the Iranian population at large becomes racially queered and disposable.

In chapter 5, "The War Machine, Neoliberal *Homo Œconomicus*, and the Experts," I discuss the production of expertise and its relationship to neoliberal self-entrepreneurship in Weblogistan during the "war on terror." The empire-building project is connected to neoliberal practices and discourses that produce entrepreneurial blogger subjects who are disciplined—and discipline themselves and others—according to the gendered and sexed norms of freedom, democracy, and the market. I contextualize the production of the neoliberal self-entrepreneur blogger in relation to the politics of democratization during the "war on terror" through a number of key sites: a documentary film about Weblogistan, a radio program that was launched as the radio of Weblogistan, and a conference that featured liberalization through blogging. Through these examples I argue that while blogger self-entrepreneurs as the war machine became "soldiers of freedom" in the market for information during the "war on terror," they were easily disposable and replaceable once they lost their political usefulness and posed a threat to the internet democratization projects.

In the coda, I discuss the 2009 "Twitter revolution" and the 2018 arrests of the "Instagram girls" and argue that the celebrations of social media mobilizations through hashtags that reduce dissent to "sexual revolution" elide the conditions that render the Iranian population killable. The hype around "internet revolution," censorship, freedom of speech, and the mobilizations of civil society in social media overshadows the sanctions and the pending war that subject the Iranian population to the politics of rightful killing. Rather than an optimism that seeks potentiality in bare life, I suggest pessimism as the possibility of transformative politics.

[1]

Weblogistan and the Iranian Diaspora

*Nation and Its Re-territorializations
in Cyberspace*

Shortly after English-language blogs started to proliferate in the mid to late 1990s, Salman Jariri published the first Persian-language blog in September 2001. One month later, Hossein Derakhshan (also known as Hoder), an Iranian immigrant living in Canada, published instructions on how to make a blog in Persian by using a Persian-language template.[1] Derakhshan posted some basic blogging tools for Unicode (an international standard used to encode texts), enabling many Iranians in Iran and its diaspora to use free blog-hosting services (Doostdar, 2004). Hoder began to encourage his friends in Iran and Toronto to start their own blogs. Soon after, a number of servers for Persian blogs became available inside and outside of Iran, and an increasing number of Persian-language blogs emerged. The large number of Persian-language blogs came to be known as Weblogistan, the Iranian blogosphere. By 2005, Weblogistan included an estimated 700,000 Persian-language blogs, of which roughly 100,000 were estimated to be active.[2]

It is not clear who coined the term *Weblogistan*. Pronounced "veblah-gestahn" in Persian, the term literally means the land of weblogs, a cyber-territorial designation naming the fastest growing cyber sphere in the Middle East (Hendelman-Baavur 2007). Although limited access and the expense of personal computers meant that only a small percentage of Iranians in Iran were internet users in early 2000s, the proliferation of Persian-language blogs written by Iranians in Iran and its diaspora since September 2001 put Persian-language blogging in fourth place in blog-ranking systems.[3] Not all of the 100,000 active Persian blogs were written by Iranians. Nor did all Iranian bloggers write in Persian. At the time of my research, blog search engines such as Technorati estimated the number of blogs based on language-indexing methods and keyword search. These methods did not take into account that Persian is a language also spoken in Afghanistan and a few Central Asian countries such as Tajikistan.[4] Also, even though most Iranian bloggers wrote in Persian (because it is the national language), some blogs were written by Iranians in Kurdish, Turkish, Armenian, English, French, and other languages that are spoken in Iran and its diaspora. However, the statistics provided by blog-hosting services in Iran highlight the fact that the number of Persian-language blogs written by Iranians in Iran and its diaspora in the mid-2000s was quite significant (Khiabany and Sreberny 2007). Although the "net" has not covered many rural areas and is not accessible to economically disadvantaged urban Iranians, the transnational encounters between a group of educated Iranians in Iran and its diaspora, along with the infrastructural changes in the Iranian communication industry, have made computer-mediated communications a significant means of transnational communication between computer-savvy cosmopolitan Iranians in Iran and those in different parts of the world.[5]

At the time of my research, most Persian blogs were individually written, but there were also several group blogs (*veblohg-e goroohee*) with several authors (e.g. *hanooz, hezaar-too*). Some blogs resembled diaries, with the bloggers reporting their daily thoughts and activities for a public audience. However, most blogs comprised a combination of subjects (including politics, sports, music, arts, science and technology, religion, news, and culture) and genres (from short story to memoir to poetry). Other bloggers wrote topic-specific blogs (*weblog-e takhassosi*) on one subject and using technical terms. A few bloggers wrote about their children and their children's daily activities; some even named their blogs after their children. Most blogs in Weblogistan were text based, but the use of images was also common. Some bloggers chose not to publicize their blogs and instead wrote a diary anonymously for themselves or for their children.[6] Many Persian blogs were hosted by Iranian blogging services, or by free and paid non-Iranian blogging services such as Blogger and Movable Type.[7] Even though most Persian blogs were written in Iran, North America, and Europe, Persian blogs and blog readers were geographically dispersed. Some of the readers of my blog were commenting from Saudi Arabia, Turkey, Bahrain, Indonesia, Malaysia, Czech Republic, Azerbaijan, Japan, and India, among other locations.

Blogging as a dialogic phenomenon (Doostdar 2004) relies on user comments and hyperlinks that connect blogs and readers to one another. One of the elements that distinguishes a blog from a website, other than the frequency with which it is updated and its format, is its interactive character. Users interact with one another in a number of ways: commenting on posts in *commentdooni* (the comments section), hyperlinking to other bloggers in their own posts, and adding bloggers to their *linkdooni* (link dump), which is a list of links to other blogs. One of the ways that bloggers expanded their blogging circles was to maintain a blogroll. Bloggers added a long list of blogs to their blogroll, either to increase their blogging circle or because they felt obliged to do so out of politeness. However, just as blog fights or disagreements did not translate into offline adversity, adding another blog to one's blogroll did not necessarily indicate friendship or agreement. At times, bloggers would add an unfavorable blog to their blogroll in order to monitor the other blogger's activity. Blogroll was an effective way to know who had updated their blog. When a blogger "pinged" (i.e., updated) their blog, the blogroll service would move their blog to the top of the blogroll column. Another mode of interacting was the use of "trackbacks." By adding one's URL (uniform resource locator) to the trackback under someone else's blog post, a blogger would let others (including the author of the trackbacked blog) know that they had either written a response or a post that was related to the other blogger's post. Following links on the blogs that one read regularly was yet another way to connect to a wider network of blogs in Weblogistan.

As a reciprocity ritual, commenting is an effective way to connect and communicate with other bloggers. As Alireza Doostdar has suggested (2004), leaving comments on another's blog resembles a *deed-o baazdeed*: a customary Iranian social ritual that refers to reciprocal visiting and literally translates into "seeing and seeing again." Even though not reciprocating a visit in deed o baazdeed is considered to be impolite within Iranian social conventions, some "star bloggers" who got a lot of visitors did not respond or leave comments on their visitors' blogs. Sometimes, "trolls" would leave inappropriate or insulting comments by using another blogger's name and/or email address.

In order to relieve themselves from the responsibility of *baazdeed* (to return the visit) and the hassle of being pranked, a few popular and controversial bloggers made it publicly known that they did not leave comments on anyone's blog.

At times, a blogger who wanted to be known by another would leave a comment such as "I came here by accident, and I like what you write. Please pay me a visit." Other times, a blogger would leave a comment such as "With your permission, I gave you a link" to indirectly signal the expectation of reciprocity. If a reader made a comment that indicated careful reading and contemplation (rather than a generic flattering remark), it often meant that they were interested in establishing a blogging relationship with the host. In some cases, when a reader did not like a blogger's post, they would leave challenging or hostile comments. This was the main reason that some bloggers (especially women who were targeted by sexist comments) "filtered" incoming comments before approving them. Some bloggers who faced hostility in their comments section chose to close this section altogether.

Many bloggers self-censored by avoiding subjects that transgressed social conventions, disappointed readers, or jeopardized their respectability (I will discuss this in detail in chapter 4). At times, comments functioned as normalizing techniques, wherein readers participated in regulating bloggers' conduct according to the norms that established the acceptable contours of Iranianness in Weblogistan. Comments such as "I did not expect such vulgarity from you," "A lady does not use such words," or "Why use a manly language?" reminded female-bodied bloggers that they were under surveillance by readers who deployed gendered notions of civility and propriety to discipline them. As I will discuss in chapter 4, discussions about internet censorship in Iran often focus on state repression while ignoring gendered forms of normalizing, disciplining, and censorship that are imposed by bloggers and readers in Weblogistan. During my research, it became clear to me that the disciplining of bloggers did not just take place in the commentdooni but extended its reach to bloggers' offline lives. Many Iranian bloggers in Iran and its diaspora wrote with their real names, which often meant that the content of their blogs had tangible consequences in their offline lives. While the famous *New Yorker* cartoon by Peter Steiner depicts a computer-literate dog telling another dog, "On the Internet, nobody knows you're a dog," in Weblogistan many popular bloggers did not hide their identity.[8] Indeed, in order to lay claim to one's individuality—a much-celebrated feature of blogs—not only did many bloggers write with their real names, but they also shared private matters that were uninteresting to many readers but seemed important to the bloggers' sense of their uniqueness.

Transparency and telling one's "truth" were often celebrated as a practice of democracy. The desire to prove commitment to democracy and transparency compelled many bloggers to write in a confessional mode. One of the "truth-telling" practices in Weblogistan was known as *baazi-ye veblogi* (blog game). To initiate a game, a blogger would pose a question and invite a list of bloggers to participate by tagging them. Questions had different themes but often demanded a confessional-style answer, where the invitees were expected to respond to the question truthfully. Some of the questions posed in baazi-ye veblogi in Weblogistan during my fieldwork included "What is your fondest memory of childhood?" "What are you up to these days?" and "What is homeland to you?" After responding to the posed question in a post, the invited bloggers would invite a number of other bloggers to participate. In this way, through the domino effect a large number of bloggers would write about the same topic. While not every invited blogger told the truth in these games, the offline connections and the fact that many bloggers wrote with their real names compelled them to write in a confessional mode.

Censorship

In the past few years, internet censorship in Iran has attracted international attention. Even though dial-up internet became available in Iran in the mid-1990s, it took until 2001 for the Iranian Supreme Cultural Revolution Council to start monitoring the internet and issuing guidelines for acceptable internet content.[9] By 2002, this council had implemented strategies to limit access to websites that were considered to endanger national security and/or Islamic values (a process known as filtering). It did not take long for Iranian internet users to circumvent the Iranian state's filtering system by using proxy servers (or virtual public networks) and software known as *filter shekan* (filter breaker).[10] The Iranian state blocks a number of sites that it considers to be antithetical to the Islamic values of the state. Ironically, the Iranian state has purchased certain filtering software from private U.S. companies.[11] At times, to outdo the state, private internet service providers (ISPs) filter URLs that contain certain words. For instance, in 2005 some ISPs filtered the word *zan* (woman). Enraged by this censorship by private ISPs and to protest the Iranian state's filtering of several women's-rights organizations' websites, many

FIGURE 1.1 "Censorship is obscene, not woman."

feminist women bloggers posted a banner on their blogs that read "Censorship is obscene, not woman."

Through a contract with an internet "security" company, Anonymizer, the U.S. International Broadcasting Bureau (IBB) provided (and continues to provide) free filter-breaking proxies to enable access to blocked sites.[12] The URLs for these proxies were publicized by different media such as Radio Farda, a station run by the International Broadcasting Bureau, which is the U.S. government's overseas news and propaganda arm. Proxies were also sent through bulk emails that Anonymizer sent to IP addresses in Iran. Radio Farda's website (itself filtered) also included instructions in Persian. Some human rights groups and other "nongovernmental" entities provided the addresses.[13] Ironically, despite the claims of its providers, filter-breaking proxies did not allow limitless surfing. The U.S.-provided proxies themselves filtered certain words such as *gay* to deter the Iranian internet users from visiting gay porn sites.[14] The word *ass* was among the blocked items by the U.S.-sponsored proxies. Ironically, in its efforts to break the Iranian state's filters, the U.S. freedom/security apparatus did not realize that all words and terms that contained the letters "a-s-s" (including "American Embassy") were unsearchable.[15]

While the Iranian state's internet censorship practices started soon after the popularization of the internet in Iran, the increased restriction of access to sites such as Facebook, Twitter, and Google was mainly a reaction to the proliferation of regime-change discourses during the 2009 protests (also known as the "Twitter revolution"). During the same period, the U.S.-Israeli cyber-attack (using the Stuxnet virus) damaged Iranian computers that worked with nuclear technology.[16] This gave license to the Iranian state's intelligence apparatus to detain activists and protesters on charges of espionage and in the name of national security. In 2009 the Working Group to Determine Instances of Criminal Content on the Internet—an entity that includes members of the president's cabinet, Intelligence Ministry, Guidance Ministry, and the Islamic Republic of Iran Broadcasting (IRIB) Agency—was formed to prosecute "criminal" internet activity.[17] FATA, the Iranian cyber-crimes police unit, was formed in 2011 to counter "cyber-crimes" and terrorism. The death of Sattar Beheshti, a low-profile Iranian blogger who died while in FATA's custody, culminated in the removal of the commander of the cyber-police unit.[18] In 2012 the Iranian state formed the Supreme Cyberspace Council to oversee compliance with Islamic principles and to ensure national security. In 2016 the first phase of the national internet plan was launched.[19] While the national internet was partly designed to increase surveillance under the rhetoric of national security, the sanctions against Iran had a significant role in the emergence of this plan, as the comprehensive sanctions imposed by the United States blocked access to countless websites owned by private companies.[20] As I discussed in the introduction, with the increased censorship and security measures of the Iranian state, lifting Iran's "electronic curtain" became the official language of the U.S. democratization projects.[21]

The market for liberating the internet in Iran attracted a range of state and nonstate organizations and individuals who found an apt opportunity in the regime-change industry. For example, shortly after the 2009 street protests in Iran, Austin Heap, a young self-described "internet junkie," announced that he and Daniel Colascione would be launching software called Haystack to provide uncensored internet for the Iranian people.[22] Despite the sanctions against Iran, U.S. Secretary of the State Hillary Clinton announced that the Department of the State had granted an accelerated license to Heap's company to export Haystack to Iran. Heap's nonprofit organization (the Censorship Research Center) received grants from civil society groups (such as the global advocacy group Avaaz.org) to provide internet freedom for Iranian internet users.[23] Heap was lauded as the "innovator of the year" by the *Guardian* and hailed as the leader of the "Twitter revolution" in Iran by the BBC. Despite the publicity and enthusiasm that Haystack received, it became clear that it had jeopardized the Iranian internet users' identity soon after it was tested.[24]

While hacking and viruses are often seen as progressive antiestablishment cyber-activism, these practices have been co-opted by the empire to serve the geopolitical and neoliberal economic interests that deploy human rights, freedom, and democratization. As Seb Franklin argues, "One cannot take the overall function of computer viruses as a model for radical politics or critique"

(2012, 165). Even though Franklin focuses on the technical aspect of computation to argue that hacking and viruses rely on the data bank characteristic of control societies (Deleuze 1995) and centers the individual as the hero who acts against injustice, his analysis is helpful in understanding how movements for "justice" are co-opted to serve neoliberal and militaristic uses of the internet. Franklin sees the progressive potential not in attacking or exceeding the informatics society but in that which cannot be coded, measured, and therefore not co-opted (167). Franklin's suggestion may lead us to think beyond the frameworks that excavate potentials of subversion in data-oriented "control societies." As viral democracy projects in the Middle East demonstrate, the optimism that sees the viral as exceeding human-centric activism, or considers it a gesture of civic hacking, turns a blind eye to the recentering of the neoliberal individual hacker/entrepreneur while erasing the co-optation of cyber-activism by the neoliberal war machine. Given that democratization experts have hailed the internet in the Middle East as one of the most important agents of civil society, and considering that the internet is deployed as a technology of calculation and surveillance in the region, cyber-enthusiastic approaches to social movements in the Middle East may be exaggerating its subversive potentials. Hailing the internet as the bedrock of revolutionary movements in the Middle East misses the point that Weblogistan and other sites of civil society in cyberspace do not escape forms of governmentality, including state and nonstate security measures and insurance technologies that reproduce the militarized neoliberal logic. It is this logic that sanctions the politics of rightful killing to secure the future of the market against a risky present.

During my fieldwork, many bloggers circumvented filtering by using RSS (rich site summary or really simple syndication) feeds, which include the full text of the blog with the name of the author and the date of the post in a simple readable format. Unlike blogs, which could be blocked individually, RSS feeds were not easily blocked: in order to block a feed, the whole server had to be blocked. Filtering was not the only reason that bloggers were drawn to feeds. By subscribing to an RSS feed, users could keep track of their favorite blogs in one news aggregator without having to check those blogs manually. Feeds provided the text of various blog posts, saving readers from having to visit individual blogs, a convenient and time-saving strategy for those who were interested in reading a large number of blogs. Moreover, with broadband limitations in Iran and the fact that high-speed internet was not available to many people, it could take a long time to upload a blog if it was "heavy."

After I stopped blogging, many bloggers moved to feed-reader tools such as Google Reader (also known as "Goder" among Iranian bloggers) or FriendFeed (also known as "Ferfer" among its Iranian users), a real-time feed aggregator that brought together a group of RSS feeds from a variety of social networking websites and blogs.[25] It was/is common for some bloggers to use a variety of social networking tools, such as Facebook, Orkut, Flickr, Ferfer, and Goder.[26] In order to increase readership, some bloggers registered their blogs with these tools or gave links to their blog entries on other social networking tools. As a result, blogs increasingly obtained visibility through other social networking media. At times, older media forms such as television, radio, and newspapers used blogs (and other social networking tools) to access real-time news. Because these older media had a wider audience, blogs reached a large number of people who relied on older media forms.

A popular link-sharing tool among Iranian bloggers and blog readers was Balatarin ("the top/the highest").[27] Created by Mehdi, a Stanford postdoctoral fellow in computer science and a blogger at the time, Balatarin allowed registered users to "vote" on a link, thus increasing its rating. The post with the highest number of votes would appear on the top of the list of articles on the Balatarin site. A couple of years before Balatarin was launched in 2006, Mehdi told me that he was interested in building a site that enacted democracy in Weblogistan, where people's votes would determine the popularity of a blog post. In 2008 I learned through email about a voting controversy that erupted when Hoder, a popular and highly controversial Iranian blogger, complained that Balatarin had blocked him because of a post in which he had accused another blogger (a friend of Mehdi) of complicity with the U.S. militaristic agenda against Iran. After protesting his being blocked by Balatarin, Hoder questioned the website's claims of democracy. Almost a year after this incident, a blogger friend told me that in the aftermath of the 2009 presidential election, Mohsen Sazegara, a former postrevolutionary politician who had left Iran and worked for the conservative pro-Israel think tank the Washington Institute for Near East Policy, was repeatedly featured at the top of the Balatarin list. Sazegara's instructional YouTube videos in Persian about "nonviolent struggle," which were translated from Gene Sharp's strategies for "color revolutions" in Eastern Europe, advocated similar results in Iran.[28] Disapprovingly, this blogger friend who was concerned about the popularity of a regime-change proponent (albeit under the guise of "nonviolence") in Balatarin told me, "This tells you who votes in Balatarin." Regardless of the critiques of Balatarin, it remains a useful tool for reading news, and its blogs and websites receive the highest number of clicks from Iranian internet users.

Blogger Types

Some researchers insist on categorizing bloggers into types and groups.[29] However, because of the dialogic and transnational character of Weblogistan and because of multiple fragmentations and overlaps, it is impossible to easily categorize bloggers. For example, to categorize bloggers into secular and religious types not only reifies an artificial divide but also ignores that the content of actual blogs cannot be so easily categorized. The representation of Weblogistan as a uniformly secular anti-Iranian "regime" erases a number of bloggers with different degrees of religious devotion who may or may not be supportive of the Iranian state. Many bloggers with conservative, reformist, or secular positions may have heated disagreements over one issue (for example, their desired presidential candidate, which I will discuss in chapter 2) but be in alliance when it comes to another issue (for example, the naming of the Persian Gulf, which I will discuss later in this chapter).

The political inclinations of bloggers span a wide range. Despite differences in politics and opinions, strategic alliances are not uncommon among bloggers. For example, while I had a heated confrontation with a reformist blogger in Iran over issues of gender and sexuality, we formed an alliance during the 2005 Iranian presidential elections. Similarly, despite my disagreements with a blogger who lived in Europe and was an avid advocate of free markets and neoliberal economy, I joined him and a few other bloggers to launch *Iranians for Peace*, an English-language group blog that advocated against a military attack on Iran during George W. Bush's presidency. Regardless of the inflammatory nature of political conflicts in Weblogistan, online friendships extended offline. During my fieldwork in Toronto I noticed that a number of bloggers who often had hostile interactions online were extremely friendly to one another in person. For example, two Toronto-based bloggers who had heated blog fights over issues of gender and sexuality often socialized offline as friends and consulted each other about different issues. During the controversy about the "Mohammad cartoons,"[30] one of them was invited to a radio debate with Irshad Manji, a Canada-based lesbian of Muslim background who identifies as a "Muslim refusenik."[31] Despite his blog fights with the other blogger, he called her to get help with talking points. I was present when the woman blogger gave advice to her online adversary over the phone. She frequently interrupted her phone conversation to ask my opinion about the best way to challenge the conflation of homophobia with Muslims. Alliances like this were not uncommon in Weblogistan. This messiness (not apparent if one only observed online interactions) made any clear categorizations of blogger types practically impossible.

Similarly, the differences of opinion among bloggers in Iran and in diaspora cannot be reduced to resident bloggers versus diaspora bloggers. There are vast differences in class and politics within and between both of these groups. An Iranian resident blogger may be more politically aligned with an Iranian diasporic blogger than with another blogger in Iran. Despite political differences, nationalist sentiments at times aligned Iranian bloggers in different parts of the world. As I will discuss later in this chapter, during the mobilizations around the naming of the Persian Gulf, bloggers who had different political positions formed alliances through transnational performances of nationalism. Even though one cannot divide bloggers into homogenous categories of "bloggers in Iran" and "diasporic bloggers," politics of location certainly matters in the complex dynamics of power in Weblogistan. This was particularly apparent when some Iranian resident bloggers ridiculed diasporic bloggers who had a skewed understanding of the political atmosphere and life in Iran by calling them *dor-e gowd nesheen* (one who sits around the wrestling pit and orders the wrestler to grab the opponent's leg).

Just as one cannot easily categorize bloggers as diaspora bloggers or resident bloggers, class categorizations are almost impossible. Even though economic inequality is a reality of Iranian people's life (regardless of location), differences in the articulation of class in Iran and diaspora, changes in upward or downward mobility after immigration, formal and informal connections to centers of power, and the tendency to save face (*aberoo negah daashtan*) by downplaying one's hardship or one's economic privilege online make clear-cut class categorization in Weblogistan impossible. One can make a similar argument about categorizing bloggers based on their gender or sexuality. Even though I initially went to the field with the assumption that organizing men's focus groups and women's focus groups would reveal differences among bloggers based on their gender, I came to realize that categorizing bloggers as such would limit my research to the binaries that I had set forth based on the hegemonic categorizations of gender. Rather than assuming that women bloggers had a unique blogging style or that their blog contents were similar because of their shared gender, a more productive approach, I decided, was to see how competing and compatible national and transnational discourses in Weblogistan produced normative notions of gender and sexuality that came to regulate gendered subjects.

As I will discuss in chapter 2, a dominant trend in mainstream representations of Weblogistan is to characterize it as a unified "voice" against the Iranian state. For several reasons, this is an inaccurate understanding of Weblogistan, not least of all because Iranian state officials themselves were drawn to blogging. For instance, Mohammad Ali Abtahi, the former Iranian vice president, maintained one of the most popular Persian blogs.[32] During the 2005 presidential elections, many candidates, including the reformist candidate, Mostafa Moeen, and the Abaadgaraan candidate, Mahmoud Ahmadinejad, started their own blogs. The multiplicity of voices in Weblogistan was not limited to the diversity of political positions among Iranian bloggers but concerned multiple subject positions that bloggers occupied in different discursive fields. Unlike the popular assumption that blogs give bloggers (in particular women) an outlet to express their authentic voice or that women reveal their true selves on their blogs, there is no inherent truth that is awaiting excavation through online confessions. As fragmented subjects, bloggers' online voices were often different from their offline voices among friends, intimates, family, coworkers, and strangers. To assume that blogs reflect bloggers' "true" voices erases their multiple subjectivities, neglecting the performative aspect of blogging.

Infrastructure

The popularization of the internet and the growth of the "information society" in Iran cannot be separated from the infrastructural and economic policies of the Iranian state and the globalized communication industries (Khiabany and Sreberny 2010). In *Digital Capitalism: Networking the Global Market System* (1999), Dan Schiller provides a historical account of networks in the United States and in the transnational context. Schiller shows that the neoliberal market economy was essential to the expansion of telecommunication infrastructure and argues that since the 1960s, network applications were guided by corporate demand and military strategies in the United States. In the 1980s and 1990s and with the U.S. push toward deregulation, a series of transnational initiatives came into being. Iran was not an exception to this trend. From the 1960s until the late 1970s, Iran was a key center of information technology in the Middle East. The Iranian software industry had developed mainframe computing and had signed many contracts with foreign software and IT suppliers. After the 1979 revolution, the mainframe sector, handled by major multinational corporations such as IBM and NCR, sold out; despite U.S. sanctions, the telecommunication industry in postrevolutionary Iran opened to privatization and foreign contracts.

While the 1980s saw an increased use of computers, it was in 1992 that the Institute for Studies in Theoretical Physics and Mathematics used the internet for the first time. This internet connection was enabled through the BITNET network via Iran's membership in the Trans-European Research and Educational Networking Association (TERENA).[33] The internet connection was further developed with TERENA's assignment of five hundred IP addresses across the country and acceptance of Iran as a Class C node.[34] After 1994, the number of long-distance channels increased, and the number of main lines in the urban system significantly increased. These developments were consistent with Iran's changing economic policies after the eight-year war with Iraq. As the communication industry grew, a series of contracts was signed between the Data Communications Company of Iran (DCI) and transnational companies such as Minitel and Intelstat.

Because Iran's economy saw liberalization after Rafsanjani's presidency (1989–97), middle-class Iranians in diaspora who did not face the same regulations as foreign investors took advantage of the opportunity to conduct business in Iran.[35] Some diaspora Iranians participated in Tehran's stock market and invested in Iran's communication technologies.[36] Also, the political aspirations of Iranian diaspora groups and individuals motivated them to take advantage of communication technologies and to form political alliances in Iran. For example, in August 2001 Goli Ameri, an Iranian American member of the board of Republican women's organizations in Oregon and the founder and president of eTinium (a consulting and market research firm specializing in the telecommunications industry and advising for firms such as Lucent Technologies and Nortel Networks), was invited to the first Telecommunications Conference and the Ministry of Telecommunications in Iran to discuss deregulation in the Asian telecom market.[37] The fact that a Republican corporate investor in the communication industries was providing consultation to the Iranian state is a reminder that the role of the Iranian diaspora in Iran's economic, infrastructural, and cultural changes should not be ignored in analyses of Iranian civil society.

While the internet in Iran was initially limited to research institutes and universities, it was later made available to the public. Despite slow connections, internet use increased very rapidly in urban areas. Some reports indicate that by 2003, the number of internet users had reached 4.3 million (from 250,000 in 2001) and that by 2004, more than 5,200 internet hosts existed in Iran.[38] The number of private internet service providers that offered internet cards, DSL, and wireless connection continued to rise in Iran, as the internet provided a lucrative business for the private sector.[39] By the early 2000s, internet cafés in urban centers flourished (mostly in upper-middle-class neighborhoods), and relatively inexpensive internet cards that provided access from a personal computer for a limited time (up to ten hours) had become popular.[40] Despite this increase, internet users in Iran constituted only 8 percent of the population during the time I conducted my fieldwork in 2005.[41]

Diasporic Blogging

After September 11, 2001, Persian-language blogging was popularized among a group of educated and computer-savvy Iranians in Iran who had regular access to the internet. But some of the first and most popular bloggers, several think tanks and foreign-government–funded Persian media that were interested in Persian blogging, and many Iranian opposition groups that found a revolutionary potential in Persian blogging were concentrated in North America and Europe (and not Iran). Weblogistan's emergence in 2001 enhanced the connectivity of Iranians throughout Iran and across its diaspora. Blogging created a renewed sense of belonging to the "homeland" for those educated Iranians living in the United States, Europe, and Canada who could not easily travel to Iran because of visa restrictions, finances, politics, and the fear of return. Toronto, in particular, hosted a large number of popular Iranian bloggers, even though the largest population of Iranians living outside of Iran resides in Los Angeles. The significance of blogging from Toronto compelled a famous Iranian blogger and journalist in Amsterdam to associate a style of controversial blogging with *maktab-e Torentoyee* (the Toronto school).

At the time of my research, Toronto had an Iranian population of approximately 57,178.[42] According to the 2006 census, the number of Iranians in Canada had increased by 38 percent since 2001, a factor that explains the large number of Persian-language blogs written by young, computer-savvy Iranians in Toronto.[43] Because of the need for skilled workers in Canada and the relative ease (in comparison to the United States) of obtaining a professional visa for certain classes of workers (with software engineering as one of the most needed skills), in the early 2000s young professional Iranians tended to immigrate to Canada rather than the United States. Mostly professionals, recent immigrants in Toronto are both computer-literate and fluent in Persian. Los Angeles has a larger population of Iranians who fled Iran immediately after the 1979 revolution. However, because of harsher immigration policies in the United States, Los Angeles has seen fewer recent immigrants than Toronto has.[44] The older immigrants in Los Angeles are fluent in Persian but (with a few exceptions) not as keen about blogging. Many younger Iranians in Los Angeles grew up in the United States and, for the most part, do not have the Persian-language skills required for Persian blogging. While there are some Iranian Persian-language bloggers in Los Angeles, the demographics of Toronto made it a hub of Persian blogging for recent Iranian immigrants who used blogging to keep their connection to friends and family in Iran, to engage with the politics of homeland, and to find other Iranians in their new cities.

There are a variety of factors contributing to the emigration of Iranians, chief among them the sociopolitical events of the 1979 Iranian revolution and the subsequent fear of persecution by the newly formed Islamic government.[45] By the first decade of the twenty-first century, the United States contained the largest number of Iranians outside of Iran.[46] According to a 2004 report by MIT's Iranian Studies Group (ISG), the per capita income level of Iranian Americans ($30,143) in 2000 was 50 percent higher than the U.S. national average, and their educational attainment likewise surpassed the national average.[47] According to the ISG, Iranian Americans have founded—or are employed by—many Fortune 500 companies (Mostashari and Khodamhosseini 2004). Of course, dominant representations of Iranians in the United States do not take into consideration Iranian refugees who do not find their way into mainstream surveys and media reports. Mehdi, one of the ISG members and an active blogger, told me that the purpose of the 2004 study was to show the economic contribution of Iranian immigrants in the face of anti-Iranian/anti–Middle Eastern sentiment in the United States. According to Mehdi, ISG was aware of the erasure of the underprivileged segments of the Iranian immigrant community, but the goal of this survey was to highlight the "success" rate of the Iranian immigrant communities in order to boost the confidence of Iranians who, unlike many other immigrant communities in the United States, have not formed networks.

While these data do not account for Iranian refugees and immigrants who may not be counted in census reports and do not enjoy the privileges of middle-class life in the United States, one could argue that the majority of Iranian immigrants come from urban, middle-class backgrounds in Iran

(Ansari 1988; Modarres 1998). They are, for the most part, professionals, entrepreneurs, and scholars who contribute to the establishment of a "transnational civil society" (Moallem 2000) and who participate in the politics of "homeland."[48] Postrevolutionary changes in Iran's state structure and shifts in political power have been affected by the increasing links of diaspora Iranians with Iran through communication technologies and/or the back-and-forth movement of people. Furthermore, changes in the sociopolitical fabric of the nation-state have in turn affected the ways that Iranian diaspora communities relate to Iran by increasingly engaging in homeland politics via communication technologies, exchange of capital, and mobility. Nevertheless, it is wrong to assume that all diaspora Iranians have equal access to the internet.

While a large group of Iranians in the United States and Europe have access to the internet, many Iranian refugees live under dire conditions (and often "illegally" in Turkey and other locations). These refugees are not as mobile and may not have easy access to computers as they wait for the United Nations Human Rights Commission (UNHRC) to recognize them as "true refugees."[49] In addition, despite the large number of educated diaspora Iranians in North America, many Iranians (such as older immigrants) who live in the United States and Europe do not use internet-mediated social media, either because of lack of computer literacy or because they do not have access to computers. Thus, as David Morley has argued in the context of satellite television (2000, 176), while the internet has produced "new definitions of time, space, and community, these are not necessarily erasing but are rather overlaying our old understanding of distance and duration." The "time-space compression" (Harvey 1990) under conditions of postmodernity is not experienced the same way by everyone. Different histories of migration, immigration policies, and market needs, among other factors, make generalizations about Iranians in Toronto and those in Los Angeles impossible. These factors not only influence the number of bloggers in Toronto compared to Los Angeles, but also the different forms of identification and politics in relation to the "homeland." Because many of my interlocutors in the United States and Canada were young, recent immigrants, their sense of Iranianness and politics differed from those who had immigrated immediately after the 1979 Iranian revolution. Second-generation Iranian Americans and first-generation Iranian Americans who emigrated at a young age immediately after the revolution are often not fluent in written Persian. Therefore, for the most part they usually do not write or read blogs in Persian. As I mentioned above, the older generation of Iranians who migrated soon after the 1979 revolution are generally not as internet savvy as younger immigrants. At the time of my research, with a few exceptions, these immigrants were not active bloggers or blog readers. The forced nature of departure for some of the older Iranians in Los Angeles has resulted in their common self-characterization as exiles.[50] Many Iranians who came to the United States as political refugees have since become legal permanent residents (LPRs) or U.S. citizens. While some still fear traveling to Iran, many started to travel back and forth between Iran and the United States after the Iran–Iraq war.[51] Nonetheless, exile continues to be an overarching discourse among a large number of Iranians who live outside of Iran. This self-characterization might be a result of the ambivalence toward living in Iran under an Islamic state or a strategy of survival in the face of anti-Iranian racism in the United States. Some reactionary Iranian "exiles," especially royalists, MEK (*Mojahedeen-e Khalq*), traditional leftists, and younger Iranians who are relatively detached and unaware of the changes in the political situation in Iran over the past four decades, completely reject reform within the context of the Islamic Republic and find regime change to be the only solution to Iran's problems. While the opposition to the Iranian state is not limited to these reactionary groups, for the sake of simplicity, in this book I use the term *opposition* to refer to these groups and the political career opportunists who have left Iran more recently to join regime-change forces.

As I will discuss, although many recent immigrant bloggers broke away from simplistic representations of Iran that are frozen in the time of revolution, some considered themselves to be exiled. One blogger considered herself to be "self-exiled" because she could not travel to Iran because of U.S. anti-immigration laws that made it difficult for many Iranians on student visas to return if they visited Iran. Other reasons that compelled some bloggers to identify as exile included postimmigration political activism and subsequent fear of persecution by the Iranian state, the need to produce proof of political endangerment for asylum claims, and class and gender connotations of the terms *refugee* and *exile*. For example, a famous blogger and artist who identified as an exile had initially traveled to Canada for an exhibition that was organized and paid for by the Iranian Embassy in Ontario. He eventually applied for asylum in Canada, claiming that his life was in danger in Iran. This blogger, who refused to identify himself as a refugee (*panaahandeh*) and preferred the term *exile* (*qorbat*), explained to me that *panahandeh* implied weakness. Unlike the feminized refugee, exile carries an aura of masculine intellectualism and political subjectivity.[52] Identifying as an exile is also informed by the reality that one's legitimacy in the country of asylum relies on exaggerated accounts of persecution in Iran. On several occasions, I found discrepancies between the public accounts of persecution narrated by self-identified exiles and the actual experiences of those exiles.[53] For instance, Musa—a former journalist in Iran—fabricated his academic qualifications, assumed a position with a conservative think tank in Washington, DC, as an expert on Iranian affairs, and provided policy recommendations to the U.S. Department of State. Needless to say, his political involvement with "regime-change" organizations and his cooperation with the U.S. Department of State and a pro-Israeli think tank after immigration have made his return to Iran impossible. His partner, a blogger who traveled back and forth between Iran and the United States, also referred to herself as an exile.[54]

Diaspora

The concept of diaspora has gained much currency as a result of the confluence of transnational, postcolonial, and British cultural studies. Although some uses of diaspora have romanticized displacement and hybridity, or have equated it to cosmopolitan travel (Watney 1995, 53–70), diaspora as a theoretical concept is useful in interrogating essentialist notions of home, origin, nation, and belonging. The currency of the use of the modernist and gendered definitions of "exile" in describing the "Iranian community" often homogenizes the multiplicity of experiences of displacement. Hamid Naficy is right in arguing that "Iranian exiles have created via their media and culture a symbolic and fetishized private hermetically sealed electronic communitas infused with home, past, memory, loss, nostalgia, longing for return, and the communal self; on the other hand, they have tried to get on with the process of living by incorporating themselves into the dominant culture of consumer capitalism by means of developing a new sense of self and what can be called exilic economy" (1993, xvi). Unlike Naficy, who theorizes exile as "a process of becoming" and a "period of liminality and in between-ness," I believe that exile often remains a term of "being" for cosmopolitan middle-class Iranians who, despite their multiple travels to Iran, insist on an exilic identity against an idealized imagination of home before exile. The exilic economy is established not through challenging the dichotomy of the here and there, local/global, but through a masculinist hegemonic situating of the "uprooted" self "here/in exile" in relation to the authentic and fixed "there/home." In this contest for authenticity, a link between people and place is naturalized, while its loss is mourned and grieved by the estranged exile. The exile story, the perpetual suffering, and the pains of "uprooted-ness" naturalize a sovereign nation-state as the destination for the Iranian exile. As Fortier (2000b, 53) argues, this "immigrant condition" of grieving the homeland is the result of the power attributed to the norms of the nation-state, wherein "all ethnic groups must be mobilized to create a territorial state, thus making the nation-state the last stage in the 'natural' development of peoples."

Problematizing the masculinist deployments of exile, many feminist scholars find diaspora to be an important theoretical framework because of the possibilities it can open in a transnational feminist approach to interrogate essentialist notions of home, origin, nation, and identity. For example, Avtar Brah rightly argues that "the concept of diaspora should be understood in terms of historically contingent 'genealogies' in the Foucauldian sense; that is, as an ensemble of investigative technologies that historicise trajectories of different diasporas, and analyse their relationality across fields of social relations, subjectivity and identity" (1996, 180). Although I agree with Brah that the liminal diaspora space and "the intersectionality of diaspora, border, and dis/location as a point of confluence of economic, political, cultural, and psychic processes" have the potential of challenging the nativist articulations of difference, I am skeptical of the uses of diaspora that tend to flatten and homogenize this concept to include all forms of border crossings. I am also weary of easy celebrations of diaspora as a necessary transgressive shift away from the nation or as a disruptive moment in the configuration of heterosexual "family as the building block" of the nation (Gilroy 1993). Following Anne-Marie Fortier's critique of the "chic of diaspora" (2000a, 2001), I take issue with valorization of diaspora as an emblem of multilocationality, hybridity, border crossing, and multiplicity and am more interested in the collusion of diaspora with scattered hegemonies (Grewal and Kaplan 1994) that include nationalism, colonization, imperialism, and militarism.

Fortier's astute analysis of the chic of diaspora and the fixation of home versus glorified movement is quite relevant to the rise of this chic among many younger English-speaking Iranians outside of Iran, who have increasingly replaced the term *exile* with *diaspora*.[55] As I will argue in chapter 4, this new naming may be caused by increased movement and multilocationality of Iranians after the end of the eight-year war, the emergence of a generation of younger Iranians who were born and/or raised outside of Iran and therefore do not consider themselves to be exiles, or the arrival of more-recent immigrants who do not share the resentments of their predecessors.[56] Despite this shift from exile to diaspora, the uncritical uses of this term tend to romanticize displacement and hybridity vis-à-vis a fixed homeland. The assumption that the Iranian diaspora is uniformly in opposition to the nation-state undermines the ideological, financial, and political support that the Iranian nation-state receives from some diaspora Iranians or the support that some Iranian diaspora groups receive from nation-states that have a vexed relationship with the Iranian state. While many diaspora Iranians may be resistant to the Iranian Islamic state, they can be complicit with various nationalist constructions of Iranianness, including the state's official nationalism. As such, diaspora does not translate into an inevitable transgressive shift away from the nation and its gendered and raced exclusions.

The Desire for *Kharej*

Just as some stories of exile exaggerated accounts of oppression and demonized Iran, a number of well-known bloggers sketched a skewed image of success and freedom in *kharej* (outside, foreign lands), which often meant North America or Europe. The glorification of freedom and of the comforts of living in North America by these newcomer immigrants was not surprising to me. Many bloggers in North America were educated Iranians (mostly computer science, engineering, and other mathematical sciences) who migrated with student visas to continue their higher education. Others were professionals who were admitted through work visas. Most bloggers lived relatively comfortable, middle-class lives, and many experienced fast upward mobility in suburban areas. Those who worked as engineers in information technology and engineering companies or those who were hired by think tanks were able to buy property shortly after arriving in Canada or the United States.

Living relatively sheltered lives, some generalized their own limited experience and constructed a glorified image of life in North America. Some newcomer Iranian bloggers who experienced hardship and downward mobility in North America or Europe also took part in portraying an ideal image of life after immigration because they were embarrassed of *kheet shodan* (failure). For example, an Iranian blogger told me that he would not write about his downward mobility and his difficult days of working below his qualifications in Canada because he was embarrassed to be considered a failure by friends and family in Iran who were quick to admonish him for leaving. Pointing out that his role as a breadwinner gave him the responsibility to succeed, he told me, "*Nemikhaastam khaanevaadeh too Iran fekr konand kheet shodam*" ("I didn't want my family to think that I failed").

For some bloggers, focusing on positive aspects of life in North America was a way to give hope to the Iranian youths who desire immigrating to "America."[57] Disillusioned with the failed promises of justice by the postrevolutionary Iranian state and the reformists, and having experienced hardship caused by the economic sanctions against Iran, Iranian youths yearn for a range of possibilities that, depending on class, level of education, and politicization, may not be easily available to them in Iran. These possibilities may include a (depoliticized) consumer lifestyle, postgraduate educational opportunities, employment, upward mobility, and certain social freedoms. Some young middle-class bloggers, who often lack lived memory of the prerevolutionary dictatorship, fantasize about such opportunities in America. Blog posts by diasporic bloggers are often consumed as generalizable accounts of life in kharej. To borrow from Lisa Rofel, the desiring subject functions as a "normative ideal and a horizon of possibility—or impossibility" (2007, 6). The "successful" transnational Iranian citizen subject is produced through historically and culturally situated postrevolutionary experiences that give rise to desire for "America" and longing for consumer identities. As such, the desire for America is produced in transnational encounters that are mediated through the internet, satellite television, and radio.

While youths in Iran often mock Los Angeles–produced Iranian cultural productions for being outdated and fossilized, especially the Persian satellite television programs that air uninformed political commentary, shows, and music videos, Persian radio and television programs funded by the U.S. Department of State (such as Radio Farda and Voice of America [VOA]) are more popular.[58] Aware of the irrelevance of Los Angeles satellite television programs to Iranian youth, who constitute more than 70 percent of the Iranian population in Iran, VOA and Radio Farda hire young, recent immigrants (some of whom are bloggers) as reporters, researchers, and television program hosts, not only to give these media a hip and relevant image but also to have access to the events in Iran through a computer-literate and socially networked staff. Voice of America and Radio Farda circulate images of America as the land of freedom, equality, and economic opportunity. Unlike the older cold war propaganda strategies, these programs are not politically didactic. Instead, through their heavy reliance on the internet and social media, they focus on news, pop culture, music videos, political satire, and other cultural productions that appeal to youths and represent a lifestyle characterized by "tolerance," freedom, and democracy. Ironically, a D.C.-based blogger who worked at VOA told me that these programs do not allow any critique of U.S.-style democracy.[59]

In discussing the production of middle-class Indian (South Asian) and American subjects, Inderpal Grewal argues that "America functions as a discourse of neoliberalism making possible struggles for rights through consumerist practices and imaginaries that came to be used both inside and outside the territorial boundaries of the United States" (2005, 2). Grewal rightly points out that the "appropriation of neoliberal discourse was only possible for particular subjects gendered, classed, and racialized in specific connectivities within which knowledge moved and could be accessed" (2005, 3). In Iran's case it is also different forms of classed, gendered, and raced transnational connectivity that produce varying imaginaries for subjects. For example, the seemingly apolitical (yet very political) stance of VOA may appeal to a group of upper- and middle-class Iranians who deliberately distance themselves from politics and desire a consumer lifestyle that "America" represents. More-politicized youths who do not enjoy the class comforts and aspirations of VOA may not consider it to be a credible source. Moreover, many young people who prefer programs that critique the Iranian state from within associate VOA with an outdated monarchist (*saltanat-talab*) opposition.[60] While not as one-sided and geopolitically driven as the U.S. propaganda media, during my research some diaspora media, including blogs, also participated in the democratization frenzy of the "war on terror." Neoliberal discourses of freedom, democracy, and civil society circulated in blogs, with frequent comparisons between Iranian and "Western" lifestyles.[61] It was in this context that blogs became a site where desire for American democracy and freedom was reproduced, even as U.S. imperialism was acknowledged or even critiqued.

It was in rehearsals of the "art of longing" (Rofel 2007) that the idea of "America" as a desired destination and a fantasy was reproduced by diasporic bloggers. For example, in a blog post, Mehdi, a recent immigrant and a Stanford postdoctoral engineering student at the time, accused me of having "anti-American" tendencies because of my posts about racism, anti-immigration legislation, and cuts in social services in the United States. He protested that writing about racial and class injustices in the United States disillusioned the Iranian youths who were enthusiastic about the prospect of coming to America, and he criticized me for sketching a negative image. Mehdi believed that I was hypocritically writing from the comfortable position of privilege in the United States while criticizing the negative aspects of U.S. democracy. He wrote that I resembled someone who drives a Mercedes-Benz while telling those who drive a Peykan (i.e., the unprivileged) that Mercedes is a bad car and that they should be happy with their shoddy Peykans.[62]

While Mehdi's point about the privileges of living in the first world is legitimate, his assumption about equal access to resources in the United States ignores the fact that not all immigrants enjoy the same socioeconomic privileges.[63] Furthermore, keeping silent or denying racism against communities of color, including Iranians, may not serve those who desire America as a destination. This bitter truth became tangible for Mehdi when a group of scholars and alumni from the Sharif University of Technology—a school with an international reputation—were detained and deported at the San Francisco International Airport in August 2006. The invitees and their families had received visas to attend the Sharif University of Technology Association (a California-based alumni organization of an elite university in Tehran) meeting in Silicon Valley. Despite holding valid visas, Sharif scholars, alumni, and their families were denied entry, and their visas were revoked. They were detained and deported the following day without explanation. Mehdi, himself a Sharif alumnus, was repulsed by this racist exclusion of Iranian scientists by the U.S. Department of Homeland Security.[64] This incident was a sobering realization that despite cyber-visits to virtual homes, racialized bodies do not move as freely offline as they do online. As a matter of fact, during my research many Iranian bloggers in the U.S. and Canada experienced lack of mobility because of post–9/11 U.S. immigration laws.[65]

Diasporic Nationalism

The suffix -*istan* connotes a physical location, often demarcated by borders. Despite the connotation of territoriality, Weblogistan is a collection of mainly Persian-language blogs written by Iranians across the world. In this sense, Weblogistan both repeats and expands the meaning of nationalism suggested by Benedict Anderson (1983, 5–7), who defines *nation* as a political community that is imagined as both limited and sovereign. It is imagined because members will never know most of their fellow members, "yet in the minds of each lives the image of their communion" (6). And it is imagined as a community because it is "conceived as a deep, horizontal comradeship" (7). It is limited because it has "finite, if elastic boundaries, beyond which lie other nations" (7). According to Anderson, nations are sovereign because they were born in the age of Enlightenment, when freedom became an emblem of breaking away from a hierarchical dynastic realm. While not limited by the physical borders and boundaries of the Iranian nation-state, Weblogistan extends Iranian nationalism to the "borderless" zones of cyberspace. What separates members of the imagined community of Iranian bloggers in Weblogistan from other bloggers is their belonging to the Iranian national imagination. As such, Weblogistan repeats and recuperates a sense of territorial boundedness while expanding its reach beyond national territories in seemingly borderless cyberspace. As such, "digital capitalism" (Schiller 1999) and "mass publicity" (Warner 1992) rather than "print capitalism" are the organizing force of transnational nationalism (Moallem 2005b) in Weblogistan, where a deep horizontal comradeship is established through postmodern "time-space compression" (Harvey 1990). In Weblogistan the politics of the local and the global were intertwined in the deployment of ahistorical narratives that conjured heteronormative imaginations of "Iran" and "Iranianness." Weblogistan was not just a collection of Persian-language blogs, but to borrow from Fortier (2000b, 11), it was also a site of "manufacturing bodies" that inhabited the spaces that were claimed as Iranian belongings. The repetition and reification of nationalist conventions—as well as the desire for and allegiance to homeland—were performative acts (Butler 1993) that created a complicated sense of transnational subjectivity for bloggers in Iran and its diaspora. Indeed, performances of nationalism in Weblogistan seemed to be an everyday occurrence. However, a few events highlight nationalism's gendered, raced, ethnic, and sexed exclusions in a highly celebrated sphere where Iranians were purported to "practice democracy."

On June 11, 2006, during the FIFA World Cup games in Germany, I drove Ava and Dara, two popular Iranian bloggers in Toronto, from the North York district of Toronto to a sports bar, where other Iranian bloggers and students had gathered to watch the Iran-Mexico soccer game. Mehri Khanoom, Ava's mother, who was a regular blog reader, had attached a large postrevolutionary Iranian flag to a broomstick and handed it to us on our way to downtown. The available Iranian flags in Toronto's Iranian stores were either plain tricolor flags with no emblem or flags with the old emblem of the crown, lion, and sun, which for many Iranians is associated with the prerevolutionary Pahlavi monarchy.[66] Ours was neither. It was the postrevolutionary Iranian flag, with an Allah emblem in the middle. As we drove through the congested streets of Toronto, navigating through cars adorned with different national flags, Dara, an openly gay Iranian man who was proudly holding the huge Iranian flag from the backseat window, asked me to make a detour to drive through an Israeli neighborhood. Naively, I asked why I would want to drive through an Israeli neighborhood when we could take Yonge Street all the way to downtown. Ava and Dara laughed. Dara shouted, "Vaaah? What do you mean why? To skip traffic and to annoy the Zionists because they hate Iranians!" While Dara was tickled by annoying Zionists, Ava mischievously enjoyed irritating secular nationalist Iranians in Toronto's North York neighborhood, as she stretched her torso out of the passenger window and incessantly shouted, "Doodoodoo doodoo doo Iran! Doodoodoo doo doo doo Allah!" Neither Ava nor Dara was religious or favored the Islamic state. Even as the postrevolutionary Iranian nation-state excluded queer subjects, Dara and Ava were making a point by holding the Allah flag as a way to claim their space as Canadian citizens with dual Iranian citizenship in Toronto, a city that prides itself for its multiculturalism, even as it criminalizes Muslim immigrants, especially after September 11.[67]

When we arrived at the bar, we saw a group of Iran fans, many of whom were bloggers or blog readers. We sat next to "Saghar," an avid Persian blog reader in her early thirties who maintained an unpublicized English-language blog to practice writing in English. Saghar had moved to Canada through a work visa in 2001 and was an engineer in an urban construction company near Toronto. She read Persian blogs as a way to stay connected to Iranian politics. When she saw Ava's large Allah flag, she asked how we had managed to find an Allah flag in Toronto. Apparently, Saghar had gone through a lot of trouble to find a small flag of what she called the "real Iran." Earlier that week, she had walked into an Iranian deli/grocery store to order food. In anticipation of the World Cup, the store owner had displayed the prerevolutionary Iranian flags for sale. Saghar told us that she ordered her food and left the restaurant to buy an Islamic Republic flag from a young Afghani man who was selling flags across from the restaurant. When Saghar saw the prerevolutionary Iranian flags among the pile of national flags, she asked the young man if he had any current Iranian flags. To her delight, he took one out of a box and handed it to her. She bought the Iranian flag from the Afghani peddler and went back to the restaurant to pick up her food. This is how Saghar described her interaction in the restaurant: "These ladies who were wearing huge diamond rings the size of my head . . . the types of *Iroonis* who drive BMW SUVs, you know . . . started to pick on me for holding an Allah flag in my hands and said, 'what the hell is this?'" Saghar, who was annoyed with the restaurant owner who had half-jokingly asked her to state her political affiliation before entering the restaurant, continued: "I told him that this flag is the flag of those twenty-two human beings who are playing football in Germany. They went to the playing field with this flag; the *Toronto Star* has this flag as the Iranian team's flag; and I will carry this flag! If next year, they put a carrot in the middle of the flag, I will take that flag and rally on the streets to support our team!" Saghar, who was amused by her own carrot joke, went on to say that "I was praying that they [monarchists who detest the Allah flag] wouldn't throw rotten eggs and tomatoes at me!"

Fortunately, we did not have to worry about conflicts with royalists over the kind of flag that Ava was carrying. It happened that the Iranian fans in the bar either had no flags or were carrying the current Iranian flag. Some were wearing T-shirts with a cartoon design of a lion, a soccer ball, and the words "Iran World Cup 2006" that a Toronto blogger had designed. Ava admired this design because unlike the muscular lion on the prerevolutionary Iranian flag, she thought that this lion was *kooni* (faggy) and transgressed the ideals of Iranian masculinity. Despite different political inclinations and varying religious devotions, the Iranian fans at the bar were mostly recent immigrants who found the royalists' absolute rejection of all postrevolutionary matters to be irrelevant to the Iranian political realm. The Iranian fans expressed a sense of unity by encouraging their team and rhythmically shouting, "Iraaaan, Iran!" As it is the case with many sports events, some of the chants were humorous, and some bordered on being offensive and homophobic. One particular chant, "*Sheer-e samovar too koon-e daavar*" ("The samovar faucet up referee's ass!"), is a common way of protesting a referee who appears to favor the opposing team. A few bloggers, including Ava and Dara, shouted this chant to express their anger at the referee every time that he favored the Mexican team. The affective power of nationalism seemed to have put conflicts over gender, vulgarity (I will discuss this in chapter 3), and homosexuality (chapter 4) to rest, bringing together bloggers who shared their love for the nation in front of a large-screen television monitor in a Toronto bar. By the end of the game, Mohsen, a self-identified right-wing Iranian blogger who looked upset and depressed because of the Iranian team's loss, draped the Allah flag over his head as he exchanged a few words of consolation with the visibly sad Dara, who identifies with the "left" reformist movement. These two bloggers, who had a history of political and religious differences and disagreements online and offline, were united under the same flag in Toronto.

This was not the first time that nationalism had united bloggers. In November 2004 the eighth edition of the *National Geographic Atlas* included the words *Arabian Gulf* in brackets next to the Persian Gulf, a body of water that is an extension of the Indian Ocean and is located between Iran and the Arab Peninsula. The naming of the gulf is a contentious issue that has ignited nationalist outrage in offline and online debates in Iran and its diaspora. Soon after the publication of this atlas, a petition was written by a group of diaspora Iranians who were outraged by National Geographic's naming of the gulf as "Arabian." Ultimately, more than 117,000 cyber-signatures were gathered for the Persian Gulf petition and sent to the National Geographic Society, asking the organization to remove the words *Arabian Gulf* from the map. It did not take long for a massive number of Iranian bloggers to circulate a "Google bomb" designed by an Iranian blogger in Toronto in response to the National Geographic's misnaming. "Google bombing" is meant to influence the ranking of a particular website in Google search results. Google bombs can produce successful results if a large number of web pages link to a specific site. Using the Google search algorithm, which brings the most visited page for a search result to the top, the Iranian blogger who designed the Google bomb encouraged others in Weblogistan to click repeatedly on a link that he created. Consequently, a Google search for the keyword "Arabian Gulf" would lead to his "404/not found" error page: "The gulf you are looking for does not exist. Try Persian Gulf." The message further noted that "the gulf you are looking for is unavailable. No body of water by that name has ever existed. The correct name is Persian Gulf, which always has been, and will always remain, Persian."[68]

In addition to this symbolic protest, many bloggers posted negative ratings on Amazon.com's advertisement page for the *National Geographic Atlas*.[69] As a result of all of these actions and the Iranian state's protest, National Geographic finally removed the term *Arabian Gulf* from its maps. Weblogistan, as a seemingly de-territorialized online community, enabled the massive mobilization of territorial nationalism from different parts of the world.

The nationalist mobilization around the naming of the Gulf culminated in the circulation of anti-Arab sentiments on the internet through gendered imagery and text.[70] During the nationalist mobilizing around the naming of the Persian Gulf, cartoons that portrayed Iran as a woman being attacked by Arab invaders circulated online. The depiction of the land as a female body in need of protection goes back to the rise of Iranian nationalism in the nineteenth century. Najmabadi (2005) argues that in the nineteenth century, Iranian nationalism was constructed around the notion of *khak-i pak-i vatan* (the pure soil of homeland), figured as a female body. As is often the case in nationalist

FIGURE 1.2 "The Gulf You Are Looking for Does Not Exist."

discourses, the homeland is imagined as a female body to kill and die for. What further complicated this sense of nationalism in the case of the Persian Gulf was the outrage around prostitution and trafficking of Iranian women in the Arab states. Some nationalist diaspora Iranian opposition groups have blamed the Islamic Republic for its impotence and incompetence in protecting the national honor and not doing enough to stop Iranian women's prostitution in the Gulf States. Denying any agency to women sex workers, these groups have gone as far as accusing the *Arab-parast* (Arab-worshiping) Iranian regime of selling Iranian women to Arabs. Despite this antagonism, however, the Iranian state and many opposition groups often become aligned in their nationalist mobilizations. The Iranian state banned the sale of *National Geographic* magazines in Iran until the society changed the name to the "Persian Gulf." The state threatened to restrict Al Jazeera after the network used a cartoon to poke fun at the Iranian state's extreme reaction to the naming while being indifferent to religious strife in the region.[71] Subsequently, the cartoon was removed. The state also announced the first Persian Gulf internet contests for best animation and blogs. Mohammad Ali Abtahi, the Iranian president and a popular blogger, praised the Iranian bloggers for initiating the reaction to the National Geographic Society's naming of the gulf.[72] The Ministry of Culture and Islamic Guidance announced the 10th of *Ordibehesht* (April 30) to be National Persian Gulf Day. Interestingly, Iranian bloggers in diaspora (including those who consider themselves to be a part of the "opposition" to the Iranian state) played an important role in these nationalist mobilizations. As Khachig Tölölyan argues, diaspora "communities are sometimes the paradigmic other of the nation-state and at other times its ally, lobby, or even in the case of Israel, its precursor" (1991, 5).

In modern discourses regarding Iranian nationalism, the controversy over the naming of the gulf is partly due to the long-term historical resentments toward the seventh-century Islamization of Iran by Arabs. In *Refashioning Iran*, Mohamad Tavakoli-Targhi (2001, 76–95) demonstrates that the rewriting of the pre-Islamic past by the neo-Mazdean Azari movement of the late sixteenth century and the seventeenth century in response to repressive religious policies of the Safavids (1501–1722) engendered a shift in Iranian historical consciousness. The emergence of modern Iranian identity was closely linked to the reconfiguration of national history that was informed by pre-Islamic mythical texts, and it involved the purification of language and geographical territorializations of an immemorial past. Tavakoli-Targhi (94) points out that nineteenth-century history texts, which were influenced by *dasatiri* texts of the Azari movement, deployed a discourse that became pervasive in nineteenth-century history writing. The trope of Muslim conquest and Arab invasion was seen as the reason for the dispersion of Iranians from their homeland (*vatan*). Nineteenth-century nationalist discourses also drew from the pre-Islamic past to fashion an enlightened Iranian identity prior to the advent of Islam in Iran. This anti-Arab territorial nationalism intensified during the Pahlavi period and became even more prevalent among some Iranians in Iran and its diaspora who saw the Islamic revolution of 1979 as the "second Arab invasion." Nationalist mobilizations among the Iranian diaspora, or what Moallem has called transnational nationalism (2005b), have become even more feasible in cyberspace, where the fast circulation of information gives nationalism increased vigor.

The example of the "Arabian Gulf" error message, which is often cited as the most successful Google bombing, was not the only time that nationalism surfaced in Weblogistan at a moment of crisis.[73] Nationalism was the underlying element in many blogging discussions. For example, in 2007 one of the bloggers started *"baazi-ye veblogi"* (a blog game) and asked a list of people to write what homeland (*vatan*) meant to them.[74] The famous Toronto-based blogger and cartoonist Nikahang Kowsar participated in this game and bitterly expressed his feelings about *vatan* by writing this:

What is my *vatan*? To whom does it belong? I feel like my *vatan* is a harlot.... Every minute [she is] in a different person's possession.... Every time, we have given it away to a new man of war and each time we have taken her out of his, his sons', or his friends' hands with a lot of trouble.... Look at our history.... We have given away our home to the foreigner.... Here in another's *vatan*, I, the one with no *vatan*, will do any job and accept any humiliation so that I am not in my own *vatan*. I consider here [Canada] to be my *vatan*, yet refuse to call it my *vatan*.... I should be the owner of my *vatan*, but I am not. As it has always been, I/we have given *vatan* to those who do not deserve to own my *vatan*'s body. And as always, these owners have sacrificed the bodies of the youth of *vatan* for *vatan*'s soil. As if this *vatan* is a tramp whose hunger would be satisfied with our bodies and her owner wants to feed her with me, the fool in-love.[75]

Kowsar's hetero-normative nationalist fantasy conjures a fetishized homeland complete with vulnerable yet deceptive feminine soil. The righteous owners (Kowsar and other sons of vatan who are exiled), the unqualified owners (the Iranian statesmen), and the enemy (foreigners) are all imagined as men, while vatan is figured as a vulnerable and seductive female body that is prostituted to the foreigners by the incompetent and unqualified owners. Kowsar's mourning reiterates the hegemonic exilic discourse that maintains "Iranianness" within an essence through constructing difference (against the Arab Other) and homogeneity (of a unified Iranian nation dispersed around the world). In a self-victimizing mourning of a glorious pre-Islamic past, the more Islamophobic articulation of this form of nationalism considers the 1979 revolution as a "second invasion" and refers to the proponents of the Islamic state as "Arab worshippers."

Anti-Arab racism in nationalist discourse does not just construct Arab men as predators who violate Iranian men's honor by threatening the purity of Iranian women. In an absurd twist on the supposed foreignness of homosexuality, Arabs are held responsible for this "vice" and other "premodern" perversions. For example, in his blog *Noqteh Sar-e Khat*, Nasser Khaledian (a famous blogger and satirist) denied the history of homosexuality in Iran and relegated it to a foreign import brought to Iran by non-Persian invaders (Greeks and Arabs) and by those in the Iranian diaspora who have adopted homosexuality from the "West."[76] Khaledian believed that the discussions about homosexuality in Weblogistan were propaganda attempts to ruin the love between a man and a woman. These discussions, he argued, create dangerous tensions between husbands and wives. In a post that received much praise, he wrote the following:

The culture of sexual freedom has never belonged to us and we cannot accept such things in the name of freedom, because we don't have sexual freedom even in its normal form (woman + man). [We] have not resolved that yet; let alone the abnormal type (man + man and woman + woman). So, we should not become mesmerized and fooled by these few gays and lesbians who assume that because they live in a free environment, we too have to be like this in Iran! I wish someone would write an analytical essay about the sexual deviance and homosexualism [sic] among some diasporic Iranians, and its connection to the Western culture and mental paradoxes resulting from it. I mean cases of those who have voluntarily become deviants and not those who are inherently (biologically) that way.[77]

Khaledian's post is an example of the way that the othering of nonheteronormative subjects as "un-Iranian" is entangled with racial discourses of Iranianness that produces Arabs as inferior deviants. Ironically, in response to nineteenth-century European orientalists who considered Iranian sexual practices, including the "vice" of homosexuality, to be backward and barbaric, modernist Iranian elites actively sought to erase any trace of homoeroticism and homosexuality from the Iranian national memory. Najmabadi argues that anxieties about sexuality in modern Iran in the twentieth century shifted the discourse on homosexuality and led to the simultaneous production and exclusion of "abnormal" types such as *amradnuma* (adult man who made himself look like a young beardless man), *obne'i* (passive male), and *fokoli* (bowtie-wearing dandy) and also led to the heterosexualization of Iranian national culture.[78] While Khaledian's abjection of homosexuality repeats this dominant discourse, his nationalist sentiments are rooted in discourses that, as Tavakoli-Targhi (2001, 143) argues, assume continuity between ancient and contemporary Iran, and involve "the taxonomic partition of the history and destiny of peoples residing in the bounded territories of Iran from those of Arabs, Indians, and Turks."

The gendered discourses of nationalism not only construct a feminized, vulnerable, and promiscuous homeland, in need of protection by the heteronormative masculine citizens; they also produce and erase ethnic and gender differences in terms of the nation's internal others. In May 2006, Mana Neyestani, an Iranian cartoonist, was arrested for the publication of a cartoon in the children's section of the *Iran* newspaper.[79] Neyestani's cartoon outraged many Azeri Turks, resulting in riots in the northwestern provinces of Iran. The cartoon depicted a boy attempting to talk reason to a cockroach, who in return responds in Azeri by saying, "*Namana?*" ("What?"). While the Azeri Turkish word *namana* has become a part of the colloquial Persian lexicon in recent years, the utterance of the word by a cockroach, a creature that symbolizes inferiority, was interpreted as a discriminatory insult against Azeris. The government-owned *Iran* newspaper was shut down, and its editor and the cartoonist were arrested. Iranian President Mahmoud Ahmadinejad and Supreme Leader Seyyed Ali Khamene'i condemned the riots as foreign plots to disrupt Iran's efforts to acquire peaceful nuclear technology. Neyestani's cartoon, the Azeri protesters' reaction, and the Iranian state's response should be contextualized within the particular historical moment in which they emerged. Azeri separatist organizations such as the Southern Azerbaijan National Awakening Movement (SANAM), led by Mahmudali Chehregani—who was supported by neoconservative U.S. Senator Sam Brownback and was hosted by the U.S. Defense Department in Washington in 2003—have been advocating for the merging of the Iranian province of Azerbaijan (referred to as Southern Azerbaijan) with the former Soviet Azerbaijan (referred to as Northern Azerbaijan).[80] The alliance between the Republic of Azerbaijan and the United States, the Republic of Azerbaijan's plans to establish diplomatic relations with Israel, and the opening of an oil pipeline for fast transport of the Caspian Sea oil from Azerbaijan to Turkey—supported by the U.S. secretary of energy—contributed to the tensions around Mana Neyestani's cartoon.[81] The installment of two U.S.-funded radar facilities over the Caspian Sea, which enable the surveillance of communications inside Iran, was another source of anxiety for the Iranian state about the U.S. infiltration via Azerbaijan. It was against this background that Neyestani's cartoon set the ethnic tensions ablaze.

The reports of the unrest and the subsequent arrest of Neyestani were quickly spread in Weblogistan. Many bloggers inside and outside of Iran warned their readers about the separatist agenda and defended Neyestani, who had become the scapegoat in the volatile political situation. Despite their opposition to the Iranian state, many diasporic bloggers warned the Azeri protesters against the danger of disintegration, fueled by the separatist Baku-based groups. While some opposition groups appropriated this incident as an indication of ethnic discrimination against Azeris by the Islamic state, many Azeri and Persian bloggers, including those critical of the Iranian state, disputed these claims and reminded their readers that the Persianization of school textbooks was a Pahlavi-era initiative and not exclusive to the postrevolutionary state. Some pointed out that Khamene'i (the supreme leader) and many Iranian officials are themselves of Azeri descent.

The nationalist mobilizations around this incident highlighted the dominance of the Persian superiority complex as some bloggers, in their attempt to recuperate national unity, deemed the riots as the proof of Azeri gullibility. Azeri protesters were portrayed as having been easily duped by the foreigners.[82] For example, repeating the "simpleminded" stereotype of Azeri Iranians, the author of *Alpr*, a popular blog, wrote that "the simple-mindedness of the Turkish speaking student compatriots caused this innocent cartoonist to lose his job."[83] He then advised Azeri students to learn from Shahryar (1906–1988), the Iranian Azeri poet whose "*ala ey Tehrani*" addresses Persians in Tehran. In his poem, Shahryar admonishes Tehrani Persians for their arrogance and prejudice toward ethnic minorities, and repeatedly asks the rhetorical question "Who is the ass, you or me?" In the third stanza, Shahryar asks, "Why would one who is less than a woman, claim manhood? You, Tehrani be the judge: who is the ass, you or me?" Interestingly, in his attempt to subdue the Azeri rioters through reciting Sharyar's poem, *Alpr* not only takes a patronizing stance toward his Azeri readers but also deploys misogynistic nationalist discourses of Iranianness as a way of fraternal camaraderie.

As Afsaneh Najmabadi has argued (2005), ethnonational and religious "minorities" in Iran arose from the modern moment of the nation in the nineteenth century. Unlike protonationalist movements of the thirteenth century, where the allegiance of the subject was to the king, the late nineteenth-century and early twentieth-century nationalism shifted loyalty from the king to the claim of rights over "*terra iranica*." Najmabadi argues that "as Iranianness became dependent on a notion of territorial integrity (*tamamiyat-i arzi*), separatism became a politically expedient concept with which to discipline dissidence among non-Persian Iranians" (15–16). With the consolidation of a sense of Iranianness bounded to a geo-body (imagined as female: "*Iran khanom*"), the movement of nomadic tribes across borders became a marker of their non-Iranianness and was linked with "foreign interventions and loss of national body" (17). The riots over Neyestani's cartoon then retrieve the long-existing tensions between national unity and ethnic sovereignty. Firoozeh Kashani-Sabet (2000, 103) has noted that in the Iranian constitutional era of the twentieth century, themes of freedom, citizenship, law, and unity became a part of Iran's frontier experience, as the concept of *mamalik-i Iran* (provinces of Iran) was transformed to *mamlikat-i Iran* (country of Iran). Different ethnic groups were encouraged to form a unifying category of "Iranians" in order to maintain territorial unity. Iranian intellectuals' efforts to forge a national unity involved harmony between the state and the people on one hand and the singularity of the country on the other (108). Kashani-Sabet also shows that mytho-history, along with claims to the Aryan race, Persian culture, Islam, and language, were used as legitimate diplomatic strategies to win territorial reparations in the postwar Versailles negotiations in 1919. The disillusionments with the state after the Great War challenged Iran's national fictions and resulted in many separatist movements, such as Shaykh Muhammad Khiabani's uprising in Azerbaijan in 1920. Reza Khan's ascendance to power after his military coup in 1921 disarmed the tribal and separatist movements. Reza Khan's centralization of the government deployed the violent nationwide Persianization of language at the expense of the erasure of ethnic languages and in the name of the territorial legitimacy of the nation.

During the "war on terror," the fear of the loss of territorial cohesion and the anxieties over a possible attack on Iran contributed to the intensification of nationalist discourses in Weblogistan. For example, some of the posts submitted to the group blog *Iranians for Peace* resorted to nationalist sentiments as a response to a possible war imposed by the United States. An Iranian blogger in Canada, who opened an English-language blog named *Over Our Dead Bodies*, encouraged Farsi bloggers to participate in an antiwar letter campaign on the anniversary of the nationalization of oil by Mohammad Mossadegh in 1953. While the fear of U.S. intervention and the specter of disintegration were legitimate, the calls for national unity gave new life to Persianization and hegemonic nationalist imaginations of exclusionary Iranianness. Iran's territorial integrity reactivated nationalist contestations over culture, language, and land in Weblogistan, where the reaction to the naming of the gulf culminated in anti-Arab sentiments among some bloggers.

Mobilizations and protests that take place in the digital realm are often celebrated as examples of the robustness of civil society and digital democracy in a de-territorialized space. The Persian Gulf Google bomb and other nationalist mobilizations in Weblogistan show that neither cyberspace nor diaspora necessarily subvert the nation, but can draw from the affective power of nationalism. Considering the role of the nation-state in enabling and regulating internet infrastructure, celebrations of the internet as the subversive opposite of the nation are simplistic, to say the least. In other words, digital citizenship does not supersede the national; it is one of its modalities. Neither bodies nor information moves freely across national borders. If anything, digital technologies have enabled more sophisticated surveillance and security measures by treating bodies as bundles of data. Diasporic nationalist mobilizations in Weblogistan demonstrate the way that the formation of "democratic" subjects in

Weblogistan relied on national mobilizations that, as Rofel has argued, "draw their dynamic energies from global encounters" (2007, 20). While Weblogistan was often represented as a space to "practice democracy" for an undifferentiated body of bloggers, hegemonic nationalist tropes of gender, race, and sexuality excluded those who were unfit for a democratic future and exceptional citizenship.

Conclusion: Diasporic Nationalism after Weblogistan

The civilizational discourses and practices in North America that produce immigrants as threats to national security compel some diaspora Iranians to disavow Arab-ness (and by extension the Islamic Republic) and to insist on an imagined whiteness. Even as narratives of Aryan ancestry in the nationalist discourses of Iranianness have histories that precede the present moment, the anti-Iranian sentiment in the aftermath of the 1979 Iranian revolution and the intensification of those sentiments during the "war on terror" add layers to this problematic misidentification. That is, the desire for proximity to whiteness among some Iranians in diaspora is simultaneously a distancing and survival tactic. Whether it is the disassociation from the "Islamic regime" and an appeal to the greatness of a Persian past—because of the anti-Iranian hate violence in the aftermath of the Iranian revolution and the "hostage crisis"—or a strategy to reject any affiliation with Muslim-ness or Arab-ness after September 11, 2001, the dominant trend among the Iranian diaspora (who often identify as "Persian") is to distinguish themselves from Arabs. Notwithstanding this distancing, the fact remains that Iranians are subjected to discriminatory policies that include sanctions or immigration restrictions such as the "Muslim ban."

As David Palumbo-Liu (2002) argues, the civilizational thinking that became prevalent after September 11, 2001, is mobilized as a result of the merging of national identity and international civilizational thinking. The weakening of the cold war and the economic crisis led to the emergence of culture as a mediator of difference in international affairs in 1970s in the United States. The increased pressure on multilateralism for international economic and cultural relations, on one hand, and the various subaltern pressures on the national level (which called for a national-identity order), on the other, produced a crisis of governability of democracy. The U.S. multiculturalism of the 1980s and 1990s emerged as the result of the civil rights era, third-world antiwar movements, the feminist movement, the gay and lesbian movement, and the development of a multilateralism that took the shape of economic neoliberalism. However, celebrations of diversity shifted during the "war on terror." The post–September 11 incarnation of civilizational thinking added the civilizational enemy without (Islam) to the one within (ethnic and diasporic populations). The Patriot Act and the tightening of anti-immigrant laws under the Bush, Obama, and Trump administrations were all justified under the rhetoric of national security against the external and internal enemies. In the post–September 11 era, national-security screening systems have been expanded. Data systems have become accessible to immigration officials and local law enforcement. "Secure Communities," a program launched by the Bush administration, enabled coordination between local law enforcement, the FBI, and the Department of Homeland Security. This has enabled the matching of the fingerprints of those who are arrested by local law enforcement with federal and immigration databases. As a result of this centralized data collection, in fiscal year 2008 almost 360,000 immigrants were subjected to formal removals; 234,000 of these removals were not at the border but from the interior of the United States. Even though Obama's administration rescinded some Bush-era policies, other immigration restrictions (such as increased formal removals and the harsh implementation of secure communities in all U.S. jails and prisons) were put in place, giving Obama the "deporter in chief" reputation.[84]

Trump's administration followed Obama's footsteps by taking harsher measures to prevent the immigration of "undesirables."[85] In January 2017, Trump signed executive order 13769 to restrict the entry of visitors from Iran, Iraq, Libya, Somalia, Sudan, Syria, and Yemen for a period of ninety days. Given that the countries mentioned in the executive order are majority Muslim, Trump's order became known as the "Muslim ban." To avoid legal challenges to his Islamophobic order, he reintroduced Muslim Ban 2.0 and Muslim Ban 3.0. While the ban on Chadian nationals was lifted on April 10, 2018, seven countries, including Iran, remain on the "banned" list. From the onset of the Muslim ban, several civil rights groups and Iranian diasporic organizations organized protests and online petitions. Protesting the religion/national-origin–based discrimination, on February 8 four Iranian American organizations—Pars Equality Center, the Iranian American Bar Association, the Public Affairs Alliance of Iranian Americans (PAAIA), and the National Iranian American Council (NIAC)—filed a lawsuit against Trump's order (*Pars Equality Center v. Trump*) and amended the lawsuit after Trump's new order on March 8, 2017. As the amendment states, "For decades, this country has made a commitment to Iranian immigrants and their families to allow them to live free from fear and political repression and allow them to contribute to American society. These immigrants and visitors have flourished on American soil and contributed immensely to our society: Iranian Americans today include doctors, mathematicians, diplomats, artists, scientists, lawyers, journalists, athletes, professors, and entrepreneurs. They exemplify the vitality of this nation of immigrants, a nation bound together not by a common ethnicity or religion, but by the democratic principle of equality before law."[86] The documents presented in the lawsuit drop names of successful Iranian American entrepreneurs and, especially, tech-company executives. These four organizations, which had never in the past joined forces, issued a press release on April 5 proclaiming that "as members of the Iranian diaspora, we are proud of our heritage and have deep connections to our ancestral homeland. We are committed to proactively engaging to protect the interests of our community and the values of this country."[87]

The model-minority discourse has become quite prevalent in a time when Iranians are specifically named as undesirable immigrants in policies such as the "Muslim ban." Despite the strategic deployment of this discourse, its deployment by the cosmopolitan Iranian diaspora (exemplified in the reality show *The Shahs of Sunset* and the celebration of millionaire entrepreneurs such as Uber's CEO, Dara Khosrowshahi, and the e-Bay founder, Pierre Omidyar) is contingent on an amnesia that erases any traces of Islam, while recuperating a pre-Islamic Persian Empire as the source of national pride. As Semira Nikou (2017) argues, during the 2017 Iranian new year in March, the internet was flooded with articles, images, and (mytho)historical accounts about Chaharshanbeh Suri and Norouz that emphasized the non-Islamic origin of these holidays.[88] Nothing captured the desire for the revival of Iran's pre-Islamic glory more than the installation and unveiling of the "Cyrus Cylinder" statue in Los Angeles on July, 4, 2017, shortly after Trump signed the Muslim ban.[89]

The $2.2 million sculpture was unveiled by Ali Razi, an Iranian American developer and the founding chairman of the Farhang Foundation (Culture Foundation). This 20,000-pound piece, made from gold and silver, is a permanent fixture in Los Angeles's wealthy Century City, near the Westfield Century City Mall and at the gateway to Beverly Hills. The sculpture is inspired by and represents the much-celebrated "Cyrus Cylinder," a 2,500-year-old artifact which was unearthed by British archaeologists in southern Iraq in 1879 and has been kept at the British Museum ever since. The clay cylinder is a

FIGURE 1.3 The Freedom Sculpture in Los Angeles, http://www.latimes.com/local/lanow/la-me-freedom-sculpture-20170704-story.html.

Babylonian account of the conquest of Babylon by the Persian king Cyrus in 539 BC. It is supposed to attest to the Persian king's empathy for the people and religions that were deported from Babylon. The grotesque Cyrus Cylinder in Los Angeles is not just a reminder of Iran's glorious past, but it inevitably demands a historical amnesia that erases Islam from Iran's image while distinguishing Iranians from their Arab and Muslim neighbors, in hopes of joining the ranks of the "man" of liberal democracy. Drawing on Rey Chow and Susan Koshy's work, Jasbir Puar (2007, 25) has rightly noted that the "ascendency of whiteness" through biopower incorporates complicit multicultural ethnic bodies. It is through management of difference that certain cosmopolitan ethnics (often heteronormative or homonormative, wealthy, and exceptional patriots) are tolerated while those suspected of terrorism (often marked with "pathological" sexuality) are deemed as "intolerable ethnics." The inclusion of some immigrants through the model-minority discourse and market individualism gives the illusion of diversity, even as disadvantaged minorities are denied social services. Proximity to whiteness becomes a matter of class, while cultural difference is abrogated through proximity to class-based whiteness. Puar argues that "for the ethnic with access to capital, both in terms of consumption and ownership, the seduction by global capital is conducted through racial amnesia, among other forms of forgetting" (2007, 26). The unveiling of the silver/gold statue of the cylinder on Independence Day in Los Angeles is not only a symbolic move to pledge allegiance to the United States, but the statue's unnecessary extravagance also signals the "market virility" (Nast 2003, 943) of cosmopolitan diaspora Iranians who identify with the pre-Islamic (read Aryan) Persia while actively dis-identifying with Iran's Islamic past and present. The unveiling of the statue also points to the fact that to be assimilated and desirable, immigrants have to prove their loyalty by becoming docile patriots who testify to the greatness of U.S. exceptionalism. It is by no accident that the Cyrus Cylinder—which is often anachronistically described as the "first human rights document"—was unveiled on the Fourth of July. Razi, who unveiled the statue, did not miss the opportunity to pay allegiance to the United States by repeating the myth of the immigration-friendly nation and claiming that "America is great because of all the beautiful cultures brought by immigrants."[90] The irony of the Muslim ban and the profit-producing prisons that increasingly incarcerate "unwanted" immigrants and refugees is glaringly palpable in this universalist celebration of human rights.

Interestingly, the objections to the Muslim ban forged alliances between Iranian advocacy groups and other Middle Eastern and Muslim immigrants, even as many Iranians in the United States often distanced themselves from Arabs and Muslims. As Nikou argues, "While many Iranian-Americans previously had shunned a 'Middle Eastern' and/or 'Muslim' identity (and some continue to do so), Iranian-American individuals and organizations are increasingly relying on these broader identities to navigate the political and judicial process. Underscoring this necessity is the fact that in order to challenge the travel ban as a civil rights issue, they have to do so as 'Muslims.'"[91] The current political atmosphere has created a dilemma where the Iranian diaspora emphasizes its difference from Arabs while having to form alliances (even if reluctantly) with Arab immigrants who are marked as "terrorist suspects." The anti-immigrant policies, which are not new and predate Trump's blatant xenophobia, have made some Iranians in diaspora realize that despite their desire for whiteness and exceptional citizenship, they remain risky citizens who may have no choice but to build alliances with other immigrant communities (Muslim immigrants in particular) for judicial and political processes. Wearing Zoroastrian Farvahar pendants or changing one's name from Islamic names such as Mohammad and Asghar to pre-Islamic names such as Arsham and Sepanta (or Americanized Moe or Oscar) will not grant the desiring nationalist Iranian diaspora subject the status of exceptional citizenship. Using Ahmed's notion of hate's affective economy, Puar argues that fear does not reside in an object but slides across signs and between bodies, thus endlessly deferring the injury to the future. Unlike the body that contains the fear of an imminent attack (and is thus subjected to white violence through projection of fear), the passing body does not contain fear. The resemblance between feared bodies allows fear to stick and slide to bodies that could be terrorists. Fear contaminates and multiplies as it slides through passing bodies, "a sliding that works metonymically to ooze and seep these bodies into one another" (2007, 185). Therefore, it is the fear of not knowing rather than knowing that leads to the control of entire populations who not only "look" dangerous but also "feel" dangerous. This is why, despite the Iranian diaspora's efforts to substitute a menacing image with positive images of Iranians (whether through wealth, scientific contributions, or seductive and self-orientalizing representations of food and cultural heritage on the internet), the affective economy of fear contaminates Iranian and Arab alike. If the risk of terror oozing from feared bodies is not completely containable, that risk may be reduced and managed through biopolitical and ethicopolitical practices in the realm of civil society. I will discuss these practices in forthcoming chapters.

[2]

Civil Society (*jaame'e-ye madani*), Soccer, and Gendered Politics in Weblogistan

The 2005 Presidential Election

In June 2005 a group of Iranian Toronto residents, many of whom were bloggers, rented a bus to go to the Iranian Embassy in Ottawa to vote in the Iranian presidential elections. Upon arriving at the embassy, they were met by a demonstration by Iranian opposition groups who perceived participation in the elections as a sign of approval of the Iranian Islamic state. As Ava, a feminist blogger who had traveled to the embassy, told me, "When I got off the bus, I was attacked verbally by the royalists and some old-school leftists (*chap-e ghadeemee*). In particular, one of my classmates [the author of a blog in English] called my name and shouted, "*baa roosari bee roosari khaak-toosari*'" ("with or without hijab, you are pathetic"). Ava (who does not wear the hijab) pointed to the double standard in which male voters were not shamed and in which even women protesters (many of whom were self-identified feminists) shamed women voters for being "brainwashed by the Iranian regime." Dismayed by the inconsistency of Iranian secular liberal feminists in diaspora,

Ava shrugged her shoulders and said with a sarcastic tone, "*Mardaa ham keh khob tabi'atan mardan!*" ("Of course, [to them] men are men, naturally!") To Ava, it was hypocritical that liberal secular opposition to the Islamic Republic enshrined voting as a right and responsibility of modern citizens and as a marker of women's liberation, except when it came to voting in the Iranian presidential elections.

The royalist and antireform opposition groups' extreme rejection of the postrevolutionary Iranian state is informed by an understanding of "civil society" as a purely oppositional antistate formation. This wholesale rejection or phobia of the state—what Foucault in *The Birth of Biopolitics* (2010) has called the "inflationary" critique of the state—involves the assumption of "the intrinsic power of the state in relation to its object-target, civil society" (187). The Iranian opposition groups that completely reject reform often conflate the reformists with the "regime" while recognizing (and subsequently appropriating) as the "will of the people" (where people are assumed to stand in opposition to the Islamic state) only particular moments of contestation by activists and scholars in Iran and its diaspora. In contrast, the processes of negotiation and reform within the state are seen as contaminated by the state's oppressive nature and thus are excluded from the fantasy of a pure civil society. This emphasis on "the people," which is indeed a part of the liberal political project, has gained currency in Iran in the post-Khatami era, where "the people" (and not necessarily the homeland) have become the fetish for the opposition groups in exile. As Benedetto Fontana has argued, "However different in intellectual content and in political-ideological direction, modern interpretations of liberalism share a common political/historical substratum, as well as a consistent set of interrelated political/intellectual ideas. This substratum is the emergence of 'the people'—or the 'masses'—in history as a force in politics" (2006, 59). The valorization of civil society as the realm of unified opposition to a homogenously oppressive state not only discounts the violent conflicts and exclusions within civil society but also aggrandizes its subversive and antistate potentials. Furthermore, what opposition groups uncritically call "the regime" is actually a fragmented and dynamic formation that, at times, relies on civil society for its disciplinary and regulatory work, and that is always characterized by contradiction and internal conflict.[1] Along with other informal enclaves, the fissures within state have *enabled* spaces in which contestation and reform have become possible.[2] However, most academic accounts that are critical of the Iranian state portray Iranian civil society as independent and in opposition to the state (e.g., Alavi 2004; Amir-Ebrahimi

2004; Boroumand 2007; Milani 2005). These discussions focus on the women's movement, the student movement, and the labor movement as elements of a growing civil society that stands against an Iranian state that is always already imagined to be repressive, uniform, and unchanging.

By eliding the socioeconomic and political factors that led to the 2005 victory of Mahmoud Ahmadinejad after two terms of the reformist president Mohammad Khatami, these critics represent the 2005 election as staged and utterly undemocratic, while portraying different movements in Iran as symbols of a newly formed civil society that is in natural opposition to the state and in need of support by "democratic" states. In addition, when the 2009 reelection of Ahmadinejad was met with charges of election fraud and street protests by proponents of the reformist candidate, Mir Hossein Mousavi, some diaspora opposition groups opportunistically hijacked the Green movement for their own political agenda. Wary of this appropriation, many reformists inside and outside of Iran emphasized that they do not need the support of "first-world" states and "regime-change" advocates. Mousavi himself warned against malicious appropriation, emphasizing that protecting the establishment (*nezaam*) and fighting for justice and the rule of law should be the goal of his supporters. And Mohsen Kadivar, the Iranian reformist cleric who was previously jailed in Iran, told a reporter that "we don't need any special support from you. The green movement for democracy and liberty in Iran is independent and we don't need anything from the foreigners. We should get democracy ourselves."[3]

There was a proliferation of statements and petitions to support the Iranian civil society in the name of defending the rights of "the Iranian people." For many diaspora Iranians who worked at think tanks, the internet became a site where the Iranian people could practice democracy. For example, Ladan Boroumand (2007, 74) claimed, "The core of the new movement consists of people between the ages of 25 and 45. They are truly a postrevolutionary generation; most were children or not even born as of 1979. Their numbers are enormous given Iran's vast 'youth bulge.' They lack their parents' predilections for Islamism, nationalism, or radical leftism; their commitments are to human rights and nonviolence, with not much ideological baggage beyond that. They feel connected to the world through media such as the Internet, and this bolsters their advocacy of civil rights."[4] If civil society connoted progress, democracy, and freedom in these accounts, the internet was not only the index but also the vehicle for achieving civil society, and Weblogistan was the representative of the opposition to a unified "regime" (Alavi 2005; Boroumand 2007).

However, it is important to remember that the exchange of ideas (what has been referred to as "practicing democracy") in Weblogistan was actually enabled by a history of struggle that preceded the "internet revolution" in Iran. Indeed, the much tweeted and subsequently televised 2009 election was not the first time that the student movement, the women's movement, and other social movements in Iran had demanded social freedoms. Contrary to technocentric approaches that perceive blogs in particular and the internet in general to have enabled the massive expansion of civil society in Iran, blogging became popular *precisely because of* an already-existing robust civil society. The emergence of Weblogistan as a site of transnational civil society did not occur outside of postrevolutionary Iran's political and economic events. The factional politics and the social changes in postrevolutionary Iran prove that Iranian civil society was thriving long before the popularization of blogs in Iran in the early 2000s. The fragmented nature of the state and the emergence of political factions and social movements that came out of internal conflicts complicate hegemonic accounts that juxtapose a uniformly fundamentalist state to a unified Iranian civil society.[5] Reformists such as Akbar Ganji, Abdolkareem Soroush, Seyyed Mohammad Khatami, and Mohsen Kadivar, as well as some reformist women's-rights advocates such as Azam Taleghani, Faezeh Rafsanjani, and Zahra Rahnavard, came from *within* and held key positions in the Iranian state.[6] Progressive civil rights organizations that initiated student protests such as the Islamic Society of Students (*anjoman-e Islami*) were initially conservative, state-sponsored entities in the universities. Some of the secular Iranian women's-rights activists have also emerged from within Islamic organizations and the reform movement.

The term *jaame'e-ye madani* (civil society) was popularized during the presidency of the reformist Seyyed Mohamad Khatami (1997–2005). Jaame'e-ye madani was deployed by reformist intellectuals who appropriated the term from the West, while adapting it to Islamic philosophical thought. Reformists who advocated jaame'e-ye madani used John Locke's concept of civil society as well as the theorists of commercial society and the Hegelian moment. As Sunil Khilnani explains, civil society "entered into English usage via the Latin translation, *societas civilis*, of Aristotle's *koinonia politike*" and "in its original sense, allowed no distinction between 'state' and 'society' or between political and the civil society" (2001, 17). For Locke, civil society stood against the state of nature but was synonymous with (legitimate) political society and the (benign) state: political legitimacy was built on trust between the ruled and the rulers; civil society was the domain of law (18). As Khilnani observes, for Locke, "If there was to be any possibility of securing a civilized society, certain minimal conditions were clearly necessary: these included a representative political order, a system of private property rights, and toleration of freedom of worship (although this did not... extend to freedom of speech...)" (19). Civilized society was that which would discipline its conduct to fulfill the order of God (a concept that appealed to Iranian reformist advocates of civil society).

On the other hand, the post-Hobbesian concept of the state, which informs our current understanding, is a structure of authority (Khilnani 2001, 18). In this tradition, civil society as the sphere of freedom and consensus is seen as a counterweight to the state. The formation of the modern bourgeoisie, which undermined the church and enshrined the secularization of thought, gave rise to the ascendance of the state as "ethicopolitical" and free of interests. The natural law theories, which were based on communal bonds between state and society, in the work of Hobbes changed into social contract, individualism, liberty, and individual property rights (Fontana 2006). In the liberal political theory of Hobbes and Locke, property is essential to personhood, and the role of the state is to protect the private property of individuals in civil society. For Hobbes, the sovereignty of the individual and self-interest in the state of nature—where every individual is considered to be a competition and an impediment to the liberty of the other individual—necessitate an ethical state ("Leviathan") to ensure the security of civil society to cultivate culture and arts and to accumulate private property and expand the free market.

For the secular eighteenth-century commercial-society theorists such as Adam Smith, "The fundamental modality of human interaction... was not trust, but need" (Khilnani 2001, 20). However, a realm of human interaction based on choice and voluntary association rather than mere self-interest characterized commercial societies, which were juxtaposed to precommercial societies, characterized by nonvoluntary associations such as bonds of kinship (21). Civilized society, in this view, was possible through commitment to a system of justice through laws, which were enforced by political authority. For Smith, commercial society was both a moral and social order. However, the moral order was secular in that it was established through natural social interactions resulting from the market and not from the fear of God (20–22).

The Hegelian notion bifurcated the concept of civil society (Khilnani 2001, 17). In Hegelian and subsequently Marxist traditions, civil society is oppositional to the state while also necessary for it as its socioeconomic foundation. While for Hobbes and Locke the state and laws (contracts) protect liberty and property in a community of consensus, Hegel points to the conflicts arising from the accumulation of private property and self-interest. The state for Hegel is an institution that channels antagonistic interests toward reason and is the realm of liberty and reason where the particular and the universal are reconciled. The individual is free as a political being, for liberty is necessarily political. Hegel sees individuality (as an achievement of the modern world) to be necessary for the formation of civil society, where self-interest dialectically "turns into the mediation of the particular through the universal," resulting in a system in which individual pleasure and earning benefits all (quoted in Femia 2001, 133). The state guarantees security in civil society while going beyond the particular interests of society. Hegel's redefinition of civil society did not equate it with political society but "defined it on the one hand as distinct from family, and on the other (and most crucially) from the state" (Khilnani 2001, 23).

The dominant notion of civil society in Iran does not follow such a bifurcated logic. The notion of civil society, which was popularized by religious intellectuals (*roshanfekraan-e deenee*) and deployed by Khatami, is not oppositional to the Islamic Republic. Khatami's approach to civil society, which both resonated with and differed from Western traditions, and his deployment of Soroush's writings on Islam and democracy, were reflected in his speeches, which emphasized the harmony of freedom and religion, the importance of civil society, and the prominence of democracy. Iranian intellectual reformists such as Soroush, who stood in opposition to the conservative factions of the Islamic state, used *ijtihad* to aid the reassessment of orthodox and static perceptions of Islam, thus enabling the possibility of synthesis among Islam, civil society, and democracy within the context of the Islamic Republic (Ansari 2003b, 17).[7] By drawing a distinction between secularism and laicism, Soroush along with other scholars (including some clergies within the state) reclaimed secularism and gave it legitimacy within the Islamic discourse. Drawing from de Tocqueville, reformist intellectuals argued for religious democracy as a right and advocated for an Islamic democracy from below. Using reformist hermeneutics, Khatami, the reformist president, popularized a range of terms such as *civil society (jaame'e-ye madani)*, *legality (qaanoonmandi)*, *citizen (shahrvand)*, *rule of law (qanoonsaalaari)*, and *political development (tose'e-ye siyaasi)*, all of which have become a part of reformist political discourse in Iran. For Khatami and the Iranian reformists, civil society does not stand in opposition to the state but is a realm of public interest through political participation and the rule of law.

Although the term *jaamee-ye madani* was popularized during the reform movement in Iran, the emergence of postrevolutionary Iranian public space preceded that moment. As Fariba Adelkhah (2000) argues, the emergence and growth of a public sphere in postrevolutionary Iran is reflected in a number of arenas: social activism among women, expression of dissent, emphasis on individual autonomy, rule of law, and the modernization of the religious sphere. In the years after the Iranian Revolution, women started taking an active role in discussions about Islam and democracy, and five seminaries were founded to train women as *mujtahids* (interpreter-jurists). This created possibilities of women's ijtihad in sociopolitical matters and enabled their contestation to judicial rulings of the *faqeeh*.[8] Following the changes in Iran's sociopolitical and economic conditions during and after Rafsanjani's presidency, a new "social being" was disciplined and regulated in a public space that emerged in postconstruction Iran.[9] These changes included increased urbanization of the landscape, increased internet use among the middle classes, women's increased access to education, a rise in the population of young people, and decreased illiteracy rates among youths. Adelkhah focuses on the institutionalization of strategic practices of giving and receiving (*javanmardi*) in the form of financial networks as an important factor in the formation of a highly political public space. She demonstrates that these practices have been institutionalized in the Islamic Republic as individual acts are mediated through bureaucratic organizations (such as the *bonyaad-e mostaz'afeen*/Foundation of the Disinherited) (55). The differentiation and bureaucratization of the religious sphere, rationalization, individualization, commercialization, and advertising in social, political, religious, and economic realms, along with the growing autonomy of the private sphere, strengthened the idea of citizenship in postrevolutionary Iran (172–73).

Adelkhah's in-depth analysis of everyday practices of *javanmardi* is an important and innovative intervention in historicizing civil society in Iran. In particular, her analysis challenges cyber-enthusiastic accounts that assume Weblogistan to be where the Iranian civil society flourishes. However, her analysis has some key limitations. Although Adelkhah's choice of *javanmard* (literally, "young man") as the "changing same" (a consistent ethos that changes with time) disrupts the conventional norms of historiography, it inevitably privileges a masculinist approach to history and events. Equally important is Adelkhah's lack of attention to the transnational nature of the civil society in Iran. The companies (*sherkats*) that flourished during Rafsanjani's presidency were mostly established and staffed by the technocrats who were educated abroad. The postwar call for the return of the Iranian diaspora for *saazandegi* (construction) of Iran gave rise to the increased exchange of bodies and capital between Iran and its diaspora. Internet technologies further accelerated and expanded communication between the Iranian diaspora and resident Iranians. The increased emigration of Iranian students and reformists during the second term of Khatami's presidency and after Ahmadinejad's election also changed the geographical scope of organizations and networks; some of the key journalists and activists continued their activism and collaboration with those who stayed in Iran.

To supplement Adelkhah's analysis, in the remaining parts of this chapter I discuss Iranian women bloggers' participation in Iranian electoral politics. By discussing the debates around the 2005 presidential election, the women's-rights activists' sit-in at Tehran University, and their illicit entry into Azadi Stadium, I situate Weblogistan not merely as a public space where dialogue and consensus become possible but also as a facet of transnational civil society, and as such a site of conflict and inequality.[10] The contentious discussions around the 2005 presidential election did not appear in Weblogistan out of thin air but were rooted in an already-existing transnational Iranian civil society. In other words, Iranian women's participation in political discussions in Weblogistan was not sui generis but became possible because of women's existing practices of citizenship in postrevolutionary Iran, long before the emergence of Weblogistan.

The 2005 Presidential Election

The June 2005 presidential election that culminated in the presidency of the former mayor of Tehran and the member of the conservative *Abaadgaran* Party, Mahmoud Ahmadinejad, was a surprising turning point after two consecutive landslide victories (1997 and 2005) by Seyyed Mohammad Khatami, the reformist president and the Participation Front candidate who succeeded with the massive support of women and students.[11] Out of more than one thousand candidates who registered to run for presidency, the Guardian Council qualified only eight—all of them men.[12] Two reformist candidates, Mostafa Moeen and Mohsen Mehralizadeh, were initially disqualified but were later reinstated because of the supreme leader's intervention. The reformists, whose campaign was dominated by the demands of the middle class, pushed for social freedoms. Yet the reformist camp (which included several parties) was more divided than before in its approaches to social and economic issues, so the reformist votes were split between several candidates, including the reformist Mostafa Moeen, the pragmatist Akbar Hashemi Rafsanjani, and the moderate pro-reform cleric and advisor to the supreme leader, Mehdi Karrubi.[13] As a result of this division, reformists failed to win enough votes in the preliminary stage of the election.[14] In the runoff, Ahmadinejad won 61.7 percent of the votes, in comparison to Rafsanjani's 35.9 percent. Ahmadinejad promised to change the financial corruption and unchecked wealth accumulation that Rafsanjani symbolized at that time. His campaign appealed to those Iranians disillusioned by the reformists' lack of economic solutions.[15] In his promise to correct economic problems that had caused discontent among many Iranians, he said, "People think that a return to revolutionary values is only a matter of wearing the headscarf. The country's true problem is employment and housing, not what to wear."[16]

Because of Iran's young population (70 percent under the age of thirty), many candidates tried to appeal to the young, urban middle class, with some candidates tapping into the internet. For example, Rafsanjani (moderate pragmatist), Rezai (conservative *Jebhe-ye Moqaavemat*/Resistance Front), and Qalibaf (conservative *Osoulgara*/Principlist Party) used new strategies to appeal to young people through advertisements that included pop music and fashion, or conveyed secular nationalist messages by invoking Ferdowsi's *Shahnameh*.[17] In their campaigns, some candidates, including Rafsanjani, employed young women with fashionable clothing—what would normally constitute "*bad hijabi*"/improper hijab, in the eyes of conservatives—to give the impression that if elected, they would take a liberal approach to women's freedom.[18] While Rafsanjani appealed to youths through such strategies, Moeen, a reformist candidate and the former minister of science and technology, emphasized the importance of the "information society" and even established a blog. Mehralizadeh, another reformist candidate and the minister of sports under Khatami, allowed a small group of women protesters (many of whom were bloggers and journalists) to attend the Iran-Bahrain soccer game at Tehran's Azadi Stadium.

Unlike the extravagant advertisements of the pragmatics and the reformists that appealed to young, middle-class voters, Ahmadinejad used humble images, promised to advocate on behalf of the poor, and presented himself as the "man of the people." When voters found themselves in the position of choosing between Rafsanjani and Ahmadinejad in the runoff, many Moeen supporters voted for Rafsanjani, fearing Ahmadinejad's victory. Regardless of this alliance and to the dismay of reformist voters, Ahmadinejad won the 2005 election.

In Weblogistan, Ahmadinejad's victory came as a shock to many political bloggers who had turned their blogs into campaigning tools for Moeen. Disillusioned with blogging for political mobilization, a few of them shut down their blogs. Sanam Dolatshahi—a feminist activist who had immigrated to the United States, lived in Florida at the time, and was one of the first Iranian women bloggers—advocated for Moeen in the first round of the election. Disappointed with the results of the first round, she wrote in her blog, *Khorshid Khanoom*, that "I have no hope that the situation will change. I am starting to doubt that I am Iranian and that Iran is my homeland. I feel like I have no homeland. Nowhere is my place. I feel like I can never do anything for Iran. I will not advertise for Rafsanjani. My words have no influence. But I will go and vote for Rafsanjani, only for the sake of Farnaz, Parastoo, Asieh, Shadi, Arash, Hamid Reza, Parisa, Kathy, Khosrwo, Nima, Omid, and other friends who live in Iran. And I will never forgive myself for voting for Rafsanjani."[19]

Pointing to the shortcomings of the reform movement before and during the election, Dolatshahi expressed that she nonetheless saw voting as an important act of political participation. She condemned boycotters for accusing voters of complicity with the Islamic state, and in turn she blamed them for the defeat of the reformists in the first round of the election. By emphasizing the importance of participation in the elections, Dolatshahi challenged the claim that Iran does not have a democratic system:

> When the final results [of the first round] were announced, we saw that 28 million people had voted. Mo'in's votes to "give legitimacy" [to the system] were only 4 million. . . . If you say the system is a dictatorship, then what is the meaning of the "legitimacy" argument? In a dictatorship legitimacy does not have a meaning, does it? If we believe that it is a dictatorship, the least we can do is to try and alleviate the pain of others [who live] under dictatorship. If we believe that legitimacy is important, then it means that we believe that it is a democracy and one must vote in a democracy. But does it even matter now?

The election boycotts left many fearing the loss of social freedoms that had been gained during the reform era. After the results of the first round were announced, Fataneh Kianerci, a feminist blogger who had traveled to Iran from Austria to vote in the 2005 elections, posted on her blog, *Qasedak*, in large letters, "*tahreem tarheem-e Azadi shod*" ("boycott became the funeral of freedom").

Women Bloggers and the Iranian Presidential Election

As is usually the case in the months preceding a presidential election in Iran, the 2005 election brought increased social freedoms and provided the opportunity for feminists to put pressure on candidates to advance women's rights. Some of the significant events that many feminist bloggers discussed during the 2005 election included the meeting of a group of women's-rights advocates with the presidential candidates, a sit-in by a group of feminists in front of the University of Tehran, and the entrance of a group of women and women's-rights activists to Azadi Stadium to watch a men's soccer match (at which women are usually not allowed).

During the 2005 presidential election, a group of women presidential nominees, women's-rights organizations, and nongovernmental organizations (NGOs), including the Women's Society of the Islamic Revolution (*jam'iyat-e zanaan-e inqilab-e Islami*), gathered in front of the president's office to protest the discriminatory interpretation of the Arabic word *rejal* ("political personalities") in the Iranian constitution. Article 115 of the Iranian Constitution indicates that "the President must be elected from among religious and political personalities [*rejal*] possessing the following qualifications: Iranian origin; Iranian nationality; administrative capacity and resourcefulness; a good past-record; trustworthiness and piety; convinced belief in the fundamental principles of the Islamic Republic of Iran and the official *madhhab* [religion] of the country."[20]

For years, Iranian women activists and scholars have been challenging the masculinist interpretation of *rejal* in the constitution's definition of "*rejal-e siyaasi*" (political personalities). The Arabic term *rejal* can be translated into Persian as "*mardha*" ("men") or as "*ashkhaas-e siyaasi*" ("political personalities"). Azam Taleghani—a former member of the Iranian Parliament and a well-known Islamist women's-rights advocate—was the first woman to challenge the Guardian Council's interpretation of *rejal* as "men" by running for the presidency in 1997.[21] The Guardian Council disqualified her in 1997 and continues to do the same to her and other women who persistently nominate themselves as an act of protest. This symbolic act is meant to pressure the

Iranian state to change the (mis)interpretation of the word *rejal* as "men."[22] Consistent with the previous elections, the Guardian Council disqualified eighty-nine women nominees in 2005. Women's-rights activists and bloggers organized meetings with the reformist candidate, Moeen, to ask him to support Iranian women's demands to eliminate discriminatory laws (including the interpretation of *rejal-e siyaasi*) in the Iranian constitution. In addition to this meeting, around the same time, roughly a thousand women gathered for a sit-in in front of the University of Tehran to demand changes to the constitution to guarantee equal rights for women. Many bloggers (both women and men) supported the protest against the Guardian Council's interpretation of *rejal*. Mohamad Ali Abtahi—a blogger, reformist cleric, and President Khatami's former parliamentary deputy—described women's disqualification as unjust: "Of course, the problem remains that some of those whose qualification was denied were disqualified for no reason. Examples such as Dr. Yazdi and others, and ladies who were eliminated altogether."[23]

Although largely successful in publicizing its message in the social media, the sit-in ended early because various people tried to opportunistically hijack the women's-rights activists' gathering by shouting slogans that were irrelevant to the organizers' demands. In addition, the sit-in coincided with the explosion of bombs in Tehran and Ahvaz. Several popular blogs such as *Khorshid Khanoom* (*Lady Sun*) and *Zan Nevesht* (*Woman's Writing*) featured posts about the sit-in, expressing concern about the unknown forces that wished to jeopardize the democratic movements in Iran by creating chaos. As Masoumeh Naseri—a women's-rights activist, blogger, and journalist—wrote in her blog, "Those who were saying they can no longer wait [for things to change through reform]. Those who were saying if Khatami does not do anything they would enter the arena themselves. They are exploding it."[24] Pointing to the expected enhanced security measures by the state in the aftermath of the bombings, she continued: "Do you know where the [state] decision resulting from these explosions will land? Surely, the smoke [from the explosions] will burn our eyes. [We will pay for it]!"[25] In response to the opportunistic unrest during the sit-in, the feminist website Zanan-e Iran reported the following: "That the gathering got chaotic had nothing to do with the organizers of the women's sit-in. We neither know those who shout political slogans, nor do we know about their goals."[26] According to this report, once there were people shouting political slogans from outside the women's gathering, Mahboubeh Abbasgholizadeh, a women's-rights activist, addressed the crowd by saying, "Political gentlemen have sufficient tribunes to speak. It is us women, who do not have a tribune to make our voices be heard by the people, and have to resort to these sit-ins."

Civil Society and Its Discontents: Half of Freedom

On June 9, 2005, shortly before the presidential election, a group of women challenged the ban prohibiting women from attending men's soccer games in Iran. After four hours of waiting behind the doors of *stadium-e Azadi* (Freedom Stadium) for the Iran-Bahrain match and shouting slogans such as "My share, woman's share, half of freedom," and "shame, shame!" ("*khejaalat, khejaalat!*"), women pushed through the gates behind the bus that transported the national team. Finally, the reformist candidate, Mohsen Mehralizadeh, who at the time was the sports minister in President Khatami's cabinet, allowed women to enter and sit in the VIP section of the stadium, where they would not be harassed by male soccer fans. Although Mehralizadeh attempted to use this event to portray himself as sympathetic to women's rights, most of the women bloggers who reported about this incident in Weblogistan were supporters of the reformist candidate, Mostafa Moeen. Aware of Mehralizadeh's political motivations and the appropriation of women's rights by a candidate who had otherwise not shown support for women's rights, Parastoo Dokouhaki, a feminist blogger and journalist, critiqued the women who were using the protest to shout pro-Mehralizadeh slogans: "I forgot to say that a large number of women in the stadium came with Mehralizadeh's invitation. They were shouting slogans in his support and campaigning for him. It wasn't a pleasant move at all. It was offensive."[27]

Dokouhaki was not the only blogger who took issue with the appropriation of women's rights by politicians. Fereshteh Ghazi, another feminist blogger and journalist, was also enraged that candidates were appropriating women's causes for their electoral agendas: "In the heat of the elections, it is as if everyone is appropriating any movement in favor of their candidates."[28] Rejecting the charges that women who entered the stadium were pawns of presidential candidates, a feminist blogger and reformist journalist, Geesoo Faghfoori, recounted the events at the stadium:

> We entered the Freedom stadium. We watched the second half of the Iran-Bahrain game. With our entrance, the national team scored a goal. We entered *Azadi* [Freedom] as a group of ordinary women and Iranian citizens.

> We got one of our small rights. We gave a casualty for it. Asiyeh accompanied our injured member and had to miss the pleasure of watching soccer in the stadium. We put effort. We waited and at the end of the first half, we entered the VIP section. We did not have VIP tickets. We were regular people. We were not Mehralizadeh's guests. We were not artists and actors. We were journalists, but we did not use our journalist permits. We were a group of Iranian women citizens without [equal] civil rights who entered this stadium.[29]

Critiquing Mehralizadeh's propaganda campaign, she continued: "We also did a little bit of campaign work. When women who were Mehralizadeh's fans cheered for him, we sang '*Ey Iran*.' I had not at all forgotten that I wanted to vote for Moeen." "*Ey Iran*" ("*Marz-e Por Gohar*") is a patriotic song that was composed in 1944 and is at times used as a de facto Iranian national anthem. Because neither the official national anthem during the Pahlavi period nor the postrevolution anthems hold the same nationalistic significance in the cultural realm in Iran or its diaspora, the women activists' deployment of "*Ey Iran*" was a strategy of claiming citizenship and belonging to the nation while distancing themselves from state nationalism.

The presence of women journalists and bloggers in Azadi Stadium was a strategic move to push for equal access to public space during the state's preelection softening of social restrictions. Similarly, the participation of some women without scarves in the street celebrations that followed Iran's victory in the soccer match, and the staging of a demonstration in front of the University of Tehran by a few hundred women to demand equal rights, seized on the opportunity to occupy the political and public space that was created during the election. The women activists took advantage of this stage for strategic performances of citizenship by pushing against the masculinist imaginations of the nation (embodied in national sports) while repeating its conventions through songs and flags.

Of course, women who participated in the stadium protest were not immune from criticism from a wide range of angry bloggers and blog readers. In the comments section of Geesoo Faghfoori's blog, a commentator who identified as "Azadeh" (a woman's name meaning "Free") wrote the following:

> I was saddened to read that such combatant [*mobaariz*] ladies are pinning their hopes on a deception called Moeen. How is it that such a lady has not yet understood that the only opportunity for her liberation and the liberation of other ladies such as me from the evil of an ideological archaic regime

is to boycott and disappoint its international supporters, so that when it opens its mouth to say that they [other states] are going to negotiate with Iran, etc. etc., we slap it in the mouth! . . . I will not be satisfied with a bone that the famous Mr. Moeen throws! I deserve complete freedom. . . . I don't know about you.

Playing with the term *Azadi* (freedom), a commentator who identified as Noghteh Alef responded to Azadeh's comment in Faghfoori's comments section: "Perhaps this Ms. Azadeh has not heard that each strategy is justified in the continuum of reaching a goal, and not from thin air! And not just for the present. . . . The way that this 'free group' talks about this issue and their goal is to take away the dignity of the Iranian government in the international arena (if there is any dignity left!) and to discredit the Iranian system (and if there is any credit left, it is due to the presence of the reformists!)." After making a distinction between independent slow change through reform and regime change through occupation similar to that of Iraq and Afghanistan, Noghteh Alef continued: "No! Freedom is not something that they bring you as a gift from outside! You have to earn it! Sometimes sitting in ivy towers and belittling the living is the easiest and safest way . . . and most importantly, to drop the burden of responsibility. . . . So that whatever happens, you can say, it wasn't me! Let's not forget that it is the scent of our oil which is pleasant to the foreigners and not the wishes of our Azadehs [that they care about]."

Even though some reformists such as Noghteh Alef showed their solidarity with Faghfoori and other women voters by defending them against the opposition groups and regime-change advocates, many reformists were critical of women's-rights advocates' fight for access to the stadium and accused them of diluting the reformist cause. For example, in a post titled "*darbaare-ye Feminism-e Irani*" ("About Iranian Feminism"), Mohammad Heydari, a reformist blogger with *melli mazhabi* (religious nationalist) views, criticized Parastoo Dokouhaki, whose post about women's-rights activists' entrance to the stadium garnered a lot of support from feminist bloggers:

I don't know what pleasure these respected ladies get from this struggle for nothing? . . . I don't understand what entering the stadium has to do with the problems of this land? Rather than following the issues of the Iranian woman, Iranian feminism is going after the same elitist talks that are incidentally rooted in the same things that men say. My lords! [*sarvaraan-e man*!] For once visit the remote areas of Iran or even Tehran. I know of many places where girls are not allowed to study. Would it not be better if, instead of going to the *Azadi* Stadium, you started a movement that asked for mandatory high school education for girls and boys?[30]

Paternalistic tone aside, Heydari's point is valid insofar as the women's-rights movement in Iran has historically been a middle-class, Tehran-centered movement. By concentrating on urban middle-class women's issues, urban women's-rights activists have at times ignored forms of organizing by religious, rural, and working-class women in everyday life situations, namely the everyday practices that neither enter the realm of social movements nor are organized under the banner of "feminism." Some women use mosques or *jalasehs* (women's religious gatherings) for their activism, even though such networks may not be considered to be a part of the more formal women's-rights movements.[31] Partially because of the criticism from within and outside of the movement, women's-rights groups tried to reach out to provinces and rural areas to educate women about discriminatory laws with regard to family, marriage, divorce, and custody through the One-Million Signatures campaign.[32] However, most of their priorities still remained limited to the concerns of middle-class and secular women.[33]

While Heydari pointed to an important shortcoming of the middle-class women's-rights movement, his criticism was dismissive of the activists' issues. Dokouhaki responded to Heydari by drawing his attention to a post she had written almost a year before. On November 16, 2004, she had written about deciding whether to go to the stadium for the Iran-Laos game or to spend her time working on publishing the popular magazine *Chelcheraq*. That year, the journalists and women's-rights activists did not have an organized plan to go to the stadium for the Iran-Laos game. However, they had been prevented from entering the stadium for the Iran-Germany game earlier that year. In her 2004 post, Dokouhaki wrote, "Tomorrow is the Iran-Laos game and Iranian women behind the stadium bars have to watch Laotian women go and sit on platforms that could be their place."[34] When Ali Moazzami, a reformist blogger, criticized Dokouhaki's post (similar to Heydari's objection in 2005), expressing that the Iranian women's movement had failed to prioritize its issues according to the needs of Iranian women, Dokouhaki responded to Moazzami:

> In the past few years, as soon as we said women's issues, reformist friends would turn and say, first democracy and then other issues. To be honest, their logic was similar to yours, Mr. Moazzami. They said (and they probably still say) that resolving an important issue such as democracy in the

country has priority to resolving women's issues. It means that it has priority to everything. As far as I remember, an important part of their logic was that "until there is no freedom and cultural security women's issues would not be resolved." . . . But the view of a segment of women's movement is different. They say that one of the problems that women face is that so far others have decided on their priorities. . . . I think that women's issues (women and not woman, because the issues of a pregnant woman, an employed woman, a rural woman, or a woman student are different) include all sorts of discriminations and conditions that exist for women because of their gender (being a woman). These forms of discrimination are so general that they exist in all countries and nationalities, and sometimes they are limited to a society. . . . Going to the stadium may not be a priority among women's demands (although I can only talk on my own behalf and say that it is not so for me), but it [going to the stadium] is to eradicate an existing discrimination.[35]

Here Dokouhaki explains that women's-rights activists have different priorities and approaches and that it does not make sense to postpone the demand for one right because others have not yet been granted. Dokouhaki's response makes it clear that the women's-rights movement in Iran is neither monolithic nor monological. Finally, her post takes issue with male nationalists and reformists who accuse women of diverting the reformist movement. In fact, the dilemma that many Iranian feminist bloggers faced was the bifurcated approach to feminism and "proper politics" that either excluded women altogether from political discussions or required that women leave their feminism out of electoral politics.

While Moazzami and Heydari's responses were written in a seemingly supportive (if paternalistic) tone, framed as constructive criticism, some explicitly hostile responses by anonymous commentators were completely dismissive of the legitimacy of the women's-rights movement. Some saw women's-rights activists' concerns and agendas to be absolutely irrelevant to the "real" issues of the Iranian people. Others perceived women's-rights activism to be insufficient and ineffective because it stayed within the framework of the Islamic state. On the other hand, several bloggers in Iran and in the diaspora applauded women activists' efforts by leaving them encouraging comments or by thanking them in their blog posts.[36]

The responses that Dokouhaki and other women's-rights activist bloggers received about the sit-in at the University of Tehran and the Azadi Stadium events show that women activists are often caught between male nationalist agendas and the liberating mission of diasporic opposition groups and states that seek to appropriate the Iranian women activists' cause against discriminatory laws of the Iranian state. It is at the intersection of nationalist discourses and the civilizing mission that the Iranian women's-rights activists assert their agency through negotiating a legitimate space in Iranian politics. As Judith Butler (1993, 15) argues, "The paradox of subjectivation [*assujetissement*] is precisely that the subject who would resist such norms is itself enabled, if not produced, by such norms. Although this constitutive constraint does not foreclose the possibility of agency, it does locate agency as a reiterative or rearticulatory practice, immanent to power, and not a relation of external opposition to power."

Women supporters of Moeen refused to be labeled as Mehralizadeh supporters, even as their presence in the stadium was enabled by the state power (upon the minister of sports/presidential candidate's permission). While distancing themselves from the state, women activists tapped into the affective power of nationalism by singing *"Ey Iran,"* a song about homeland that overrides the power of the state's national anthem. The power of the song lies in its deployment of the timelessness of love for the motherland, regardless of the state's (prerevolutionary or postrevolutionary) ideological position. Women gained entrance into the stadium during the elections through their active participation and persistence, but their resistance to power was not outside of nationalist discourses that have both excluded and enabled women as subjects. Nor is Iranian women's-rights activism outside of liberal discourses of rights. In order to gain their citizenship rights, middle-class women activists tap into both international and national laws to insert themselves into the realm of Iranian political citizenship. In other words, while women's-rights activists are complicit with the Islamic state and the liberal discourses framed within the logic of universal rights of the individual, they have successfully negotiated a space within the realm of Iranian politics and citizenship by overriding these discourses through their strategies and their constant negotiations with the state.

It is important to point out, however, that not all Iranian women activists articulate their resistance to state power through the framework of universal rights. Many religious women have situated their demands within religious frameworks and have effectively challenged discriminatory laws through religious activism.[37] But these forms of participation are barely recognized as "activism" or given due credit in mainstream accounts of Iranian women's activism. For example, Farnaz Seifi, a young Iranian feminist activist and the author of the famous blog *Amshaspandan*, critiqued Azam Taleghani, the daughter of the late Ayatollah Taleghani, for her complicity with the Iranian state.[38] Born in 1944, Taleghani was imprisoned during the reign of Mohammad Reza Pahlavi. She served as a member of Parliament after the revolution, is the founder of the *Jaamee'e-ye zanaan-e mosalmaan* (the Society of Muslim Women), served as head of the Society of Islamic Revolution Women of Iran, and is the editor of a Muslim women's journal called *Payaam-e Haajar* (*Haajar's message*). In 2003 she launched a solo sit-in in front of Evin Prison to protest the treatment of prisoners, solitary confinement, and the death of Zahra Kazemi, an Iranian Canadian journalist who allegedly had a stroke as she was being interrogated in Evin Prison in 2001.[39] Taleghani has repeatedly nominated herself for the Iranian presidential elections to protest the Iranian constitution's discriminatory interpretation of the term *rejal*, which disqualifies women from the presidency.[40]

In a sarcastic critique of Taleghani's Islamic approach and self-presentation, Seifi confessed that she had burst into laughter upon seeing the old chador-clad Taleghani. Nazli Kamvari, the author of *Sibil Tala*, wrote a post titled "*baraay-e maatik va chador*" ("For Chador and Lipstick") in which she criticized what she considered to be Seifi's dismissal of Taleghani's contributions to the Iranian women's movement. Addressing Seifi, Kamvari wrote the following:

> I want to tell you about *haaj khanoom*'s characteristics.[41] ... Which *haaj khanoom* [you ask]? Yes, *haaj khanoom* Taleghani. The same one at whom you laughed. Please don't take it personally, because generally speaking, I am your fan. But, back in the day, when you did not know how to spell feminism, *haaj khanoom* was nominating herself in every presidential election.... I don't want to rank [activism], but what *haaj khanoom* has done for the women's movement in Iran is valuable and so is Ms. Kar's [contribution].[42] Now, *haaj khanoom*'s work is the Islamic feminism and Ms. Nooshin's is the secular version.[43] ... It is useless to compare Nooshin Ahmadi Khorasani and *haaj khanoom* and to put value [on one or the other]. In the peculiar Iranian society, we need both Nooshin and *haaj khanoom*.[44]

By acknowledging Taleghani's long-term activism, Kamvari challenges the assumption that Iranian women's activism is always already secular and

NGO-based. Kamvari moves beyond the bifurcated configuration of Islamic versus secular feminism and acknowledges the important contributions of seemingly opposing approaches to the Iranian women's movement. Even as Islamic feminism has been instrumental in challenging the masculinist laws of the Islamic Republic, some feminist activists and scholars consider Islam and feminism to be incommensurable. As Minoo Moallem (2005b, 177) argues, "Bringing Islam and feminism into the same frame of reference has caused a predictably hysterical reaction from Iranian modernists as well from anti-West fundamentalists." Many Iranian feminist activists resist the dichotomy of "secular" and religious, for such dichotomies do not follow the realities of everyday life and feminism in Iran (Moallem 2005b, 178; Najmabadi 2000, 32). The dismissal of Islamic feminists who challenge the Iranian state wrongly assumes that activism and resistance could be pure, and that the state could be uniform. What the glorified fantasy of pure activism ignores is the fact that state power also enables seemingly "nongovernmental" activism, often producing the conditions of possibility. As is the case outside of Iran, many women's NGOs (secular or religious) in Iran have been supported and funded in one way or another by either the Iranian state or a foreign state. Despite their claims of being nongovernmental and regardless of whether they receive state funding, NGOs are often part and parcel of governmentality in national or transnational assemblages that include multiple state and nonstate actors. As elements of civil society, NGOs that disperse state funding (as was the case with the Dutch state funding for several Iranian organizations) participate in the art of governing populations through biopolitical and ethicopolitical practices that may include normalization of the population according to democratization discourses, Eurocentric secularism, and liberal feminist ethos. Furthermore, resistance to state power is not the only way to gain agency as a citizen subject. As Saba Mahmood (2001, 203) has argued, despite the important insights that a notion "of human agency in feminist scholarship that seeks to locate the political and moral autonomy of the subject in the face of power" has enabled, this model of agency "sharply limits our ability to understand and interrogate the lives of women whose desire, affect, and will have been shaped by nonliberal traditions." What is often dismissed as docility and complicity with the "regime" may very well be an expression of agency for many Iranian women activists (feminist or not) who form their politics in relation to the conditions of possibility of activism and scholarship.

Are We Iran?

Iranian voters have long engaged in passionate discussions about the elections and in a number of public and private settings: at home, in *baqqaali* (grocery stores), in *naanvaayee* (bakeries), in taxicabs, on buses, on college campuses, at religious *jalasehs*, in *masjids* (mosques), to name a few. Weblogistan emerged as one more site where Iranians with different political positions held heated discussions. But the online discussions provided an opportunity for a wider reach and allowed transnational connectivities between Iranians in Iran and diaspora Iranians (who enthusiastically participated in the politics of homeland from different parts of the world). Whether in Iran or in diaspora, bloggers had different takes on the 2005 presidential election. Several disillusioned reformists who had left Iran, some bloggers in Iran, and the old-Left opposition groups in diaspora boycotted the elections. Others, including those who were critical of the Iranian state, publicly announced their support for different candidates. Some bloggers reluctantly announced that they would vote for Rafsanjani in the second round to prevent a backlash against the relative freedom they had gained during Khatami's presidency.[45]

However, these discussions were far from being univocal. Several bloggers who had announced that they were voting received accusatory emails or comments from those who saw participation in the election as complicity with the Islamic Republic. It was not uncommon for women bloggers who voted to be called "*jendeh-ye molla*" ("whore of a mullah") in the comments section of their blogs. When Nazli Kamvari—a feminist woman blogger in Toronto who wrote about sexuality on her blog—announced publicly that she was going to vote for Moeen, she was accused of being *jendeh-ye molla*, backward, or an agent of the "regime". On the other hand, some comments were from Moeen's supporters who thought that the support of "whores" and "tramps" would damage Moeen's reputation. To Nazli's surprise, some of the attacks came from secular feminists in diaspora who considered the Iranian "regime" to be inherently hostile toward women.

I was also subject to online aggression. Without explicitly mentioning my name, Shadi Amin—an Iranian feminist lesbian based in Germany—quoted from one of my blog posts in which I had mentioned that I had voted for Moeen in the first round and was voting for Rafsanjani to stop the conservative candidate (Ahmadinejad) from winning in the runoff: "Backwardness outside of the country has its spokespeople. From a lesbian who in her weblog in the U.S. passionately advocates for Moeen (*sang-e Moeen raa beh sineh mizanad*) and publishes the address for voting polls (a woman whose existence is denied and death penalty awaits her in this Islamic Republic) to disillusioned leaders who never regret anything."[46] Amin also accused voters of being *amaleh haa-ye regime* (regime construction workers): a classist form of insult, ironically deployed by a socialist. Using a civilizational approach that deems any association with Islam, Islamic feminism, or voting in the presidential elections as signs of backwardness, she considered voting to be an act of complicity with "the regime" and perceived those who voted to be brainwashed and uneducated. Like many boycott advocates who assume for themselves the higher moral ground, Amin foreclosed the possibility of an in-between position, conflating participation in political processes with collusion and backwardness.

Many feminist bloggers who had chosen to vote challenged the elitist position of diasporic advocates of boycott such as Amin. Disappointment with the results of the first round of the election led many reformist voters to strategically vote for Rafsanjani, who seemed to be the only viable option in the face of an imminent conservative backlash. A day before the second round of the election, Masoumeh Naseri, a journalist and blogger, admitted that while she had criticized Rafsanjani's supporters in the first round, she found herself in a position where she had no choice but to vote for the pragmatist candidate in the second round. In a post titled "An Intellectual without Action Is Like a Bee without Honey," Naseri responded to a blogger from London who had accused voters of being complicit with the "regime":

> You have the right to sit there in your world of free press. But you don't have the right to stop me, and others, from going [to vote]. And [you do not have the right] to consider our solution as ignorance, when we do not have any other choice [but to vote]. . . . Because, we are still supposed to at least have the right to walk in the lovely streets of Tehran. You too, go and vote, if you wish, so that we can think about the strategies to challenge the future president. These ways are the minimum of what we, the resident Iranians, have learned during eight years of [living with] the reformist government in Iran.[47]

The absolutist logic that condemned bloggers who voted in the presidential election also appeared in *We Are Iran: The Persian Blogs,* an English-language book by Nasrin Alavi (pseudonym) that attracted much attention soon after its publication in the United States in 2005. *We Are Iran* represents Weblogistan as a unified body of bloggers who stand univocally against the Iranian state, even as many of the bloggers quoted in the book would not support such an agenda. Alavi, who excludes those blogs that challenge this politics, such as religious ones, frames Weblogistan as a frontier for regime change. In the last section of the book, Alavi focuses on the boycotts of the 2005 Iranian presidential election. Claiming that the supreme leader's intervention to convince the Guardian Council to reinstate Moeen discredited the reformist candidate, Alavi writes, "Mo'in's decision to stand following the supreme leader's intervention made a total mockery of his subversive stance and neutered his chances with the majority of the electorate who once again saw reformists as all talk and no action" (2005, 310). Alavi's claim about the disappointment of the "majority of the electorate" with Moeen presumes that his supporters saw him as a candidate who stood against and outside the "regime," not as a candidate who had worked toward reform from within. Alavi undermines bloggers who had voted in the election by writing that "having watched for eight years as the so-called reformists struggled to overturn hardline opposition, many bloggers openly stated that they had lost hope for bringing change through the ballot box" (312). As with many of the decontextualized quotations, Alavi selectively quoted from a post by Foroogh, a resident Iranian blogger: "I don't regret not voting. I only wish that circumstances were different and my choice hadn't been one between bad and worst.... If Ahmadi'nejad can keep only a few of his promises [such as the fight against poverty,] then I will be happy that I didn't vote for Rafsanjani.... They [the poor] are hungry and tired ... and only want financial security" (ellipses and brackets in Alavi, translated by Alavi 2005, 314).

The quotation is part of a longer post written by Foroogh on June 26, 2005. Alavi selectively cited Foroogh's concern about voting for Rafsanjani, thus giving the impression that Foroogh had not voted at all. The fact is that Foroogh had not boycotted the 2005 election but had voted for the reformist candidate (Moeen) in the first round. In the second round, however, Foroogh chose not to vote, as she was not convinced that Rafsanjani would be a suitable president for working-class Iranians. Ahmadinejad's victory seemed to be a wake-up call to Foroogh, who had come to realize that her reformist politics and her concerns for social freedoms might have overlooked the economic realities of the majority of the Iranian society. Here is the full-length post to provide the necessary context for Foroogh's decision in the second round:

> I am not sorry that I did not vote. I only wish that circumstances were not such that I would be forced to choose between bad and worse. I did not want to give up my right to vote. I acted based on my beliefs. Perhaps

it is stupid. But I still think that I did the right thing. In the first round, there was a ray of hope. I thought it was possible to be hopeful. But this time, all my beliefs went under question. It has passed any way. One cannot think about death. This is what democracy means. That if you give up your right to vote, others will decide for you. . . . I don't think about [election] fraud. Fraud is a possibility for one million votes. But the [vast] difference indicates a reality in which fraud fades. People did not say their big "no" to fascism. That expected "no" was said to lies and deception and to the undeserving movement [reform movement] that did not think of anything but its own interests every time it came to power. The big "no" was said to us [the reformists] so that we understand how far we are from the heart of the society. With Rafsanjani's defeat, perhaps many of us will lose what we have, but the man who goes home embarrassed [for being empty-handed] to his wife and child did not have anything to lose by consoling himself with Mr. Mayor's [Ahmadinejad's] welfare slogans. The promise of 50,000 Tomans is more tangible to him than the ten million-Toman promise of free stock market share. If Ahmadinejad can act on a small fragment of his slogans, I am very pleased not to have voted for Rafsanjani. Also, I don't think that the story is as horrific as they have painted for us in one week. Those who voted for Ahmadinejad were not worried that headscarf, short mantua, film, and music would jeopardize their Islam. They are hungry and tired. And they just want material welfare from him. In the midst of this, like other governments we have had, we will surely witness the appearance of opportunists and new people who want to bag money. But their story is different than those who voted. To legitimize overlooking Rafsanjani's past mistakes, many people said that the past 8 years have made him wiser; that he would act better than before. If this much ability to change is possible in a person like him, then it is possible in Mesbah Yazdi as well.[48]

Foroogh's disheartened realization about the small number of votes for the reformist candidate and the overwhelming support for him in Weblogistan seemed like a sobering concern shared by several reformist bloggers. This realization subdued the hype about the potential of blogging as a miraculous tool in creating political change, highlighting the fact that Iranian bloggers who engaged in political discussions constituted a small fragment of the Iranian population. Many bloggers expressed their disillusionment with vanguardist and patronizing approaches to social change. A day after voting in Ottawa and realizing that Moeen had not gotten enough votes, Kamvari wrote on her blog that "the Persian Weblogistan is consisted of a group who are far from [the Iranian] people. If you want to issue verdicts about the situation of the people in Iran, make sure to talk to the grocer, the baker, the vegetable vendor, the car driver. My personal ruminations [*ifaazaat*] about issues pertaining to Iran are worthless."[49]

Consensus or Conflict?

The selective and decontextualized quotations from disillusioned reformists that appear in *We Are Iran* erase the reality that reformist blogger voters were acknowledging the bitter fact that a select group of middle-class bloggers did not represent the Iranian population at large. While *We Are Iran* portrays bloggers as a unified online community against an oppressive state, those bloggers who supported the conservative candidates did not find their way into this imagined community. While most popular blogs were critical of Ahmadinejad, a number of bloggers defended him. For example, the author of the *Rooznameh Nevis* (*Journalist*) blog repeated Ahmadinejad's campaign slogan, "Yes, we can and it is possible," in order to portray him as a "man of the people" who, against all odds, had promised to stand up to corruption.[50] He mocked Rafsanjani's supporters by posting pictures of fashionable urban upper-middle class young women and men on their roller skates wearing "Hashemi" (Rafsanjani's middle name) stickers. He also posted pictures of Rafsanjani in his extravagant residence, juxtaposed with photos depicting the humble Ahmadinejad and his supporters.[51] Even though in Weblogistan the number of Ahmadinejad supporters was not nearly as large as the number of popular reformist bloggers and boycotters, this number grew during Ahmadinejad's presidency.

On the second anniversary of Ahmadinejad's election, a group of pro-Ahmadinejad bloggers started a *baazi-ye veblogi* (blog game) where they wrote about "*hemaaseh-ye sevvom-e Tir*" ("the legend of June 24"), referring to his 2005 victory.[52] Pro-Ahmadinejad bloggers recalled their memories and described June 24, 2005, as the day of the struggle of people-oriented Ahmadinejad against the well-financed propaganda of Rafsanjani and the well-dressed Qalibaf.

The conservative bloggers were not the only group of bloggers who were rendered invisible in mainstream articles and books about Weblogistan; any blogging that challenged the dominant narrative of Weblogistan as a united site of protest against the "Iranian regime" was often excluded. For example, reformist bloggers' internal disagreements about the question of boycott were omitted in mainstream accounts about Weblogistan.[53] While some boycotters were segments of the Iranian opposition groups that believed there was no difference between a reformist candidate and a conservative one, more-nuanced discussions took place among those who explored boycott as a strategy of reform. This group of reformists considered boycott to be a strategy for protesting the disqualification of reformists in the Parliament and the presidential processes. There were heated discussions among reformist boycotters and the voting reformists in Weblogistan. Reza, a reformist sociology student in Iran, wrote this in his blog:

> The boycott movement criticizes the structure of the establishment and the constitution and subsequently avoids any political activism based on and within this framework. But it seeks votes from the disenfranchised and discontent masses whose philosophy of political opposition and lack of presence in elections is limited to this concept: "we voted all this time and what has happened? Khatami was one of their own!" The boycott movement produces an opposition which believes that "this regime is illegitimate and Khamene'i has to go." But when it comes to the masses, it turns into a passive discourse that says, "leave it alone.... They are all cut from the same cloth" ("*baba vel kon . . . hamashoon sar o tah ye karbaasand*").[54]

Reza also criticized Akbar Ganji—a journalist[55] who was imprisoned between 2001 and 2006 and had gone on a hunger strike in 2005—for appropriating human rights and for pushing his boycott agenda by using the reformists who had defended him when he was in prison: "The most unfortunate characteristic of the boycott movement in Iran is the establishment of a parasitical existence with the reformists. The meaning of parasitical existence here is that their livelihood is dependent on feeding from social forces and the political outlook of the reformists. But their role has been nothing but to weaken and thin the body of reform. The boycott movement has been shaped in the margins of the reform movement.... But they [boycotters] have seen them [reformists] as their competitors."[56]

Unsurprisingly, most of the disapproving responses to Reza's post came from those who had boycotted the elections. Nikahang Kowsar—a boycotter living in Toronto who was one of the most vocal and harsh critics of the reformists—wrote a series of responses to Reza and criticized the governmental reformists (*Eslaah talabaan-e hokoomati*) for not including Rafsanjani supporters in their circles during eight years of Khatami's presidency.[57] In his first response, by pointing to the pivotal role of the pragmatists (Rafsanjani's camp), whose alliance with the reformists in 1997 helped Khatami's victory, Kowsar wrote that "to expect from everyone to always be with us and approve of us is slightly far from reason. To call others parasites is irresponsible."[58]

The arguments were not limited to those within the opposition. Some reformist bloggers who had not boycotted the elections also disagreed with Reza's harsh criticism of Ganji and other disillusioned reformist boycotters. Ali-Asghar Seyyed Abadi, a reformist journalist in Iran who managed *Hanouz*, a blog belonging to a group of journalists, complicated the seeming binary between the boycotters and those who were in favor of voting:

> In both [Reza] and [Kowsar's] arguments, the reformists are positioned against the boycott forces. However, one can be both a reformist and a boycotter. Perhaps one cannot call all boycotters reformists, but a segment of them are without doubt, reformists. If we accept reform as a method, then we have to position it against concepts such as "regime change"; because reform is a method that sees change within a governmental framework. But it does not mean that it has to accept all the workings within the government. The best example is the 7th parliament elections during which the reformists within the government were divided to two groups: A group, like the Participation Front and the *Mojahedeen* [*Mojahedeen-E Inqilab*], did not participate in the elections, and a group, like the *majma'-e roohaniyoon* participated.[59]

Seyyed Abadi's intervention is informed by a long history of factional politics that challenges facile assumptions that to vote is to be co-opted and/or that boycott as a strategy is deployed only by regime-change advocates. His post is a good example of the multiplicity of political positions that exceed the simplistic representations of Weblogistan as a platform for regime change. Posts such as Seyyed Abadi's, which never appeared in the mainstream international media, show that Weblogistan, as a manifestation of transnational civil society, is a site of conflict and disagreement, not necessarily a unified front against the state. The very possibility of debate in Weblogistan (one of *many* sites of Iranian civil society) was enabled because of an already existing history of civil society and reform in Iran, with its rich and varied array of public spaces for the creation of networks. Weblogistan has undoubtedly enabled a transnational linkage of resident and diaspora Iranians who are technologically literate and have regular access to computers and the internet to participate in political discussions and activism.

Celebrations of Weblogistan as a site of consensus, as a conduit for transnational forms of connectivity that have radically shifted notions of citizenship and community, and as a unified front where civil society flourishes and poses a challenge to the state overlook the manifold ways in which it is also a site of violent conflict, exclusion, and disagreement. In discussing the Eritrean diaspora website Dehai, Victoria Bernal (2005b) argues that new forms of technological and geographical mobility have given way to new public spheres "that transform the meaning of community, citizenship, and nation" (660). Bernal claims that Eritreans in diaspora merged the utopian promises of nationalism and technology in order to imagine a hopeful future for Eritrea in cyberspace: "Eritreans on Dehai are writing in the margins and experimenting with political freedoms and a new kind of transnational political community in ways that might suggest new forms of citizenship, democracy, and the public sphere emerging out of the new technologies and the heightened mobility of the 21st century.... It [Dehai] sheds light on the emergence of counterpublics and spaces of dissent in which unofficial views are voiced and alternative knowledges are produced" (661, 672).

Positioning Dehai as a new public sphere, Bernal suggests that the public sphere is not just the venue for "rational discussion" but also an arena of nonviolent conflict and a vehicle for mobilizations in times of conflict. Challenging the Habermasian notion of the public sphere, where individuals gather to discuss societal issues and participate in politics through consensus, Bernal argues that conflict helps produce community, identity, and the public sphere. As such, for Bernal, Eritrean cyberspace represents "ordinary people [inventing] a public sphere that made possible the articulation of ideas and sentiments that could not be expressed elsewhere" (662). However, the argument that cyberspace and the public sphere "allow diverse actors to call into question the terms of knowledge production, relations of authority, and the politics of representation and the ways they give rise to alternative knowledges and counterpublics" (672) fails to take account of the ways that they reproduce violent gendered, raced, and sexed exclusions in nationalistic performances of community.

Bernal rightly points out that the new public sphere enabled by the internet opens opportunities for nonintellectuals who were historically excluded from print publications prior to the popularization of blogging. It is true that blogging has allowed many "ordinary people" to circumvent the formal publishing processes and to surpass the state and nonstate print media conventions and regulations. However, this relative inclusiveness does not translate into equality in cyberspace. As I will discuss in the next two chapters, the elite/nonelite and intellectual/nonintellectual divisions are repeated and (re)produced through the use of gendered language and blogging practices that can keep blogging circles exclusive. In Weblogistan, diverse actors may question terms of knowledge production, but subjugated knowledges often do not find their way to mainstream national and international media and decision-making think tanks. This point is closely related to how elite bloggers and intellectuals are constituted in Weblogistan. The way that a blog gets popular often relies on the number of links that a blogger receives from other popular bloggers, as well as the recognition of that blog by the mainstream digital and nondigital media. Bloggers whose readership skyrockets overnight have either been mentioned by a mainstream radio station, a television program, or a website.[60] The fact that Weblogistan as a new public sphere relies on older mainstream forms is an example of how digital "counterpublics" may not be as subversive as cyber-enthusiasts would like to believe.

More importantly, what does not make cyberspace exceptional in transgressing lines of authority, knowledge production, and representation is the fact that offline power dynamics are often repeated in online political discussions, a point that is not lost on women bloggers. On a Sunday afternoon, after I held the first focus group for women soon after my arrival in Toronto, several bloggers, blog readers, and I decided to go to a nearby café for a less formal meeting. The format of the focus group was such that bloggers assumed their public (more formal) personae and spoke about women's roles and women's issues in Weblogistan. As we walked to the café, several women bloggers who had not met one another in person prior to the focus group exchanged jokes and engaged in gossip about Weblogistan. By the time we got to the café, the formal intellectual discussions about blogging at the focus group had given way to *gheybat* (gossip). Before too long, women bloggers were sarcastically referring to each other as "*ostaad*," "*doktor*," and "*khanoom mohandess*" (professor, doctor, and Ms. engineer) as a way to mock elite male bloggers who regularly address each other (and almost never women) by these titles of respect. Political male bloggers linking to one another is certainly a community-building practice of Weblogistan; like many imagined communities, however, blogger communities can exclude those who are deemed unfit to participate in debates about politics and other subjects that are often assumed to be the turf of men.[61]

Women bloggers' political participation often made them vulnerable to forms of violence that become possible only in online spaces where a commentator (blogger or not) can anonymously troll a woman blogger in her comments section. In her early days of blogging, Nazli Kamvari compared her comments section to the walls of a *mavaal* (public bathroom). Explaining that writing on the bathroom walls reminded her of school days in Iran, where "debate" took place in a space that is simultaneously private and public, Kamvari announced that she preferred to leave the mavaal door open (by not filtering her comments) so that ideas could be exchanged freely. However, the decision to leave her comments section unfiltered left the door open to many abusive comments that used violent language to insult her. These comments often sexualized her, even when she wrote about "proper" political matters such as the presidential election. Distraught and tired of receiving verbally abusive and violent comments, Kamvari closed her comments section after four years of blogging. Kamvari's decision (like that of many other feminist women bloggers) points to the fact that Weblogistan is not a utopian space of equal and democratic exchange where bloggers (especially women) practice freedom of speech. While blogs may be relatively affordable and accessible to educated, urban, and middle-class users, gendered norms of modern Iranian citizenship often set the limits of discussion.[62]

The utopian understanding of Weblogistan as a new public sphere and a site of consensus and transgression calls for more critical analyses. Jodi Dean's examination of cyber society as a site of inequality, conflict, and violence is instructive in understanding Weblogistan as cyber civil society. For Dean (2001, 252), civil society is a platform for political action, but it is not necessarily in opposition to the state or disconnected from state and economy. Challenging the dominant understandings of the public sphere, Dean suggests that civil society rather than the public sphere is a more applicable analytical framework for understanding cyberspace. As Dean argues, Seyla Benhabib's notion of salon is the sphere of friendship that offers the cultivation of intimacy. While Benhabib's salon as public space challenges the Habermasian "rational public," Benhabib shares with Habermas the assumption of an equality based on shared humanity and disregard for status (245).[63] Dean rightly asserts that both versions of salon fail to adequately deal with cyberspace because of their shared assumption about inclusivity based on equal access to the salon as a public sphere.

Dean argues that the dominant theory of the public sphere as universal and antihierarchical has been enshrined by internet enthusiasts who claim the internet as the most ideal speech institution for offering universal access and cultivating public opinion through discussion and freedom of speech. She points out that unequal access to computers and the internet, the dominance of English, surveillance, and incompatible protocols, among other factors, prevent the internet from living up to the ideals of the public sphere. Rather than focusing on the shortcomings of cyberspace as counterpublic, however, she questions the concept of the public sphere itself: "To territorialize cyberia as the public sphere is to determine in advance what sort of engagements and identities are proper to the political, and to use this determination to homogenize political engagement, neutralize space, and sanitize popular cultures. Such a territorialization, moreover, configures those excesses of the internet that resist compilation into a normative vision of the public sphere as pathologies and exceptions that do not apply to, that are outside of, that bound this public sphere and so continues to reassure the public sphere's claim to freedom and democracy" (246, 247).[64]

As Dean argues, "whereas the ideal of the public sphere relies on abstracting norms of equality, inclusivity, publicity, rationality, and authenticity from a few, usually elite, social locations, the notion of civil society embeds interaction in the media, associations, institutions, and practices that configure contemporary politics" (247). The analytical privileging of civil society over the public sphere is not to enshrine a pluralist concept of democracy, where different yet impartial discussions by various groups are assumed to compete in multiple public spheres on equal footing. Civil society is inevitably exclusive, unequal, partial, and a site of conflict and argument. It produces multiple subjectivities that engage in political participation, where political participation is neither purely free of nor always oppositional to the state.

Dean also argues that the state is organized around administrative power while civil society is organized around communicative action (252). The impetus for Dean to delink economy from civil society is to challenge the Lockean convergence of economy, wherein economy is an element of society and outside the political domain (Taylor 1990). Dean argues that to allocate economy to the turf of civil society ignores public opinion and its political possibilities. For Dean, the economics-based thinking about civil society runs the risk of depoliticization through a self-regulating economy that relieves the state from its economic responsibilities and makes society into a technologically managed entity that is organized around economic ideals. While Dean's concerns are valid, divorcing civil society from economy and limiting it to the turf of communication and public opinion may ignore the fact that many civil society entities often bridge the economic distribution between state and society, to the extent that this distinction is not as transparent and clear. For example, *Bonyaad-e Shaheed* (Foundation for the Martyrs) and *Bonyaad-e Mostaz'afeen* (Foundation for the Dispossessed) were formed as para-state entities (*nihads*) to distribute economic resources to the families of the martyrs and/or the poor.[65] Not surprisingly, some of the economic tycoons in Iran who have managed these nihads have state affiliations. Furthermore, the artificial economic division between civil society and the state impedes any meaningful analysis of the "nongovernmental," when many NGOs, including some Iranian women's organizations, inevitably rely on state (Iranian or European) funding for their operations. The state also relies quite heavily on communicative action, which includes the state and non-state-sponsored media and websites, a fact that makes a state/economy versus civil society/communication binary meaningless. Despite this separation between the civil society and economy, Dean rightly argues that the analytical distinction between state, economy, and civil society should not lead to the assumption that civil society is a domain free from power (as the public sphere is assumed to be). Dean departs from the Habermasian approach to communicative action as oppositional to power, and she instead emphasizes the way that the circulation of information is imbued with power (253–54). In her later work, *Democracy and Other Neoliberal Fantasies* (2009), Dean examines the hegemony of democratic rhetoric in networked communications and the fetishization of speech and democratic participation by the American Left and Right alike. Dean argues that unlike the claims of democratization in the United States, "Communicative capitalism materializes and repurposes democratic ideals and aspirations in ways that strengthen and support globalized neoliberalism" (17). As I will show later in this book, unhinging civil society from a top-down (state-society) vertical model of power is crucial to understanding techniques of surveillance and disciplining within civil society. Practices of democracy in Weblogistan are forms of neoliberal governmentality in a seemingly horizontal civil society where bloggers who embody neoliberal digital citizenship participate in forms of politics that enshrine the ideals of democracy and freedom.

Conclusion: Transnational Cyber-Civil Society and Governmentality

Rather than celebrating Weblogistan as a new, liberating public sphere and a uniform body of bloggers mobilized against a repressive state, in this chapter I have argued that Weblogistan was an extension of an already existing Iranian civil society. Moreover, as a site of transnational Iranian civil society, Weblogistan was not merely a platform for debate and consensus but also a site where violent conflict and gendered inequalities were repeated. The political discussions in Weblogistan among Iranians in Iran and its diaspora show the existence of a vibrant Iranian civil society that had a transnational character and was a site of conflict and disagreement. Weblogistan, as an element of civil society, was also where gendered citizenship was performed through inclusion and exclusion. In Weblogistan there was no equal footing when it came to discussions about politics and access to policy centers and mainstream media. Even though disagreement was not unusual in passionate offline political discussions, the anonymity of the comments in Weblogistan allowed a measure of violence that was harder to perpetuate in face-to-face debate. As in any civil society, there was no inclusive "we" of Weblogistan. However, celebratory accounts about "freedom through blogging" created an image of an inclusive and equal blogger body mobilized against a uniformly oppressive Iranian state.[66]

The discussions around the 2005 presidential election show the way that the gendered performance of citizenship in Weblogistan used women to define the boundaries of politics through conflict, exclusion, and inequality. As Moallem argues (2005b, 61), the logic of modern citizenship, which claims equality of citizens, actually relies on gendered binaries that subject Iranian women to disciplinary practices. In Weblogistan these embodied disciplinary measures were practiced online, where disembodiment upheld the unfulfilled promise of equal citizenship for the inhabitants of the nation-state. I have also shown that unlike the assumptions of some Iranian opposition groups that perceive the postrevolutionary Iran to be an archaic place where civil society does not exist, Iranian women have been involved dynamically in the cultural and political realms of citizenship. From the beginning of the Iranian Revolution, and especially after the Iran–Iraq war, Iranian women have continued their active participation in civil society by forming organizations that work toward removing discriminatory laws and through less visible entities that work in rural areas and religious establishments to provide social and educational services to women. They have actively participated in arguments and discussions about a range of issues, from family law and women's rights to electoral politics. The Iranian women bloggers' political discussions in Weblogistan and their participation in the street protests (such as the ones I discussed in this chapter) became possible because of a legacy of Iranian women's participation in the political processes and their active role in the Iranian civil society. Iranian women have continued to challenge the discriminatory policies of the state, whether it is through street protests or less conspicuous acts. Social media and online campaigns may have contributed to the wider reach for those who have access to the internet and computers, but they have not been the mainspring for women's participation in civil society. Weblogistan emerged as one element of the transnational civil society where gendered inequalities were reproduced in online conflicts.

Even as the dominant discourse on Weblogistan represented it as a "counterpublic" and a subversive bridge to a democratic future, to consider Weblogistan as a site of the transnational Iranian civil society would require us to ask questions about the operations of power that go beyond the realm of state repression. At a time when neoliberal discourses of freedom and democracy—along with militaristic interventions in the name of freedom—produce and reproduce binary categories of free/unfree, democratic/authoritarian, secular/religious, freedom-fighting dissident/terrorist, one is compelled to ask what constitutes dissent in online and offline spaces?[67] What kinds of complicities are inevitable in the formation of new "counterpublics" that rely on naturalized secular ideals of freedom and democracy? If blogs become effective through connection to mainstream media or policy-making centers, which discussions find their way to these centers and audiences, and which remain subjugated? What forms of democracy and citizenship are promoted and celebrated, and what is singled out as an exception or as an anomaly? And last but not least, how are women activists seen as risks to the Iranian state, while becoming hypervisible subjects in democratization projects? What happens to those who refuse to occupy the subject position of victim in need of rescue? Put simply, how do activist women shuttle between being "at risk" and "posing a risk" to "national security" and the "international community"?

Iranian women's protests continue to bring to the surface the tensions that arise from competing forms of governmentality that contend with women as rights-bearing citizens, as threats to national security, as victims to be saved from the Iranian state, and as threats to the "international community." Needless to say, the examples that I discussed in this chapter were not the first or the last time that Iranian women activists mobilized street protests. On June 12, 2006, a group of Iranian women's-rights activists gathered in Haft-e Tir Square for a peaceful protest against the misogynistic laws of the Iranian state. Seventy protesters were arrested, and some received suspended sentences of up to four years. Except for Ali Akbar Mousavi Khoeini, the sixth *Majlis* MP, all protesters were released on bail within a week. On March 4, 2007, before the trial of the June 12 arrests, several women, including those who were arrested on June 12, gathered in front of the courthouse to show their support for the women who had hearings. Thirty women, some of whom were awaiting trial after the June 12 protest, were arrested and released within a few days on bail with suspended sentences of two to five years. The news of the arrests circulated widely on the internet and garnered support from a wide range of human rights organizations and opposition groups and personalities, including Farah Diba, the former empress of Iran during the Pahlavi reign. Azadeh Forghani, a Tehran University student and women's-rights activist who was arrested on both occasions, wrote an open letter to Diba, criticizing her for co-opting the Iranian women's-rights movement and jeopardizing the arrested activists' lives. In her letter, Forghani reminds Diba of her silence in response to the shah's injustices and critiques the dethroned empress for her complicity with the U.S. neoliberal and militaristic agendas: "Many times when human rights in this land has been violated in the most intense and bloody way, pretenders such as the empress and the elitist women's-rights advocates on the other side have acted as if they were snoozing. The deadly silence among circles of power, the royalty, and sympathizers from the upper echelons, in response to the killings of the left forces, the socialist-communist, freedom seekers, dissidents, and others, has been experienced before."[68] At the end, Forghani condemns the irresponsible and self-serving appropriation of the women's-rights activists' protests by the royalists and other opportunistic opposition groups:

> Mrs. empress! Examine your own conscience or take as witness the objective conscience of another and tell us what relation—any at all—have you had or do you have with the women activists of June 12 and March 4? Their commonality is in their years of struggles for true freedom, eliminating oppression, liberty, and reaching to the minimum of women's human rights.... But you, empress, under the influence of or in collaboration with those around you, jump in the middle and opportunistically and ostentatiously issue statements, as if we are with your camp. And with your actions you place us, an independent movement that does not rely on any

Open Letter to Farah Diba: "Kindly Come and Do Us a Favor, Oh Lady"

By Azadeh Forghani (translated by Niki Akhavan, Sima Shakhsari)

> **Note from the translators:** Azadeh Forghani is one of the women's rights activists who was arrested for peaceful protest on March 4th 2007 in front of the Revolutionary Court in Tehran. The following open letter was addressed to Farah Pahlavi, the empress of Iran during the reign of Mohammad Reza Pahlavi. Forghani critiques the cooptation of the Iranian women's rights movement by Farah Pahlavi and opportunistic opposition groups. The original piece in Persian was published by roozonline.com on March 13.

Azadeh Forghani

FIGURE 2.1 Azadeh Forghani, the arrested Iranian student activist, in court, http://www.payvand.com/news/07/mar/1231.html.

foreign support or on you, under suspicion and leave us to the hands of the interrogators and don't give a damn when they say: "here is the proof that you get money and orders from abroad, your work does not reflect the needs and desires of women, so there!"[69]

While the arrests of the Iranian women's activists in 2006 and 2007 were widely publicized in the international media and the human rights organizations' websites, Forghani's statement did not receive much attention.[70] This was not surprising, as the dominant representation of Iranian women on the internet is that of powerless victims in need of rescue. It is as if Forghani's self-representation in a black *chador* and *maqna'eh* (the strict form of hijab that is often worn by more religious women) rather than a *manteau* and *roosary* (a coat and a headscarf that are often wrapped loosely around one's head), her defense of the communist activists who were executed during the Pahlavi reign, her simultaneous resistance to the Iranian state and U.S. capitalism and imperialism, and her refusal to align with the opportunistic opposition groups rendered her unrepresentable in the mainstream international media. Forghani's letter curbs the enthusiasm of the liberating forces and opportunistic opposition groups that are keen on appropriating the arrested Iranian activists' cause.

But this paradox of representability is not limited to the question of visibility. It has material effects on bodies that are subjected to sanctions, bans, or imprisonment, and are ultimately excluded from the realm of rights. The immigration laws (including but not limited to the "Muslim ban") epitomize this paradox of representation. In January 2018, around the time that Trump signed the "Muslim ban," Iranian women started a solo protest movement that came to be known as "*Dokhtaraan-e Khiaabaan-e Enqelaab*" ("Girls of the Revolution Street"). By February, the Iranian state arrested twenty-nine women who stood on utility boxes, removed their hijabs, and waved them on sticks, protesting the mandatory hijab law. Even as Donald Trump banned Iranians from entering the United States through his executive order, he praised the Iranian women's protests in a Twitter message.[71] As expected, Iran's prosecutor general claimed that the protests were instigated from outside of the country.[72] Narges Hosseini, the second protester who was arrested and sent to prison, made it clear that her act of protest was not related to any outside movement, including the New York–based online campaign called "My Stealthy Freedom." Led by Massoumeh (Masih) Alinejad, a former Iranian journalist who now works for Voice of America, "Stealthy Freedom" deploys the civilizational narratives that fetishize the hijab and juxtapose it to freedom through unveiling. In her interview with Shahrzad Hemati, Hosseini said that "I wanted to disassociate my actions from Ms. (Masih) Alinejad's campaigns. . . . I tied a green ribbon to my wrist with the aim of declaring that I am not associated with any one [campaign or group], and if there is an association with any movement, then it is with the Green Movement."[73] Despite her statement, the "Girls of the Revolution Street" movement was co-opted by the opportunistic opposition groups in social media, making the women protesters vulnerable to accusations of working for foreign elements. As Sussan Tahmasebi, an Iranian women's-rights activist—who was arrested in Iran multiple times, was one of the organizers of the June 12, 2006, protest, and now lives in the United States—put it eloquently in a Facebook post, "Struggles for emancipation need to reflect the realities of those on the ground, rather than those of international audiences or media or super hopeful diaspora-based political groups who plan to ride into Iran under the banner of Netanyahu or Trump!" Repulsed by the "wishful cyber space diaspora" who had accused Shahrzad Hemati of having fabricated her interview with Narges Hosseini, forcing her to release her tapes to prove the authenticity of Hosseini's statement, Tahmasebi wrote the following:

> It is especially problematic when the fight for women's liberation becomes part and parcel of neocon supported movements for regime change by people who want to go to Iran with tanks and guns, by those who basically don't give a damn about women, only use women's status to attack their political opponents (often choosing to employ seriously sexist language) and equate the end to compulsory hejab with the end to the Islamic Republic—in other words making it a highly securitized effort. . . . Most unsettling for me however is how some of these groups, their most outspoken in fact, tend to be racist and Islamophobic.[74]

It is, indeed, unsettling to make sense of the simultaneous lionization and demonization of Iranian women—a paradox that Paul Amar's notion of "parahuman" (2013) can help explain. In discussing what he calls the emergence of the "human security state" in the "global south," Amar argues the following:

> In the universe of human security, sexuality is implicated in modes of governance that blend parahumanization (the creation of politically disabled 'victim' subjects that must, essentially, be constantly protected or rescued by enforcement interventions regardless of consent or will to be rescued),

hypervisibilization (the spotlighting of certain identities and bodies as sources of radical insecurity and moral panic in ways that actually render invisible the real nature of power and social control), and securitization (the reconfiguration of political debates and claims around social justice, political participation, or resource distribution into technical assessment of danger, operations of enforcement, and targetings of risk populations). (17)

Amar defines para-humanization as a "notion of humanized security where rights-bearing subjects of the state become suspects under the control of privatized rescue industries" (18). Following Amar, I argue that the Iranian woman protester embodies the para-human figure who needs to be rescued (as a woman) and who poses a security risk (as a foreign agent in the context of the nation-state and as an Iranian/Muslim in the transnational context). Put simply, produced as a hypervisible victim and villain, the Iranian woman protester is simultaneously at risk and risky. She is at risk of prostitution, foreign influence, or harassment in public, and thus needs protection by the security state. At the same time, she is a risky subject because she poses a threat to national security. The woman protester who is rendered at risk or risky by the Iranian state becomes hypervisible, thanks to the enthusiastic circulation of her image on social media by human rights regimes, liberalizing states, opposition groups outside of Iran, and the Iranian state's television "confessions," where protesters admit to being duped by outside forces. The hypervisibilization of the Iranian woman protester legitimizes securitization by the Iranian state, not in the name of human rights but in the name of national security and the protection of Islam and the *Umat* (Islamic community) from the danger of the foreign enemy. While Amar's analysis focuses on the security state, I suggest that the figure of the Iranian woman protester as para-human is not limited to her relationship to the Iranian state but concerns the security of the "international community." That is, the Iranian woman (protester) as para-human shuttles between the national and the transnational, wherein the "international civil society" hypervisibilizes her as a "victim" who needs to be rescued by the liberating forces (Abu-Lughod 2013). The hypervisibilization of this figure as both brave and vulnerable legitimizes the securitization measures of the "liberating states," including exclusionary immigration laws, economic sanctions, and ultimately war in the name of the protection of the "international community." Perhaps because not all Iranian women protesters can be mobilized in the civilizational narratives of rescue (Forghani and Hosseini's refusal being examples) and because the image of the menacing woman protester—epitomized by the hypervisible angry veiled woman shouting anti-American slogans during the hostage crisis of 1979—continues to haunt this rescue narrative, the figure of the Iranian woman activist/protester shuttles between rightfulness (through the universalist logic of "women's rights are human rights") and rightlessness (through the racist logic of protecting the "international civil society" against the threat posed by Muslim terrorists).[75] Even as the Iranian woman protester who is perceived to be vulnerable and in need of protection becomes hypervisible in liberationist narratives (the most famous example being Neda Agha Soltan's image during the 2009 street protests) and even as a select number of Iranian dissidents (including a select number of women's-rights activists) are hired by the U.S. propaganda apparatus and given special visas, the Iranian woman remains a risky subject. But because risk inevitably concerns the population and not just the individual, the Iranian population at large is subjected to exclusionary immigration policies, "crippling" economic sanctions, and ultimately the politics of rightful killing. Yet the virality of risk means that its management (and not complete elimination) can also be achieved virally through democratization in the realm of cyber civil society, which functions as a correlate of the technology of government (Foucault, cited in Gordon 1991, 23), a topic to which I will turn in the next chapter.

[3]

Whores, Homos, and Feminists

Weblogistan's Anti-modern Others

> Power is not so much a matter of imposing constraints upon citizens as of "making up" citizens capable of bearing a kind of regulated freedom. Personal autonomy is not the antithesis of political power, but a key term in its exercise, the more so because most individuals are not merely the subjects of power but play a part in its operations.
> —PETER MILLER AND NICHOLAS ROSE, "POLITICAL POWER BEYOND THE STATE"

In chapter 2 I discussed how Weblogistan as a site of transnational civil society is characterized by gendered inequalities, violence, and exclusions. In the rest of this book, extending Foucault's analysis of governmentality, I examine strategies of regulation and discipline imposed by complex international and transnational networks in Weblogistan, which, as I have argued thus far, is one of many sites of transnational Iranian civil society. In *The Birth of Biopolitics,* Foucault recognizes sovereignty, discipline, and government as three elements that characterize modern power (2010, 102). According to Foucault (1983, 221), government encompasses not only "political structures or the management of states" but the way in which the "conduct of individuals or of groups might be directed." In other words, going beyond sovereign power, the governmentalization of the state involves the regulation and management of populations through the language of rights and the rhetoric of natural liberties in order to generate a self-organizing and self-regulating civil society. Rather than the direct imposition of law, the modern liberal government regulates the conduct of the individual from a distance and by calculation techniques and programs implemented by nonstate agents. As such, what Foucault (2007, 108) defines as governmentality is "the ensemble formed by the institutions, procedures, analyses and reflections, the calculations and tactics that allow the exercise of this very specific albeit complex form of power, which has as its target population, as its principal form of knowledge political economy, and as its essential technical means apparatus of security."[1]

Using Foucault's insights (and Ferguson and Gupta's transnational expansion of governmentality), I define *cybergovernmentality* as a significant method of transnational governmentality (Ferguson and Gupta 2002) that operates through online and offline normalizing techniques, uses diasporas and media technologies, relies on neoliberal economy, and employs security as its mechanism of calculation to discipline and regulate populations according to the ideals of liberal democracy. In the remainder of this book I discuss modes of cybergovernmentality and digital citizenship that enable the production of an internet-savvy Iranian subject who desires freedom and democracy and aspires to reach a democratic future in Iran through "practicing democracy" in Weblogistan. During the "war on terror," a group of diasporic blogger entrepreneurs came to represent the "Iranian people" by producing knowledge about Iran. However, the creation of this idealized figure of Iranianness is contingent on normalizing techniques according to nationalist discourses and practices, alongside heteronationalist and homonationalist conventions of empire. Analyzing the way that Iranian bloggers self-discipline and are disciplined through biopolitics and ethicopolitics (Ong 2006), I argue that resident and diasporic Iranian blogger subjects as digital citizens are normalized in transnational online and offline encounters. It is in a nexus of nationalist and neoliberal discourses that the idealized digital citizenship is produced and regulated through a number of online and offline blogging practices and technologies of self: deploying confessional representation and other forms of expression that appear transparent, overemphasizing individualism and performing it against "communal traditionalism," and engaging in the conduct of the conduct of others through comments, blog posts, and offline interactions. Informed by gendered discourses of Western modernity, technologies of digital citizenship reproduce and normalize a classed, gendered, and raced Iranianness in online re-territorializations that emphasize individualism and neoliberal ideals of transparency and freedom, all under the rhetoric of "practicing democracy."

This chapter focuses on what Foucault calls the "the conduct of conduct" (2010, 186) and "technologies of the self" (1988, 16–49). In his late writings and interviews, Foucault tackled questions of subjectivity, agency, power, and the government of conduct. For Foucault, "technologies of the self" are practices and techniques that are historically situated in inevitably productive and constraining power relations that are deployed to conduct and cultivate the self. Foucault argues that technologies of self "permit individuals to effect by their own means or with the help of others a certain number of operations on their own bodies and souls, thoughts, conduct, and way of being, so as to transform themselves in order to attain a certain state of happiness, purity, wisdom, perfection, or immortality" (18). Foucault notes that even though the relationship to oneself changes with time, it is always a relationship to morality. Moral and ethical aspirations and obligations are inseparable from subjectification and the practices of self.

In Weblogistan, freedom and democratic participation were normative concepts that circulated among intellectual blogging circles. These were significant techniques used to discipline and regulate the conduct of bloggers in order to cultivate digital citizens suitable for a democratic future in Iran. The disciplining and regulation of bloggers' conduct under the cloak of freedom and democracy often revolved around gendered and sexed techniques of normalization that deployed neoliberal and nationalist ideals of selfhood. If the modernization projects of the last century used newspapers, handouts, and educational books to discipline modern Iranians and to craft a "modern, yet modest" Iranian womanhood (Najmabadi 1998), Weblogistan became a new site of the normalization of transnational digital citizens in an era characterized by postmodern time-space compression. The mass media, which as Moallem (2005a) argues replaced the print culture of modernity, became increasingly dominated by internet-mediated communications in the early 2000s. With the popularity of the internet and the increased exchanges between a group of computer-savvy Iranians whose cosmopolitanism was owed to their transnational connections enabled by internet technologies, Weblogistan became an important site where gendered ideals of Iranianness were reified by bloggers who conducted the conduct of themselves and others. In what follows I discuss some key debates in Weblogistan to illustrate how the gendered disciplining of bloggers as digital citizens (and, by extension, the Iranian population) reproduced modernist notions of masculinity and femininity.

Sibil Tala and the Ethics of Javanmardi

I was first introduced to the blog known as *Sibil Tala* (Golden Mustache) through the snowball effect. As a novice blogger in 2004, I read the "giants" of Weblogistan and followed their links to other blogs. One of these "giants" whose blog I read on a daily basis was Hoder, the "godfather" of Persian blogging. Hoder had linked to *Sibil Tala*, by Nazli Kamvari, who at the time was one of Hoder's close friends. Invoking the famous *luti* (tough guy) of the pre-revolutionary film *Paashneh Tala* (*Golden Heel*), Kamvari's blog name often misled new readers to expect the author to be a tough man.[2] In one of her first English posts and her first Persian post, Kamvari used her characteristic wit to explain that her blog name was a feminist response to modern standards of beauty (which encourage hair removal from the female body) and the Islamic Republic's regulations of female-bodied students:

> Sibiltala means golden mustache literary [*sic*]. From my Iranian parents, I inherited facial hair, a unibrow, the obesity gene, and very large bones. In my teenage years boys disfavored me (they still do), and I was advised by a peer that this is due to my mustache. So, one day I waxed my mustache off, plucked my unibrow, and I was not fat yet. So, it happened, a boy fell for me. The only problem was I was expelled from school for removing my facial hair. I was told to come back to school whenever my mustache is grown back. In the olden days in Iran, girls were not supposed to remove their facial hair before getting married. I thought to myself, no one is going to marry me with this tick [*sic*] mustache, I needed a solution. However, my first love had already shown interest and I knew it had something to do with me not having a mustache anymore. So I waited for the hair to grow back and went back to school. From that day on, I bleached my facial hair every time I had to see my boyfriend and dyed it black every morning before going to school. The bleached mustache of mine had a golden blond color, hence the name: Sibiltala.[3]

It didn't take long for me to became a fan of Kamvari's blog. I left comments for her regularly, and our blogging relationship became more reciprocal when she linked to one of my posts in which I critiqued a blogger who had argued for the control and surveillance of homosexuals. From that point on, our exchanges about gender and sexuality culminated in a productive blogging friendship. We also communicated "offline" through chat and email.[4] For instance, she sent me an email to vent about the hate mail she had received after appearing in a television interview about Weblogistan. Starting her email by saying that she wanted to *dard-e del* (tell the pain of her heart), she confided in me that many of her friends in Toronto, who had initially encouraged her to start a blog, distanced themselves from her after she talked about sex in this interview. Kamvari was particularly heartbroken that a famous blogger, who at the time was one of her close friends in Toronto, had opportunistically capitalized on the backlash by writing a post that, while seeming to defend her freedom of speech, actually boasted about his *javanmardi* (see chapter 2) and his democratic tendencies at her expense, positioning Nazli as a *jendeh* (tramp/whore) who needed to be saved by a chivalrous hero. The famous Toronto blogger's public performance of defending freedom of speech (an act of bravery for which he had received awards), Nazli believed, was his strategy to represent himself as innocent and free from any wrongdoing and to deny any association with her. In public online exchanges, she was represented as a perverted woman who deviated from the norms of proper womanhood and heterosexual monogamy, and who was rescued by the *Javanmard Luti* of Weblogistan. "It was just like Film Farsi, *bekhoda*! (I swear to God!)," she told me. Purportedly defending Nazli's right to freedom of speech, this male blogger wrote in his blog:

> Many attacked her [Sibiltala] for defacing the Iranian woman [*aberoo-ye zan-e Irani ra bordeh*] and for bringing herself down to the level of a tramp. I am one of the first critics of her ideas about out-of-the-norm relationships (*raabetehaaye kharij az orf*). She might talk against monogamy and accuse me, and others like me, of hypocrisy and contradiction. But it doesn't matter. What is important is that she has tried to express her views despite the traditional restrictions [on sexuality]. People who are close to me were upset with her presence [in the interview]. And they have a right to be upset, but this does not mean that we should block a compatriot's freedom of speech to express her particular belief! I am officially against *Sibil Tala*'s beliefs, but I respect her right to express them! Speaking about sex and sexuality seems to be eternally forbidden for Iranian women.[5]

Irritated by this blogger's insincere performance of javanmardi, Nazli wrote in her dard-e del email, "*Naamard, jaanamaaz aab kesheed*!" ("Naamard rinsed his prayer mat!"). The opposite of *javanmard* (literally, "young man"), *naamard* ("not a man") is a Persian expression used as an insult (regardless of gender) to connote lack of loyalty and disregard for ethical behavior. One who "rinses his prayer mat" is a person who commits sins or immoral acts but exonerates himself in public in order to demonstrate ethical superiority. Kamvari believed that the famous blogger's public performance of javanmardi was a duplicitous act of self-exoneration and a reification of norms of sexuality and gender.

As I discussed in chapter 2, Fariba Adelkhah (2000) shows that javanmard, a man of integrity, is an ethos (albeit not fixed) that is deeply rooted in Iran's history and involves both the assertion of the self and overcoming of the self (45). Javanmard is a social being who is involved in social action and is built up by the public opinion of his fellows (70). In contemporary Iranian society, Adelkhah argues, javanmards participate in redefining the public and private spheres. They are social beings who are respected for their selflessness and piety, and for their participation in the public sphere (5). As I argued in chapter 2, analyses of public space (and by extension the public sphere) in Iran often overlook structural gendered inequalities. While it is true that performances of javanmardi may engender social beings that redefine public and private spheres, as a social being javanmard is a masculine figure that is deployed to discipline and normalize gendered subjects according to conventions of heterosexual monogamy and the nuclear family. These conventions juxtapose the respectability of the middle-class, nuclear family with the uncivility of perverse sexualities, unsuitable for the modern Iranian public. In Weblogistan, performances of javanmardi are techniques of the self, wherein social beings come to construct themselves as democratic subjects and digital citizens, suitable for a heteronormative civil society. As I will discuss in chapter 5, these ethicopolitical practices (Ong 2006) are in line with neoliberal self-entrepreneurship in Weblogistan.[6]

Kamvari was right about the social capital that this blogger would gain in Weblogistan. Shortly after writing his freedom-of-speech post, the javanmard-presenting blogger was admired by his readers, who left comments and applauded him for not only defending a deviant's right to freedom of speech but also for upholding the moral values of the institution of family. Meanwhile, Kamvari received numerous hate messages and was accused of being a "tramp" and an embarrassment to all Iranians. Some Iranian immigrants (bloggers or not) in Toronto who knew Kamvari advised her to rectify her behavior. This was not the first time that Kamvari was subject to collective disciplining. She was admonished by online and offline friends for writing a post in which she had questioned monogamy as the only acceptable form of romantic relationship. A blogger, whose blog name indicated her role as a mother, advised Kamvari against writing openly about sexuality, warning her that she would lose her female friends if she continued to write such posts. "She told me that every man in Toronto was waiting for my partner to leave so that they would take his place," Kamvari chuckled as she told me the story. Trying to give the other blogger the benefit of the doubt, I asked Kamvari if this comment could be interpreted as a compliment. "Yeah right," she burst out in laughter and shook her head disapprovingly at my naïveté. "You are such a Turk, Sima!⁷ Are you kidding me? This is her polite, double-edged way of telling me that I am a whore and that she is the angelic mother who is worried about me stealing her husband!"

Taming the *Kulthum Nanehs* of Weblogistan

During my fieldwork, *freedom of speech* was a buzz term that was deployed by many bloggers who advocated "practicing democracy" in Weblogistan. However, this freedom seemed contingent on a modern/traditional binary. Often, male bloggers who assumed themselves to be the sole authority on the Persian language dismissed or admonished blog posts that they perceived to be "superstitious," "vulgar," "premodern," "immoral," and "dangerous." As a strategy of normalization, the modern/traditional binary was deployed to exclude those who were not considered proper subjects and good digital citizens. Because they did not comply with gendered and heteronormative notions of modern Iranianness, these "bad/risky subjects" were seen as ill-suited for participation in proper politics. In this section I discuss a debate that started as a critique of the use of sexist language in Weblogistan. This was one of the most controversial debates in Weblogistan about gender, language, and power, a dispute that culminated in heated arguments about vulgarity and proper ways of being modern. The debate was initiated by two popular and widely read bloggers: Nazli Kamvari (the author of *Sibil Tala*), who was located in Toronto, and Mehdi Jami (the author of *Sibestaan*), who lived in Amsterdam.

With a good command of Persian, Jami, who holds a master's degree in Persian language, often expressed his annoyance with what he considered the improper use of Persian in Weblogistan. He frequently corrected other bloggers' grammar or ridiculed them for not using proper Persian, thereby establishing himself as one of the authoritative voices of Persian-language blogging. For the most part, Jami engaged with mostly male, self-acclaimed intellectuals and bloggers who, regardless of their profession, referred to one another by *ostaad* (professor) and other flattering titles. As a very influential blogger, Jami was hailed by some as belonging to the *bozorgaan-e veblogistan* (the giants of Weblogistan/the older and more knowledgeable members of Weblogistan). This reputation was so widespread that in a phone conversation I had with a woman blogger in the United States about the social and symbolic power that some people enjoy in blogging circles, she referred to a male blogging circle that included Jami as the "bourgeoisie of Weblogistan."[8]

On January 6, 2006, after Ariel Sharon (then prime minister of Israel) suffered a stroke, Jami wrote a post titled "A Man Who Had Torn the Veil of Innocence" ("*Mardi keh pardeh-ye esmat dareedeh bood*"). Jami's use of the slang expression "*pardeh-ye esmat dareedan*," which has a gendered connotation and is often used to refer to breaking a woman's hymen, incited a passionate response from Kamvari and generated a debate about language, gender, knowledge production, and power in Weblogistan. Here is part of his initial post on January 6, 2006: "Sharon's [public] face is bipolar. On one side is the infinite hatred of a people who were hurt by his politics, and on the other side are countless enthusiasts and compatriots who saw in him an emperor who knows how to protect the kingdom at any cost. In *Rostam-al-Tavaarikh*,[9] there is a unique saying, which he [Sharon] knew without having read [the text]: the emperor should not be concerned with virtue, piety, grace, and innocence. What is required of an emperor are justice, beneficence, order, calculation, and protection of the kingdom."[10]

On the same day, Kamvari criticized Jami for making authoritative statements about Sharon and accused him of lacking knowledge about the subject matter. In line with her well-known sense of humor, Kamvari started her post with a sarcastic remark about Jami's use of the term *pardeh-ye esmat*, which she characterized as a *binaamoosi* word. Her use of the term *binaamoosi* (without honor, especially related to sexual matters) was a witty way to characterize Jami's language as vulgar. Admitting that she was annoyed with Jami's post, Kamvari wrote in a more serious tone, "It is as if *Sibestaan*, like a self-appointed chief editor of a newspaper called Weblogistan, has immunity to write generalizing posts about any event that happens in the real or cyber worlds. Never mind how much he knows about this subject."[11] With a subtle reference to previous instances and debates about vulgarity and language in Weblogistan (see Doostdar 2004), Kamvari continued: "It is interesting that Sibestaan has claims [of knowledge] and yet will shame many bloggers and accuses them of vulgarity. Doesn't he think that expressing these *tokhmi* (testicular, bogus) opinions about the important issues of the world is worse than any kind of vulgarity?" Kamvari deliberately used *tokhmi*, a term which literally means "of testis" and is an impolite way to refer to worthlessness and baseless objects and statements. She also used the slang *kheshtak parcham mikonad,* which literally translates into "making someone's crotch into a flag." Kamvari used this language as a type of smart wordplay to refer to Jami's public humiliation of others for incorrect and improper use of Persian.

Kamvari's sarcastic and exaggerated use of vulgar language in a serious critique aimed to disrupt the educated/vulgar binary and to "queer" the Persian language by transgressing its proper rules and conventions. This graceful/vulgar (*mateen/mobtazal*) binary, which was often used by male intellectuals in Weblogistan to critique what they considered to be a perversion of proper Persian language, demarcated the boundaries between the *roshanfekr* (intellectual/enlightened) and the *mobtazal* (vulgar) bloggers in Weblogistan: "To be honest, this pretentious gesture of 'I know Persian, so I have the right to feed people any crap I desire with my divine language' is killing me. At the end, in the style of Mehdi Jami himself, who issues general rules for Weblogistan (and of course, women), I have to say that a weblog is there for one to write whatever one wishes, but with the condition that one does not assume one's personal views to be authoritative and educated ruminations."

Kamvari's incisive critique of Jami's post did not remain unanswered. She received several hateful and humiliating comments in her own comments section, as well as in Jami's comments. Jami replied with an indirect response in the tradition of *aseeb shenaasee* (social pathology). In his post titled "Airplane, the Sign of Armageddon for Us," Jami expressed that "we" (Iranians) have not learned how to invent technological devices but have been fascinated by them and bought them from foreign powers.[12] As was usually the case with his posts, in order to build credibility and make himself sound knowledgeable, Jami wrote with an aura of expertise about Iranian history. His purple prose, which gave him authority over language and impressed many readers, was a strategy to make him appear like a rational being, even as the content of his posts were often speculative and irrelevant to his main point. In his counterattack on Kamvari and Hoder, he wrote a long post to pathologize Iranians for being out of joint with modernity. Jami wrote that Iranians got cannons from the Ottomans during the Safavid Period and now get modern weapons from the Germans, British, and Americans. He continued his account by saying that "we" relied on the Soviet Union after the revolution, but little did we know that the Soviet empire was going to collapse: "With the fall of the soviets, the world changed. We had changed too. People of the world were not the same. Before everyone else, not the intellectuals, but Bin Laden understood this. The sign of major change became September 11. September 11 was a strange Armageddon. Its sign was the airplane. This airplane was like the cannon that instead of bringing victory to the Ottomans and the Russians who owned the cannon ball, ended in their annihilation. Like a cannon ball that they fired at themselves."

Claiming that for Bin Laden, who "does not invent anything," the airplane is used only to end the world and to create ruckus in order to prepare for the Armageddon, Jami characterized the common link between Bin Laden and "us" Iranians as technological backwardness and inability to use technology properly in a rational, modern world:

> We have not entered the age of satellite and rockets. For us, the airplane is the maximum limit of progress. And our behavior with this maximum limit of progress shows the content and the future of our empire: We have borrowed the airplane and have become familiar with it through its catalogue, or at most, we have learned from the old-time elite folks who studied in imperialist countries.... We are emperors without an outfit. This airplane for us is like a spaceship that has come from other planets for cave people. The airplane is a sign of our inability; the sign of our Armageddon; The sign of our big ruckus. Exactly like the nuclear plant, which we cannot make without help from others. And it is better if we don't. Otherwise, we prepare another sign for Armageddon: Atomic explosion and nuclear contamination.

Jami ended his post with this statement: "Because the title of today's post is of interest to two of my readers, I dedicate it to both of them, meaning: Hoder, a man with a shining past; the only knowing man of Weblogistan; the one who divides knowledge and honor among other people, and who, lately, has been worried about the lack of knowledge in *Sibestaan*; and to *Sibil Tala* who is the super hero (*qadar qodrat*) of womanhood in Weblogistan; the grandmother of Persian language experts, and the pioneer of *Kulthum Naneh* literature!"

Jami's post clearly deploys the developmental narratives of "backwardness" of the "third world" and the orientalist tropes of irrationality associated with Iran (Moallem 2005a) and the Middle East in general. Reminiscent of the character studies that used social pathology to prove the irrationality of the terrorist (Puar 2007), Jami sees blogging as a technology that could be used for destructive purposes in the hands of irrational, uneducated, vulgar bloggers. Unsurprisingly, this division of the rational and irrational use of technology and language took a gendered twist in Jami's post. His sarcastic postscript dedicating the post to Hoder and Kamvari indirectly suggests that these bloggers' deployment of modern technologies (blogging) is an example of the irrational use of modern technological progress.

While Jami's sarcastic statement about Hoder's bombastic behavior was in line with his repeated ridicule of Hoder's *beesavaadee* (illiteracy), the gendered nature of his sarcastic belittling is notable. By referring to Kamvari's language as *Kulthum Naneh literature,* Jami indirectly conflated being a strong woman (*qadar qodrat*—and implicitly unfeminine) with being backward, superstitious, shameless, and traditional. As Kathryn Babayan (2008, 244-59) has described, the book *Kulthum Naneh*, also known as *Aqa'id al-Nisa* (*Women's Beliefs*), was a seventeenth-century social critique of "female superstition" written by a clergyman, Aqa Jamal Khwansari (d. 1710), during the reign of the last Safavid Shah, Sultan Husain (1694-1722). Babayan rightly argues that this book was a disciplinary text, provoking edicts and treatises on ethics and morals toward the end of the Safavid era, "on the eve of the rationalization of power and fear of independent Sufi expressions of sexuality and religiosity" (252). *Aqa'id al-Nisa* pokes fun at Kulthum Naneh and four other women, who in the author's view represent "irrational" and "superstitious" ritual customs of women and their friendships before the onset of rationalism and patriarchy in the royal court and religious seminaries. Aqa Jamal Khwansari mocks these women as *ulama* (experts), and he expresses fear and concern about women's immodest behavior.

Jami's use of "Kulthum Naneh language" to refer to Kamvari's manner of expression invokes Khwansari's disciplinary technique of regarding women's immodest behavior and language as traditional and backward. Writing about the Qajar period and the constitutional era, Afsaneh Najmabadi (1991, 1992, 1993) has shown the way that language in Iran was cleansed in order to cultivate a "modern yet modest" (1991, 91, 49) Iranian womanhood, suitable for heterosocial spaces. The disciplining of modern Iranian women aimed to produce educated housewives who behaved properly and according to the norms of the heteronormative nuclear family. As Najmabadi (1993) puts it, the unveiling of women in modern Iran entailed the veiling of their language. Gendered conventions of Iranian modernity involved the acquisition of an internal veil in women's behavior and language to replace the sartorial one. The untamed and courageous language of Iranian women during the constitution era was condemned as "backward" and traditional within the modernist discourse. The common use of the slang "*hamaam zanaaneh*" ("women's bathhouse") as a derogatory term to refer to chaotic, noisy, and loud echoes fears and anxieties of Iranian modernity around women's untamed language in homosocial spaces. Not surprisingly, the hamaam zanaaneh was the space where Iranian women discussed politics and spoke with an "unveiled" and "vulgar" (*bee-pardeh*) language during the constitutional era. Bibi Khanum Astarabadi's bee-pardeh language in the book *Ma'aayeb al Rijal* (*Men's Vices*, 1895), which was written in response to a pamphlet titled *Ta'deeb al Nisvan* (*The Disciplining of Women*), is another example of the threat that women's untamed tongues posed to the patriarchal codes of proper behavior in nineteenth-century Iran.

Jami's post, which repeats the gendered anxieties of Iranian modernity, generated many comments and posts by other bloggers. Many of Jami's readers (mostly men) expressed agreement with his position and suggested that he should not lower his standards by engaging with vulgar, insignificant, and abject people. In response to such comments, Kamvari herself left a comment for Jami, referring to herself as the royal "we" in order to emulate and mock Jami's sense of grandeur:

> Dear Mehdi, you have humbled us! God forbid! Have our *Kulthum Naneh* literature and our grandmotherly existence made you nervous, scaring you to the point that you think—may my tongue be muted—we have superwoman powers?! Am I in trouble because of the name "golden mustache"? You have seen us in our own territory [Toronto], no? [As you saw,] there was no mustache and no power. [As you saw,] we were slim, depressed, and very beautiful like all depressed women. We are exactly the opposite of the revolution: First we look like an old witch, and after they sleep with us, they see how young and beautiful we have been! In any case, if you insist on sticking a macho woman label on us, we prefer "auntie-with-balls" literature (*adabiyaat-e khaaleh khaayeh daar*).[13]

Kamvari's sarcastic comment includes coded references to Jami's previous posts, which are worth mentioning in order to provide context for this interchange. In particular, "the old witch" is a reference to an older post in which Jami had objectified women and undermined their political participation during and after the revolution. On February 10, 2005, almost a year before the above exchange, and on the twenty-sixth anniversary of the revolution, Jami opened his post titled "The Revolution Was a Beautiful Woman" by writing "Revolution—it's like conquering a woman."[14] In his (hetero)sexist national romance, Jami likened the revolution to an attractive young woman with whom "we" (Iranians) had fallen in love. Assuming the revolutionary Iranian subjects to be heterosexual cisgender men, Jami wrote that "revolution was our beloved. Revolution was a woman for whose capture we were all fighting manly." And "the major attractiveness of a woman is due to her having many suitors. She puts on makeup to add to those who die for her. . . . Woman is the jewel of conquering. . . . All conquests are women." Suggesting that a conquered object of desire no longer appeals to the conqueror, Jami continued: "When captured, a woman can fall." Claiming that the nation's men have fallen out of love with the revolution and that they have nothing to choose from except for war, coup, or sleeping with an old foreign witch, he wrote that "It's like sleeping with an old witch that makes us gag."[15] It was this post from a year before to which Nazli referred in her witty comment on Jami's blog. In her response to Jami's Kulthum Naneh post, Nazli also poked fun at another post by Jami where he had expressed that women look more beautiful when they are depressed. Kamvari's response wittily highlighted the hegemonic notions of gendered citizenship, war, and revolution that were repeated in digital re-territorializations. The deployment of woman as the figure of the object in need of protection and as a risky/seductive subject who can jeopardize the democratic future drives this modernist articulation of revolutionary desire.

Of course, the flame war over language, gender, and power did not end there. Jami published another post, which invited yet another series of responses on vulgarity, language, power, gender, and modern Iranianness. In "I Hate the Game of Hatred" ("*Az Baaziye Tannafor Motennaferam*"), Jami explained that some of his readers and friends had encouraged him to remain silent or delete the "dedication" postscript on his January 9 post.[16] Jami wrote that in Weblogistan, "where even [the] cockroach whistles," he could not remain silent. One of the fan letters that Jami published in this post condemned Jami's critics as vulgar and insignificant people. In a gesture of fraternity, this fan referred to Jami as an "older brother" while calling Jami's critics "nobodies who have found free blogs to express their worthless opinions." Jami responded to this fan by writing: "I may be able to tame one or two wild animals, but taming a herd of grasshoppers is beyond my power." Jami promised his fans that he would write a post about the "school of Canada" ("*Maktab-e Canadayee*"), whose founders and promoters, in Jami's opinion, were two bloggers (Hoder and Kamvari). He warned his readers that if "we" do not stand up to "them" (vulgar bloggers)—in the way that Nikahang Kowsar had stood up to them—"we" would lose the game to "evil nature and malice." Jami's reference to Kowsar was quite ironic given that he also lived in Toronto and often attacked feminists with language that would have been considered vulgar if used by women.

Much like Jami, his friends and fans who defended him with flattery admonished the *bee-adabee* (impoliteness) of his critics. Many of them condemned the use of foul language by women and expressed concern about women's violation of the boundaries of *hojb o haya* (demureness and shame) in Weblogistan. For example, Naser Khaledian, a blogger and well-known satirist, attacked Kamvari by calling her a lazy bum (*lash*) who does not move away from her laptop computer. Accusing Kamvari of mental and emotional deficiency, Khaledian wrote that Kamvari defaced "real feminists" by using "vulgar language" and claimed that men do not even use such language in public. In his blog, *Noqteh Sar-e Khat*, Khaledian wrote that "she has filled her writing with vulgar language, erecting genitalia and pitching it to the whole world. Surprisingly, you see that the author is a woman!"[17] On the same day, Sanam Dolatshahi, a women's-rights activist, one of the first Iranian women bloggers, and the author of the blog *Khorshid Khanoom*, wrote a response to Khaledian in which she asked why the use of curse words is considered natural for men but is surprising and shameful when used by women. She cited Kowsar as an example of a blogger who uses words such as *tokhmi* and *hasteh* (*testicular* and *testis*) without being attacked for being vulgar:

> Who defines vulgarity, dear *Noqteh*? Since when are these so called vulgar words used "barely and only in private jokes?" Why is it then, that women from the age of 10 or eleven hear these terms under different names on the street [as they are harassed by men]? Why is it that they hear it in their emails? [Why is it that they hear these words] in their comments section? Why is it that when a woman wears a little make up, she hears these words? Why is it that when a woman talks about her rights, she is called these words? Since when are men so sanitized? Which private realm are you talking about, dear Noqteh? . . . And since when are you a psychologist to diagnose those who talk about genitalia as being mentally deficient? This is an old game! When someone used to rub himself against us [women] in a taxicab and we objected, he would say without hesitation: "She has mental deficiency. She is rubbing herself to me!" And often we were forced to shut up and not say anything so that we would not be accused of mental deficiency.

Dolatshahi defended Kamvari and mentioned her efforts in raising funds to stop the execution of a woman prisoner in Iran. She sarcastically critiqued Khaledian for assuming himself to be the guardian of women's decency: "Oh, these poor helpless women are being defaced and do not have the courage to defend themselves. Polite men who only use bad curse words to refer to women in their private realm must defend women in the public realm. *Akheyyy!*"[18]

While some women bloggers critiqued the hypocritical sexism of those who had attacked Kamvari, some bloggers and blog readers defended Kamvari by arguing that the use of sexually explicit language was commonplace in modern cultures of the "West." For example, in Kamvari's comments section a woman blogger in the United States advocated for the use of the words *kos, keer,* and *koon* (pussy, dick, and ass). Claiming that talking about such matters is acceptable in "Western cultures," and repeating the logic of "backwardness" of Iranians to defend Kamvari, this reader expressed that Iranians needed to catch up with the West. Another blogger, a male journalist who worked in a U.S.-based conservative think tank, also wrote a post in defense of Kamvari. He claimed that allowing this kind of open discourse about sex is essential to becoming modern, as uprising and sexual rebellion are signs of modernity. Jami and Khaledian challenged these responses through competing ideas of what it means to be modern. Like those who defended Kamvari through the discourse of modernity, Jami and Khaledian formulated their responses through the logic of temporal lag and the modern/traditional binaries. While Jami and Khaledian desired being modern, they defended what they considered to be Iranian traditions that are noble and worthy of preservation. Not surprisingly, these traditions concerned the hegemonic gendered conventions of Iranianness. Supporters of Jami and Khaledian defended women's hojb o haya and child-rearing duties as virtues that were essential to proper forms of Iranianness. Being modern, many of them argued, meant adopting some new values while still adhering to *orf* (social codes) and *adab* (discipline).

In a January, 11, 2006, post titled "Gendered Language and the Game of Power," I responded to Jami's post and argued that certain forms of language are established as modern and rational and others are deemed traditional and superstitious.[19] I pointed out that Jami's use of *"pardeh-ye esmat dareedan,"* his allegory of "revolution as a seductress," and his characterization of *"Kulthum Naneh* language" as backward and traditional are informed by gendered discourses of the Iranian modernity. Historically, I wrote, modern Iranian men are seen as rational subjects as opposed to the figure of the traditional woman who needs to be trained and tamed to fit the modern contours of Iranianness. I cited feminist Iranian scholars and discussed the history of *Kulthum Naneh* to argue that despite its emancipating impulses, modernity in Iran (whether in its modernizing forms or as fundamentalism) has regulated women and sexuality in order to construct and institutionalize a normative monogamous heterosexuality and a tamed and docile femininity (Moallem, 1999). Jami responded to my critique in a comment, followed by a post. Jami explained that his response to Kamvari was not meant to insult *Kulthum Naneh* but sought to point out that one should not talk about modern concepts using the *Kulthum Naneh* language: "This language in its own place, and for example, in an artistic framework may be good, but in serious discussions it is lacking." When I pointed to a paradox in his logic by asking him why speaking about modern events with seventeenth-century *Kulthum Naneh* language was considered to be anachronistic and irrational, but referring to *Rostam al-Tavarikh* (also a seventeenth-century text) in his post about Sharon was perfectly rational and unproblematic, Jami attempted to show that the question of my logic in response to his comment was para-logical (*maqlateh*). In a post titled "The Rationale of Being Reductive and the Rationale of Research," Jami used ornamental language and claimed that even if my question was legitimate and even if he, like Kamvari, was guilty of being anachronistic, one should not make that mistake (speaking about modern issues with a traditional language).[20]

Ignoring my critique of the gendered connotations of referring to Kamvari's language as *Kulthum Naneh* and overlooking the history of disciplining of women in public spaces, Jami completely changed the topic and instead laid claim on the Persian language by proposing "proper" equivalents for *gay, lesbian,* and *gender*. In his post, Jami questioned the use of a term (*jensgoonegi*) that I had been using in my blog (and had adopted from a diaspora feminist journal, *Nimeye Digar*) to refer to gender and accused me of lack of knowledge about the Persian language. Saying that the term does not sound right to the ear, he mentioned that his search for the term *gender* failed to find it in the *Ashuri Encyclopedia*. Even though I had not written about the categories of *gay* and *lesbian* in my post, Jami's response on his blog focused on what he (after consulting Daryush Ashuri) considered to be the appropriate Persian terms for *gender, gay,* and *lesbian*. Ignoring that over the years several gay/lesbian and queer magazines and websites had produced a list of terms to refer to these concepts, Ashuri, Jami claimed, insisted that the terms *gay* and *lesbian* were to be translated as *narineh kaam* and *maadineh kaam* (terms that are often used for plants and animals and that reduce sexual identities to biology and essentialized notions of body and desire). I responded that while I had no claims about expertise over the Persian language, the proposed terms were problematic and almost comical. I pointed out that the lack of terminology about queerness and sexual identities in the *Ashuri Encyclopedia* revealed only that the "experts" on Persian language are unconcerned with gender and sexuality.[21]

Whether expressing praise, agreement, or disagreement, none of the comments or posts in response to Jami included sexual insults. I, on the other hand, received a few hostile comments such as "you are a whore like your friend." Despite my use of "professional" and "proper" language in my role as a graduate student at that time (my critique did not include language considered to be vulgar), as a female-bodied person I was targeted with hostile and violent sexualized comments. While some of Jami's fans squarely placed Kamvari and me in the camp of shameless (*bee-haya*) whores, other advocates of women's hojb o haya took the opportunity to pit my *mateen* (graceful) language (appropriate for women) against Kamvari's *mobtazal* (vulgar) and inappropriate language. In an interesting gesture to prove their democratic tendencies, some commentators claimed that despite their disagreements with me, they liked my graceful language. Yet this nod to my "clean" use of language eerily felt like a normalization technique that was deployed subtly to put me in my place as a female-bodied person who was assumed to be a heterosexual woman (the possibility of a queer, gender-nonconforming academic did not even occur to many of these readers).

In response to the debates that had emerged after his exchange with Kamvari and me, Jami wrote another post, titled "Against Chaos: A Critique of Intellectual Superstition" (January 17, 2006). In his post, which clearly reads as a counterattack against bloggers who had accused him of being sexist and heteronormative, Jami wrote that "all intentional riots are built on illogic and benefit from the inexperience (and in fact, limited experience) of the Iranian society in the modern world."[22] He expressed his concerns over what he considered to be an attack on Persian literature (*adabiyaat-e farsi*). He declared that any kind of deliberate chaos is rooted in ideological frameworks and is "dangerous for the mental and psychological health of the society." Positioning himself as a modern intellectual blogger against chaos and superstition, Jami proceeded to dispel myths about feminism and homosexuality:

> Lesbians and gays do not have a pornographic language. This is a myth that stems from the lack of experience among the Iranian society (in Iran and abroad). They [homosexuals] are people too. They don't see themselves

obliged to propagate vulgarity. You know that they also have priests. To equate [vulgarity with homosexuality] is very dangerous and a misunderstanding that would harm the social rights of those whose sexual orientation is *really* [my emphasis] this way. Only the inexperienced would equate these people with vulgarity: They use these individuals' rights as fun play; People who have claims on modernism, but are completely premodern.

Jami's version of authentic, sanitized, and Eurocentric gay and lesbian identities stood in clear opposition to what he considered to be pornographic, backward, inauthentic, and queerly thug-like. Similarly, he wrote that "feminists do not at all defend pornography. The clear example of it is the group, Feminists Fighting Pornography in Canada and the United States. A number of distinguished homosexuals support this movement. This movement says, 'there is no feminist issue which is not rooted in the problem of porn.'" Jami continued: "The logic of the Canadian supreme court is fascinating because they see the protection of women's rights to be more important than the freedom of speech (note to those naïve people who copied the human rights protocol in my comments section to legitimize freedom of vulgar speech)." Arguing that the West is not a place for the freedom of debauchery (*fisq o fojoor*), Jami then clarified that "this has nothing to do with the reality of the West. This heaven of chaos is only created by an oppressed mind for which the only ideal freedom is the unlimited freedom of below-the-belt (*azadi-yeh zeer shalvaree*)." Jami concluded by suggesting that "vulgar language" is premodern and in violation of civility and human rights: "The main issue in modernism is to be serious about human rights. Those who ignore our rights, whether they are the police and the judge, or our real or cyber neighbor, have not entered the modern world. Really, our problem is still that one word: the law. Without the law and in chaos, there is no modernism. Our anarchism is the sign of our inexperience [in being modern]."[23]

Declaring mainstream Western liberal white feminism as authentic feminism and dismissing queer and feminist bloggers as failed mimics were not unusual. I will argue in chapter 4 that the juxtaposition of a sanitized and authentic gay and lesbian-ness to a backward, untamed perverse sexuality was a common theme in "defense" of a sanitized homosexuality, wherein homonormativity and homonationalism became conditions of tolerance for Iranian gays and lesbians. Noticeable in Jami's post are his emphasis on civility and his insistence on the need for rehearsing ways of being modern and reaching exceptional citizenship in Weblogistan as a gymnasium for democratic fitness.

For Jami, the pitiful abject others of a democratic future are risky subjects, the queer "thugs" of Weblogistan whose elimination is necessary for the cultivation of a properly "modern" citizenship.

Agitated by Jami's authoritative tone and claims of expertise, Kamvari wrote a post on January 18, 2006, in which she translated an erotic excerpt from Samuel Delany's book *Shorter Views: Queer Thoughts & the Politics of the Paraliterary* (1999). Kamvari used a graphic passage about masturbation that might be read as pornographic to discuss Delany's distinction among the speakable, the unspeakable, and the forbidden. She wrote that repressive relations of power make certain sex acts unspeakable and argued, à la Delany, that to theorize about the unspeakable, one has to speak the unspeakable.[24] As expected, many commentators admonished her "pornographic" language. Dismissing Kamvari's discussion and her use of queer theory in making a point about vulgarity and the politics of language, a reader who attacked Kamvari by insulting her with a long list of extremely rude curse words ended his comments by saying, "No, fat lady. You cannot disguise your *Kulthum Naneh* nature with things like this!" Another commentator wrote that "you Canada residents make me sick with your lesbianism and putting out your pussy" and inserted a link to a photograph on another famous Toronto blogger's Flickr account, in which Kamvari had posed as if kissing another woman.

While Kamvari received several extremely hostile comments, not everyone attacked her by using violent language. Some expressed their dismay through "civil" advice, and others pathologized her and her behavior without using curse words. An anonymous commentator wrote the following: "The problem is that you either deny or do not understand a simple thing called *sharm o haya* (shame and being demure); or you essentially do not believe in its existence. *Sharm o haya* are among human behaviors. . . . The reason why sex is limited to bedroom is because it is [where it belongs]. Unlike animals, the human kind does not engage in sexual acts on the street, on the train, or in front of guests."

Another reader, writing under the name Ali Sadeqi, likened Kamvari's critique of normal sex as private and heterosexual to a contagious "disease" that could threaten the health of the population:

> What are you after? What will you get from taking sex out of the bedroom? Do you think such people who eat their own semen [referring to the scene from Delany's book] are ruling the society? Do you think that their rights are violated and [that is why] they are not in literature? On the contrary, they are victims of the same kind of psychological diseases that intellectu-

als such as you spread. And you prevent these unfortunate people [Iranian readers] from enjoying a healthy life. I have lived in Canada for many years and will tell you with courage that not only normal people here are not like that, but they hate your kind and the kind of conduct you spread.[25]

He added that "not having these issues in unsoiled literature, and essentially in public, is a positive thing. To discuss these issues is like spreading disease." When Kamvari asked Sadeqi why refusing to talk about sex is a virtue, he responded: "I am not a language expert, but I know that breaking the essential *hojb o haya* of sex is not an art. It is quite easy. The way you have done it. But the negative effect of breaking this essential *hojb o haya*, from the standpoint of the destruction of family, is by far more harmful than its small positive effects. The natural place of a healthy and clean sex is in the institution of family. But what is often spread in the name of breaking taboos, is not at all in this direction [the institution of family]." By identifying as someone who has lived in Canada for a long time, Sadeqi lays claim to expertise about proper speech and conduct in Canada. At the same time, by using the notion of hojb o haya to advocate against perversions of sex, he simultaneously performs Iranianness, thus asserting his belonging and sense of respectable citizenship in Iran and Canada as opposed to the deviant and pathologized others. Sadeqi was not alone in deploying hojb o haya to critique Kamvari's post as an attack on the Persian language and culture. In fact, most of the criticism of Kamvari's posts naturalized a heteronormative "Iranian culture" that was threatened by perversions of "vulgar bloggers" in an otherwise normal Weblogistan. Some bloggers expressed their exasperation at this debate (which led to yet another debate about homosexuality, which I will discuss in chapter 4) by wishing for it to end. Their logic was that the debate about vulgarity, which had turned into a critique of heteropatriarchy in Weblogistan, had gotten out of control and was no longer relevant to the "Iranian culture." It was as if the discussions that were deemed "vulgar" distracted rehearsals of democracy and delayed the attempts to reach exceptional citizenship in Weblogistan.

Not all responses to Kamvari were adversarial. In response to Sadeqi's attack, a blog reader named Kamyar defended Kamvari by reversing Jami's charge of backwardness:

> It is interesting to see some people talk positively about the lack or presence of such issues [sex] in the Iranian and Islamic culture. Don't they know the extent of "pedophilia" and "rape" that takes place in "secret" [private] in Iran? And this secret is the same as the alleged "bedroom,"

which is responsible for the "stability of the institution of family!" As long as you close your ears, you will not hear anything. It is likely that next to us, a human being is raped, but because of backward views, we will not say a word. And with our hands covering our ears we shout, "but I know that breaking the essential *hojb o haya* is not an art at all." May we all be directed to the correct path.... Mr. Sibiltala, remember that one day they will accept that "the earth is round."

Kamyar's comment, which questions the sanctity of the institution of family, falls back on the modern/traditional and backward/progressive binaries that Jami also deployed in his argument. Despite their differences, both Jami and Kamyar associate speaking about sex with progress and scientific rationality. The insistence on speaking the truth of sex, as Foucault argues, overlooks the way that sex is discursively produced. In fact, the exclusion of nonheterosexual subjects from the realm of modern Iranian citizenship has less to do with static and transhistorical imaginations of "Iranian culture" or Islam than it does with anxieties about Iranian modernity. In order to refute the charges of backwardness by European orientalists who wrote disapprovingly about sexual practices in Iran, Iranian elites have actively erased the history of non-heteronormative subjects from the history of modern Iran (Najmabadi 2005; Moallem 2005b). In the same vein, since the twentieth century medical and psychological discourses in Iran have pathologized nonnormative sexualities (Najmabadi 2014). Not unlike Jami and his fans, those who defended Kamvari through the logic of the incommensurability of Islam or the "Iranian culture" with modernity reify Western modernity's claims on the concept of "modern."

Ironically, while male intellectuals in Weblogistan did not perceive vulgar attacks on feminist bloggers as censorship or cyber-bullying, they deemed feminist bloggers' criticisms of sexist language to be censorship of the Persian language.[26] Several male intellectuals accused feminist critics of being "ideological," while assuming themselves to be neutral and free of ideology. Implicitly suggesting that the Persian language was the property of a few good men, they ordered feminists to leave the Persian language alone and spare it from perversion, superstition, and contamination. For example, a male graduate student in the United States posted a comment on my blog, accusing me of policing language (because of my critique of Jami) in the same way that the Islamic Republic censors language. This blogger later suggested that Iranian feminist scholars should leave "serious issues" (such as Foucault) to the experts and instead write about women's issues such as rape. Without naming him or linking to his post, I wrote a blog post critiquing the sexist self-righteousness of some Iranian bloggers who belittled feminist scholars. Soon after, this blogger shut down his blog, making it known to his friends that it was my response that made him stop blogging. One of his friends in Toronto, an engineer and a self-identified exiled man who exuded an aura of expertise about politics and social sciences, wrote a retaliatory post, angrily insulting women's and gender studies scholars. This blogger claimed that women's studies was neither a scientific nor an objective field. He further expressed that the "gurus" of women's studies were illiterate and insignificant, never mind the graduate students of this field. A close associate of the conservative politician Ali Larijani (the deputy minister of information and communications technology during the first term of Rafsanjani's presidency) and a Hezbollahi student at Sharif University, this blogger took pride in having helped bring the internet to Iran. In my interview with him in the early days of my field research in Toronto, he boasted about the extravagant cars he owned and the level of comfort he had enjoyed in Iran. Despite his comfortable life, he told me, he left Iran to seek what was lacking in his life: freedom and participation in a democratic civil society. This blogger's performances of "modern" manhood and ethical policing of other bloggers added insult to injury for two women, one a blogger and the other a blog reader. Both of these women were harassed/assaulted by this man but kept quiet for fear of retaliation and because they were concerned about being shamed by others. One of the two women told me that she did not expose this male blogger in Weblogistan out of concern for his wife's *aberoo* (public reputation). She was, after all, his wife's friend and colleague. When she finally told her friend (the blogger's wife) about the incident, her friend blamed her for wanting to tarnish her husband's reputation. Ironically, claims of being modern and freedom-loving worked to normalize violence against those who were seen as either too "feminist" or "too sexually permissive."

In the battle over the sanctity of Persian language and literature, bloggers who saw themselves in the position of preserving the Persian language and culture tried to discipline "vulgar" bloggers through humiliating posts and comments. Of course, this had a chilling effect in that many women bloggers practiced self-censorship as a classed performance of respectability and as a way to distance themselves from women who were seen as male-hating lesbians, whores, and vulgar feminists. As Roya, a blogger who lived in Iran, wrote in Kamvari's comments section,

> In one word: Power does not allow the unspeakable to become speakable. Power in whatever level: from family to the global society. To be mute is often a choice. For instance, if Sibil [Kamvari] wanted everyone to tell her what a good girl she was, she would have to bite her tongue [be mute], like those women who defend their own muteness and attack Sibil by saying: "why do you not respect politeness and *adab*?" Of course, this requirement only applies to women and not men. A human being often internalizes power. And even if there isn't a baton over her head, she still shuts her mouth and buries the unspeakable in her heart at any level, from politics to the family or the unspeakable sexual matters.[27]

Roya speaks to the forms of disciplining and censorship that exceed the state's attempts to "filter" women bloggers. Her response addresses forms of power that are not in a vertical relationship to subjects but operate through "choice." It points to the way that she and other women in Weblogistan willingly submit to the conventions of *adab* that define unspoken rules of heteronormative middle-class Iranianness. It is through these performances of civility and self-censorship that Iranian women bloggers participate in Weblogistan as social beings and digital citizens. As a site of civil society that is celebrated for "giving voice" to Iranian women, Weblogistan is a public platform where women (and other gendered subjects) use techniques of self and self-censorship to become intelligible as normal digital citizens, worthy of a democratic future that carries with it the promise of freedom and exceptional citizenship.

In the women's focus group that I organized in Toronto, almost every woman recounted their strategies of self-censorship and self-conduct. Mina, an assertive and strong woman blogger, expressed that she chose not to write about many issues out of her consideration for her husband: "My marriage is relatively new and vulnerable and I do not want to jeopardize it. I don't want to make my husband insecure." Niloufar, who at the time was separated but had not yet divorced from a very famous blogger, said that she hesitated to write freely because her ex-husband was always under attack by others. She did not want her posts to be used as ammunition against her ex-husband: "I have hundreds of posts that I have written and deleted. . . . There is so much that I want to write about, but I can't." Nooshin, a Persian blog reader who wrote an anonymous blog in English, said that her reason for not blogging in Persian was *harf-e mardom* (what people say). Noting that certain issues were considered to be taboo subjects if discussed by women, she had decided to avoid people's gossip and judgment by not writing for a public readership.

Zohreh, a former blogger whose husband was also a blogger, told me privately that she stopped blogging because her friends and people she did not even know would contact her to inquire about her personal life; they assumed that her critique of patriarchy was indicative of marital relationship problems. "I did not like to be under surveillance all the time," she told me when I asked her why she did not write anymore, even as she left comments for other bloggers. If the Iranian state's filtering system attempted to expurgate "objectionable content" in Iran, bloggers did the job rather successfully through the rhetoric of civility by criticizing the conduct of others and regulating their own behavior in Weblogistan.

Conclusion: Aghdam's Para-Humanity

The debates that I have discussed in this chapter highlight the way that male intellectuals who passionately invoked freedom and advocated "practicing democracy" in Weblogistan disciplined women bloggers who posed a threat to their vision of a normative democratic Iranianness. When confronted with criticism by feminist bloggers, the male elites of Weblogistan portrayed their critics as backward and vulgar impediments to modernity (assuming that Iranians have not learned how to be "modern") and invoked an idealized form of exceptional digital citizenship that would be the blueprint for Iran's democratic future. The "proper" use of technology became a sign of rationality, a sign of democratic potentiality, and a prerequisite for exceptional citizenship, while "vulgarity" became the stamp of risky citizenship in Weblogistan. Feminist bloggers' grievances about moral policing by other bloggers point to conspicuous contradictions in claims about the freedom of speech. While mainstream accounts of Weblogistan celebrated it as a platform for practicing democracy and a rare gift to Iranians who were assumed to lack freedom of speech, these rehearsals of democracy entailed forms of nonstate disciplining (often in the form of hostile comments or patronizing advice) that regulated bloggers' conduct according to the codes of heteronormative monogamy and democratic futurity. Freedom and democracy as ideoscapes (Appadurai 1996, 37) of the Enlightenment and progress became techniques of normalization in exchanges between resident and diasporic male intellectuals who injected particular meanings into these concepts. As a mediascape of a deterritorialized population, Weblogistan became a ground for nationalistic and seemingly democratic forms of normalization.

As Ong argues, there is "a fundamental shift in the ethics of subject formation, or the ethics of citizenship, as governing becomes concerned less with the social and collective management of the population (biopolitics) and more with instilling behavior of individual self-management (ethicopolitics)" (2006, 138). This ethicopolitics involves the practices of self-care and self-constitution according to moral codes and in line with particular lifestyles. Weblogistan as a site of transnational civil society was where ethicopolitical practices sought to produce proper subjects suitable for an imagined democratic future. Discourses of democracy in Weblogistan interpellated Iranians as ethical, desiring subjects who willingly submitted to its laws, thus producing forms of consciousness that compelled digital citizens to self-govern in the name of democracy and individual freedom. As Foucault has noted, one of the contracts of the Enlightenment is the Kantian principle that the "public and free use of autonomous reason will be the best guarantee of obedience, on condition, however, that the political principle that must be obeyed itself be in conformity with universal reason" (1984, 37). This "democratic" promise, as the debates that I have discussed here demonstrate, reified gendered and sexed conventions of Iranianness, while demanding the submission of the blogger individual in the name of liberty.[28] But what happens when subjects refuse or fail the biopolitical and the ethicopolitical? And how do transnational governmentality and the production of ethical democratic subjects connect to the politics of rightful killing? Who can be killed, and who can kill, ethically? Can killing be justified when those whose loaned lives are expendable are seen as risks to a healthy and ethical heteronormative population? Does suicide shooting create a crisis in the art of government through biopolitics and ethicopolitics?

Kamvari's reflections about the "YouTube shooter" are useful in highlighting the contradictions and failures of disciplinary and normalizing power. On April 3, 2018, Nasim Najafi Aghdam, an Iranian refugee, vegan activist, artist, and bodybuilder who was upset with YouTube's demonetization of her videos, walked into the company's headquarters in San Bruno, California, injuring three people and killing herself with a gun she had purchased in January.[29] Aghdam had become relatively well-known among Iranian YouTube, Instagram, and Telegram users because of her eccentric videos. Her small number of followers grew after she changed her content about animal rights and veganism and focused on responding to the hostile comments from viewers who ridiculed her. Her campy and slapstick one-woman comedy videos in Persian, Turkish, and English were a combination of exercise routines and social commentaries about animal rights, veganism, consumerism, and objectification of women's bodies, along with a critique of empty claims about freedom of speech in the United States. In the last months of her life, Aghdam produced videos that critiqued YouTube for demonetizing and filtering her four YouTube channels. In a video, where she is not dancing or being campy, Aghdam tells her viewers that while sexually suggestive videos are allowed on YouTube, her exercise video is censored for "inappropriate content."[30] In another (Persian-language) clip, she criticizes the myth of freedom of speech in the United States and tells her viewers in Iran that the United States has rampant censorship, corruption, suppression of truth, nepotism, animal abuse, and immorality. At this point, the viewer hears gunshots, and Aghdam ducks quickly to dodge video-animated bullets flying toward her. Acting relieved and thanking God that the danger is averted, she tells her viewers that because carrying guns in the United States is legal, one is always worried about not coming back home alive. At the end of the video, she is shot at by animated bullets again, giving the message that one gets killed for speaking the truth.[31]

In her article on Radio Zamaneh on April 4, 2018, Kamvari criticized the hostility and violence that Aghdam received in social media. Kamvari brings examples of Twitter posts by Iranians who called Aghdam crazy, and she critiques those who reported the eccentric animal-rights activist to YouTube. She writes the following:

> For me, as someone who was a blogger for years, was active in social media, and wrote about sexuality and gender, Najafi Aghdam's being woman [an anomaly in the trend of mass shootings] is not that surprising. There are many people like me who can write about the violence that they experienced for producing content about sexuality and gender for a Persian-speaking audience.... Nasim was put in our cycle of violence.... Search her name and you will see that [internet] users are talking about the possibility that she had a mental illness. But does saying that someone was crazy displace responsibility and exonerate us from being a part of this cycle of violence? Even if Nasim Najafi had a particular mental illness—which is unclear that it was the case—it is our social responsibility to take care of those who have special needs and live with mental illness.... Perhaps this tragic event becomes an opportunity for us to think more about bullying, violence, abuse, and degradation in the Persian language cyberspace.[32]

Kamvari's post alludes to the verbal violence that she received as a blogger woman during the heyday of Weblogistan (the reason why she disabled her comments section). As someone who now writes for Radio Zamaneh for a living, Kamvari's style of writing and her tone have changed drastically since her blogging days, perhaps an indication of the way that the disciplinary and normalizing techniques in Weblogistan have culminated in a less threatening language that is suitable for a "democratic" and tolerant civil society. Kamvari's point about the violence in the Persian-language cyberspace is an important reminder that the digital realm remains a platform for the disciplining of unruly bodies online. However, Kamvari's important reminder about social responsibility and her point about the demonization of mental illness by Persian-language YouTube users border on individuating violence rather than acknowledging YouTube's role in its normalization.

Aghdam's anger at YouTube was a result of the company's change of policy in early 2018. In order to make its service advertiser-friendly, YouTube raised the eligibility requirements for monetization to four thousand watch hours and one thousand subscribers. YouTube announced that it intended to "prevent bad actors from harming the inspiring and original creators around the world who make their living on YouTube." [33] The video-streaming service claimed that this measure would entail "strengthening our requirements for monetization so spammers, impersonators, and other bad actors can't hurt our ecosystem or take advantage of you, while continuing to reward those who make our platform great." In her videos and on her website (all deactivated now), Aghdam informed her viewers that YouTube's policy is a euphemism for censorship. "People like me are not good for big business," she proclaimed in one of her videos in which she criticizes YouTube's demonetization policy. Even if one agrees with critics who condemn Aghdam's resentment to have resulted from her narcissism and her exaggerated sense of self-importance, her claims of being censored by YouTube cannot be dismissed as paranoia or conspiracy theory. In fact, even as YouTube's content-moderation policies at the beginning of 2018 intensified, the company has removed content that it deemed inappropriate and risky since its inception. In 2006 the Google-owned company became one of the first venues where the Digital Millennium Copyright Act and Section 230 of the Communications Decency Act—which for the most part emerged as measures against "child-inappropriate" content—allowed service providers to restrict user-generated content/actions in order to reduce the risk of liability.[34] In addition, after several governments blocked YouTube, the company started to restrict content. For example, in 2007, claiming user complaints as justification, YouTube suspended Wael Abbas, the Egyptian anti-torture activist blogger/YouTube user whose videos revealed police brutality in Egypt. By the end of the first decade of the new millennium, YouTube effectively became the arbitrator of content appropriateness. Ironically, while YouTube removed videos that violated its policy against violence and hate speech, the company allowed graphically violent videos from the Green movement (Neda Agha Soltan's last breaths became a YouTube sensation) and the Arab Spring. In 2011 the company's manager of news, referring to the violent videos of the Arab Spring, claimed that while normally "this type of violence would violate our community guidelines and terms of service" and result in removal, YouTube makes an exception for videos that have educational and news value.[35] As Jillian York argues, "YouTube, whether its policymakers and executives like it or not, is already an arbiter of speech, not merely a technology company. And so, the decisions it makes reflect its values, and the values of those who make and enforce its policies."[36]

Considering YouTube's censorship record and Google's close relationship with the U.S. government's security apparatus, Aghdam was not wrong to criticize YouTube for its discrimination and censorship practices. After YouTube demonetized her channels, in her website she warned her readers, "Be aware! Dictatorship exists in all countries but with different tactics! They only care for personal and short-term profits and do anything to reach their goals even by fooling simple-minded people, hiding the truth, manipulating science, putting public mental and physical health at risk, abusing non-human animals, polluting the environment, destroying family values, promoting materialism and sexual degeneration in the name of freedom and turning people into programmed robots!"[37] In one of her parody videos titled "Islamic Republic," Aghdam is sarcastically wearing a dress with décolletage, along with a tightly wrapped hijab on her head. Animated U.S. dollars are raining on her as she dances with a repetitive move and a stern look on her face. In a sing-a-song voice she says, "at least in Iran they kill you with an axe. Here they cut your throat with cotton balls" (phrasing that derives from a Farsi proverb). She tells her viewers about her view of the United States:

> If you are oblivious and superficial, want to walk naked, and have all kinds of sex, like animals, you will think that this is heaven. . . . But if you want to act humane and delve deeply into the system, you will realize, "yuck! yuck! This is hell! This is worse than Iran!" Yes, those who want to raise awareness and go against the system and big businesses will be shut down and repressed. Like Nasim. See how they filtered her on the Internet, on YouTube, on Instagram? But bullshit pages in which someone promotes sexual corruption, reveals her ass, and reveals her tits . . . they give her more viewers and make her a celebrity.[38]

In another parody video, where she seems to be mimicking the leader of the Iranian revolution, she addresses the United States by saying, "Yo, America! You with your slogans of freedom of speech! Tell YouTube to free my four channels from filtering and demonetization and stop this ridiculous game. Otherwise, I, as the Iranian *shaakh* [a term in Iranian internet culture that literally means "horn" but connotes being popular in social media] . . . [here she pauses and changes the word *shaakh* to *Shaakhehye gol*, meaning a flower stem] will order Iran to attack America and make your roads into never-drying wet asphalt [most likely making a reference to nuclear bombs]." Once Aghdam stops her rant, she looks sternly at the camera, while a thick voice (her version of a man's voice) shouts, *"Marg bar tab'eez. Marg bar zed-e vilaayat-e Nasim!"* ("Down with discrimination! Down with the enemy of Nasim's guardianship/leadership!").[39] Aghdam's video is clearly a parody of the former Iranian supreme leader, the late Ayatollah Khomeini, whose famous speech "America cannot do a damn thing against us!" was followed by chants from the audience: "Down with America! Down with the Soviet! Down with the opposition to the guardianship of Islamist jurist! Greetings to Khomeini!" By using a parody of the famous postrevolutionary slogan, Aghdam simultaneously pokes fun at the Iranian state (she was a Baha'i refugee and seemingly against the Iranian state) and the claims of freedom of speech in the United States. Cleverly, she uses sarcasm to comment about the fear that Iranian bodies incite in the United States. Her sense of humor is lost on those who assumed that Aghdam was a "Muslim terrorist."

In one of her last videos, Aghdam appears sitting on a stool, as if in a TV show, and responds to her followers' questions. She tells her viewers that she was born in Urumiyeh/Urmia (an Iranian city in the province of Western Azerbaijan), that she likes to wear her hair short because it is easy to maintain, and that she does not have any particular physical or mental illness but lives in a planet that is filled with disease, disorders, deviations, and injustices.[40] While in this video she appears in what seems to be her everyday look, in most of her videos she appears in exaggerated feminine drag to mock what she considers to be the popular and shallow form of Iranian femininity that attracts viewers. In one of her most famous videos, titled *"Dokhtar-e mameh badkonaki"* ("Balloon-Boobed Girl"), she dances in a shiny red skirt, a purple top that reveals ample cleavage, a wig, long eyelashes, and makeup. She sings:

> Balloon-boobed girl, Balloon-boobed girl. I am very enlightened. Whatever comes to the market, I buy. . . . Breasts like balloons, lips like cheese

puffs [alluding to the prevalence of plastic surgery among middle- and upper-class Iranian women]. Yes, this is civilization. It's a form of enlightenment. I am very enlightened and smart because every few months I sell my iPhone and buy the latest system [version]. In sexual matters, I have reached the highest level of civilization. No laws, orgy, sex from behind. The law and sexual ethics mean being pious. One should be free like other animals, but not animals in the jungle, urban animals.[41]

In another video she talks about how having large breasts and buttocks and acting like a prostitute has become more attractive, while being a virgin is looked down upon.[42] In fact, in several of her videos Aghdam seems to be condemning the normalization of sexual licentiousness and meat consumption as progressive and enlightened values, while in others she complains about how her viewers judge her based on her appearance and her unconventional videos. In one video she plays two characters to compare Iranians and Americans. She puts on a cowboy hat to impersonate Americans and sports a see-through scarf, big hair, and a lot of makeup to impersonate Iranians. She mimics Iranians (most likely Iranians in Southern California where she lived) who belittle those who do not look "normal" (likely herself) by saying, "Wow, look at that girl! Look at her hair and her makeup! She looks like she is stuck in the 60s [1980s according to the Christian calendar]. Thank God we are from the 90s [2000s according to the Christian calendar]! . . . Yuck! what a bad accent she has! She looks like she's crazy! I don't get her. What's her deal?! Look at her long neck! At first, I thought she was a giraffe! Cure these people, God! It looks like she's trans. She must be trans!"[43]

In fact, many people before and after her death speculated that Aghdam was trans. In a Twitter post, Laura Loomer, an alt-right journalist, wrote that "#Nasim Aghdam, the #YouTube shooter has very muscular thighs and buff arms. oversized breasts in some of her pics look distorted w/ photoshop. I don't think we are getting the full story. And for the record, Nasim is not traditionally a woman's name. It's a boy's name."[44] Aghdam's immigration status and nationality made her alleged transness and mental illness even more menacing. Even though Aghdam had moved to the United States as a Baha'i refugee more than two decades before the YouTube incident, she was assumed to have been undocumented and Muslim.[45] While Dana Rohrabacher, a Republican California congressman, speculated that Aghdam was an "illegal alien," Laura Loomer complained that there was no mention of "the fact that the shooter was from a #TravelBan country."[46] The right-wing white supremacists such as

Loomer were happy to announce that the YouTube shooting was not a gun problem but the fault of a mentally ill travel-ban "tranny." But this transphobia was not just limited to the right-wing conspiracists. U.K. Labour Party member Jennifer James—a feminist who campaigned against trans women and who was suspended from the party for breaching the party's rules on social media—wrote that "the YouTube shooter was a man. This was male violence. Name the problem. Men can shoot, rape, kill, but we have to 'respect pronouns.' No."[47] On the other hand, liberal queer and trans organizations and individuals dispelled the myth of Aghdam's transness to distance themselves from the figure of the Middle Eastern terrorist. By pointing out the transphobia of conspiracy theorists and transphobic feminists, LGBTQ activists, eager to prove their exceptional citizenship, made it clear that Aghdam was Iranian and not trans.[48] Just as Puar argues, the cultivation of homosexual (and, in this case, transgender) subjects "folded into life, enabled through 'market virility' and 'regenerative reproductivity,' is racially demarcated and paralleled by a rise in the targeting of the queerly raced bodies for dying" (2007, xii). Aghdam's video in which she is being shot at becomes an eerie foreshadowing of being destined to die, even as she forecloses that possibility by shooting herself and the others. At the moment of shooting, Aghdam, to borrow from Puar, does not "transcend or claim the rational nor accept the demarcation of the irrational. Rather, [she] foreground[s] the flawed temporal, spatial, and ontological presumptions upon which such distinctions flourish" (2007, 218).

While for the likes of Loomer, who learned about Aghdam only after her death, she embodied the figure of the terrorist, her representational body in her daily life did not make her into what Puar (2007, 199) calls the "body of excess," read through racial and sexual excesses of the visual. Had Aghdam looked different, had she "looked like" a Muslim man or a hijabi woman (or a black man sleeping in his car in a parking lot), it is unlikely that the Mountain View Police officers—who responded to a missing-person report and questioned Aghdam in a parking lot the night before the shooting, without searching her car—would have treated Aghdam so gently.[49] One wonders if the police officers' sympathy to Aghdam's claim that she did not get along with her family and was running away from them was not related to assumptions of girl children being abused by violent and abusive Middle Eastern families. Undoubtedly, the fact that she was found in Silicon Valley, the hub of model-minority Iranian tech executives, could have also made her Iranianness less threatening. Without her animal masks, headscarves, drags, and eccentric, self-made costumes, Aghdam's visual representation offline did not make her body into a "body of excess." It was only after her death, when Aghdam was identified as an Iranian woman, an angry and eccentric YouTube user, a shooter, and a refugee that her "affective body" and her "informational body" implicated her in danger, irrationality, and terror through contagion and digital cohesion.

The alt-right's complaints about the mainstream media's hesitance to associate Aghdam with ISIS and "Islamic terrorism" may reflect the differences between her attack and other mass shootings or suicide bombings (such as the Boston Marathon bombing or the Orlando Pulse club shooting) where the attackers were Muslim men. For one, Aghdam did not kill anyone, but she injured three people (one critically). The gendered framing of her "failure" to kill reiterated the essentialist narratives of women being naturally peaceful and less violent. But the scale was not the only element that contributed to less demonizing reportage in Aghdam's case. The shooting came at a time when Trump's presidency and his attacks on "fake news" had turned the liberal media into vanguards of resistance against ultraconservatives in the United States. In contrast to previous shootings by Muslim men, the mainstream media (except Fox) were more careful in a hasty characterization of Aghdam as a terrorist. One cannot help but wonder if the fact that she was a "calm" woman in a pink hoodie sweater when the police questioned her and was a Baha'i (and not a Muslim man or a hijabi Muslim woman) contributed to the media's less hysterically Islamophobic reactions to this shooting. Yet her Iranianness haunted the coverage of Aghdam's shooting. Unlike the male Muslim suicide bomber or shooter, Aghdam was produced as a victim and as an unstable and risky subject whose Iranianness, gender, and refugeeness made her prone to madness, irrationality, and unpredictability. Even as Aghdam condemned sexual promiscuity and anal sex, and even as she was not Muslim, her quirky YouTube personality, her "deviant" behavior (video superimpositions in which she dances with herself dressed as cows, chickens, and horses), and her refusal to act as a model-minority Iranian immigrant made her into a racially queered subject destined to death. When her protest videos and letters to YouTube's headquarters failed, Aghdam resorted to self-annihilation as the only way to be heard. As Spivak (2004, 96) argues, "Suicidal resistance is a message inscribed in the body when no other means will get through." Without pointing the gun at any particular employee, she shot at "YouTube" for silencing her and for annihilating her digital life. Confused by her act, Aghdam's family repeatedly told the press that she was not capable of hurting living beings—not even an insect—let alone humans. For Aghdam, the employees were no longer "human animals" but stood as substitutes for YouTube itself. In Spivak's words, "Suicide bombing . . . is a purposive self-annihilation, a confrontation between oneself and oneself—the extreme end of autoeroticism, killing oneself as other, in the process killing others. It is when one sees oneself as an object, capable of destruction, in a world of objects, so that the destruction of others is indistinguishable from the destruction of the self" (2004, 95).

Aghdam's suicide was not for a common struggle (she did not shoot others and commit suicide at a factory farm that symbolizes animal slaughter), nor was it incited by living under siege and occupation (as in the case of female suicide bombers in Palestine). Even as it was an act of self-preservation, Aghdam did not gain cultural capital through "giving life to the future of political struggle" (Puar 2007, 216). Hers was an act of disillusionment and an attempt to reclaim individualism through a protest against censorship (ironically captured in the alt-right #CensorshipKills Twitter handle after Aghdam's death). She committed the act of suicide shooting in defense of the liberal notion of freedom of speech, while revealing the contradictions and the violence of "freedom of speech." The very same technology (YouTube) that machined together "Nasime Sabz" as a fleeting queer assemblage of human/computer, human/animal, and organic/inorganic constituted her body as an assemblage (metal/flesh) when she walked into the company's property with a gun and at the moment when a metal bullet shattered her heart into pieces. Aghdam was neither a perfect victim nor a perfect villain; neither queer because of her sexuality and identity nor a heteronormative subject; neither a perfect embodiment of fear and hate nor a figure of love. Her para-humanity is not owed to crossing the lines of human/animal, sane/insane, victim/villain, and robot/human, but to being an Iranian immigrant, a risky subject who will never be an exceptional citizen, no matter how badly she desires it.[50] Aghdam's defense of normative sexuality notwithstanding, her failed exceptionalism and affective queerness unsettle the futurity that holds the promise of freedom of speech and individualism in the realm of civil society.

[4]

Weblogistan and Its Homosexual Problem

Increasingly, some Iranian civil society groups outside of Iran have become preoccupied with defending the rights of *hamjinsgaraayaan* (those who desire their own gender) inside Iran.[1] No longer completely rejected, Iranian homosexuals are more recently put into discourse as "special groups" or minorities who should be tolerated and granted rights as humans (albeit "abnormal" humans) in Iranian civil society. Curiously, this hypervisibility of queers has not always been the case. The *chic of queer* (the sudden "tolerance" and even celebration of Iranian queers among some Iranian diasporic opposition groups) is dubious, given that Iranian queers have historically been denied a legitimate space in diasporic imaginations of the nation. Not too long before the emergence of the chic of queer, Iranian queers were deemed unrepresentable by the Iranian diasporic media, excluded from exilic opposition groups' human rights activism, and humiliated by Iranian intellectuals.

As a topic of discussion in Weblogistan, homosexuality appeared more noticeably when a series of homophobic posts appeared in June 2006, perhaps as a result of a few coinciding events. Around the same time as the gay pride celebrations in North America and Europe, a group of women activists in Iran launched a campaign to protest a section of family law granting polygamy rights to men.[2] The controversy around polygamy and family law, the debate over language and power in Weblogistan, and posts about gay parades in North America and Europe led to anxieties about family values and sexuality among some bloggers in Weblogistan. For example, a blogger residing near the "gay neighborhood" in Toronto asked in his blog *Khatt-e qermez* (*Redline*), "If lesbians like women, why do some of them dress like men?" This question culminated in a series of posts by other bloggers. Some bloggers expressed hostility and homophobia, while others regarded the subject to be irrelevant to Iranian culture and considered queers to be "Westernized." One blogger (the same woman who had admonished Kamvari for speaking openly about sex) sarcastically suggested that there should be an official job for breaking taboos. The job description, she wrote, should include defense of feminism for any reason and at any cost, along with defense of homosexuality and all messed-up and confused desires (*hamjinsgaraayee va har gooneh ghaatee paatee garaayee*); defense of divorce at any time; defense of having children out of marriage; the use of vulgar and unveiled words in any gathering; the use of vulgar jokes; and defense of piercing and tattoos. She claimed that by doing "abnormal" and strange things, one could become very famous.[3]

Some of the most hostile posts were written by Nikahang Kowsar, a famous Toronto-based Iranian cartoonist who has held jobs with some of the most popular Iranian diasporic media. He reported that he and his friends went to see the "tribe of Sodom" at the gay pride parade in Toronto and that he was thankful to God for not being one (June 25, 2006). While "there are some nice people among them who are very kind and have a poetic and artistic spirit," he claimed, "the problem is that among the Iranian gays who I know, I have not seen a [worthy] human, especially among the colorful type that hangs out under the *Si-o-seh pol*" (a famous bridge in Isfahan).[4] Kowsar continued his homophobic attack, this time by targeting Iranian lesbians and feminists: "Of course, after seeing a significant number of Toronto lesbians, and of course feminists, we could arrive at an almost statistical conclusion as to why beautiful girls do not go along with them. Essentially, from our caricaturist perspective, we didn't find any of the available lesbians to have attractive looks or body."[5] In another post (June 30, 2006), Kowsar attempted to legitimize his homophobia through a seemingly liberal gesture, explaining that he was not trying to encourage or discourage people from homosexuality and claiming that he had a problem only with those who tried to make homosexuality acceptable to others.[6]

The discussions around homosexuality in Weblogistan frustrated a few bloggers who did not think that the subject of homosexuality (whether to attack it or defend it) was the Iranian people's problem or a good use of bloggers' time. In his blog, Ali Mosleh wrote the following:

As if this is the only thing we were missing! Is the Iranian women's problem, really, to get rid of men and sleep with their own sex? ... Even if anywhere else in the world there is homosexuality, it is because there is an excess of it [sex], or perhaps because it is a social norm. In any case, it [homosexuality in these societies] comes from consciousness and they have found genetic roots for it too. But in our country, except for the genetic issue, people become homosexuals because of societal norms and limitations. And some [become homosexuals] because they lack a "suitable" place [to interact with the opposite sex]. Now, some people are sitting outside of Iran's borders and are prescribing their Western consciousness to Iranian women!⁷

Claiming that because of their "traditional" upbringing, Iranian girls do not know about their bodies and the opposite sex, so "speaking of a conscious choice to become a homosexual is ridiculous." Mosleh suggested that in a place like Iran, where "women and men cannot become roommates but two women or two men can live together for a long time without anyone bothering them," homosexuality is a form of false consciousness resulting from the restrictions on heterosociality. Deploying the modernist heteronormative logic that homosexuality is a result of traditional homosociality and the cultural limitations and taboos that discourage the mingling of the opposite sexes, Mosleh ended his post by justifying his outright disdain of homosexuality as un-Iranian and asked, "And even if we are homophobes; what is wrong with that?" Khaledian, Mosleh, and Kowsar are just a few of the bloggers who attempted to justify their homophobia by associating homosexuality with the "West." Kowsar and Khaledian repeatedly insulted queer women and feminists by referring to them as *tabaq zans* (dykes) and "lesbo-feminists." In his post, Khaledian wrote, "some man-looking and woman-looking pseudo feminists who are indeed Mujahedeen of masturbation [*Mujahedeen-e jalq*], and who, in order to save their virginity from the front, have had several experiences from their anus, suggest this method to others in order to fight the homophobes and the 'backward' Iranian people."⁸ He also accused homosexuals of corrupting the youth of the homeland (*javaanaan-e vatan*), wasting the blood of martyrs who died in the war, and disrespecting those who died for their beliefs. Cultural authenticity became a tool for the self-identified modern enlightened (*roshanfekr*) men to justify violence against queers in Weblogistan.

While such bigotry is not exceptional (in fact, homophobic violence is quite common in North America and in cyberspace), finding out that several homophobic and sexist posts were written by bloggers who were hired by diasporic media and "democracy projects" that claimed to advocate for democracy and freedom for all enraged a number of feminist and queer bloggers. For example, Kowsar was at the time employed by at least two of these media venues, including the Dutch-funded Zamaneh, which initially started its activities as the radio of Weblogistan (see chapter 5). In his blog, Kowsar often labeled women who objected to his sexist remarks as "extremist feminists" (*feminist-e efraatee*) and accused feminists of being men haters. In a series of memoir-style posts, he made derogatory comments about women who held higher positions than he, accusing them of performing sexual favors in exchange for career advancement. Kowsar repeatedly attacked Faezeh Rafsanjani, the daughter of the former Iranian president and an Islamic feminist who was the chief editor of the *Zan* newspaper, charging her with incompetence. He also made sarcastic remarks about a woman being the head of the philosophy section of an Iranian newspaper where he was employed, suggesting that it was an oxymoron to be a woman and a philosopher.[9] He accused another woman journalist of making sexual advances toward him at work, changing her headscarf in front of men, and having affairs with people (both men and women) in positions of power for career advancement.

Several women criticized Kowsar (in his comments section or in their own blog posts) for rendering women as either helpless victims or whores.[10] They also questioned his unethical exposé style of writing about the private lives of others. Kowsar responded that the public/private binary was artificial when it came to the workplace. Privacy was irrelevant, Kowsar argued, if people who deserved jobs did not advance while some undeserving women were promoted because of their sexuality.[11] To prove his feminist critics wrong, he listed a couple of "respectful" women journalists who, he claimed, had gotten their jobs because of their merit and not because of performing sexual favors. He also claimed that his posts were meant to defend and protect women who faced sexual harassment in the workplace.

In his satirical Radio Zamaneh program *Kalaaghistoon* (Crow-ville), Kowsar often made sexist comments that enraged feminists in Iran and in diaspora. For example,

> ISNA [Iranian Students' News Agency] reported that more than sixty percent of girls are unsatisfied with their own gender [*jinsiyat*], [a phenomenon] which has increased a lot compared to the past! Now, may god help men who are trapped in these ladies' net. When they [women]

are unsatisfied themselves, God help their men! Possibly, this issue is the reason for the increasing number of feminists! The anti-feminist unit in Kalaaghistoon suggests that in order to avoid creating public anxiety and to remain healthy, gentlemen should keep their distance from this sixty per cent as much as possible! I am telling you.[12]

In another *Kalaaghistoon* post, Kowsar ridiculed his feminist coworkers at Zamaneh: "It is true that in Radio Zamaneh there are some ladies who are our co-workers, but in *Kalaaghistoon* all matters are in the roosters' hands! There is no way that we should allow chickens here so that we contract the chicken flu and that kind of nonsense! Chicken flu is essentially a new feminist disease of the chicken crowd and if we roosters are careful we won't contract it."[13]

Some women bloggers objected to Radio Zamaneh for airing such sexism when it claimed to be working toward a democratic future for Iran. Monahita, the author of the blog *Javaneh-ha,* criticized the misogyny of the programming, blaming *Kalaaghistoon*'s sexism on Islam and the religious convictions of Kowsar and Jami (the chief editor of Zamaneh at the time). Nazli Kamvari posted a comment in support of Monahita on Jami's personal blog: "Even though I too, am very disappointed with the Islamophobic language in *Javaaneh-ha*, I have to say that Monahita has raised a very important point about the hiring of misogynist individuals at Radio Zamaneh. I have to write extensively about this issue, but Nikahang's satire in *Kalaaghistoon*'s page is an example of this misogynistic literature." Referring to Kowsar's sexist commentary about the ISNA report, Nazli asked Jami, "Is the best satire about this extremely bitter [painful] ISNA news, really what Nikahang has written? Is Zamaneh's goal to be a rightwing and anti-human rights [radio] that you allow the broadcasting of such idiotic and vulgar satire? Where is the aesthetic value in a satire that is philosophically based on misogyny?"[14] Jami, the chief editor of Zamaneh at the time, promised to relay Nazli's message to Kowsar and replied, "We will be careful so that Zamaneh won't have a misogynistic direction. In Zamaneh, there are first-class feminist ladies too, but they do not have your view on his work."

Confronted with objections to his misogynistic programming on Zamaneh's *Kalaaghistoon,* Kowsar decided to respond to Kamvari's comment in his own blog as a strategy to separate his public persona at Zamaneh from his *hareem-e shakhsee* (personal privacy). However, what made this distinction meaningless was the fact that his blog was one of the main reasons that he had secured a job at Zamaneh. Kowsar's blog posts were public and often included links to his *Kalaghistoon* broadcasts. In a post titled "We Are Every Woman's Devotee, Especially Angelina Jolie and the Worthy/Proper Ones [*zan haaye dorost o hisaabee*]" (August 13, 2006), Kowsar wrote the following:

> A group of nobody ass-ripped feminist crows [*kalaagh-e koon dareedeh*][15] are putting all their efforts to jeopardize gentlemen! May god not forgive these godless members of the *Tudeh* party, and the fans of the holy "*seh kaaf.*"[16] One of them, in a threatening tone, announced to us that "until you don't use the word *kos* [pussy], we will do whatever we can to annihilate you!" By the way, one dear friend has recognized that those who have problems with us are either homosexual, have homosexual friends, are bisexual, and have bisexual friends. Of course, some are also homo-bi-animal-sexual [*sic*] and those clearly have a different story! A common link shared by a significant number of them is their addiction to the vibrating stick [*dasteh khar-e larzaan*]! Now, of course, this is our friend's diagnosis and he is responsible for how wrong or right it is! In any case, we are advocates of freedom of choice for all of them. God willing, may they all find a position in the holy city of Sodom![17]

Kowsar's blatant homophobia and misogyny exemplify how violent sexist and homophobic speech is legitimized in the name of freedom in Weblogistan. The mainstream diasporic media often celebrated Kowsar and regarded him as a courageous blogger and a defender of human rights. For instance, a BBC Persian article claimed that Kowsar considers "experiencing the significance of individual choice in social life and respect for others' views to be among the influential factors in his and other bloggers' writing in this region [North America]."[18] The celebrations of Weblogistan as a new frontier where free individuals practice democracy may be blind to the ways that buzzwords such as *freedom*, *transparency*, and *democracy* were deployed to repeat the inequalities that violently excluded women and queers in a future that the modernist intellectuals of Weblogistan envisioned. It is irrefutable that conversations about homosexuality became possible in Weblogistan in ways that may not have been possible offline. However, one should not ignore the fact that these online debates in the realm of cyber civil society continuously reiterated conventions of heteronormative Iranianness. As I will discuss below, even when homosexuality was discussed in less hostile terms, the heterosexuality/homosexuality binary as prediscursive categories foreclosed the possibility of positions that exceeded the reductive logic of "for" or "against" homosexuality.

The Normative Gay Subject

Even though the most celebrated male bloggers who were praised as the champions of democracy in Weblogistan were in the forefront of attacking and excluding queers, the conversations around homosexuality were not always so blatantly inimical.[19] For some bloggers, tolerating homosexuals became the yardstick of democratic Iranianness in the modernist imaginations of a free Iranian future. One of the first open discussions about homosexuality among political bloggers took place in 2005, when the now-defunct Persian online magazine *Feminist Tribune* linked to a post by Hossein Mansour, a supporter of the feminist publication.[20] Hossein Mansour, the author of the blog *Sharh*, made a distinction between *hamjinsgaraayee* (inclination toward one's own sex) and *hamjinsbaazee* (a derogatory term meaning playing with one's own sex).[21] Mansour appropriated the term *hamjinsgaraayee* and defined it as a genetic condition with which a hamjinsgara person is born. To Mansour, hamjinsbaazee is a condition that is caused in heterosexual individuals who are not inherently homosexual but are wrongly influenced by hamjinsgaraayaan (plural form of *hamjinsgara*). In Mansour's view, while hamjinsgaraayee is not a normal inclination, it is no longer considered to be a disease in modern science and should be tolerated. However, he also suggested that hamjinsgaraayaan should refrain from forming associations and clubs—and, in fact, should be under psychiatric supervision—in order to prevent the spread of hamjinsbaazee to those who are not inherently homosexual.[22] He further claimed that women who have suffered violence in the hands of men might be inclined to become hamjinsbaaz, a mistaken reaction resulting from disillusionment, fear, and dislike of men.

As a supporter of the *Feminist Tribune*, Mansour saw it as his responsibility to defend hamjinsgaraayaan while emphasizing the need for the control and surveillance of the entire population to prevent deviancy and hamjinsbaazee among Iranians. Mansour's post repeats a common discourse about homosexuality, in which the formation of the heterosexual subject depends upon "a repudiation which produces a domain of abjection, a repudiation without which the subject cannot emerge" (Butler 1993, 3). Interestingly, as Mansour's argument demonstrates, the upholding of heterosexual/homosexual difference requires the surveillance of the population as a whole. While it is no longer necessary to quarantine the homosexual (for it is no longer seen as a disease), the population needs to be managed because of the hovering danger of homosexuality (which lies in the body of the homosexual) and the risk of developing an inauthentic hamjinsbaazee desire (which can be incited among the "normal" members of society). The modern Iranian citizen is asked to put aside her/his traditional and superstitious beliefs on homosexuality, tolerate homosexuals, and defend the rights of the homosexual minority, while practicing self-control and preventing other citizens from the dangers of becoming the inauthentic hamjinsbaaz.

As I argued earlier, modern nationalist discourse in Iran and its diaspora relies on this realm of abjection, wherein nonheteronormative sexualities are perceived to be un-Iranian and inauthentic. However, with the currency of the neoliberal parlance of democracy, freedom, and responsibility, tolerance has awkwardly supplemented the outright rejection of queers. At a time when aspirations for democracy are central in ethicopolitical practices that manage the conduct of the conduct of oneself and others, tolerance of homosexuality is seen as a progressive gesture that epitomizes one's readiness for a free and democratic Iran. Erasing the historical production of sexual difference and imposing historical amnesia about the heteronormalization of Iran, tolerance emphasizes respect for inherent difference among individuals. Tolerance for the nation's queers becomes the ticket to Iran's democratic future. By categorizing homosexuals as inherently different by nature, however, this discourse forecloses the possibility of sexualities that do not fit the heterosexual/homosexual binary. The freedom to choose one's "lifestyle" and to be tolerated becomes contingent on adhering to the realms of the "natural" desires that are sanctioned by medical and psychological discourses that hold unassailable authority in modern Iranian cultural and political realms. Deviation from heteronormativity becomes dangerous to the well-being of a democratic future and is prevented through self-control and individual responsibility in civil society.

In discussing the shift to a postsocialist China, Lisa Rofel (2007) argues that the formation of a new Chineseness involves a rejection of the repression of the past through the notion of desire. In this configuration, human nature is seen as having been inhibited and repressed by excessive and uninhibited political passions of the socialist state during the Maoist era. The formation of postsocialist Chineseness, Rofel argues, involves the cultivation of human nature and benign interests, rather than what is perceived as destructive passions of the past. Thus, homoerotic desire is no longer seen as antisocialist immoral deviance but as part of human nature that is deserving of tolerance in a democratic present. Rofel points out that the advocates of free-trade capitalism in China have argued that the success of the global expansion of neoliberalism is a result of its naturalness and its cultivation of interest. Homosexuality and homoerotic desire as benign interests (rather than destructive passions) fit quite well with the idea that global capitalism is natural. Rofel's insights are useful for thinking about the way that the new discourse of tolerance of homosexuals among Iranian intellectuals relies on the idea that natural desire is repressed in postrevolutionary Iran. Resorting to nature to defend and tolerate hamjinsgaraayee and to separate it from the unhealthy and excessive hamjinsbaazee (which is seen as an unfortunate outcome of sexual repression under the Islamic state) becomes the new and improved strategy to be a modern Iranian who is suitable for a democratic future in Iran. It is through rejection of the Islamic Republic's restrictive policies that modern Iranian intellectuals produce themselves as desiring subjects. The desire for democracy becomes entangled with tolerating other natural human desires, as long as those desires do not disturb the rational sexual norms that maintain the superiority of heterosexuality and the sanctity of the nuclear family. To tolerate homosexuals becomes a democratic chic. Perhaps this explains why some of the blatantly homophobic bloggers, whose posts I discussed earlier, jumped on the bandwagon and criticized Iranian President Mahmoud Ahmadinejad when he denied the existence of homosexuals in Iran.

Chic of Queer

On September 24, 2007, after I had moved back to Oakland, California, I received a phone call from a blogger friend in Canada who, in a rushed and upset voice, asked, "Did you see the news? Ahmadinejad has messed up [*gand zadeh*]. The bastard said there are no gays in Iran!" This friend, who was also furious about Lee Bollinger's racist response to Ahmadinejad, told me to watch the video of Ahmadinejad speaking at Columbia University. I watched the video, and even though I was no longer blogging, I read several blogs for reactions to Ahmadinejad's speech. Ahmadinejad had become the butt of jokes of many bloggers, including those who had earlier proven themselves to be extremely homophobic. Later that night, I attended a meeting of Iranians who had gathered in Berkeley to provide the U.S. Library of Congress representative with information about the cultural production of the Iranian diaspora. When the representative said that he was going to meet with a queer Iranian group in Los Angeles, people burst into laughter. "But we have no homosexuals in Iran," remarked a participant, mimicking Ahmadinejad. Everyone got the joke, as Ahmadinejad had spoken at Columbia only a few hours before. Being one of the two queer people (or at least the only one who was "out" to most members of that group), I felt the weight of unfamiliar and familiar looks. It was as if at that very moment with that sarcastic utterance, I had received the stamp of authenticity (you are living proof that Ahmadinejad lies!) and at the same time was given an opportunity to participate in a moment of group solidarity: all of a sudden, gay rights had become an issue of concern for all of "us," the intellectual Iranians in diaspora. Defending the queer was suddenly chic, especially when it came to proving the Iranian president wrong.[23]

Even though Ahmadinejad spoke about several issues, what received the most media attention was this comment: "In Iran we don't have homosexuals like in your country," a response to an audience member who had asked about the execution of Iranian homosexuals. Reports with titles such as "Ahmadinejad Says No Gays in Iran" appeared on major news websites, while television networks frantically contacted Iranian queer organizations outside of Iran, seeking to prove the fallacy of Ahmadinejad's widely publicized claim.[24] Diasporic gay Iranians were paraded on television programs, news websites, and YouTube videos to prove that gays do exist in Iran.[25] The obsession with the persecution of homosexuals in Iran is not new. President Khatami was confronted with the same question when speaking at the Kennedy School of Government at Harvard University on September 10, 2006.[26] In fact, the "Gay International" (Massad 2002) has produced representations of Iran as a grand prison and death chamber for queers since the 1979 revolution.[27] Such representations have become even more prolific during the "war on terror," when Iranian queers have become hypervisible in transnational media, especially the internet.[28] "Gays in Iran" or "transgenders in Iran" are topics that increasingly appear in blogs, websites, print, television, internet news, YouTube, international film festivals, and international television programs.

The hypervisibility of Iranian queers in mainstream international media during the war on terror as a pink-washing strategy is neither new nor surprising. However, my interest here is the sudden change in attitude of the Iranian diaspora, especially on the part of opposition groups. Iranian queers, who have historically been denied inclusion in Iranian national imaginaries, are now representable subjects in Iranian diasporic cyberspace. Increasingly, some Iranian human rights organizations, dissidents, and Iranian intellectuals outside of Iran have become preoccupied with defending the rights of hamjinsgaraayaan. Many royalists and leftists who left Iran immediately after the 1979 revolution, as well as a segment of reformists who left Iran after their disillusionment with the reform movement in Iran, have shifted their approach from outright rejection of homosexuality to tolerance. For example, in 2008, Akbar Ganji (a famous reformist dissident) published a series of online articles in Zamaneh and argued that Iranian hamjinsgaraayaan are a minority to be defended.[29]

The change in attitude of diasporic opposition groups toward queers was also reflected in an online statement that was drafted and signed by 171 academics, artists, and activists who condemned laws regarding homosexuality in Iran. The statement pointed out that "in open and democratic societies, the violation of rights and denial of social participation to homosexuals is minimized because of enlightenment, the possibility of assembly for homosexuals and their friends, and the enjoyment of rights and legal backing."[30] An Iranian queer woman in Germany, who had initially signed this statement, later questioned its sincerity and critiqued its patriarchal language after noticing that several signatories were homophobic individuals who appeared to be using the petition as a political tool.[31]

The sudden "tolerance," and even celebration, of Iranian queers among some Iranian diasporic opposition groups is questionable, given that Iranian queers have historically been denied a legitimate space in diasporic imaginations of the nation.[32] How does one account for the *chic of queer*—a recent political position among diaspora Iranian opposition groups who have suddenly decided to advocate on behalf of queers in Iran? I would argue that in addition to the desire to appear modern and democratic, two other factors contribute to this chic of queer among the Iranian diaspora: the "war on terror," which uses internet technologies in its democratization projects, and the discursive shift from "exile" to "diaspora," which is partly caused by increased transnational connectivity (Grewal 2005) between resident and diaspora Iranians. This connectivity that is enabled by internet technologies has produced a sense of unhampered mobility in cyberspace. While the celebrations of movement and borderless frontiers in cyberspace give way to the increased deployment of diaspora as an emblem of unrestricted mobility, glorification of the liberating potentials of the internet constructs cyberspace as a haven for Iranian queers who are awaiting rescue within the liberalizing and civilizational discourses of the "war on terror." In a market where information about human rights abuses in Iran may translate into funding, some segments of the Iranian diaspora seem to be eager to provide expertise and information to think tanks and democratizing states. In this race toward a free and democratic Iran, many opposition groups and individuals compete over offering the most democratic vision for the future of Iran, which includes queers at this historical moment. However, this inclusion or tolerance is restricted to particular forms of representable queer subjectivities, namely those who are complicit with homonationalist (Puar 2007) discourses that legitimize the "war on terror."[33]

From Homoerotics of Exile to Homopolitics of Diaspora

> Now living in a safe country, I still consider myself first and foremost an Iranian. I can never forget that I am in exile due to my own sexual orientation. This situation is both a burden and a tremendous personal responsibility for me. In May 2005, as I crossed the border out of Iran into Turkey I promised myself, my nation and my people that I would one day return to a free, open and democratic Iran. To that end, I promised that I would fully devote my labors toward achieving for myself and my fellow citizens in Iran the treasured dream and desire of so many millions around the globe, and which so many in the West take as for granted as breathing: freedom.
>
> —ARSHAM PARSI

The mainstream international media has deemed Arsham Parsi,[34] founder of the Canadian-based Iranian Railroad for Queer Refugees (IRQR), the "expert" on the persecution of queers in Iran. Before establishing IRQR, which purports to help Iranian queer refugees across the globe, as a nonprofit organization in 2008, Parsi had started two other queer organizations, both of which relied on the internet as a tool of both dissemination and recruitment: in 2001, while still in Iran, the Rainbow Group, a Yahoo! group that consisted of Iranian gay men, and in 2003 the Persian Gay and Lesbian Organization (PGLO), a small group that was registered in Norway. Parsi relocated to Toronto, and in 2006, in collaboration with a group of Iranian Canadian activists, he changed the name of PGLO to the Iranian Queer Organization (IRQO).[35] In 2008, accused of alleged budget mismanagement and misconduct by the board of directors of IRQO, Parsi "fired" the board and left IRQO. Not too long after his dispute with the IRQO board, he formed the Iranian Queer Railroad.

Parsi, who repeats the trope of escaping the home of oppression (Iran) to come to freedom in the "West," has been the center of attention in international mainstream media and cyberspace. So widespread is his fame as the representative of Iranian queers that a Google search with the key words "Iran and queer" produces either articles about Parsi or images of "gay hangings."

Despite his self-promotion as the first Iranian gay activist, there were several diaspora Iranian queer organizations in existence long before Parsi became the poster child of the Iranian queer advocates. Starting in the early 1990s, Iranian diaspora queer groups such as Homan, Hasha, and Iran Shademan held conferences, produced magazines, and provided moral and legal support to Iranian queers who lived inside and outside of Iran. While elided in the few historical accounts about Iranian queers in postrevolutionary Iran, networks such as Homan (the Group to Defend the Rights of Iranian Gays and Lesbians) produced the lexicon that characterizes much of the discourse on homosexuality in Iranian diasporic cultural circuits today.[36]

Two main factors can explain the hypervisibility of PGLO, IRQO, and IRQR in comparison to earlier groups such as Homan: the role of the internet and the activist strategies of new organizations during the "war on terror." The wide reach of the internet—together with Parsi's effective use of email lists, YouTube, and blogs—has given him a much larger audience than that of Homan. In fact, Parsi has claimed that the internet saved his life and enabled him to connect with other queers inside and outside of Iran.[37] The emergence of online Iranian gay and lesbian magazines such as MAHA, *Cheraq*, and *Neda* shows the use of the internet by Iranian LGBTQ groups.[38] In addition, internet-mediated images and information are often picked up by television and radio programs to reach a wider audience than those who have access to the internet.[39]

The hypervisibility of Iranian queers in cyberspace is enabled by the "war on terror," in which Iran has become increasingly demonized in mainstream international media. Despite the emergence of a diasporic Iranian gay/lesbian network soon after the 1979 Iranian revolution, it was only after the "war on terror" and the popularization of the internet that Iranian queers became highly visible. It was in this key political moment that Parsi took advantage of the internet to circulate the preexisting normative notions of sexual identity and hegemonic discourses of oppression in Iran. While representations of Iran as a grand prison for queers are not new or particular to the internet (Homan also portrayed Iran as a "backward" and traditional place, in need of "modernization" and liberation), the broad reach and the fast circulation of images and ideas in cyberspace accelerate and enable mobilizations of identity and politics on a larger scale. This is not to say that the civilizational narratives around homosexuality in Iran (queer-friendly and civilized "West" versus homophobic and backward Iran) are new. In fact, as Moallem (2005b) has argued, civilizational discourses that deemed the sexual practices of Iranians perverse have a colonial history in Iran. However, forms of representation that produced Iran as a grand prison for homosexuals after the 1979 revolution emerged as a part of the knowledge-production apparatus that included international gay and lesbian organizations such as the International Gay and Lesbian Human Rights Commission (IGLHRC), the International Gay and Lesbian Association (ILGA), and Iranian gay and lesbian organizations such as Homan. When George W. Bush announced that Iran belonged to the "axis of evil" after September 11, 2001, these forms of representation escalated significantly.

An example of the way in which Parsi has been instrumental in producing highly sensationalized accounts of gay persecution in Iran is the widely publicized case of the hanging of two young men, Ayaz Marhouni and Mahmoud Asgari. Marhouni and Asgari were hanged on charges of raping a male minor (*lavat beh onf*) in the city of Mashad, on July 19, 2005. While it is unclear if the two young men were "gay," the international media, international gay and lesbian organizations, and diasporic Iranian opposition groups publicized the case widely on the internet, alleging that Marhouni and Asgari were hanged because of their sexual orientation.[40]

Several groups, including the International Gay and Lesbian Human Rights Commission, Human Rights Watch, and Amnesty International, issued statements and disclaimers about the lack of credible information about Marhouni and Asgari's sexuality or the reasons for their execution. Scott Long, a human rights activist with an extended history of working on Iranian cases, argued that the investigations into this case (and similar "gay" cases) are merely based on speculations and are not rooted in any evidence. However, the Human Rights Campaign, the Log Cabin Republicans, and Britain's Outrage!, along with PGLO, insisted that Marhouni and Asgari were executed for being gay. The massive representation of this case as "gay hangings" on the internet was not limited to international gay and lesbian human rights groups but also included Iranian opposition groups in diaspora. In particular, as Scott Long (2009) has argued, the National Council of Resistance of Iran (NCRI)—the political wing of the extremist militant organization *Mujahedin-e Khalq-e Iran* (MKO)—had a crucial role in initiating this claim by mistranslating an online report issued by the Iranian Students News Agency (ISNA).[41] Other diasporic Iranian organizations, including queer ones, also jumped on the bandwagon by circulating inaccurate news about the hangings on the internet, thus representing this case as an example of gay executions in Iran. In fact, many international gay and lesbian organizations claiming that Marhouni and Asgari were gay received their information from PGLO—and, later, IRQO—both of which acted as "authentic" and reliable sources.

On July 19, 2006, the first anniversary of the Mashad hangings, protests were organized internationally, and the main organizers of the protests, Outrage! and IDAHO (International Day against Homophobia), declared July 19 to be the International Day of Action against Homophobic Persecution in Iran (IDAAHOPI).[42] Parsi, the executive director of the IRQO at the time, was the contact person for the Toronto protest. He appeared on several radio and television shows and sent out press releases, claiming that Marhouni and Asgari were arrested at a gay house party. While there were more critical conversations in Persian blogs and on email lists during the international protests against Iran, these accounts did not receive much attention in online and offline media.[43] Doing fieldwork in Washington, DC, at the time of this campaign, I was struck by the life-size poster of Marhouni and Asgari's execution in the window display of a major gay bookstore in Washington's DuPont Circle. The image was also printed on the first page of the *Metro Weekly*, the metropolitan gay newspaper.

Information about the internet-organized worldwide protest was readily available in bookstores, in cafés, and on street corners. I attended the event as a counterprotester and arrived with a blogger friend with signs that questioned the legitimization of imperialism and militarism in the name of Iranian queers. Incidentally, two young recent immigrants from Iran who worked for Voice of America Persian were present at the event to videotape the rally for their news program.[44] Even though the reporters interviewed us, the report of their interview was never aired on VOA Persian. Later, I learned from another blogger who worked for VOA Persian that the supervisors refused to air the report, claiming that it was culturally inappropriate to show a report on homosexuality to an Iranian audience. According to this blogger, who later quit VOA for its undemocratic practices, the managers felt that showing the report would lead viewers to assume that VOA condones homosexuality. Ironically, shortly after this incident, VOA Persian produced several programs about homosexuality in Iran, repeatedly showing images from the Mashad hangings. Gay pundits such as Parsi, who provided the dominant narrative about gay persecution in Iran and freedom in the United States, were frequently invited to speak about the violation of gay rights in Iran.

Voice of America Persian's shift is consistent with the changing attitude toward homosexuality among the Iranian opposition groups in exile. Even

FIGURES 4.1 AND 4.2
"Iran Stop Killing Gays."
Lambda Rising Bookstore,
DuPont Circle, Washington, DC.

as some queers, such as Parsi, identify as exiles in order to emphasize the forced nature of their departure and the pain of alienation from a troubled homophobic homeland, Iranian opposition groups in exile consistently excluded Iranian queers until Bush launched his "war on terror." In 1996 the organizers of the "Conditions of Transition from Religious Jurisprudence to Democracy" conference refused to include or read a statement by Homan.[45] The organizers, who had invited a wide range of opposition groups and individuals in exile, explained to Homan members that they did not want people to assume that "a bunch of faggots had organized this conference."[46] Even though Homan clearly situated itself in opposition to the Islamic state, it was consistently rejected by the opposition forces in exile. *Homan* magazine often included at least one article about the frustration of being rejected by Iranian opposition forces in exile. For example, in an article that embraced orientalist discourses, the editor of the sixteenth issue of *Homan* wrote the following: "The humiliating attitude of all the so-called opposition forces towards the oppression of gays and lesbians is owing to these groups' incomplete and partial understanding of human rights. It also shows their lack of concern about freedom, the individual's right to life, and democracy.... They continue to lounge in their Eastern and Asian traditions. Traditionalists and cowards, who choose such non-offensive politics, cannot be called the opposition to the Islamic Republic.... They squirm in the collective swamp of ignorance of the Third World."[47]

The resentment toward Iranian opposition groups in *Homan* magazine was mainly a result of the heteronormative imaginations of nation and exile among these groups. The idealized and romanticized *qorbat* (exile) often connotes a painful separation from the homeland, the loss of which, more often than not, is accompanied by imaginations of an idealized original home, mourned and fetishized in nostalgic remembrances. In the Iranian exilic discourse, the importance of nuclear family is emphasized to construct "homeland" as inherently heterosexual. This heterosexualization of homeland, however, does not translate into a complete rejection of homosexuality. Home as a lived space in "exile" flirts with a foreign queerness through jokes about homosexuality outside of Iran.[48] While these flirtations construct an image of the perverted "West," they also create an innocent heterosexual homeland, one that disavows any possibility of homoerotic desire in Iran. This *homoerotics of exile*—the disavowal of homoeroticism in exile versus a heterosexualized imagination of homeland—becomes necessary in imagining a coherent heterosexual nation and a fixed homeland.

However, this exilic discourse has increasingly faded over the past three decades, and *diaspora* has come to replace the older deployments of *exile*—a shift that has ironically enabled the representability of exilic gay subjects such as Parsi. This shift may have to do with the emergence of a newer generation of Iranians outside of Iran who do not share their parents' sentiments of exile. Unlike the earlier generation of self-identified exiles who left Iran in the aftermath of the 1979 revolution, the Iranian diaspora includes a younger generation of internet-savvy Iranians who may not share their parents' dogmatic sentiments. The shift to using the term *diaspora* could also be a result of the immigration of a large number of Iranians during the eight-year war with Iraq, the increased mobility of Iranians after the end of war, and the immigration of a group of educated and internet-literate Iranian professionals who left Iran in the late 1990s and early 2000s, partly because of disillusionment with the reformist government. Changes in the sociopolitical fabric of the nation-state after the rise of the reform movement have affected the way that Iranian diaspora communities relate to the "homeland" by increasingly engaging in its politics via communication technologies, capital investments, and travel to Iran. In addition, the Iranian diaspora's increased ability to exchange information in cyberspace has heightened feelings of mobility, multilocationality, and border crossing. Unlike the generation of Iranian exiles (be they ultranationalists, royalists, or some leftists) whose forced departure immediately after the Iranian revolution encouraged their fixed imaginations of Iran's politics and culture, the Iranian diaspora is seemingly more receptive and tolerant toward queers.

But the tolerance of homosexuality in Weblogistan and among the diaspora opposition groups also owes its emergence to the "war on terror," when civilizational thinking (Moallem 2005a), coupled with a neoliberal market economy, produced individual self-entrepreneurs (Brown 2003). As I argue in the next chapter, one cannot ignore the ambitions of some diaspora Iranians who take advantage of this particular moment when knowledge production about the Middle East creates opportunities for neoliberal self-entrepreneurship and "expertise." In a competition over "democratization," defending the rights of women and queers reflects aspirations for becoming exceptional subjects and likely candidates to receive funding from liberation projects.

All of the above factors may have not only contributed to the inclusion of queers in some opposition groups' imagination of Iranianness but also to their hypervisibility as victims of the Iranian state's homophobic policies. In a sense, there has been a shift from the *homoerotics* of exile to the *homopolitics* of diaspora, where the Iranian homosexual is transferred from the position of the lowly abject to that of the representable political subject in transnational realms. The shift to homopolitics not only involves Iranian opposition groups but also a select number of Iranian diasporic queers who have historically been excluded from the heteronormative imaginations of the nation and thus willingly take the opportunity to insert themselves into national imaginations in diasporic re-territorializations. In this process, while the modern heteronormative binaries of gender and sexuality are reified, the exceptional Iranian homosexual is produced and deployed as the marker of freedom in civilizational discourses and practices that divide the world into binaries of liberated/repressed, free/unfree, and democratic/theocratic. Testimonials by a few gay informants become necessary for a counternarrative to Ahmadinejad's statement about the absence of homosexuals in Iran. As such, "outness" through dissemination of testimonials and images via the internet becomes the condition of being and belonging to the nationalist imaginations of diaspora Iranian opposition groups that deploy human rights discourses, in what some Iranians humorously have called "*dokoon-e hoghoogh-e bashar*" ("the human rights shop").

Conclusion: Queer Death

While nationalist discourses in Weblogistan continued to produce and normalize a heteronormative Iranianness, homosexuality, transsexuality, and queerness as hot topics of discussion increasingly appeared in Weblogistan and, later, in the Iranian diasporic media and social networks. For example, in 2007 Farid Haerinejad, the Canadian Broadcasting Company (CBC) producer who made the award-winning film *Blogger's War* (see chapter 5), made another sensationalizing CBC film titled *Inside Iran's Secret Gay World*. After leaving the CBC in 2009, Haerinejad acted as the editor in chief of Radio Zamaneh, and in 2012 he became the Iran project manager for the International Gay and Lesbian Human Rights Commission (IGLHRC). IGLHRC has produced many publications in Persian, including a guide for language that the journalists should use in covering queer and trans issues. In 2014, a Toronto-based blogger who later worked as a contractor with different Iranian diasporic media such as Radio Zamaneh, and as an independent researcher for the International Gay and Lesbian Human Rights Commission (now OutRight Action International), gave an hour-long webinar in Persian about the proper language to use in reporting about queer and transgender issues for journalists at Radio Zamaneh.[49] In 2013 Haerinejad made a film for Radio Zamaneh about Iranian queer and transgender refugees titled *Out of Iran: Iran's Unwanted Sons and Daughters.*[50] While these attempts in fighting homophobia and transphobia in the "Iranian culture" are admirable, they become complicit in homonationalist discourses that constitute queerness as the yardstick for the normalization of perverse populations that are marked as exceptionally homophobic and transphobic. This logic, which normalizes certain queers through folding them into life, simultaneously produces, to borrow from Puar, "queerly racialized" (2007, xii) populations that are destined to die. In other words, the hypervisibility of the queer or trans Iranian as victim to be saved is inevitably implicated in biopolitical, ethicopolitical, and necropolitical practices that underlie the division of populations into those who are exceptionally deserving of life, those who are marked as risk populations and live a precarious life, and those who are deemed killable.

Perhaps one of the most salient examples of the paradoxical relationship between visibility and necropolitics is that of queer suicide. In July 2008, shortly after my fieldwork, I returned to Toronto to attend the Iranian Studies conference. On the first day of the conference, I learned from a friend that Sayeh (Atrian), an Iranian transgender woman, had quietly taken her life in her subsidized Toronto apartment a few days before. Sayeh, who had lived under dire conditions in Turkey for more than a year while waiting for the United Nations High Commissioner for Refugees (UNHCR) to process her refugee case, had become disillusioned with the promise of a better life in Canada and was unable to afford to go back to Iran. While in Turkey, in an interview with the Iranian Queer Organization, Sayeh had said, "My life is not like a cigarette that you can smoke and then put away, as I will live and suffer in its ashes. We are (we live). The world has a forgettable mind, and I will be forgotten very quickly. I might get to Canada, or I might not. But I will never forget that all my rights were taken away from me and there are even no selected individuals who I can blame for this. From now on, I want to build my life."[51] Sayeh was the subject of several documentary films (such as *Be Like Others, Birthday,* and *I Know That I Am*) about transgender life in Iran. Screened at international film festivals, distributed through YouTube, or broadcast on television outside Iran, most of these films juxtapose a repressed life in Iran to a free life in North America and Europe. In most of these films, the suffering of working-class Iranian transgender women, who are ostracized by their families and subjected to social discrimination, is showcased, rendering it visible to the mostly non-Iranian audience. Sayeh's statement "I know that I am" became the title of an award-winning Canadian documentary film that represents transgender Iranians as victims of a fundamentalist state and in need of rescue by the "free world." The film repeats a narrative that Anne-Marie Fortier has aptly called "queer homecoming": the familiar story of queer flight from the home of oppression to seek refuge in the home of freedom in "West." Through documentary-style testimonials and the juxtaposition of words and images, the film creates a stark opposition between freedom in Canada and oppression in Iran. This narrative style is very prominent in the promotional video of the film.[52] While transgender Iranians are portrayed as powerless victims, in a slow-motion caption the white Canadian immigration attorney is literally depicted as a saintlike figure whose image is juxtaposed to subtitled lyrics that interpellate her as a "savior angel." Not surprisingly, the image of a cleric is accompanied with lyrics that construct him as the unsympathetic enemy. Ironically, Hojjatt-al-Islam Karimnia, the cleric depicted in this film, is a religious transgender-rights advocate and has played a key role in removing the stigma around sex change by arguing that sex-reassignment surgeries are religiously sanctioned. While Sayeh's life in Iran and Turkey was of immense interest to many filmmakers, her death in Canada did not get any coverage.[53] It wasn't until two years after her death that that ILGA and an Iranian queer diaspora organization finally wrote about her death, misrepresenting her gender and ignoring the hardship that she experienced in Canada.[54] On July 31, 2008, almost two weeks after Sayeh's death, the codirector of the film *I Know That I Am* wrote on his blog that "I would like to take this opportunity to share with all my good friends the good news of a first prize Audience Award for the documentary, I Know that I Am."[55] Ironically, the director did not acknowledge that Sayeh, the transgender woman whose life was the subject of the film and whose utterance of "I know that I am" had inspired its title, no longer was.

The silence around the suicides of several Iranian queer and transgender refugees in cosmopolitan gay destinations stands in stark opposition to the hypervisibility of deaths of queer and transgender individuals in Iran. The unspeakability of Sayeh's death and the hypervisibility of Ayaz and Mahmoud's deaths point to the economy of queer death in relation to biopolitics and necropolitics. The representability of some queer deaths and the unspeakability of others complicate biopolitics and necropolitics, pointing to the killability of loaned lives that are simultaneously imbued with and stripped of liberal universal rights—lives that are subjected to the politics of rightful killing. The biopolitical and necropolitical significance of these representations (the silent "victim" death and the hypervisible "barbaric" death) becomes even more pronounced when one compares them to the heroic death of exceptional gay subjects. As Puar and Rai (2002) have observed, immediately after the September 11, 2001, attacks, one of the most publicized stories in the mainstream media was that of Mark Bingham, a successful gay white businessman with a bicoastal firm who lost his life as he allegedly thwarted the plan of the hijackers to crash a plane into the White House. While the hypervisibility of the post-9/11 American nationalism emphasized the heteronormativity of the nation through images, language, and nationalist practices, queer forms of American nationalism had an overarching presence in gay and lesbian websites. As multicultural America hindered the exclusion of racialized and gendered sexualities through the myth of equality, it reified the sovereignty of the figure of the exceptional citizen subject versus its victimized Muslim queer. The willing American queer subjects who were historically excluded from the realms of the "normal" exercised belonging to the national culture through performances of normative citizenship and against the figure of the dangerous terrorist or the victimized refugee. The events of September 11 provided an opportunity for American queers to insert themselves into the imaginations of the nation, thus becoming exceptional citizens in a moment of crisis when particular forms of queerness became tolerable and even encouraged in the American nationalist discourse.

Bingham's hypermasculinity became an ideal to which the exceptional queer was expected to aspire (Shakhsari 2012). After September 11, coming out to honor Bingham became a patriotic act that designated a spatial and temporal division within a Manichaean logic, wherein the United States signified freedom/democracy/progress and the Muslim world stood for homophobia/gay oppression/backwardness. In this dual field of signification, the exceptional American queer citizen as protector (of the nation) and protected (from the Muslim enemy) was constructed through difference and commonality against the figure of the victimized Muslim queer. As Minoo Moallem argues, "The barbaric other is there to legitimize and give meaning to the masculine militarism of the 'civilized' and his constant need to protect. Protection enables an alliance between the protector and the protected against a common foe" (2002, 300). The common foe to the heterosexually imagined American nation, the homogeneously imagined visible gay subject, and the victimized queer refugee continues to be the barbaric and homophobic Muslim, whose racial queerness makes him disposable.

While technologies of normalization subject the *individual* to the management of life and death through biopower, as Foucault has argued, it is the *population* that is the target of the art of governmentality through biopolitics, where the management of the life of one is inevitably connected to the death of another. During the "war on terror," hegemonic representational practices not only produce universalized sexual identities that are mobilized according to the logic of U.S. homonationalism (Puar 2007), but they also contribute to the management of the life and death of entire populations. If, as I have argued earlier, the Iranian population at large is subjected to the politics of rightful killing, how does the Iranian transgender refugee figure in the state of normalcy that characterizes the "war on terror"? Here, Agamben's (1998) argument that declarations of rights presuppose man as the natural bearer of rights and a citizen, thus bringing together the biological and the political and making the bare life central to politics in modernity, is instructive. If, as Agamben argues, camp is the nomos of modernity where the state of exception becomes the rule of law, the transgender refugee as a paradigmatic figure of *homo sacer* further complicates the naturalness of rights and the link between the biological and the political. Camp as the state of exception signifies both the body in excess and the location that one occupies as a refugee and as such can highlight the limitation of rights associated with the converged notions of natural and political. Shuttling between life and death, the transgender refugee is caught between biopolitics and necropolitics, where her body is produced and managed through religious, medical, psychological, and geopolitical discourses, and her death is sanctioned in the state of exception as a refugee (outside the nation-state) and transgender (outside the naturalized binaries of sex). Just as the insistence on revealing the truth of her gender/sex is necessary to the maintenance of norms of gender and sexuality—because the transgender body's ambiguity translates into deception and concealment of the truth of one's sex and gender (Beauchamp 2009)—the insistence on visibility and testimonies of oppression becomes necessary to the civilizational narratives of queer oppression in Iran and liberation in North America and Europe. It is in this context that the Iranian transgender refugee is at once politicized as a victim of backward homophobia and depoliticized as *homo sacer*: one whose life is disposable once it loses value in neoliberal economies and geopolitical discourses. This is not to assume the exceptional victimhood of the transgender Iranian but to point to the way that the figure of the risky citizen as para-human is necessarily produced as a hypervisible victim. Victimhood is not only the condition of representation but also the condition of life itself. Yet victimhood is not absolute: the risky citizen as victim can at any point become a burden to the neoliberal economy or a threat to the security of the nation. That is when the Muslim enemy and the risky queer, who once epitomized victimhood as opposed to the Muslim terrorist, become indistinguishable and interchangeable. Until then and forgotten at death, the Iranian queer and transgender victim's testimony (as a condition of life) becomes a valued commodity for diaspora entrepreneurs, in a market where information about human rights abuses in Iran may translate into funding by think tanks, democratizing states, and the human rights regimes.

[5]

The War Machine, Neoliberal *Homo Œconomicus*, and the Experts

On May 16, 2006, while conducting fieldwork in Washington, DC, I attended a press conference across from the U.S. Capitol Building that was organized by Ghazal Omid, the author of *Living in Hell: A True Odyssey of a Woman's Struggle in Islamic Iran against Personal and Political Forces* (2004). Omid—who had immigrated to Canada in 1995—had heard that the U.S. Department of State was funding Iranian civil society groups and hoped to receive funding for an organization that would educate Iranian women.[1] In her press conference Omid portrayed Iranian women as traditional and oppressed victims of a savage Iranian patriarchy who are forced into arranged marriages and raped by their kin. These men rob Iranian women of any agency, she claimed. Omid added that "the Iranian woman" (*zan-e Irani*) needs to be educated in order to realize her rights as an individual. After the press conference, I approached Omid and introduced myself as a researcher. I told her that her account of women in Iran was significantly exaggerated and inaccurate. I asked her if she knew about women's-rights activism and scholarship in Iran and, if so, why she didn't talk about those issues in her press conference. Realizing that I was not a media representative who would give her publicity, she stood up to signal the end of our interview and said impatiently, "*Azizam* [darling], you cannot be a good businesswoman or a politician if you are this ethical."

Omid's shockingly honest statement about the economic gains of political participation through providing expertise is an example of the deployment of women's rights during the "war on terror," when "liberation" projects are delivered not only through direct military intervention but also through the participation of diaspora self-entrepreneurs who provide expertise in the democratization market. Weblogistan was not exempt from the competition to provide information in this lucrative market. As I discussed in the introduction, during the "war on terror," and especially in the first decade of the twenty-first century, Persian blogs received notable attention from think tanks, policy institutes, and diaspora opposition organizations. Not surprisingly, some bloggers tapped into the funding opportunities that the "war on terror" created for Iranians in Iran and its diaspora. In this chapter I argue that discourses of militarism and neoliberalism interpellated the *representable* Iranian blogger as a neoliberal *homo œconomicus* who became militarized as a "soldier of freedom" in the market for information during the "war on terror."[2] While being subjected to hate crimes and anti-immigrant laws, some diaspora Iranian bloggers took advantage of the opportunities provided during the hype of Persian blogging in the aftermath of September 11, 2001, to market themselves as sources of valuable information. These opportunities, which were enabled by the need for "expertise," testimonials, and staffing for the private and governmental security industries and propaganda services, offered upward mobility, awards, career options, and at times immigration and visas to Europe and North America. At the end of the chapter, I illustrate that despite being a self-entrepreneur and an expert informant, the Iranian diasporic blogger as *homo œconomicus* can become disposable when social solidarity is replaced with neoliberal self-interest.

Blogger Entrepreneurship

Since its emergence, blogging has increasingly been used as a source of revenue.[3] During my years as a blogger, entrepreneurship took different forms in Weblogistan, including the posting of commercial advertisements. Popular bloggers whose blogs were visited in large numbers could generate income by posting advertisements on their blogs. Some of the bloggers I interviewed obsessively tracked the "counter" on their blogs and bragged about their readership. For example, at the end of my interview with Nikahang Kowsar, I asked him if there was anything else that he wanted to talk about. He enthusiastically told me to ask him about the number of visitors.

NK: "Ask me how many visitors I get a day!"

SS: Tell me!

NK: "Five thousand hits a day!" (smiles victoriously)

Barely disguising his happiness, he waved his hand in a nonchalant manner, as if to curb his enthusiasm: "I don't even check my counter. I don't care about the hits!"[4] Kowsar had become a popular blogger because of his satire, his cartoons, and his memoir-style posts about the world of journalism in Iran. He began when Hoder encouraged him to start a blog and promised to help him construct it, using Moveable Type, in exchange for the proceeds from advertisements on Kowsar's blog. Once Kowsar realized that he could use ready-made templates, he refused Hoder's offer. Hoder encouraged many of his friends to start blogging in 2001 in order to popularize blogs among Iranians. Not too long after Hoder made a Persian template available to the Persian-speaking public, he gained popularity in online democratization projects that deemed him an expert on Iranian politics.

Not only did the popularity of a blog signify social capital; it also granted the blogger opportunities for employment in venues that were funded by various democratization projects. While posting advertisements was a form of entrepreneurship for some bloggers, my interest here involves the promotion of Persian blogging as a revolutionary phenomenon in the market for information during the "war on terror." That said, even as I suggest that blogger self-entrepreneurship became possible because of the opportunities that the war on terror provided, I consider complicity and co-optation to be inevitable for many diasporic subjects whose survival is contingent on their successful integration into the norms of the nation-state and the neoliberal market. Therefore, I do not want to suggest that the bloggers in the discussion to follow were indifferent about the people of Iran or were knowingly complicit with the war machine. The war on terror, the emphasis on security, and the attendant criminalization compel those who are caught between "homeland" and "destination" to make "rational choices" as responsible individuals in a militarized neoliberal market that enshrines freedom. While some prioritize self-interest at any cost (even to the point of offering a show of support for the bombing of Iran), others make choices to market information about Iran from a deep desire for freedom in the homeland, even if this desire is often articulated in terms that reify the heteronormalization of the homeland and its future. In the discussion to follow I examine three cases that illustrate a group of diasporic bloggers pitching Weblogistan as a liberalizing site, worthy of investment for governmental and nongovernmental entities that have been involved in democratization projects: *Blogger's War*, a documentary about Weblogistan that features several famous Iranian bloggers in Toronto; Radio Zamaneh, a Dutch government–funded website and radio broadcaster, which started its activity as the radio of Weblogistan and has become one of the most popular Persian media outlets; and the Votes, Bits, and Bytes Conference at Harvard University's Berkman Center for Internet and Society, where Hoder, a famous Toronto-based blogger who was hailed as the "godfather of Weblogistan," was featured as an expert in the "Global Voices" segment of the conference.

Weblogistan Goes to War

Shortly before the 2005 Iranian presidential election, the Canadian Broadcasting Corporation (CBC) aired *Blogger's War*, Farid Haerinejad's documentary about Iranian bloggers in Canada and Iran who oppose the Islamic Republic of Iran.[5] From the beginning, *Blogger's War* reproduces the binary geopolitics of freedom in the "West" and oppression in Iran: "There are those who are fighting a very different kind of hi-tech battle against Iran's repressive regime, and these revolutionaries are launching their fight from right here in Canada. . . . They're reaching millions of Iranians; they believe they can do what no one else has done: bring democracy to Iran. It's called the Blogger's War, and this is how Nikahang Kowsar became one of the generals" (*Blogger's War*). The narrator then marks the beginning of this "war" with a 2000 controversy in which Kowsar, a cartoonist for one of Iran's newspapers, sketched a conservative clergyman (Mesbah Yazdi) and mocked his claims about reformist journalists' having received money from the CIA. The film includes images of angry protesters, giving the impression that there were widespread riots in the aftermath of the cartoon. The narrator also tells the audience that "that little cartoon forced Kowsar to flee to Canada."

The story that Kowsar told me during my interview was slightly different. In 2005 I met with him several times to talk about his blog, his past, his reasons for migration, and his experience in prison. Kowsar, who came to Canada in 2003, was imprisoned for six days in 2000 after publishing the Mesbah Yazdi cartoon in a newspaper in Tehran. He told me that he was released from prison because of his father's connections to *kalleh gondeh* (big shots/influential) people.[6] While the narrator of *Blogger's War* leads viewers to think that "that little cartoon forced Kowsar to flee to Canada," my interview with him indicates that he actually did not "flee" Iran. He stayed in Iran for three years, and when he left, he did so with the full knowledge of the Iranian state. The Iranian Embassy in Ottawa had organized a cartoon exhibition in 2003 in response to the American invasion of Iraq. Kowsar told me with an impish grin that "I asked them [the Iranian Embassy in Canada] to organize an exhibition for me during this conference, so that I could defend Islam outside of Iran."[7] This was not the only time that Kowsar had left Iran after his arrest in 2000. He had traveled to Canada in 2001 to receive the "Courage for Editorial Cartooning" award from the Cartoonists Rights Network in Canada. In 2003, however, despite his wife's objection, he decided to stay in Canada and apply for asylum, as he felt that his life was in danger in Iran.

The manner in which Kowsar's story is told in *Blogger's War* repeats the civilizational tropes that represent refugees as those who flee violence in the "Third World" to come to the safety of the "first world." Exploring the refugee discourse in Canada, Sherene Razack (1998, 99) argues that the gendered imperial stories in asylum cases reconsolidate the "racist notion of the first world helping the third world out of barbarism and social chaos." Yet despite the fact that most refugee movements take place between neighboring nation-states in the "third world," the "south-north" narrative is the prevalent representation of refugee discourse. *Blogger's War*, with its testimonial-style interview with Kowsar and other bloggers, participates in this civilizational narrative. The anchor reminds the teary-eyed Kowsar, who is upset about leaving his daughter behind and coming to Canada to work as a blue-collar worker (as opposed to his prestigious job in Iran), that he is safe and free in Canada. It is as though the requirement to tell the story of flight from Iran as the home of oppression to Canada as the home of liberation is inextricably tied to a refugee's claim to legitimacy of presence in Canada.

In *Blogger's War*, the anchor tells us that upon his arrival in Canada, Kowsar finds "something revolutionary: an internet-based underground movement that's fighting back against the mullahs of Iran." By hailing bloggers as participants in an "underground" movement, the documentary misleadingly portrays Persian blogging as a subversive act in an organized movement that is actively working to overthrow the Iranian state. Bloggers who wrote about their day-to-day activities or those who frequented Iran and lived in Canada are portrayed as revolutionaries whose lives were in danger in Iran.

While there were bloggers who explicitly favored regime change in Iran, many did not. Indeed, none of the bloggers whom I interviewed in Washington, DC, and Toronto, including those who participated in the CBC documentary, expressed any desire for regime change.[8] In their blogs and interviews, Nazli Kamvari (the only woman included in *Blogger's War*) and Bahman Kalbasi, a former student activist who is hailed by the narrator as a "revolutionary," explicitly opposed regime change: they considered that concept to be neoconservative. Even Kowsar, who had boycotted the 2005 presidential election, was against regime change, for the term often connoted foreign intervention through military action or "velvet revolutions." Indeed, it was not necessarily the Iranian "regime" that Kowsar attacked in his memoir-like blog posts. As I argued in previous chapters, Kowsar's attacks often targeted women journalists, reformists, feminists, and Iranian queers, whom he accused of moral and sexual misconduct.

Bloggers' decisions to participation in mainstream projects about Weblogistan cannot be reduced to regime change. Some took part simply because they were approached by a friend who asked them to participate as a personal favor (this was the case with at least one person in *Blogger's War*). For others, getting paid for writing reports or "starring" in films was a strong motivation.[9] Because many bloggers took pleasure in the social capital that came with a large readership, they participated in mainstream media's programming in order to boost the number of hits on their blogs. The increased traffic, which showed in bloggers' statistical reports, could potentially provide opportunities for entrepreneurship. For example, with the producer's help, one of the bloggers in the documentary who had no prior experience in journalism was hired by the CBC and later moved on to become a well-known BBC reporter. The producer of *Blogger's War* continued to make other sensationalized films on Iranian queers, Iranian transgender people, and stoning, hot topics that won him awards, promotion, and job opportunities with other diasporic media such as Zamaneh.[10]

The Politics of Representation and Gendered Soldiers: Toppling the Regime with the Regime of Sex

Like many representations of war, *Blogger's War* offers a highly gendered account of its subjects. While Kowsar is called the "general" of the war for freedom and Kalbasi, a former student who was imprisoned in Iran, is called "revolutionary," Kamvari, the only woman among the group of six bloggers included in this documentary, is hailed as a "taboo breaker." In response to the interviewer's question about the content of her blog, Kamvari says, "I break taboos. . . . I write about sex. I have had premarital sex." It is this discourse about sex that separates the liberated Iranian woman who owes her liberation to Canada from her "repressed" counterpart in Iran. If the masculine soldier takes freedom to Iran through his active participation in proper politics (enabled by his freedom of speech in Canada), the woman blogger finds freedom of expression in writing about sex and telling the truth of her sex in a confessional mode. Ironically, in its account of this war over freedom of speech, *Blogger's War* itself practiced a form of censorship through selective editing. Kamvari told me that "'I write about sex' was not all that I said. I said so many things that were kindly edited out. The final version was a two-minute controversial sexy sex theme thing."[11]

Not surprisingly, *Blogger's War* reproduces a gendered binary that positions men (assumed to be heterosexual) as agents of politics and women (also imagined to be heterosexual) as subjects of sexual liberation. While this film highlights Kamvari's sexual life, it is silent about the sexuality of male bloggers. Even though one of the men in this film is openly gay, it is his political participation and not his sexuality that is discussed in this film. Gay men were represented, of course, in CBC's later film, *Out in Iran: Iran's Secret Gay World*. In both films, women (represented as victims in need of liberation) and queers (also represented as victims and mostly as cis men) can enter the realm of politics only through confessions about their sexuality.

Even as the only subject position available to Kamvari in this video is her role as a sexually repressed woman who finds liberation through blogging in Canada, her participation in Weblogistan goes beyond this selective and popular representation. *Blogger's War* was broadcast just as the 2005 presidential election in Iran was approaching. As I showed in the previous chapters, Kamvari enthusiastically encouraged people to vote and publicly announced that she would vote for the reformist candidate, Moeen. As a result, like many other women bloggers who encouraged others to vote, she became the target of attacks by those who boycotted the presidential election. As I discussed in chapter 2, such attacks illustrate that while men's participation in the political field is deemed to be natural, women's participation is caught between nationalistic discourses of protection and honor and the neoliberal discourses of liberation from local repression. It is in this war of representation that women negotiate their subjectivity while shuttling in and out of local and global politics as both subjects of politics (markers of sexual freedom and oppression) and political abjects (not worthy of political participation).

The main character of *Blogger's War*, Kowsar, is portrayed as a hero who has made a sacrifice by leaving his family and homeland behind to fight for freedom. Kowsar hoped to sell his company and have his wife and daughter follow him to Canada. Kowsar's wife, a manager in his company, refused to sell their house in Iran and decided to stay and run the company on her own, using her income and his share of the company to pay for their mortgage. Kowsar, who seemed to be extremely unhappy about his wife's decision, jokingly said that "the moral lesson is not to include your wife in your house title." Kowsar's resentment toward his wife seemed to be rooted in his sense of shame in losing his status as breadwinner, a grievance that he connected to his downward mobility (working initially in the service industry and living with a family member) and refugee status in Canada.[12]

On his blog, *The Letters of an Iranian Exile*, Kowsar downplayed his refugee status and emphasized his identity as an *exile*. Kowsar expressed to me that he did not like to identify as a refugee, a category that he saw as signifying weakness. His complaint about his wife's decision, his refusal to identify as a refugee (*panaahandeh*), and his insistence on identifying as an exile (*tab'eedee*) point to his anxieties of emasculation as a refugee. Kowsar's refusal to identify as a refugee rather than an exile highlights the gendered connotations of these terms. While "exile" is associated with a cosmopolitan masculine individual who often suffers from the pain of alienation (Gilroy 1999, 294), the feminized "refugee" connotes vulnerability and need of outside protection. Despite Kowsar's self-representation in *Blogger's War* as a hero who makes sacrifices by giving up his home, his family, and his job to fight for freedom from afar, his hypermasculine blog posts seemed to be strategies of self-making in Weblogistan, where participation in homeland politics recuperated his masculinity as an exilic subject who refused association with the vulnerabilities of being a refugee.[13]

Kowsar's popularity in Weblogistan and his connections to other Iranians who had left Iran during Khatami's presidency helped him with employment opportunities. For example, he joined a group of diaspora Iranians that were working on launching a satellite television network in Persian. That group included many powerful "exiles": a former journalist, a former Iranian president's consultant, a former employee of the ministry of guidance, and a senior fellow for the Washington Institute for Near East Policy in Washington, DC. The group asked for and received a substantial amount of funding from the

European Union for its project.¹⁴ The circumstances were ripe for the proposal, partly because Farah Karimi, an anti-Islamic Republic diaspora Iranian, was a member of the Dutch Parliament at the time. The project, which according to Kowsar got 150 votes from the Parliament, passed with no opposition and received fifteen million euros. Kowsar told me that because launching the television network was so laborious, the group decided to start with a website called Rooz Online.

Rooz Online was not the only job opportunity that Kowsar's blog and his experience as a cartoonist afforded him. He had also been approached by a U.S.-based Iranian opposition group that had received funding from the U.S. Department of State to start a website. While he refused to disclose the name of the organization, Kowsar told me that he rejected the proposal. He also rejected offers by Voice of America and Radio Farda, for he believed that being hired by the U.S. Department of State–funded media would have been detrimental to the well-being of his wife and daughter, who at that time were still living in Iran. "*Estekhareh kardam bad oomad*" ("I consulted the Qur'an, and it wasn't auspicious"), he told me.¹⁵

Radio Zamaneh: Timely Entrepreneurship

Radio Zamaneh, a Dutch government–funded radio and website that initially started its programming as "the radio of Weblogistan," provided yet another job opportunity for Kowsar and several other bloggers who took advantage of the emerging funding sources. Radio Zamaneh introduced itself in its inaugural press release as attempting to tap into the energy and voices of the Iranian blogosphere: "Radio Zamaneh intends to increase and intensify working relations with online bloggers. This strategy is based on the observation that the Iranian blog sphere is an active web community which is considered 'the preserve of young urban Iranians both inside and outside the country.' Through its own website, Radio Zamaneh serves as a platform for Iranian bloggers, hoping to reflect and disseminate their opinions and ideas for social change."¹⁶ As such, Radio Zamaneh's focus on bloggers was a result of the widespread assumption that blogs crystallized the revolutionary potential of young Iranians in Iran and its diaspora.

The funding for Radio Zamaneh was handled by Press Now, an NGO project of the Royal Tropical Institute (KIT), based in Amsterdam.¹⁷ Because the Iranian state had cracked down on foreign investment, receiving funds directly from a foreign government was not an option. To circumvent this hurdle, several organizations in Iran received funding from the Dutch government through "middleman" NGOs. Press Now and Hivos were two such organizations that either provided training for Iranian journalists and women's-rights activists in Iran or provided funding for Iranian diasporic media projects such as Radio Zamaneh and Rooz Online. According to Press Now, "On the basis of an amendment by the Dutch Parliament for substantial support of free media for Iranians in 2004, the Dutch government agreed to fund a selection of new media initiatives by Iranian journalists. Radio Zamaneh was one of these initiatives."[18] It was proposed to the Dutch Parliament by Mehdi Jami, a blogger who lived in the United Kingdom at the time and who had previous journalism experience with the BBC.[19] Jami told me that he started writing the plan for Radio Zamaneh in April 2006 and submitted it to the Dutch government the next month. The plan was approved for funding by June 2006, with Radio Zamaneh and *Shahrzad News* receiving most of the earmarked funding available through Press Now. During my fieldwork in Amsterdam, as I spent long hours at Radio Zamaneh, I met a researcher who had been directed by the Dutch government to investigate and assess the success of Radio Zamaneh. He told me that Jami was fortunate to be the only one to come up with a viable project.

Jami interviewed several blogger/journalists from Iran in Turkey, hired some, secured their work visas, and trained them in the Netherlands. Many of the staff I interviewed had no previous radio experience but were journalists in the reformist Iranian newspapers such as *Shargh*. Jami also selected a group of thirty bloggers and journalists from the United States, Europe, and Canada to attend the training session in the Netherlands. Most of the staff, from across the globe, were hired as contract workers. At the time of my fieldwork, fewer than fifteen people worked full-time in Radio Zamaneh's office in Amsterdam. Rather than having an open hiring process, Jami invited and hired the bloggers and journalists whom he thought were suitable for the job. Despite the initial criticism of and accusations of nepotism against Zamaneh, it turned out to be a popular website and radio broadcaster. It was one of the few reliable diasporic media stations that seemed to be less sensationalizing than opposition media such as Voice of America. From the beginning, Jami announced that he was more interested in social issues than state-related politics. He told me that the funders always had an unspoken expectation that Zamaneh would take particular political positions (i.e., against the Iranian state) but that its focus on social issues rather than state politics might have created dissatisfaction among certain conservative Dutch Parliament members and extremist Iranian opposition groups who believed that Zamaneh was not sufficiently critical of the Iranian regime.

Because Zamaneh was Jami's brainchild, some staff jokingly referred to it as "Radio Mehdi," commenting on the way that he controlled every aspect of the operation. Jami viewed the staff of Zamaneh as a "family," which meant that they had regular social gatherings and were expected to work beyond their paid hours. One night, over drinks with Jami and some Zamaneh staff after a long day of work, I took the opportunity to voice a concern that I had heard from several people at Zamaneh: in his quest for human rights and democracy, Jami might be violating the rights of his overworked staff.[20] My comment, which was posed as a lighthearted "teasing" remark, received several nods. As a "guest" (and not a paid employee), I was able to ask this question without being concerned about the consequences. However, the staff remained silent during this exchange and smiled while sipping their beer. Not amused by my comment, Jami responded that Zamaneh was a family and operated according to the traditions of the Iranian family. Like a family business, Jami claimed, working beyond regular hours should not be judged according to formal "Western" concepts. The irony of this response was not lost on me or on the Zamaneh staff. Jami, who frequently criticized "traditional" Iranians for not learning to be "modern" (see chapters 3 and 4), was defending his labor practices by invoking tradition. While there were tensions between Jami and some staff, his social skills and his age helped him push the logic of family and belonging. In his role as patriarch of Zamaneh, Jami used affective bonds as a business strategy.

In 2008, immediately after Jami returned from a fund-raising trip to Canada, the board of directors of Radio Zamaneh fired him on charges of mismanagement and budget deficits. When I visited Zamaneh in 2007, I learned that Jami had been having regular meetings with Press Now and the members of the board of directors, and was actively lobbying the Dutch Parliament to extend Zamaneh's budget. While he did not receive full funding from the Dutch government, he negotiated a budget for three years. Almost a year after being fired, Jami told me that the budget deficit of approximately 250,000 euros in the first two years could hardly be a legitimate reason for his dismissal, as the deficit amounted to less than 4 percent of his total budget. He planned to close the budget gap by reducing expenses (such as through cuts in salaries) and fund-raising. Jami told me that he was open to receiving money from any state but Iran. He attempted to generate funds by appealing to Canadian, German,

Swedish, and U.S. funding sources but was fired before he was successful. In Jami's opinion, it was highly likely that the board's decision was the result of the resentment of extremist Iranian groups such as the MEK and the Communist Worker's Party (*hezb-e kommonist-e karegari*). These groups, Jami suggested, had made negative commentaries about Zamaneh, accusing it of serving the Islamic Republic. He expressed that his lack of fluency in Dutch had put him at a disadvantage regarding the rivals who were actively lobbying against him.

Jami also believed that the new conservative Iranian ambassador in the Netherlands, who had replaced the reformist ambassador, had put pressure on the Dutch government to defund Zamaneh. In 2009 the Center for Organized Cyber Crimes of the Islamic Republic's Revolutionary Guard Corps (IRGC) "unraveled" a plot accusing hostile governments of plans to overthrow the Iranian government through the internet. Referring to the Dutch government's allocated budget, the statement claimed that "one such country, which has supported the opposition movement financially in recent years, is the Netherlands, which passed a budget addendum in 2005 sponsored by Farah Karimi, an Iranian-born representative in the Dutch parliament and a member of the leftist Green Party."[21] Referring to this statement, Jami asked me, "Why do you think they mention Zamaneh first? It was because the rest of the projects were silent. Zamaneh was effective."[22] Not convinced that he was fired because of budget mishandling, Jami believed that the Iranian diaspora leftist groups and the Iranian state's extremist elements were responsible for his ouster.

For many months after being fired, Jami was hopeful that through negotiations he would be reappointed. He was extremely shocked by the speedy firing process and the refusal to be given a second chance to improve his performance. "There was no reassessment," he told me as he criticized what he considered to be an undemocratic decision by his employers. In the end, Jami reached a legal settlement with Zamaneh's board of directors but was not rehired. To his disappointment, Zamaneh lost many of its original staff after he was removed from his position. Some were fired, and others quit. Many former Zamaneh employees found jobs in the Netherlands, some were hired by Radio Farda and the BBC, and others returned to Iran. According to Jami, after he was fired only three original Zamaneh staff were still employed by the organization; two of them were, according to Jami, part of the "coup d'état," and the other, his wife, was not only retained but also promoted.[23] Jami told me that the original staff was fired before reaching their third year of employment because it is extremely difficult to fire an employee after three years of employment in the Netherlands. The Board appointed a Dutch person as interim director of Zamaneh. Farid Haerinejad, the producer of *Blogger's War*, was hired on a six-month contract as the editor-in-chief. Jami started his own media-consulting firm to design new Iranian media projects in the United States, Europe, and Malaysia. In 2009, a year after being fired, Jami told me that he had reached the conclusion that Iranian media should be owned by Iranians, not by foreign governments.[24]

Jami's enthusiastic efforts to tap into opportunities provided by democratization projects point to the way that he banked on—and actually helped create—the hype around blogging as a revolutionary front for social change in Iran. His unexpected firing shows that cosmopolitan diasporic self-entrepreneurs are disposable and can be replaced at any moment, when they lose their political usefulness. While human rights is the currency in this neoliberal democratization market, where competition replaces social solidarity, what is valued is not the humanity of the actors or their labor, but the profit that they produce.

Global Voices: Blogging Iran Free with the *Abol-Blogger*

On December 9, 2004, the Berkman Center for Internet and Society at Harvard Law School held "Votes, Bits, and Bytes," a two-day conference about the effect of the internet on politics. Sponsored by corporations such as eBay and organizations such as the Open Society Institute, the conference drew business investors, U.S. politicians, military personnel, and entrepreneurs, as well as internet enthusiasts, bloggers, activists, internet geeks and software developers. Hossein Derakhshan (Hoder), whose popularization of Farsi blogging from Canada had earned him the title of "*abol-blogger*" (the father of bloggers) or the "godfather" of Weblogistan, was a speaker in this conference. Hoder's significant role in popularizing Farsi blogging had made him famous among internet enthusiasts. A cosmopolitan traveler with dual Iranian and Canadian citizenship, he was frequently invited to conferences in Europe, the United States, and Israel to talk about the liberalizing potentials of blogs in Iran. A novice blogger at the time, I had learned about the conference by seeing it posted on Hoder's blog, which he aptly had titled *Editor Myself*. I decided to attend the conference to meet the "godfather" and to learn more about the world of blogging.

Upon entering the conference, I was handed a folder that included a briefing report. The report argued that the internet provides the tools to empower the individual to participate in the political process. "Semiotic democracy," the report maintained, is one of the positive impacts of the internet. This form of democracy refers to the recoding of cultural meaning by an "energized citizenry" that is empowered by digital technologies. Semiotic democracy through the internet advocates for an energized citizen who adopts an active relationship with information and processes it in creative ways. The impact of the internet on politics and civic life was emphasized in two areas: using the internet to "jazz" the classical political campaigns, and the "empowerment of the individual."

An overarching theme of the conference was "wiring democracy," where democratic participation on a global level is assumed to be the natural outcome of networking through ideologically neutral internet technologies.[25] On the first day of the conference, attendees met as a whole; during the remainder, the program was divided into three separate tracks: citizenship, business, and "global voices." In the first conference session, Hoder participated on a panel with an American military officer (Miliblogger) and two Iraqi brothers, Omar and Mohammad, who had created the blog *Iraq the Model*.[26] Omar and Mohammad had also helped design the Arabic Blogging Tools software. According to its creator, Spirit of America, this software "gives voices to those working for freedom and democracy in the Arab world." [27] These two "exemplary Iraqis" glorified "Operation Iraqi Freedom" and talked about the importance of blogging in the "liberation" of Iraq. They were represented as living proof of the liberating role of the internet in the "war on terror."[28] "Through blogging we can spread love," Mohammad said, arguing that the media creates hate by overemphasizing images of "an American soldier punching an Iraqi." Mohammad said that his blog allows him to tell the story of "people [who] go up to American soldiers and shake their hands." Mohammad claimed, "Just about everyone in Iraq has access to the Internet."

Hoder's talk, "How to Build a Blogosphere," emphasized the popularity of Farsi blogs among young Iranians, who constitute 70 percent of Iran's population. Working on the premise that internet users in Iran were representatives of the entire population, Hoder expressed his enthusiasm about the world of blogging and its liberalizing potentials in Iran. According to Hoder, unlike in other countries where the internet preceded blogs, blogs showed Iranians the greatness of the internet as a medium. Repeating the dominant narrative that civil society is nonexistent in Iran, Hoder claimed that because there were no parties and no freedom of press in Iran, the internet had not yet had a significant impact on Iranian politics: "Weblogs are creating social and cultural change, which could be translated into political change in a few years."[29] Speaking to an enthusiastic audience, he said that "thanks to weblogs, Iranian women for the first time are free to express themselves."[30]

Hoder used three metaphors to describe Persian blogs: windows, bridges, and cafés. Identifying with the mostly American audience, he stated that blogs were windows through which "we" could see what happened inside Iran. These windows, Hoder claimed, also gave Iranians the opportunity to see the "outside world." Excited by the idea of learning about what Iranian bloggers wrote about, several participants suggested translating Persian blogs so that "we know how they think." Believing that blogs were starting a revolution in Iran, Hoder announced enthusiastically that blogs were "preparing the ground for the real and effective change in Iran in the next, maybe, couple of years." This, in Hoder's view, had resulted in the crackdown on the internet and the arrest of bloggers in Iran. In the end, Hoder advocated for the localization of technology, Persian blogging tools, and fast internet access in Iran.

After the first session, I attended Global Voices to listen to Hoder's next presentation. Without exception, all the sessions in Global Voices assumed the unproblematic presence of freedom in the West, the lack thereof in the "third world," and its natural transmission through the internet to societies living under "totalitarian" rule. Hoder's talk was well received, and he was celebrated as a visionary who had discovered the internet's democratic potentials. Jeff Jarvis, a participant blogger as well as an associate professor and the director of the Interactive Journalism Program at CUNY's new Graduate School of Journalism, simultaneously blogged Hoder's talk and commented about his metaphor as "particularly important in a developing nation." Curious and sympathetic questions were posed to Hoder, who by now had assumed the position of expert on Iranian politics. "What can we do to help?" asked one audience member who, I learned later, worked with North Korea Watch. The same person commented, "We need to help those who do not enjoy the freedom of speech that we enjoy in this country."[31]

During this conference, Hoder blogged in English about his future plans for "using blogs as a means of sociopolitical change in Iran." (Among his plans were traveling to Israel to initiate an Iran-Israel peace project, helping provide dialogue between Iranian and American bloggers, and blogging the old diaries of Iranians from the mid-1970s, "when Iranians [had] the highest amount of social freedom and economic well-being." According to Hoder, "the new generation of Iranian[s]; those who were born after the revolution are more after individual and social freedoms, and economic well-being, rather than political openness. But since they've never seen [freedom], they have low expectations and as a result [they have] no will or effort to change the status quo, and thus, [this explains] the political apathy."[32] Hoder was surrounded by fans during the conference breaks. I found an opportunity to approach him and exchange a few words about the recent debates in Weblogistan. I had to wait to have a more detailed conversation with the godfather a few months later in Toronto.

Banning the Godfather from New York

Hoder's role as the "godfather of Weblogistan" and his networks among cyber-enthusiasts in the United States and Europe made him the self-appointed representative of Iranian bloggers in the mainstream international media. His extreme secularist politics and his antagonistic position toward the Iranian state were represented in the mainstream media as the unified position of Weblogistan against the "Iranian regime." Many bloggers who did not fit within the dominant accounts of a secular and/or antistate Weblogistan were lost in Hoder's shadow and remained unrepresented. During my fieldwork in Toronto, a year after I met him at the Votes, Bits, and Bytes Conference, I got the chance to know Hoder better. Sitting in a hipster café in downtown Toronto, he told me his reasons for actively promoting blogging among other Iranians. Hoder, who used to write a tech column for an Iranian tech paper prior to his migration to Canada in 2001, firmly believed that blogging was an effective way to counter stereotypes about Iranians: "I wanted to show that Iranians in Iran were friendly towards the U.S."[33] That is why he decided to teach his Iranian readers to convert the Blogger template into a Farsi blog template by inserting a few codes in the HTML format, he said. The Hoder that I met in person was much less self-absorbed than how he appeared on his blog. An intelligent and ambitious young man, Hoder had made many fans and enemies because of his disregard for flattery among the male elites of Weblogistan, who considered him to be arrogant and bombastic.

Hoder was raised in a very religious family of wealthy merchants (*baazaari*). His paternal uncle was one of the seventy-two leading officials of the Islamic Republic who died in a bomb explosion at the Islamic Republic Party headquarters on June 28, 1981 (7 *Tir* 1360). Over the years, streets, major squares, buildings, and schools (including my high school) were named "Shohadaay-e haft-e Tir" (martyrs of the 7th of Tir). That day has never escaped my memory, not only because for a significant part of my childhood and teenage years my birthday coincided with a national mourning day but also because of what followed that day. The bombing led to the massive persecution of many leftist activists in the 1980s in what has come to be known as "*daheye shast*," the most oppressive decade of postrevolutionary Iran. Twenty-five years later, I was sitting with the nephew of one of the Islamic Republic Party leaders who at the time of his death represented an oppressive Islamic government to me as a young socialist. It was ironic to listen to Hoder's strong anti-Islamic sentiments and his dismissal of the reform movement on the grounds of complicity with the "regime," and to be accused by him of being sympathetic to the "regime" for defending the reform movement.

In the first few months of my fieldwork in Toronto, Hoder was rarely in Canada. He had fallen in love with New York City and rented an apartment there. I had abandoned the idea of seeing Hoder in Toronto and planned to arrange a phone interview with him. He seemed to be inaccessible as he was constantly on the move. As a star blogger, he was enjoying a cosmopolitan life, traveling to give speeches about the unique potential of Weblogistan as a tool for freedom. However, on his way back to New York from Europe, Hoder was denied entry for overstaying his visa. Frustrated by this rejection, he came back to Canada and stayed with blogger friends (including me) in Toronto while he looked for ways to get back to New York. On his second attempt to cross the Canada-U.S. border in a car, a U.S. immigration officer interrogated him and looked up his English blog. Hoder was barred from entering the country because of his sarcastic remarks on his blog about getting paid by the U.S. government. To his surprise, it was not censorship by the Iranian state that impeded his cosmopolitan mobility (at least not yet). What restricted his freedom to move was surveillance by the U.S. immigration services, enabled by the very technology that Hoder had celebrated as the highway to freedom.

Despite Hoder's faith in the liberalizing potentials of the internet and his infatuation with the promises of liberal democracy, he was one of the many Iranians who were subjected to limitation of movement as a result of new immigration policies resulting from the fear of a terrorist threat. As Davina Bhandar (2004) argues, the new border-harmonization programs between the United States and Canada in the aftermath of September 11 resulted in new ways of organizing and controlling citizens and noncitizens. The discourse of the "new normal" has implications for the formation of new subjects in relation to disease, fear, risk, loss of security, the call for increased surveillance of bodies and the population, and the formation and maintenance of the technoscientific capitalist democracy (Bhandar 2004, 261-62). The new normal necessitates constant invocation of risk, fear, and danger, thus normalizing the disappearance of the promise of liberal democratic freedoms (266). This increased surveillance has become possible because of the very technologies that promise freedom elsewhere through internet democracy projects across the world.

Disillusioned with the United States and banned from reentering it, Hoder traveled to the United Kingdom, where he studied for a year to get his master's degree at SOAS University of London. His political position changed drastically, from desiring regime change in Iran to publicly defending the Iranian state, the supreme leader, and Iranian President Mahmoud Ahmadinejad, whom he portrayed as a hero in the struggle against neoliberalism and imperialism. The change in Hoder's position was so surprising that some bloggers and blog readers commented on his change of position in his comments section. Some of his readers accused him of being a spy hired by the Iranian state. Others suggested that Hoder's change of position was strategic, as he was planning to go back to Iran. They believed that Hoder had changed his ways to distract the Iranian state's attention from his trips to Israel in 2006 and 2007, and to compensate for his previous insults to the Iranian supreme leader. A few people believed in his genuine transformation and engaged with him in his comments section about his new position, which he characterized as "postcolonial."[34]

Hoder became extremely critical of the segments of the Iranian diaspora who received money from the U.S. state. He revealed the details of the cooperation of a few diaspora Iranians with U.S. Department of State–funded entities. Mehdi Khalaji, a former blogger (he unexpectedly erased his entire blog) and a senior fellow at the Washington Institute for Near East Policy (WINEP) who advocated for a military attack on Iran and was often invited to the White House as an "expert" during George Bush's presidency, filed a defamation lawsuit against Hoder. Hoder's investigative posts went so far that he no longer distinguished between the likes of the Washington-based Khalaji and women's-rights activists in Iran. He accused anyone who had received any support (even in the form of a statement) from the U.S.-funded organizations of treachery and treason. This frustrated many women's-rights activists who saw Hoder's accusations as unfair and detrimental to their cause. When I first met Hoder at the Votes, Bits, and Bytes conference, we had a discussion about Shirin Ebadi, an Iranian woman lawyer and the 2003 Nobel Peace Prize laureate. At that time, Hoder, who perceived Islam to be irreconcilable with democracy, found Ebadi's statement about the commensurability of Islam and democracy to be unacceptable, accusing her of complicity with the Iranian "regime" and referring to her as "Ayatollah Ebadi." After his drastic shift in politics, he accused her of being complicit with neoconservative and imperialist politics.

Ebadi was not the only Iranian feminist who was the target of Hoder's accusations and shaming. In 2008, *Zanan*, an Iranian feminist journal, was shut down by the Iranian state. Despite the fact that *Zanan* had for years challenged the Iranian state on issues such as inheritance, child custody, women's political participation, and other issues pertaining to women in Iran, many secular feminist and opposition groups and diasporic individuals refused to recognize its important interventions because they saw it as promoting Islamic feminism. However, after it was shut down by the state, several groups, including opportunistic diasporic opposition groups that had rebuked the magazine in the past, took the opportunity to issue statements condemning the Islamic Republic. Hoder did not hold back from shaming the journal's editor, Shahla Sherkat, for having been defended by some opposition groups that received funding from the U.S. Department of State.[35] Not unlike his position before his drastic political shift, Hoder was oblivious to the fact that Iranian women activists and scholars are often caught between absolutist politics (which accuses them of being tools of colonialism) and the secular fundamentalist position (which sees Islamic feminists as pawns of the "Islamic regime"). Before his political transformation, Hoder, who believed that blogging had given Iranian women the platform to speak their mind for the first time, ignored the fact that women such as Sherkat had been vocal for years without being heard by opposition groups or being represented in mainstream international media.[36] After his political shift, he continued to dismiss Iranian women's activism by accusing them of being complicit with imperialist projects.

The widespread crackdown on women's organizations by Iran was mainly a result of the polarizing politics that accused all activists alike of being complicit with regime-change agendas. Opportunistic funding and/or support statements by "liberating" forces and opposition groups exasperated the Iranian state and gave ammunition to the state's national security measures, thus jeopardizing women's, labor, and student organizations. As Emad Baghi, a prison-rights activist, wrote in a July 2007 statement, because the U.S. funding for Iranian opposition groups was not transparent, the Iranian government's crackdown on recipients included not just those who had actually received funding but many activists and organizations that did not.[37] The security measures and paranoia that were incited in response to "regime-change" activities resulted in journals being shut down and the arrest of activists who were accused of receiving foreign funding.

Despite accusing others of receiving foreign funding and support, Hoder himself became the target of these heightened security measures of the Iranian state. Almost a year after his political transformation, Hoder announced that he was going to travel to Iran and asked his readers not to campaign for his freedom were he to be arrested. After arriving in Tehran, he blogged about Iran and seemed to be enjoying his life as a visitor in Iran. Considering his recent trips to Israel and his insults to the supreme leader in his earlier days of blogging, many were surprised to read his blog posts that made it clear that he roamed freely in Tehran and its suburbs. But this luxury did not last for long. In November 2008, a few months after his arrival in Tehran, Hoder was arrested. During his trial in 2010, he was sentenced to nineteen and a half years in prison. He was released for two days in 2010 on a $1.5 million bail. After spending six years in prison, he was pardoned by the supreme leader, Ayatollah Khamene'i, and released in November 2014.

Soon after Hoder's arrest, his family and lawyer asked diasporic bloggers and organizations not to jeopardize his case by defending him, as they hoped to strike a deal with the judicial and intelligence authorities.[38] Several groups, including diasporic opposition groups and individuals who had earlier strongly criticized him for his change of position, wrote an online petition in English, declaring that "freedom of expression is sacred for all" and asking the Iranian authorities to release Hoder (see the appendix). Discussions about Hoder's arrest and the petitions that were issued after his arrest generated a range of commentary in Weblogistan. Some bloggers argued that even as some signatories were genuinely committed to the notion of "freedom for all," others were ethical narcissists who only aimed to prove their fairness and democratic tendencies, or had taken advantage of yet another opportunity to demonize the Islamic Republic of Iran. Some believed that while international human rights groups had not hesitated to issue press releases when the Iranian state arrested other journalists or bloggers, they kept quiet during Hoder's arrest. They rejected the human rights organizations' claims about respecting Hoder's wish, and argued that these organizations had never paid attention to similar requests by families of the arrested individuals in the past. Hoder's critique of the complicity of human rights organizations with the empire-building projects, they argued, was the reason why human rights groups did not adhere to their claims of equality of human rights. A group of bloggers objected to the petition, arguing that the statement did not help Hoder in any way. They argued that the petition was yet another empty internet campaign that glorified abstract ideals of freedom and democracy and was not meant to convince the relevant authorities who could release Hoder.[39]

Internet mobilizations to defend Hoder were not limited to those who were critical of the Iranian state. In March 2009 a group of Muslim bloggers who had announced their commitment to the Islamic Republic wrote an open letter in Persian to the head of the judiciary, asking for justice in Hoder's case. They started the letter with this verse from the Quran: "O you who believe! Stand out firmly for God as just witnesses; and let not the enmity and hatred of others make you avoid justice. Be just: that is nearer to piety; and fear God. Verily, God is well-acquainted with what you do."[40] Acknowledging Hoder's change of position, the authors of the letter stated:

> The Persian language news media outside the country, contrary to their routine methods, did not create any commotion after his arrest, and refrained for a long time from even reporting the smallest news about him. The signatories of this letter do not have any knowledge about the contents of the case against Hossein Derakhshan. However, it appears that his long detention is not appropriate for the accusations that have been formally discussed in relation to him, especially given that with his recent positions and actions, Derakhshan was clearly taking steps to make up for his past. Without doubt, if he had not been detained during the brutal attacks of the Zionist regime in Gaza, he would have used his pen and blog to further expose those crimes and to defend the innocent people of Gaza. We wonder, if Derakhshan has changed his ideas and actions in earnest, then what message does this way of dealing with him send to Derakhshan and others like him?[41]

Interestingly, this letter, which was translated by Niki Akhavan into English, received no press coverage in the transnational mainstream media. Hoder, who was the most represented Iranian blogger in the international media in the past, seemed to have lost his political usefulness in discourses that relied on binaries of freedom and repression. This example attests to the fact that regardless of their intentions or level of participation in the democratization industries, diasporic self-entrepreneurs may easily become disposable and replaceable. As Aihwa Ong (1999, 2003) argues, different forms of citizenship give way to different forms of governmentality, in which individualism and collectivity are negotiated in the processes of subject formation. Neoliberal individuals are constructed as self-responsible rational entrepreneurs with free choice. These ethics of "compulsory individual freedom" are not limited to "advanced capitalist societies" but travel through a form of "transnational citizenship" in borderless markets and sites of civil society. These "global citizens," as Ong rightly points out, "do not rely on a specific citizenship status to make a living but travel the world to perform globalized functions in the nodes of a far-flung archipelago. They are substitutable for one another in any given site, members of a circulating intellectual 'labor aristocracy' (including writers and professors) who serve the contemporary demands of global capital" (2006, 239). Much like the "global citizens" in Ong's analysis, bloggers who marketed themselves as Iran experts could easily become disposable and replaced by other self-entrepreneurs.

Conclusion: Job Insecurity and the Security Business

Despite Obama's announcement in 2013 that the "war on terror" had ended, the U.S. militaristic interventions continued under the rhetoric of targeted attacks.[42] The legacy of the "global war on terrorism" proves that it is not solely fought within the national boundaries of the "enemy" but acquires a global face where multiple states, nonstate institutions, and individuals participate in a battle against "evil." Such a spatially ambiguous war employs diasporas who act as "native informants" and experts in academic circles, think tanks, media, policy institutes, and other elements of the international civil society.[43] As Minoo Moallem (2005b) argues, the presence of Muslim immigrants in the West and the "threat" of "Islamic fundamentalism" that fills the void of the cold war have given rise to new security concerns that have created a need for expertise in the form of testimonies in media, academic scholarship, and political discourses. Moallem argues that in claiming both "here" and "there," Iranians in diaspora struggle to find a legitimate space to engage with political and cultural issues while they are subjected to disciplinary measures of the nation-states.

One cannot dismiss the fact that many Iranians in North America, who often face discrimination, took advantage of the opportunities to provide expertise during the "war on terror," when information about the "enemy" was a marketable commodity. In particular, in the first decade of the twenty-first century, the privatization of security in a neoliberal economy translated into an economic boom for the willing Persian-speaking self-entrepreneurs. During my fieldwork, the participation of diaspora Iranians in the knowledge-production industry during the "war on terror" varied in degree and scope. While some took translation jobs in the security industry, a few others actively worked to market themselves as dealers of information and obtained jobs in neoconservative think tanks or media. Others took advantage of this opportunity by providing testimonials and acting as human rights "experts" in what some people in Weblogistan have called "the human rights store" ("*dokoon-e hoghoogh-e bashar*").

It is not surprising that almost all of the results for "Farsi" as the search key term in the employment listings of the *New York Times* in 2006 were in the security industries. The first few jobs listed were posted by the CIA. Other jobs included policy-analysis and security positions at firms such as DFI International, a security firm that in 2007 merged with Detica to form the U.S. Government Division in order to solve "complex analytical, policy, and technology challenges confronting America's national security."[44] Another job listing appearing near the top of the list was from SAIC: From Science to Solutions, a firm that provided a range of services, "from geospatial information and signals intelligence to data mining software and visualization tools," in order "to help the intelligence community fight the global war on terror."[45] SAIC was one of three companies that were given five-year contracts by the U.S. government in June 2005 "to develop slogans, advertisements, newspaper articles, radio spots and television programs to build support for U.S. policies overseas. Each contract had a maximum value of $20 million per year for a total of $300 million."[46] The job opportunities that were available to Persian-speaking individuals in North America and Europe illustrate that during the "war on terror," when discourses of "national security" produced and represented Middle Eastern and Muslim immigrants as risks to the security of the nation, a paradox arose as the same immigrants became valuable commodities in the market for information.

Diaspora Iranians who tapped into the opportunities provided during the "war on terror" knowingly or unknowingly participated in the war machine. As Deleuze and Guattari (1986) argue, the war machine is not necessarily an extension of the apparatus of the state but may include proxies that stand outside and against the state and may not have war as their objective. The militant organizations and proxies (such as the MKO/MEK) that were funded by the "liberating" states were not the only elements of the war machine during the "war on terror." Think tank experts and nonmilitant "dissident" groups that desired "regime change" also participated in this war apparatus through providing expertise. Despite their intentions, segments of the Iranian diaspora—including some bloggers—who may not have desired regime change took advantage of the economic opportunities that the market for information about Iran provided, thus participating in a war machine that used liberation as its legitimizing force and employed neoliberal self-entrepreneurs as its proxies. In a sense, Weblogistan as a site of civil society and the modus operandi of what Deleuze and Guattari call "control societies" became where the assemblage of data enabled biopolitical and necropolitical practices that divide populations into those that are folded into life and those that are killable.

In the United States, where proper subjects are expected to be self-responsible individuals and entrepreneurs, it is inevitable that some among the Iranian diaspora take jobs in private and state security industries. Yet not all of my interlocutors took advantage of the opportunities provided during the "war on terror." Nor did those who tapped into the knowledge-production and security industries do so without feeling conflicted. Some recent immigrants, who lacked work experience or fluency in the language of the "host" country, felt uneasy about taking jobs in these industries. Several of my interlocutors had no choice but to take jobs with security firms, the U.S. propaganda media apparatus (such as the Voice of America), "nongovernmental" organizations that worked toward regime change in Iran, or academic programs that were commissioned by the U.S. Department of State to provide Persian lessons for U.S. government employees in the military and the intelligence sector. One of my informants, Soodabeh, a blogger and graduate student in Washington, DC, expressed that she had no choice but to work for Voice of America Persian: she and her husband needed the money. She indicated that VOA had hired her and several other recent immigrants only because of their language skills in Persian and not because of their experience in television or other media. Soodabeh told me that on rare occasions they were given permission to produce reports or programs. However, their programs went through intensive monitoring and editing by the higher-rank staff to ensure that the outcome was in line with the portrayal of democratic life in the United States. Mahboubeh, another recent immigrant and a blogger in Washington, DC, told me that her limited English was the only reason she agreed to tutor U.S. officials in colloquial Persian at an academic institution that received Department of State funding after September 11. Mahboubeh, who had no illusions about the U.S. government's political and economic motives for funding media, academic departments, and "nongovernmental" organizations, viewed the situation as an inevitable fact with which one had to come to terms. Quoting a professor who had accepted State Department funding to run this program, Mahboubeh told me that "if we don't take the money, somebody else will."[47] Sharareh, a U.S. citizen and a blogger who had lived most of her life in the United States, was hired as a contractor to translate the manuscripts of taped phone conversations in Persian. Despite the conflict she found between her politics and her position, Sharareh—who was an antiwar and human rights activist blogger in Washington, DC—told me that she accepted the contract job because she needed the money. The salary that she and her husband earned from doing nonprofit work was insufficient to cover their living expenses.

As scholars of neoliberalism have argued, a significant aspect of neoliberal governmentality is the coupling of notions of freedom and democracy with the economic agendas of neoliberalism.[48] Wendy Brown (2005) rightly points out that the "liberalism" in neoliberalism resembles the pre-Keynesian assumptions about the generation of wealth through minimizing state intervention, but with a crucial difference. The "neo" in neoliberalism carries a social analysis, which if deployed as a form of governmentality, "reaches the soul of the citizen subject to education policy to practices of empire" (2005, 39). Neoliberalism, as Brown argues, is not just a series of economic policies but involves the dissemination of market values to all social action. Unlike classical liberalism, neoliberalism does not conceive rational economic behavior as natural but postulates it as organized by law and in need of political intervention.

While the market, rather than the state, becomes the regulative principle of society, rational action on behalf of every member of the society and legal protection become necessities for a successful economic mechanism within the neoliberal language that privileges economic growth (Brown 2003). State legitimacy becomes contingent upon the extent and speed of implementation of this economic rationality. As Brown argues, market rationality is spread through imperialistic practices under the guise of American democracy. Unlike classical liberalism, neoliberalism extends the economic domain to every sphere of life and constructs individuals as entrepreneurial actors (Brown 2003). As such, the free rational individual becomes responsible for their actions and is seen as one who chooses between the economic options rather than seeking to change these options.[49] Profit becomes the measure of good governance, and moral subjects become individual entrepreneurs who are responsible for their own self-care.[50]

Even as the Hegelian notion of civil society is predicated on the movement from appetite and utility (*homo œconomicus*) to reason and consciousness (*homo politicus*) (Fontana 2006, 67), the political subject suitable for freedom and democracy in the neoliberal world is also an economic man. As Foucault argues, like classic liberalism, in neoliberalism, there is "a theory of *homo œconomicus*, but he is not at all a partner of exchange. *Homo œconomicus* is an entrepreneur, an entrepreneur of himself" (2008, 226). As such, free rational individuals become responsible for their actions and choose between economic options rather than seeking to change these options.

In the market for information and expertise during the "war on terror," when intelligence and security are privatized, the diasporic Iranian expert becomes an entrepreneur who participates in the production and marketing of a particular form of knowledge about Iran. The autonomous free individual blogger as *homo œconomicus* and *homo politicus* becomes the active netizen/entrepreneur who desires self-advancement and can be governed through his or her desire for freedom. Profit becomes the measure of good governance, and moral subjects become individual blogger entrepreneurs who are committed to the logic of compulsory freedom. As such, neoliberalism fuses *homo politicus* and *homo œconomicus* when individual self-interest and rights become inseparable. The disposability of Iranian self-entrepreneurs who willingly participate in "democratization" projects points to the fact that despite their aspirations, they remain risky subjects whose loaned life can be sacrificed to "protect" the interests of the "international civil society."

[Coda]

Revolutionary Ends

Weblogistan's Afterlife

> This is an opportunity for the Trump Administration to learn from the Reagan Administration, which used the telecommunications tools of the 1980s to spread information behind the Iron Curtain. The tools then were short wave radio, satellite news and fax machines. Today's dissenters need software to evade the regimes's [sic] internet firewalls.
> —"IRAN'S INTERNET IMPERATIVE," *WALL STREET JOURNAL*, JANUARY 17, 2018

> To Iranian President Rouhani: NEVER, EVER THREATEN THE UNITED STATES AGAIN OR YOU WILL SUFFER CONSEQUENCES THE LIKES OF WHICH FEW THROUGHOUT HISTORY HAVE EVER SUFFERED BEFORE. WE ARE NO LONGER A COUNTRY THAT WILL STAND FOR YOUR DEMENTED WORDS OF VIOLENCE & DEATH. BE CAUTIOUS!
> —DONALD TRUMP'S TWITTER PAGE, JULY 22, 2018

Over a decade after I first started my research on Weblogistan and just about the time that I was working on the final revisions of this book, Donald Trump tweeted what looked like a *Games of Thrones* movie poster: a stern-looking and triumphant image of the president with words that read "Sanctions Are Coming, November 5." A day after Trump's tweet went viral, Qasem Solimeni, the commander of the Quds Force (the Iranian Revolutionary Guard's extraterritorial

FIGURE C.1 Source: *Washington Post*, https://www.washingtonpost.com/arts
-entertainment/2018/11/03/i-will-stand-against-you-trump-iran-crisis-is-literally
-unfolding-through-game-thrones-dialogue/?utm_term=.61acbdb95f49.

operations unit), mimicked Trump's representational style, replacing Trump's image with his own and responding with the tweet "I Will Stand Against You."[1] The hypermasculine social media display of military might and civilizational logic deployed by the U.S. president and the response to it by a conservative representative of the Iranian military are good reminders that the cyber civil society is implicated in the war assemblage that is fought online and offline. Trump's hostile tweet in November 2018 was not unfamiliar to Iranian Twitter users. Just a few months before this bizarre trivialization of deadly sanctions, he used Twitter to send a warning in capital letters to the Iranian president, Hassan Rouhani.[2] The warning went viral on July 22, the same day that U.S. Secretary of State Michael R. Pompeo delivered a speech titled "Supporting Iranian Voices" for a select group of Iranian diaspora and "civil society groups" in Simi Valley.[3] Royalists and members of the militant MKO were among the audience.

Though worrisome, Trump's warning is not inconsistent with either his presidential style or his hostile stance toward Iran.[4] The U.S. withdrawal from the 2015 Comprehensive Iran Deal, the exclusion of Iranian visa holders from entering the United States under the "Muslim ban," the immigration laws that seek to deport "legal permanent residents" for minor crimes and revoke citizenship from naturalized citizens, the U.S. and Israeli strikes on the Iranian forces in Syria without congressional approval, and the strengthening of the Saudi-Israel-U.S. alliance, among other events under Trump's presidency, have intensified the anxieties about an imminent war.[5] At the same time that the U.S. hawks beat the war drums, the Iranian conservatives threaten to break the nuclear deal if the European parties do not adhere to the terms of the agreement.[6] Regime-change enthusiasts among the Iranian diaspora advocate for the reinstallation of the sanctions and even war, while those who fear a war on Iran increasingly circulate photos, video, and articles on the internet about Iran's exceptional status as a non-Arab—and even Aryan—nation with a rich heritage.

It is against this background that the news about the protests in Iran have been circulating in social media networks and the international media. In December 2017, days after President Hasan Rouhani's new budget bill, protests against the state's austerity measures broke out in several Iranian cities. Iran's economic crisis, largely caused by the sanctions that have prevented foreign investment in Iran (despite the nuclear deal), the unequal distribution of wealth, corruption, unemployment, the underemployment of the highly educated Iranian population, and the austerity measures imposed by the state to remedy the economic crisis resulting from the sanctions, has given rise to massive protests.[7] Israeli Prime Minister Benjamin Netanyahu and U.S. President Donald Trump—who, like his predecessors, made a distinction between the Iranian people and the "regime"—have used social media to show their support for the Iranian protests.[8] Overjoyed about the prospect of regime change, Reza Pahlavi, the dethroned Shah's son and the leader of the royalist opposition groups, and Maryam Rajavi, the cult leader of the militant opposition group MEK—which was removed from the U.S. terrorist list in 2012 and has close ties with both the CIA and the FBI—sent messages of support on social media, asking the United States and the UN Security Council to intervene.[9] During the December and January protests, Iranian President Rouhani acknowledged the protesters' valid grievances about the economic situation, while Ali Shamkhani, Iran's Supreme National Security Council (SNSC) secretary, announced that a "proxy war" was being waged against the Islamic Republic on streets and via social media.[10] Instagram and Telegram were banned as national security measures, counterprotests against foreign intervention and infiltration resulted in violence, and the state responded harshly to street protests.[11]

In 2018 the drastic drop in the Iranian currency value as a result of sanctions and the lack of access to clean water in the southern provinces of Iran resulted in more protests. The Iranian state's hasty decisions in implementing "independent development" to remedy the "crippling" sanctions have culminated in homegrown technologies with devastating environmental consequences. For example, after Obama's penalties for the sale of oil to Iran resulted in a 75 percent decrease in Iranian imports, the Iranian state started to refine its own oil. As Kaveh Madani and Nazanin Soroush point out, "Aggressive development of water infrastructure and handing substantial subsidies to farmers are other examples of strategies developed under pressures caused by the 1980–88 Iraq-Iran war, international sanctions and the resulting threats to national food security."[12] These homemade measures have resulted in land and air degradation, culminating in the production of petrol and diesel that contain ten to eight hundred times more contaminants than the international standard.[13] The rampant air pollution that has increased levels of cancer (especially breast cancer) in Iran, along with lack of access to lifesaving cancer treatment (because of the sanctions), has subjected the Iranian population to slow death.[14] The economic pressures on the farmers and working-class urban Iranians have given rise to protests in different parts of Iran. The "water protests" (which, unsurprisingly, were hijacked by the U.S. and Israeli propaganda media and regime-change enthusiasts) were deemed as national security threats and faced severe reaction from the state.

The circulation of news on social media about the protests in Iran often omits this background, reducing these grievances to an "anti-regime" rhetoric that fixates on liberal notions of freedom. The opportunistic appropriation of the Iranian protests by some Iranian diasporic opposition groups, the U.S. hawks, and the Israeli state continues to incite the Iranian state's crackdown on social media. An example of this crackdown came in May 2018, when a few popular Instagram "influencers," known as *"shaakh-haaye Instagram"* (literally, the "horns of Instagram"), were arrested and released after being questioned by the Iranian security forces.[15] On July 7, 2018, Masih Alinejad, an Iranian dissident who works for the Voice of America, posted the news of the arrest of Ma'edeh Hojabri, a popular eighteen-year-old Instagrammer whose photos and dance videos have made her an "influencer" on Instagram. Hojabri, who allegedly had 600,000 followers, was arrested for "damaging public virtue" and spreading immoral and "anticultural" activities. Soon after Alinejad's Twitter post in English, the news of Hojabri's arrest went viral in the social media outside of Iran. On July 9 Amnesty International tweeted that "we're with the people of Iran, saying that #DancingIsNotACrime. Dance with us?"[16] Amnesty posted a video of its London staff dancing on the street, holding signs with the hashtag #DancingIsNotACrime and #برقصیم_تا_برقص ("Dance so that we dance"). People from inside and outside of Iran posted their dance videos in support of Ma'edeh Hojabri. Even though the news of Hojabri's arrest went viral in July, she and the other the "Instagram girls" were arrested and released in May, more than a month before the online dance campaigns. In a YouTube video posted from Canada, Elnaz Ghasemi, a Canadian citizen and one of the three arrested "Instagram girls," expressed her surprise at the delayed response to her (and other two women's) arrest. Hinting to the opportunistic instrumentalization of Instagram arrests, Ghasemi emphasized that she did not "say a word" about her arrest on her Instagram account because she did not want to get involved in "peripheral" controversies around the issue.[17] Assuring her followers that despite the rumors, she and the other two women were fine, in her video Ghasemi stated that it was only after the Iranian state television (IRIB Channel One) released a reality show–style "documentary" on social media that the news of the Instagram arrests went viral.[18] It was indeed from this state-produced documentary that Alinejad got the news.

The Channel One segment to which Ghasemi refers in her video is a thirty-minute program titled *Beeraheh* (astray/deviated path). The program, which is aired on Monday afternoons, takes an *aseeb shenaasee* (pathology) approach in order to address a range of topics, such as murder, prostitution, smuggling, illegal dance, illicit music studios, and fortune-telling, that the producers of the show consider to be social vices. With a focus on family values, the show features examples of remorseful "criminals" and "victims" of prostitution, drug use, embezzlement, and identity theft to teach the Iranian population moral lessons through public humiliation. The episodes titled "Social Media" and the "The Damage of Cyberspace," produced in a collaboration between Channel One's "social team" and the "security forces social branch," combine different modalities of power to discipline the criminal and normalize the Iranian population through biopolitical and ethicopolitical techniques.[19] In several cases, interviewees' faces are cast in shadow and against the image of a dark spiderweb, perhaps to protect the identity of the repenting "criminal" and to convey a sense of danger awaiting the naive youths who fall prey to the dark web of social media networks.[20] "Experts," including psychologists, cyber police (FATA), academics, and clergies, talk about how social media can deceive gullible users. The not-so-subtle message is that late marriage, loneliness, family dysfunction, and lack of family supervision will likely result in the abuse/misuse of social media by gullible youths, who are easily tricked by cyber criminals. Having divorced parents, living with two working parents, not having a father, and living away from one's family are recurring themes in the "confessions" of "Instagram girls" that are relayed as cautionary messages to the Iranian audience.

The release of this documentary outraged many Iranian MPs and politicians who criticized the Iranian state television for violating the rights of Iranian citizens by broadcasting their interrogation videos, humiliating a young woman by making her cry on television, and deliberately overlooking the rampant corruption and embezzlement committed by powerful figures in the Islamic Republic. As Mohammad Sadeghi, the Tehran MP, wrote on his Twitter page, "I suggest that the esteemed head of the IRIB orders an interview with the victims of sexual assault perpetrated by the Qur'an recital coach. Disappointed with the lack of justice in the hands of the Iranian Judiciary system, they [victims] want to appeal to foreign courts."[21] The public outrage in response to this program resulted in an investigation by the Council to Oversee IRIB and a meeting with the representatives of the three government branches. IRIB was given a warning for releasing the interviews without a permit from the judiciary branch. Yet the council also excused this violation by stating that the IRIB has the professional responsibility to enlighten the public about foreign-led illicit activities that violate norms and Islamic codes of behavior.[22]

Despite the highly controversial release of this show in Iran, nuanced critiques of the state from within were overshadowed by the opportunistic groups and individuals outside of Iran who appropriated the Instagram dance videos and portrayed them as regime-change activism in social media. The hype around the online mobilizations on behalf of the "Instagram girls" is perhaps the most recent example of the way that the Iranian cyber civil society, since the emergence of Weblogistan, has been celebrated as "revolutionary" and subversive. This hype, in large part, is caused by the fetishization of revolution, sex, or their amalgamation, "sexual revolution." Jason Rezaian, a journalist who was accused of espionage and arrested in Iran in 2014 (he was released in 2016 and returned to the United States), commented on the Iranian state's reaction to the "Instagram girls" by writing that "sexuality—especially of the female variety—is this regime's Achilles' heel (and always has been). Controlling it has been an obsession since the Islamic republic came into power in 1979. And now the establishment is obviously losing that 40-year war of attrition."[23] The twin correlate of "internet revolution," "sexual revolution" has been deployed by some opposition forces to argue that a regime change in

Iran can be achieved through targeting sex—the weak spot of the regime, according to the sexual revolution enthusiasts.[24] Celebrating "sexual liberation" as the most effective way to fight the regime, these enthusiasts privilege the sanitized, modern, and upper-class sexuality of urban Iranians while condemning what they deem to be untamed, perverse, traditional, rural, and backward Islamic sexuality. In other words, conflated with tradition, Islamic sexuality (and, by extension, the sexuality of the terrorist) comes to mean bestiality, sodomy, pedophilia, and polygamy, while a heteronormative (and more recently homonormative) sexuality is constructed as modern and revolutionary.[25] The assumption is that the young, economically privileged, urban Iranians—who are celebrated as the new and energetic face of the Iranian civil society—challenge the "theocratic regime" by having sex, making videos about sex, or by talking about sex. What made Ma'edeh Hojabri into a social media hero (perhaps despite her annoyance with appropriations of her videos by some opposition forces) was her arrest and her "bravery" for publicizing her dance videos with sexual undertones. Not surprisingly, the celebration of a classed notion of sexual freedom (with its orientalist legacy) on social media overshadowed the more effective challenges to the state that do not fit in the hype around internet and sexual revolutions. While transgressions of a select few cosmopolitan Iranians who become the *"shaakhs* of Instagram*"*—thanks to the popularity afforded to them by the Iranian state and its opposition— become news headlines and hot topics in social media, forms of contestation that are attentive to sanctions, war profiteering, and environmental degradation, while critiquing the Iranian state for failing to respond to social and economic grievances, are erased in the annals of social media.[26]

The hype around "internet revolutions" in Iran started with the celebrations of Weblogistan. Even though by the end of the first decade of the new millennium Weblogistan lost its appeal, the vestiges of enthusiasm for "democratization" projects through the internet carried through in the celebrations of other social media. After the dispute over the 2009 Iranian presidential election and subsequent street protests, the "Twitter revolution" was hailed for its assumed mobilizing power and liberalizing potentials. John McCain—a pro-war U.S. senator, an ardent supporter of "freedom" projects through the internet in the Middle East, and a proponent of neoliberal communication policies such as the "Internet Freedom Act"—paid tribute to Neda Agha Soltan, a bystander who was shot during the protests that followed the Iranian presidential elections. Celebrating YouTube and Twitter for circulating the video footage of Agha Soltan's death, McCain, like other U.S.

politicians, appropriated the Iranian protests for their hawkish policies.[27] A range of Iranian opposition groups and individuals also hijacked these videos to take advantage of the political climate. Neda Agha Soltan's fiancé used the opportunity to flee Iran, pronouncing himself the Iranian people's ambassador and participating in the Israeli state's propaganda machine against Iran.[28]

The Iranian protests soon became a hot topic on Twitter, as 98 percent of the site's links during the first week of the Iranian protests were Iran-related. The Twitter hype hijacked the street protests, interpellating the Iranian people's movement as the "Twitter revolution."[29] However, this description was far from accurate. According to Sysomos, a social media platform, there were 19,235 Twitter accounts that stated their location to be in Iran.[30] This number, which accounted to 0.025 percent of the Iranian population at the time, included Twitter users outside of Iran, who in a "cyber war" to confuse the Iranian state, altered their Twitter setting location to Tehran (or other Iranian cities) and changed their time zone to GMT +3.30.[31] In fact, the *Zero Anthropology* blog called the Twitter hype "America's Iranian Twitter revolution," stating that there were only forty-five Twitter accounts in Iran during the 2009 Green movement.[32] Evgeny Morozov (2012), quoting *Aljazeera*, has argued that there were only sixty active Twitter accounts in Iran during the first week of the protests. Soon after the Twitter hype, Mehdi Yahyanejad, the founder of the Balatarin site, warned that Twitter's impact in Iran was zero. Golnaz Esfandiari, the Iranian journalist and a senior correspondent with Radio Free Europe, reflected a year later that the "Twitter revolution" led by those outside of Iran hurt the Green movement and jeopardized the protesters' lives on the street by spreading misinformation and rumors.[33] Yet, in what can be characterized as simulacrum (Baudrillard 1981), the "Twitter revolution" became a reality for media, internet users, and U.S. politicians alike. One of the most retweeted accounts was that of the conservative gay blogger Andrew Sullivan. In his blog post titled "The Revolution Will Be Twittered," published in the *Atlantic* on June 13, 2009, Sullivan who is notoriously Islamophobic, ends his praise of Twitter with *"Allah o Akbar"* ("God Is Great"), a chant that is reminiscent of the 1979 Iranian revolution and was shouted by some Green movement protesters on the rooftops in 2009.[34] The co-optation of a religious chant that Islamophobes often associate with "Islamic terrorism" exemplifies the opportunism of cyber-enthusiastic regime-change advocates who appropriate local movements and hail them as internet revolutions in the service of "democratization" projects.

The manufactured "Twitter revolution," which was taking place outside Iran while Iranian protesters were risking their lives on the streets, received tremendous support from the U.S. politicians. Jared Cohen, senior staff member at State Department Policy Planning, sent an email to Twitter asking the company to delay scheduled maintenance so that the Iranian Green movement would not be interrupted. Mark Pfeifel, the deputy national security adviser for Strategic Communications and Global Outreach at the National Security Council, suggested that Twitter be nominated for the Nobel Peace Prize for its role in the Iranian Green movement.[35] Ironically, at the same time that the Iranian people were subjected to aggressive life-depleting sanctions imposed by the United States, Neda Agha Soltan's tragic death was used as an affective strategy by politicians and journalists to incite outrage and valorize the liberating role of Twitter.

Morozov describes "the enthusiastic belief in the liberating power of technology accompanied by the irresistible urge to enlist Silicon Valley start-ups in the global fight for freedom" as the "Google Doctrine" (2011, 14). As a former enthusiast himself, Morozov admits that the exaggeration of the role of Twitter in the Iranian Green movement backfired as the Iranian state also used these tools for surveillance against the protesters.[36] As Morozov points out, despite Twitter and Facebook's claims of freedom, they refuse to join the Global Network Initiative (GNI), a pledge by the technology industries to act in accordance with the tenets of freedom of speech and privacy and with respect to the Universal Declaration of Human Rights. Even though Google is a GNI signatory, the questionable privacy record of this company and its cooperation with the National Security Agency (NSA) makes it less than neutral. Because of the close relationship between these industries and the U.S. Department of State, the Iranian intelligence ministry associated Twitter, Facebook, and Google with the U.S. regime-change agendas and accused the Iranian protesters of complicity with foreign governments.[37] A group of journalists and activists who had left Iran to attend the U.S.-funded trainings were not able to return to Iran, fearing arrest on charges of treason. While the Iranian state's excessive force against the protesters is deplorable, the track record of the U.S. regime-change activities in Iran—from the 1953 U.S.-backed coup that toppled the democratically elected Mohammad Mossadegh to the regime-change budget and trainings after the 1979 Iranian revolution and the "war on terror"— makes the Iranian state's suspicions of the U.S. activities in Iran understandable, if not justifiable.[38] The U.S. policies have not only jeopardized the Iranian protesters' lives, but they have also made autonomous democratic movements within Iran extremely difficult and nearly impossible. During the 2009 street protests the Iranian police published the social media photos of several protesters, asking the public to identify them in the interest of national security. In an uncertain and chaotic climate, when misinformation abounded in social media, many Iranians stopped attending the street protests. It was no longer clear if the information circulating on the internet was initiated by the conservative Iranian state and para-state elements, the U.S.-backed regime-change agents, or genuine protesters. The fear of continuing the protests was twofold: on the one hand, many protesters feared violence perpetuated by conservative elements of the Iranian intelligence who saw the protesters as foreign agents; on the other hand, citing the history of the U.S.-backed coup of 1953 and the more recent occupations in Iraq and Afghanistan, many warned about the U.S. interest in instigating unrest in Iran. In a way the myth of the "Twitter revolution" and the circulation of misinformation on the internet effectively hijacked and extinguished the Iranian Green movement.

...

My sister, Mojgan, who took me to my very first protest during the Iranian revolution in 1979, and who was forced to bury her Marxist books during the witch hunts against leftists in *daheye shast* (1360s), had come to appreciate the importance of the reform movement in Iran over the years. Like many Iranians, thirty years after the revolution she took part in the street protests in 2009, hoping for a better future in Iran. Soon after the street protests were hijacked, she stopped attending, as it was no longer clear who was creating chaos during the protests. Shortly after the 2009 street protests, Mojgan was diagnosed with stage IV breast cancer at the age of forty-seven. Despite the sanctions and the scarcity of cancer medications, she decided to go through treatment. Her radiotherapy treatment was disrupted because of a U.S. cyberattack that shut down Iranian computers that worked with nuclear energy. Having no choice, she continued her treatment at a different hospital with an outdated machine that burned her lung, causing more damage and resulting in multiple lung surgeries. Despite all of the challenges of living with cancer under the sanctions in Iran, Mojgan continued to translate books about environmental justice and participated as an editorial board member for the Children's Book Council of Iran, an ironically forward-looking genre that is predicated on futurity. However, her fight to live was not out of an optimism that awaited salvation. Optimism, even in its "cruel" form, is not afforded to those who live a loaned life. Hers was a pessimism that places death on the same plane as life, for and with others.[39] A life that is not indebted to "freedom" or liberation, but carries on day to day, without the romance of revolution or salvation. An "Immanent life" (Deleuze 2005, 29) that captures a lived ethics. Mojgan was not an unintended casualty of the sanctions in a "total war" that deems civilians as enemy combatants. Her death, like the deaths of many Iranians, was the intended effect of the politics of rightful killing. Even if her story of resilience does not enter the register of the liberalizing accounts of a past of suffering and a future of freedom, it is a part of an alternative world making, a present that exceeds the limits of human rights. That is a present that the first sentence of a children's book about the Cuban Revolution—a book that Mojgan gave me when I was twelve and she was seventeen—encapsulates: "Because we love life, we fight for it to death." This unfathomable pessimism is the possibility of the politics of the present, where neither death nor revolution is the end.

[Appendix]

Statement by Iranian Bloggers on Hossein Derakhshan

We, the undersigned, view the circumstances surrounding the Iranian authorities' arrest of Hossein Derakhshan aka Hoder, one of the most prominent Iranian bloggers, as extremely worrying. Derakhshan's disappearance, detention at an unknown location, lack of access to his family and attorneys, and the authorities' failure to provide clear information about his potential charges is a source of concern for us.

The Iranian blogging community is one of the largest and most vibrant in the world. From ordinary citizens to the President, a diverse and large number of Iranians are engaged in blogging. These bloggers encompass a wide spectrum of views and perspectives, and they play a vital role in open discussions of social, cultural and political affairs.

Unfortunately, in recent years, numerous websites and blogs have been routinely blocked by the authorities, and some bloggers have been harassed or detained. Derakhshan's detention is but the latest episode in this ongoing saga and is being viewed as an attempt to silence and intimidate the blogging community as a whole.

Derakhshan's own position regarding a number of prisoners of conscience in Iran has been a source of contention among the blogging community and has caused many to distance themselves from him. This, however, doesn't change the fact that the freedom of expression is sacred for all not just the ones with whom we agree.

We therefore categorically condemn the circumstances surrounding Derakhshan's arrest and detention and demand his immediate release.

SOURCE: HTTPS://MRONLINE.ORG/2008/12/19/STATEMENT-BY-IRANIAN-BLOGGERS-ON-HOSSEIN-DERAKHSHAN/

[Notes]

Prologue

1 Sima Shakhsari, *Farangopolis*, December 15, 2004. I launched *Farangopolis* in English and Persian in December 2004 and wrote my Persian blog until May 2007. My short-lived English blog was written for an English-speaking readership and had a completely different content than my Persian blog. I stopped blogging in English because I was more interested in the Persian blogs and the political discussions among Iranian bloggers in Weblogistan.
2 Variations of the terms *Frank*, *Farangi* (foreigner), and *Farangistan* (foreign land) are used in Iran to refer to foreigners, especially Europeans.
3 After meeting several bloggers who had just left Iran, I noticed the extent to which English words have become integrated in colloquial Persian. Perhaps a class marker and a product of movement of information through satellite television, the internet, and traveling bodies, Pinglish is quite popular among the younger generation of urban resident Iranians.
4 For an excellent analysis of the way that violence constitutes belonging, see Adi Kuntsman's *Figurations of Violence and Belonging: Queerness, Migranthood and Nationalism in Cyberspace and Beyond* (2009).
5 Ethnography of cyberspace as a new field site has challenged ideas of location, culture, place, and the field (Boellstorff 2008; Eichhorn 2001; Hine 2000; Kendall 1999; Markham 2004). These studies have helped challenge fixed notions of the "field," exposing the way that the boundaries of the anthropological field are much more porous and fragmented than traditionally conceptualized. While feminist anthropology and postcolonial anthropology have questioned notions of field and culture (Abu-Lughod 1991; Visweswaran 1997) by unsettling the binary of the West as the center of knowledge and the "third world" as the exotic site of culture, ethnographies of the internet further complicate notions of travel, field, and home. Adi Kuntsman's work on notions of belonging, violence, and home in cyberspace is an important intervention in ethnography. Using feminist

scholarship that conceptualizes fieldwork as "homework" (Martin and Mohanty 1986) and feminist cyber-ethnography that theorizes fieldwork at home and about home (Fay 2007; Gajjala 2002), Kuntsman argues that while cyberspace "can bring together physically dispersed people, provide a space of communication for socially marginalized groups and serve as a resource for community organizing" (Kuntsman 2004, 3), homes and fields in cyberspace should be approached critically. Kuntsman questions the assumptions of equal power relations in cyberspace and rightly asks which subjects get a voice and who is left out. While my online and offline ethnography among Iranian bloggers highlights the inequalities of power online, the offline component points to the silences, ruptures, and affective intensities that may be lost in an online discourse analysis.

6 In chapter 5, I provide a detailed account of neoliberal entrepreneurship and the way that some diasporic bloggers tapped into the market for information about Iran during the "war on terror."

7 Unless quoting an English blog or website, I have translated all blog contents and interviews from Persian into English.

8 While there were several laat/thug characters in this blog, it was unclear whether there was actually more than one actual author.

9 Later, after I launched the offline part of my research, in an outing with a group of young women bloggers and blog readers in Toronto, I was told that this blogger used a *ketaabi* (bookish) Persian in his blog to compensate for his lack of knowledge in English, which he could not conceal in his offline life. These young women bloggers associated the anxieties around loss of privilege with the deployment of language in reclaiming masculinity in Weblogistan.

10 For example, as I discuss in chapter 3, a first-year graduate student in the United States repeatedly made sexist comments about Iranian women feminist scholars by critiquing their scholarship in a condescending manner. Poking fun at two Iranian feminist scholars' books, he suggested in a post that Iranian feminist women scholars should just write about issues such as rape and leave the "serious matters such as Foucault" to the experts in the field.

Introduction

1 "Iran's Blogging Boom Defies Media Control," Brian Murphy, Associated Press, February 19, 2004. The article was initially published by CNN at the following link, which is no longer accessible: www.cnn.com/2004/WORLD/meast/02/19/iran.blogging.ap. The article can be accessed at https://usatoday30.usatoday.com/tech/world/2004-02-19-blogging-in-iran_x.htm, accessed July 31, 2017.

2 For other examples of such news articles, see N. Alavi, 2004, "Freedom in Farsi Blogs," *Guardian*, December 20, accessed July 31, 2017. https://www.theguardian.com/technology/2004/dec/20/iran.blogging; Sepideh Parsa, 2008, "Weblogistan Key to Democratization in Iran," October 20, accessed July 31, 2017, http://archive.atlantic

-community.org/app/index.php/Open_Think_Tank_Article/%22Weblogistan%22_Key _to_Democratization_in_Iran; Sean Kenny, 2006, "The Revolution Will Be Blogged," *Salon*, March 6, accessed July 31, 2017, https://www.salon.com/2006/03/06/iranian _bloggers/; and Brian Murphy, 2004, "On Iranian Blogs, No Mask Is Needed," *Houston Chronicle*, February 20, accessed July 31, 2017, https://www.chron.com/business /technology/article/On-Iranian-blogs-no-mask-is-needed-1960673.php.

3 Ben Macintyre, 2005, "Mullahs versus the Bloggers," *Times*, December 23, accessed July 31, 2017, https://www.thetimes.co.uk/article/mullahs-versus-the-bloggers-k23nk 7z7n0k.

4 During my research, the assumed role of Weblogistan in changing the Iranian cultural and political landscape was exaggerated to the extent that in his message to the first University Students' Blogging Festival, Abbas Ma'roufi, a well-known Iranian writer who lives in Berlin, called blogging the "turquoise revolution," accessed April 6, 2019, http://old.khabgard.com/?id=1115269394.

5 For a discussion of civilizational thinking, see Moallem (2005a).

6 Moallem's astute analysis examines the production of a gendered Islamic subject by tracing the history of subject formation in Iranian modernity. She covers four historical periods: nineteenth- and twentieth-century civilizational imperialism, the period between Reza Khan's coup d'etat (1921) and the nationalization of oil and the subsequent U.S.–sponsored coup (1953), the period between 1953 and the 1979 revolution, and the postrevolutionary period. I add to this list the events after 1989 that gave rise to new subjectivities. These events include the liberalization of Iran's economy after the eight-year Iran–Iraq war, the rise of the reform movement, the acceleration of neoliberalism in the region after the "fall" of the Soviet Union, and the popularization of the internet.

7 Shortly after the 1979 revolution and the toppling of the dictatorship of the Pahlavi monarchy, a provisional state headed by Mehdi Bazargan was established. By 1981, after bloody conflicts among different political parties, the state was established as Islamic, with power falling into the hands of pro-Khomeini groups. In the 1980s (1360s according to the Iranian calendar), many communists and socialists were executed by the Islamic Republic.

8 The postrevolutionary events in Iran can be divided into four periods, roughly corresponding to decades. The first period, 1979–89, starts with the Iranian revolution and ends with the death of Ayatollah Khomeini and the subsequent shift in centers of power in the state level. In the last two years of his life, Khomeini increased the populism of the state and issued secondary decrees to override some laws, thus favoring the Left's state-interventionist policies. He also accepted the cease-fire with Iraq and set the tone for a less revolutionary and more pragmatic government. The year 1989 is also significant as it marks the end of the eight-year war between Iran and Iraq, the fall of the Soviet Union, and the intensification and universalization of neoliberalism. The 1989–97 period signifies the postwar era, economic reconstruction, and liberalization under the presidency of Hashemi Rafsanjani. The 1997–2005 period marks the rise of the reform movement, the student movement, the women's movement, and two terms of

the reformist president, Seyyed Mohamad Khatami. Finally, the 2005–10 period is the heyday of Weblogistan, during which I conducted the bulk of my field research.

9 The increasing gap between the political and economic elites and the working class, the dramatic increase of the birthrate in the 1980s, and the increased social and economic participation of women during the war led to the mobilization of laborers, students, and women during Rafsanjani's administration. Rafsanjani capitalized on these forces and encouraged relaxed attitudes toward youths and women. With the increasing rift between the Right factions (conservatives and Rafsanjani's reconstructionist party), fifteen members of Rafsanjani's cabinet announced that they would run for the fifth parliamentary elections in order to continue Rafsanjani's postwar reconstruction policies. This group called themselves *Kargozaaraan* and advocated economic development, pluralism, civil society (*jaamee'e-ye madani*), and "human rights." Kargozaaraan sought an alliance with the Left, an alliance that weakened the conservative Right (still in majority) in the fifth *Majlis* (Parliament). Kargozaaraan members, along with the Left, declared Khatami as their candidate for the next presidential elections. The May 23, 1997 (*dovvom-e khordad*), victory of Seyyed Mohammad Khatami over Natiq Nuri (the conservative speaker of Majlis) in the presidential election was a result of massive support by women and students who equated Nuri with the Taliban. As a turning point in postrevolutionary politics, the massive turnout of voters, which led to Khatami's election, was neither a change trickling down from the level of the state to society nor a movement that was completely independent of the state. Legislative changes and debates between different factions reflected the changing face of the Iranian polity. Some of these changes were related to people's access to satellite television, the internet, videos, and other communication technologies and goods, made available to them (mostly to the urban middle classes) during the period of massive imports. The policies of reformists during Khatami's presidency included political rationalization as a prerequisite to economic development, economic restructuring to promote a shift from mercantile to industrial capitalism, the enhancement of the Majlis, popular participation, decentralization and depersonalization of power, the establishment of religion as the foundation for democracy, the institutionalization of civil society, and reintegration into the "global society" (Ansari 2003b, 114–16).

10 While for Hegel civil society requires the interest-less state, for Marx the state is the representative of the dominant class, and civil society is where class struggle happens. Marx critiques autonomous reason and argues that class antagonism arising from private interests makes such objective reason impossible because of the way that the interests of dominant groups within state and society are protected under capitalism. To Marx, the economic inequality and class struggle within society inevitably translated into the guarantee of the interests of dominant groups within the state and society. Rather than combining the universal and the particular (as is the case in Hegel's idea), dissolving civil society and universalizing the particular through socializing labor and public ownership are the way to freedom and ending alienation (Femia 2001, 137).

11 In the second half of the eighteenth century, liberalism as a historical political philosophy in Europe emphasized civil society as the natural realm of freedoms and activities

immune from the limited power of state authorities. Fostering a self-organizing and self-regulating "civil society" as the realm of "natural liberties" became the task of the government. Subjects were no longer administered solely by the state but were governed in the domain of civil society that shaped the "private" realm according to the morals of family and market, and within the language of rights. Rather than the direct imposition of law, the modern liberal government regulated the conduct of the individual from a distance and by calculation techniques and programs implemented by nonstate agents (professionals). During the first half of the twentieth century in the United States and some parts of Europe, a "welfare state" was established in which the state intervened in the economy and promised to provide high levels of employment, social security, and economic growth. After the 1970s, however, a neoliberal form of governing social and economic life emerged.

Unlike welfarism, where the interventionist state seeks to guarantee mechanisms of social security, neoliberalism highlights the inefficiencies of state-regulated economy and emphasizes the market. It retains some liberal principles, such as limiting the political authority of the state in government, and replaces state planning and regulation with calculations of market and entrepreneurship. However, neoliberalism does not require the withering of the state as much as it reorganizes its political rationalities according to neoliberal technologies of government. As Peter Miller and Nicholas Rose argue, "The State must be strong to defend the interests of the nation in the international sphere and must ensure order by providing a legal framework for social and economic life. But within this framework, autonomous actors—commercial concerns, families, individuals—are to go freely about their business, making their own decisions and controlling their own destinies. Neoliberal political rationalities weave these philosophical themes into an operative political discourse" (Miller and Rose 1992).

12 These approaches (and their combinations) are rooted in the historical developments of the concept of civil society in the West, tracing back to John Locke, the Scottish theorist of commercial society.

13 In *The Birth of Biopolitics*, Michel Foucault argues that the transition from traditional eighteenth-century liberalism to nineteenth-century liberalism includes a shift from exchange to competition, where rather than a free exchange (which relies on equivalence of values), economic rationality is defined through competition. Both eighteenth-century liberalism and nineteenth-century liberalism functioned through laissez-faire, where the state at most supervised the smooth operation of the market. Twentieth-century liberals departed from the naturalism of early liberals by refuting laissez-faire as the political consequence of natural competition and advocated for intervention so that competition would be produced by active governmentality (Foucault 2008, 119–21). Foucault argues that Keynesian policy, social pacts of war, and the growth of federal economic and social programs are three elements against which American neoliberalism was formed. American neoliberalism is not just an economic policy: It is a "whole way of being and thinking" with a foothold in both the Right—with its criticism of the socialist policies—and the Left—with its struggle against the development of a military and imperialist state (Foucault 2008, 218). Following Foucault, Peter Miller and

Nicholas Rose (1992) have rightly argued that governmentality, as a historical process, includes strategies and desires of authorities that work toward forming the conduct of others in civil society by distributing tasks to different sectors. These sectors (e.g., military, educational, religious, family, and medical institutions) act according to particular political rationalities and moral justifications in changing discursive fields. Miller and Rose suggest it is through examining the connections between political rationalities and governmental technologies that we can understand how individuals, groups, and organizations are connected to the ambitions of authorities in the advanced liberal democracies of the present.

14 For an excellent analysis of *The Shahs of Sunset*, see Alex Shams, "The Shahs of Sunset . . . and the Rest of Us: 'Persian Money' in an Era of FBI Surveillance," Ajam Media Collective, February 9, 2012, accessed July 17, 2018, https://ajammc.com/2012/02/08/the-shahs-of-sunset-and-the-rest-of-us-2/. For Netanyahu's praise of Silicon Valley Iranians, see https://www.youtube.com/watch?v=e48YzZf1gGA, accessed July 17, 2018.

15 Focusing on "risky citizens" is not to suggest their exceptionality. Rather, I use them as paradigmatic figures that encapsulate my analysis of Weblogistan as a site of transnational civil society—and therefore governmentality—in the new millennium.

16 The CPD was founded in 1950 "as a bipartisan education and advocacy organization dedicated to building a national consensus for a strong defense against Soviet expansionism." It became inactive with the end of the cold war but was reactivated in response to the "war on terror." The CPD membership included over 100 former White House officials, ambassadors, cabinet secretaries, academics, writers, and other "foreign policy experts." See The Committee on the Present Danger, "Committee on the Present Danger: About Us," October 9, 2007, accessed July 31, 2017, https://web.archive.org/web/20071009234735/http:/www.committeeonthepresentdanger.org/AboutUs/tabid/363/Default.aspx. At the time of my fieldwork, the CPD was cochaired by George Shultz (secretary of state under Ronald Reagan) and R. James Woolsey (director of the CIA under Bill Clinton). Senators Joe Lieberman (D) and Jon Kyl (R) served as honorary cochairs. For a list of members, see The Committee on the Present Danger, "Committee on the Present Danger: Our Members," October 9, 2007, accessed July 31, 2017, https://web.archive.org/web/20080124113829/http://www.committeeonthepresentdanger.org/OurMembers/tabid/364/Default.aspx.

17 Michel, "The Islamic Republic Takes on the Internet: Iranian Bloggers under Fire," *Google Groups*: soc.culture.iranian, July 11, 2008, accessed July 31, 2017, https://groups.google.com/forum/#!topic/soc.culture.iranian/c8bbvlYBm0A. Also see The Committee on the Present Danger, "Committee on the Present Danger: Iran Update," October 21, 2007, accessed July 31, 2017, https://web.archive.org/web/20071021153814/http://www.committeeonthepresentdanger.org/IranUpdate/tabid/668/Default.aspx.

18 See John Kelly and Bruce Etling, "Mapping Iran's Online Public: Politics and Culture in the Persian Blogosphere," Berkman Center Research Publication no. 2008–01, April 2008, 3. More information on the Internet and Democracy Project can be found at Berkman Klein Center, "Internet and Democracy," July 2, 2018, accessed July 31, 2017. https://cyber.harvard.edu/research/internetdemocracy.

19 This research indicates that there are sixty thousand active blogs in the Persian blogosphere. The researchers divide the blogosphere into four network formations or poles: secular/reformist, conservative/religious, Persian poetry/literature, and mixed networks. They situate diaspora blogs in the secular/reformist pole, which is the turf of several discussions (including politics) while the conservative/religious pole is where distinct "sub-clusters of religious issues and politics" are placed. The research results, which are based on social network analysis (detecting links), point out that a minority of bloggers who discuss politics in the "secular/reformist" pole blog anonymously and that "blocking of blogs by the government is less pervasive than they had assumed. Most of the blogosphere network is visible inside Iran, although the most frequently blocked blogs are clearly those in the secular/reformist pole."

20 For example, see NIAC Staff, "Iranian People Are Our Allies, Pressure on Regime Needed, Experts Testify at House Hearing," NIAC (blog), February 18, 2005, accessed July 31, 2017, https://www.niacouncil.org/iranian-people-are-our-allies-pressure-on-regime-needed-experts-testify-at-house-hearing/.

21 See my post on "No War on Iran" about this statement: Sima Shakhsari, "No War on Iran!: Insurance Brokers," *No War on Iran!* (blog), February 20, 2005, accessed July 31, 2017, http://no-war-on-iran.blogspot.com/2005/02/insurance-brokers.html.

22 See Center for Constitutional Rights. 2009. "Restore. Protect. Expand: Stop Warrantless Wiretapping," 2009, accessed July 31, 2017. https://ccrjustice.org/sites/default/files/assets/files/CCR_100days_Wiretapping.pdf.

23 The report further tells us "the truth is that Iran soon can and will get a bomb option. All Iranian engineers need is a bit more time—one to four years at most. No other major gaps remain: Iran has the requisite equipment to make the weapons fuel, the know-how to assemble the bombs; and the missile and naval systems necessary to deliver them beyond its borders." See Sokolski's testimony here: Henry Sokolski, 2005, "Getting Ready for a Nuclear-Ready Iran," NPEC, February 16, accessed July 31, 2017, http://www.npolicy.org/article.php?aid=305&rtid=8.

24 For the National Iranian American Council's response to McCain, see http://www.niacouncil.org/index.php?option=com_content&task=view&id=1163&Itemid=59, accessed July 31, 2017.

25 See "U.S. Senator John McCain on Iran and Tribute To Neda Agha-Soltan," YouTube, June 22, 2009, accessed July 31, 2017, https://www.youtube.com/watch?v=biAlyEa6l9E.

26 Stephen McInerney, 2012, "The Federal Budget and Appropriations for Fiscal Year 2013: Democracy, Governance, and Human Rights in the Middle East and North Africa," Washington, DC, Project on Middle East Democracy.

27 See "U.S. President Barack Obama vows to breach Tehran's electronic curtain promising a U.S. push to ease Iranian access to the Internet," YouTube, March 8, 2013, accessed July 31, 2017, https://www.youtube.com/watch?v=pVta3sN41Cc. For a cartoon in Persian and English about the "electronic curtain" in Iran, see "Behind the Electronic Curtain," YouTube, April 12, 2012, accessed April 6, 2019, https://www.youtube.com/watch?v=Y63ElHWhG9g&t=1s, YouTube.

28 Even though P5+1 (the UN Security Council's five permanent members which include China, France, Russia, the United Kingdom, and the United States, plus Germany) signed the "Iran deal" in 2015, a slew of U.S. sanctions remained in place. In 2018 Trump signed an executive order that reversed Obama's nuclear agreement with Iran. Trump's order required that the harsh sanctions be reimposed within 90–180 days.

29 See the text of CISADA here: https://www.govinfo.gov/content/pkg/BILLS-111hr2194enr/pdf/BILLS-111hr2194enr.pdf, accessed April 6, 2019.

30 See Thomas Erdbrink, "Iran Sanctions Take Unexpected Toll on Medical Imports," *New York Times*, sec. Middle East, November 2, 2012, accessed April 6, 2019, https://www.nytimes.com/2012/11/03/world/middleeast/iran-sanctions-take-toll-on-medical-imports.html.

31 See Paul Carsten, 2012, "Barack Obama Condemns Iran for Creating 'Electronic Curtain,'" March 20, 2012, accessed April 6, 2019, http://www.telegraph.co.uk/news/worldnews/barackobama/9155783/Barack-Obama-condemns-Iran-for-creating-electronic-curtain.html.

32 One might recall the "common good" and "collective interest" in Hegelian notions of civil society.

33 For example, in an edition of Hicks File titled "Gaddafi's Bloody End: Sodomy, Summary Execution and Islamic Law in Libya," after showing graphic images of Gaddafi's execution, Joe Hicks, a conservative political commentator on PJTV.com, claims that "Putting several bullets through Gaddafi's head while the whole world watches may have been emotionally satisfying, but it strikes me as an unseemly start to an era of supposed liberty and stability in Libya. The summary execution of that nation's dictator continues a legacy of Islamic religious brutality and sets a low standard which begs a simple question: Are Muslims ready for democracy?," accessed May 22, 2013, https://www.youtube.com/watch?v=pIpAS_EKAVw.

34 See Spirit of America, http://www.spiritofamerica.net/site.

35 "Arabic Blogging Tool, Viral Freedom," http://www.spiritofamerica.net/cgibin/soa/project.pl? rm=view_ project&request_id=78.

36 For information about "Friends of Democracy," a project of Spirit of America that is based in Iraq and has funded a workshop for women, see http://www.spiritofamerica.net/cgi-bin/soa/project.pl? rm=view_project&request_id=75. The project claims that it "extends the goodwill of the American people to assist the women advancing freedom, democracy and peace in Iraq."

37 See "United States Policy on Democratizing Iran: Effects and Consequences," January 26, 2011, accessed April 6, 2019, https://www.hivos.nl/united-states-policy-on-democratizing-iran-effects-and-consequences/.

38 By no means do I intend to generalize the analysis of Weblogistan in the first decade of the new millennium to other contexts. To understand the way that civil society and governmentality articulate new forms of citizenship in the Middle East, one needs to pay attention to the historical particularities, which include distinct state formations, civil society compositions, nationalisms, histories of dissent/revolution, multiple and contentious relationships to colonialisms, American imperialism, neoliberalism, secu-

ritization, and uneven encounters with secularism. Nevertheless, the porousness of national boundaries and the relative fluidity of the movement of ideas, bodies, and capital before the rise of the modern nation-states in the region; shared colonial and anticolonial histories in some parts of the Middle East; the historical exchange of ideas (about modernization, anticolonial movements, and Islamic movements); and economic and political alliances, conflicts, and solidarities may have culminated in some similarities in the region's encounters with neoliberal digital citizenship, cybergovernmentality, and internet democratization projects. Perhaps this is where the insights from this ethnography could be most useful in understanding the "internet revolutions" in other parts of the Middle East.

39 As Morozov has argued (2012), the same companies that provided social networking tools in Egypt enabled the Mubarak dictatorship's surveillance technologies.

40 Annie Alexander and Miriyam Aouragh's critique is particularly noteworthy. Deploying a Marxist analysis of revolution, they "reject the false polarization of utopian/dystopian views of the Internet and recognize that the Internet is both a product of imperialist and capitalist logics and something that is simultaneously used by millions in the struggle to resist those logics" (2011, 1344). Pointing out that without offline political action, online protests have no meaning, they write, "To a large extent, Internet spaces and tools were the choice of young revolutionaries in Egypt because they were already the spaces and tools that people of their generation had chosen for communication in daily life" (1345). They argue that the Egyptian cosmopolitan internet-savvy *shabab-al-Facebook* (Facebook youth) and the activists who became known as "Twitter pashas" were far less in touch with the economic pressures that brought the poor and working-class Egyptians to the streets. The accounts that reduce the Egyptian intifada to a "Facebook revolution" ignore the economic crisis and the long-term discontents with the Mubarak regime in Egypt, while undermining the agency of the millions of people who participated in the protests (1344).

41 Deleuze and Guattari's description of the "smooth space" as "finite networks of automata in which communication runs from any neighbor to any other, the stems or channels do not pre-exist, and all individuals are interchangeable, defined only by their state at a given moment—such that the local operations are coordinated and the final, global result synchronized without central agency" (1987, 17) was seen as a prophecy for the future of the internet. For example, in his "Rhizome@Internet," Hamman (1996) claims that the internet encapsulates all principles of the rhizome: connection and heterogeneity, multiplicity, asignifying rupture, not being amenable to any structural or generative model, and resemblance to a map with multiple points of entry.

42 For example, the Electronic Disturbance lays out this anarchist strategy as a way of nomadic resistance: "Nomadic power must be resisted in cyberspace rather than in physical space. A small but coordinated group of hackers could introduce electronic viruses, worms, and bombs into the data banks, programs, and networks of authority, possibly bringing the destructive force of inertia into the nomadic realm. Prolonged inertia equals the collapse of nomadic authority on a global level. Such a strategy does not require action in numerous geographic areas" (25).

43 Hardt and Negri (2000, xii) engage with the concept of empire as a new form of sovereignty, "composed of a series of national and supranational organisms united under a single logic of rule.... The passage to Empire emerges from the twilight of modern sovereignty. In contrast to imperialism, Empire establishes no territorial center of power and does not rely on fixed boundaries or barriers. It is a decentered and deterritorializing apparatus of rule that progressively incorporates the entire global realm within its open, expanding frontiers. Empire manages hybrid identities, flexible hierarchies, and plural exchanges through modulating networks of command."

44 Hardt and Negri assume the rise of the post-Fordist multitude to represent the struggle between the constituted and the constituent power. For them, similar to capitalism, the forces that define the empire will be destroyed through self-organized democracy, for which the constitutive element is the multitude.

45 As several scholars have argued, Hardt and Negri's analyses of decentralized and networked empire and multitude remain U.S.-centric (Buchanan and Pahuja 2004; Laffey and Weldes 2004). Buchanan and Pahuja (2004) have pointed out that not only Hardt and Negri's dismissal of the nation-state ignores the hegemony of the international law as a mode of sovereignty; it also naturalizes the world market by undermining its reliance on the state (78–83). The distinction between the "new" empire and old imperialism further mystifies the decentralization of the empire that the vanishing borders are assumed to engender. The strict immigration laws and the U.S. hegemony attest to the fact that the "smooth surface" of the networked and diffuse empire is nothing but a fiction. Unlike the idealized notion of multitude as nomadic, the material effects of immigration laws on racialized immigrant and refugee bodies render the romanticized notion of a mobile and networked multitude a Eurocentric fetishization of mobility (Dunn 2004). Hardt and Negri's nomads are closer to the privileged cosmopolitan elites, who—to borrow from Aihwa Ong—practice flexible citizenship.

46 Using the Foucauldian notion of biopower and biopolitical governance, Hardt and Negri rightly argue that the implication of the formation of the international human rights regimes in the twentieth century is an extension of the biopolitical. They also use Deleuze and Guattari's notion of the control society to argue that control has become more "democratic" as it operates through the brains and bodies, where it is immaterial labor that organizes social relations through affect and communication networks. Hardt and Negri argue that the empire is incapable of encapsulating and controlling all aspects of social life. This inevitably leads to "the uncontainable temporal variability of the event" (2000, 26). They suggest that we have to accelerate the process of globalization through "counter-globalization" and "desertion, exodus, and nomadism" (2000, 206–12). As Passavant and Dean (2004) have pointed out, it is not clear how the multitude will automatically self-organize in a horizontal manner, especially if the multitude is not to counter the empire.

47 Gerbaudo (2012) maintains that contrary to the assumptions of spatial dispersion, internet-mediated protests produce a sense of unity through the "choreography of assembly," a process in which physical bodies assemble through emotional scripting in a symbolically constructed public space. He argues that while social media may have a role in announcing protest locations, providing instructions and directives, and constructing

an emotional narration to appeal to those who frequent social media, they are neither replacing street protests, nor are they the force behind the protests. Gerbaudo's analysis challenges the accounts that exaggerate the role of social media in the Arab Spring, pointing out that the blackout imposed by the Mubarak regime had a limited effect on the street protests. While Gerbaudo is right in highlighting the role of social media in the choreography of street protests, the notion of "soft leadership" does not engage with the complex operations of power in relationship to "internet democratization" projects in the Middle East.

48 Jodi Dean's "Communicative Capitalism" (2005) provides one of the most useful critiques of what she—with a nod to Marx—aptly calls "technology fetishism." Discussing the foreclosure of politics through this form of fetishism, Dean defines communication capitalism as "the commonplace idea that the market, today, is the site of democratic aspirations, indeed, the mechanism by which the will of the demos manifests itself" (54). As Dean argues, the circulation of communication has a depoliticizing effect, as it displaces political participation. Technological fetishism operates through "condensation," meaning that the "complexities of politics—of organization, struggle, duration, decisiveness, division, representation, etc.—are condensed into one thing, one problem to be solved and one technological solution" (63). The immediacy of sharing files, which contributes to technology fetishism, Dean argues, excludes the possibility of politicization (65).

Chapter 1: Weblogistan and the Iranian Diaspora

1 Derakhshan was arrested in 2008 in Iran. His original blog was erased, but he has been blogging in English and Persian again since July 2015, after his release in 2014. He is currently a research fellow at Harvard University's Kennedy School. See his blog, accessed June 19, 2018, www.hoder.com.
2 See Duncan Riley's article, "The Blog Herald Blog Count October 2005: Over 100 Million Blogs Created," Blog Herald, October 10, 2005, accessed July 31, 2017, http://www.blogherald.com/2005/10/10/the-blog-herald-blog-count-october-2005.
3 The 2009 ONI (Open Network Initiative) report claims that internet use in Iran had increased to 34 percent. During my research, the CIA country report and the ONI report listed 8 to 10 percent. Iran's communication ministry still reports the number of internet users to be at 11 percent. See "Statistics for the Iran Communications Company," accessed July 31, 2017, http://www.internetworldstats.com/me/ir.htm.
4 For a critique of blog statistics and their accuracy, see Khiabany and Sreberny (2007).
5 Because of Canada's "professional visa" program, which attracts a younger generation of computer-savvy Iranian immigrants, Toronto has a large number of Iranian bloggers.
6 For example, one Toronto blogger wrote an unpublished blog that she intended for her son to read later.
7 Bloggers may use the same service for publishing and hosting or use different publishing and hosting software/services. Comments can also be managed by a different software/service than the blog-hosting service. Some Iranian bloggers use the ready-made

templates and alter them slightly by changing the HTML code. Others design their own templates (or pay someone to design a template) and then host it on a free or paid blog-hosting service. The Iranian blog hosting services are Persian Blog, Blogfa, Blogsky, Mihanblog, Parsiblog, and Persianlog. Blog Count ranked Persian Blog second globally, sparking the attention of private investors and creating competition for blog-hosting services in Iran.

8 For more on this cartoon, published in the July 5, 1993, issue of the *New Yorker*, see https://www.washingtonpost.com/blogs/comic-riffs/post/nobody-knows-youre-a-dog-as-iconic-internet-cartoon-turns-20-creator-peter-steiner-knows-the-joke-rings-as-relevant-as-ever/2013/07/31/73372600-f98d-11e2-8e84-c56731a202fb_blog.html?utm_term=.8da284fe471f, accessed July 31, 2017.

9 Subsequently, in 2003 the Committee to Determine Illegal Websites and a branch for internet affairs to identify and prosecute "criminal" internet activity were formed. The circulation of regime-change discourse at the onset of the "war on terror" gave rise to national security concerns by the Iranian state. During the 2009 street protests in Iran, threats to national security were used to legitimize the arrest of several journalists/bloggers who were accused of participating in antiestablishment activities.

10 For different ways that Iranians circumvent filtering, see http://www.computerworld.com/article/2482074/technology-law-regulation/four-ways-iranians-are-beating-internet-censorship.html, accessed August 2, 2017.

11 See the Open Network Initiative report titled "Internet Filtering in Iran 2004–2005: A Country Study," accessed July 31, 2017, https://dash.harvard.edu/bitstream/handle/1/2794837/Internet%20Filtering%20in%20Iran.pdf?sequence=2.

12 IBB, the parent agency of Voice of America, provides funding for Tor and Psiphon, two internet anticensorship projects.

13 See "US Sponsors Anonymizer if You Live in Iran," accessed July 31, 2017, http://www.theregister.co.uk/2003/08/29/us_sponsors_anonymiser_if_you.

14 See "Unintended Risks and Consequences of Circumvention Technologies: The IBB's Anonymizer Service in Iran," ONI Advisory 001, modified May 5, 2004, accessed July 31, 2017, http://opennet.net/advisories/001.

15 This became the subject of jokes about how the U.S. Department of State's heteronormative security measure that sought to eliminate the "asses of evil" came back to bite it in its own ass.

16 See "An Unprecedented Look at Stuxnet, the World's First Digital Weapon," *Wired*, November 3, 2014, accessed July 31, 2017, https://www.wired.com/2014/11/countdown-to-zero-day-stuxnet.

17 See "Internet in Chains: The Front Line of State Repression in Iran," International Campaign for Human Rights in Iran, November 2014, accessed July 31, 2017, https://www.iranhumanrights.org/wp-content/uploads/Internet_report-En.pdf.

18 See "Head of Tehran's Cybercrimes Unit Is Fired over Death of Blogger," *New York Times*, December 1, 2012, accessed July 31, 2017, http://www.nytimes.com/2012/12/02/world/middleeast/after-death-of-sattar-beheshti-iranian-blogger-head-of-tehrans-cybercrimes-unit-is-fired.html.

19 See "Iran Rolls Out Domestic Internet," BBC, August 29, 2016, accessed July 31, 2017, http://www.bbc.com/news/technology-37212456.
20 See "How Iran Is Building Its Censorship-Friendly Domestic Internet," *Wired*, September 23, 2016, accessed July 31, 2017, https://www.wired.com/2016/09/how-iran-is-building-its-censorship-friendly-domestic-internet.
21 See "U.S. Announces Measures to Fight Tehran's 'Electronic Curtain,'" Radio Free Europe, March 20, 2012, accessed July 31, 2017, https://www.rferl.org/a/obama_says_electronic_curtain_divides_us_iran_peoples/24521934.html.
22 See "Austin Heap: How I Helped Iran's Citizens to Beat the Censor," *Guardian*, March 21, 2010, accessed April 9, 2019, https://www.theguardian.com/technology/2010/mar/21/austin-heap-haystack-iran.
23 See "Censorship Research Center," accessed July 31, 2017, https://www.causes.com/censorshipresearch.
24 See "The Great Internet Freedom Fraud," *Slate*, September 16, 2010, accessed July 31, 2017, http://www.slate.com/articles/technology/technology/2010/09/the_great_internet_freedom_fraud.html.
25 The increasing use of FriendFeed and Google Reader caused some bloggers to update their blogs less frequently and instead use real-time social networking, a phenomenon that a friend jokingly called the "post-Weblogistan" era. A year after I stopped blogging, a blogger friend invited me to join Ferfer. Making the argument that "serious" political discussions take place in Ferfer, she told me that "Facebook is child's play!" Even though I did not open a Ferfer account, I monitored it occasionally during the 2009 presidential election. The speed with which news of street protests traveled in Ferfer was indeed incredibly fast: people would immediately feed news from direct participation, from state news, or from their phone conversations with friends at the protests. While Twitter was used by some Iranians in Iran during the 2009 election protests, it was not widespread among resident Iranian internet users.
26 Google Reader was discontinued because of low rates of use. The Iranian government has attempted to block Google several times and has made it difficult for Iranians to access Goder in different periods. It remains to be seen if alternative feeders can circumvent the Iranian state's censorship efforts. See http://www.washingtonpost.com/blogs/worldviews/wp/2013/03/15/irans-web-censors-vs-google-reader, accessed July 31, 2017.
27 See the Balatarin website, accessed May 31, 2017, https://www.balatarin.com, accessed May 31, 2017.
28 Gene Sharp, who to some is known as the "Machiavelli of nonviolent struggles," is a U.S.-based political scientist whose writings were used in the training of movements that resulted in "color revolutions" in Eastern Europe. For more information see "Nonviolence, Power, and Possibility: The Life of Gene Sharp," in *The Progressive*, accessed July 31, 2017, http://progressive.org/magazine/nonviolence-power-and-possibility-the-life-of-gene-sharp.
29 For example, see a report produced by Bruce Etling and John Kelly (2008) at the Berkman Center. The authors divide Persian blogs into secularist, religious, poetry, and mixed categories.

30 In September 2005 the Danish newspaper *Jyllands Posten* published what have become known as the "Mohammad cartoons," which depicted Prophet Mohammad (and by extension, Muslims) as a violent misogynist terrorist. Outraging Muslims across the world, this led to massive protests in early 2006. For a time line of the controversy, see http://www.telegraph.co.uk/news/worldnews/europe/france/11341599/Prophet-Muhammad-cartoons-controversy-timeline.html, accessed July 31, 2017.

31 For a critique of Irshad Manji's work, see Saadia Toor, "Gender, Sexuality, and Islam under the Shadow of Empire," S&F Online, accessed July 31, 2017, http://sfonline.barnard.edu/religion/print_toor.htm.

32 Abtahi was arrested and imprisoned in the aftermath of the 2009 presidential election. Oddly, he was allowed to update his blog from prison, after his public "confession" of endangering national security.

33 For more on this issue, see http://www.iranian.com/Sep96/Web/InternetIran/InternetIran.html, accessed July 31, 2017.

34 IP addresses classification was used between 1981 to 1995 to divide internet protocol addresses based on the network size. Class A belonged to large corporations; Class B belonged to medium networks, such as universities; and Class C belonged to small businesses. For more information on how the classification of IPs works, see http://computer.howstuffworks.com/internet/basics/question549.htm, accessed July 31, 2017.

35 Changes in foreign investment laws in 2002 increased investment in non-oil sectors. Despite liberalizing foreign trade since Rafsanjani's reconstruction plans, the International Monetary Fund (IMF) has pushed Iran to further liberalize and dissolve its protection of import-substitution sectors and labor-protection laws (IMF 2003). A bill to reduce regulations on the labor market was opposed by the Left in the fifth *Majlis* (Parliament). The Iranian government abided by the requirements of the WTO officials, such as the privatization of state-owned companies. The tightening of sanctions on Iran significantly reduced foreign investment.

36 While keeping track of diaspora Iranians' investment in Iran is impossible because of the unofficial ways that money is transferred to and from Iran, these investments grew as the result of the removal of expatriate Iranians' investment restrictions; the post–September 11, 2001, concerns about keeping savings in the U.S. banks; and the high return on investment in Iran. While I could not locate the Central Bank of Iran's records of Iranian expatriates' investments, I was told by an Iranian consulting firm (Atieh Bahar) that even though keeping track of the Iranian diaspora's investments in Iran is impossible, the records showed a large increase of investment by Iranian expatriates, especially those in the United States, in Iran's construction and communication technologies.

37 Ameri also became George Bush's appointed delegate to the United Nations Human Rights Commission in 2005.

38 See the CIA *World Factbook* on Iran: https://www.cia.gov/library/publications/resources/the-world-factbook/docs/whatsnew.html.

39 Brian Nicholson and Sundeep Sahay, researchers who were contracted to write a report for Vetus Systems—a private-sector IT organization based in Tehran—write that "liber-

alization and attention to ICT has been caused in part by recognition that the country needs alternative strategies to reliance on oil revenues. The Iranian economy relies on the oil and gas industry, which accounts for over 80 percent of its export earnings. Second, drawing from the examples of Malaysia and Singapore, there has been recognition of the need to take action to obtain some of the benefits of developments in the 'network society'" (Nicholson and Sahay 2003). By deploying a "software export success model," the authors suggest that the IT strategy should be focused on creating a climate conducive to foreign investment. The strategies recommended by these contracted researchers include developing "competence in a list of different service offerings for domestic and international markets ranging from body shopping, [establishment of] call centers," collaborating with software firms in India or Russia, and making connections with the "unexploited diaspora-based links." In January 2003 a team from Iran traveled to India and met with NASSCOM, the "nonprofit" industry that "is the apex body for the 154 billion-dollar Indian IT industry." See http://www.nasscom.in. Subsequently, the Iranian authorities invited NASSCOM to Iran to conduct a workshop and establish a formal memorandum of understanding for further future collaboration. The development of an IT park is also under way in Tehran. See http://unpan1.un.org/intradoc/groups/public/documents/NISPAcee/UNPAN015616.pdf, accessed July 31, 2017.

40 In 2003 a ten-hour internet card could be purchased for 2,500 to 5,000 tomans ($2.50 to $5.00).

41 This figure rose to 21 percent in 2009.

42 The actual number may be significantly higher because of the fact that some Iranians may choose other categories in the census. Of course, many people do not participate in the census at all.

43 Of the 95,420 Iranians who immigrated from Iran, 27,600 arrived between 2001 and 2006. Most of my interlocutors in Toronto immigrated to Canada in this period.

44 The estimated number of Iranians in Los Angeles is 300,000 to 500,000.

45 While the twentieth-century migration of Iranians began in the 1950s (students, visitors, political exiles, etc.), the 1990 census reports that 30.9 percent of Iranian immigrants came to the United States between 1985 and 1990, 18.5 percent between 1980 and 1988, and 34.2 percent between 1975 and 1979.

46 According to the Iranian Studies Group at MIT, the U.S. census underestimates the number of Iranians in the United States. For example, at the time of my research the Iranian Studies Group estimated the number to be 690,000, rather than the 338,000 reported by the 2000 U.S. census (Mostashari and Khodamhosseini 2004).

47 The percentage of Iranian Americans with a bachelor's degree or higher was 57.2 percent in comparison to the 24.4 percent national average.

48 The existing scholarship has provided demographic data on the Iranian diaspora (Bozorgmehr 1988, 1998), concentrated on sociological classifications of Iranian exiles and immigrants (Bozorgmehr and Sabbagh 1989), focused on issues of entrepreneurship (Dallalfar 1996; Moallem 1991, 1999, 2000), explored gender and sexuality (Bauer 2000; Dallalfar 1994; Hanassab 1998; Mahdi 2002; Moallem 1991, 1999, 2000; Tohidi 1993), examined generational issues (Chaichian 1997; Mahdi 1998), analyzed assimilation and

identity (Ansari 1992; Ghaffarian 1987; Mostofi 2003), explored "exilic" cultural productions (Naficy 1991, 1993, 1998), or produced biographical anthologies on the Iranian diaspora (Sullivan 2001). My research benefits from this literature and adds to it by exploring more-recent social formations as a result of the immigration of a new generation of Iranians in diaspora who often come from universities in Iran to pursue their postgraduate studies in North America and Europe.

49 Because there is no U.S. embassy in Iran, many Iranians go to Turkey to seek student visas or asylum in the United States, Canada, Australia, and Europe.

50 The currency of modernist and gendered definitions of exile in describing the "Iranian community" often homogenizes the multiplicity of experiences of displacement.

51 Needless to say, this mobility is contingent on class, gender, and changes in the visa regulations between Iran and the United States.

52 Problematizing the masculinist deployments of exile, many transnational feminist scholars find diaspora to be a generative theoretical framework for interrogating essentialist notions of home, origin, nation, and identity. Moreover, in the past few years the term *diaspora* has gained currency among Iranians who formerly described themselves as "exiles." This new naming may be the result of a number of factors: increased movement and multilocationality of Iranians after the end of the Iran–Iraq war, the emergence of a generation of younger Iranians who did not leave Iran in the aftermath of the 1979 revolution as adults and therefore do not consider themselves to be exiled, and recent immigrants who have migrated to the United States, Canada, or Europe for work or education. As I discuss in chapter 4, the shift from exile to diaspora has done little to change these exclusions in new territorializations. The uncritical uses of diaspora tend to romanticize displacement and hybridity versus a fixed homeland. Yet diaspora is not necessarily a transgressive shift from the nation and its gendered configurations.

53 During my fieldwork I encountered several of these exaggerated stories. A blogger friend told me that she was asked to write a letter of support for a grant application. The applicant—a woman who had no history of involvement in the women's-rights movement in Iran—claimed that she was one of the leaders of the women's-rights movement.

54 After the 2009 presidential election and the massive street protests by voters who accused the Ahmadinejad government of election fraud, the regime-change apparatus outside of Iran appropriated people's movement, thus jeopardizing the pro-reform protesters in Iran. Many Iranian bloggers/activists who once traveled between Iran and the United States were no longer able to do so, fearing arrest.

55 I discuss the chic of diaspora in chapter 4.

56 The literature on the Iranian diaspora in the United States has grown in its volume and nuance as a result of the increasing number of Iranian diaspora academics in humanities and social sciences. Some of this literature has provided demographic data on the Iranian diaspora (Askari 1977; Bozorgmehr, 1998; Bozorgmehr and Sabbagh 1988; Momeni 1984). Other scholars have concentrated on sociological classifications of Iranian exiles and immigrants (Bozorgmehr and Sabbagh 1989) and their internal ethnic groupings (Bozorgmehr 1997; Feher 1998; Ungar 1995). Other sociological works have concentrated on issues of entrepreneurship (Dallalfar 1996; Mobasher 1996), gender

and sexuality (Ahmadi 2003; Dallalfar 1996; Hanassab 1998; Hanassab and Tidwell 1989; Mahdi 2002; Tohidi 1993), generational issues (Chaichian 1997; Mahdi 1998), and assimilation and identity (Ansari 1992; BiParva 1994; Ghaffarian 1987; Gilanshah 1990; Mostofi 2003). A few scholars have taken a cultural studies approach to exile (Naficy 1993, 1998; Nazeri 1996) or have produced biographical anthologies on Iranian diaspora (Karim and Khorrami 1999; Sullivan 2001).

57 I use "America" as a construct that is also used by Iranians to refer to the United States. I am aware of the erroneous usage of the term, which hides the history of U.S. settler colonialism and subsumes Central and South America by centering the United States. "America," as Grewal (2005) has aptly argued in the case of South Asian diaspora, is "a nationalist discourse that produced many kinds of agency and diverse subjects. America functioned as a discourse of neoliberalism making possible struggles for rights through consumerist practices and imaginaries that come to be used both inside and outside the territorial boundaries of the United States" (2).

58 Fully funded by the U.S. government, Voice of America is a multimedia source (radio, television, and internet) that provides programming for audiences outside of the United States. Initially established as a cold war propaganda entity, it continues its programming in many languages, including Persian. Voice of America Persian started its activity after the 1979 Iranian revolution. Radio Farda is another U.S. government–funded Persian radio, television, and website, based in Prague. A branch of Radio Free Europe/Radio Liberty, Radio Farda started its Persian-language programming in 2002. Both of these U.S. government–funded media produce cultural and political programs to advance U.S. interests and foreign policy. While Radio Farda had less hawkish programming than VOA, a group of journalists who had collaborated with Radio Farda were arrested in Iran in 2010.

59 This blogger, who was a recent immigrant and whose job choices were limited, found herself in a position to accept a job at VOA. She told me that she and her colleagues were not allowed to do any programming independently or to challenge biased representations of Iran. Programs by staff went through several levels of approval by supervisors, who were from the older generation of Iranian immigrants and opposition forces.

60 Despite its efforts to represent itself as apolitical and nonideological, Voice of America's cold war history is transparent to politically informed Iranians.

61 Overlooking the history of modernity in Iran, the narrative in these comparisons follows a sharp binary between traditional Iran and modern West, a topic to which I will return in chapter 3.

62 From 1967 until 2005, Peykan was considered to be the national Iranian car. Until the 1979 revolution, Peykan parts were manufactured by a British company and assembled in Iran. Parts were increasingly manufactured and assembled in Iran after the revolution. Peykan's production was discontinued in 2005. While it was a popular car for its affordable price, it was not considered to be a high-quality vehicle.

63 After Mehdi wrote this post, I was attacked by many hostile commenters who called me an IRI (Islamic Republic of Iran) spy. Mehdi wrote another post in my defense, in which he clarified that despite his disagreements with me, he did not condone abusive and accusatory comments.

64 See "No California Reunion for Iranian Visitors," NPR, August 7, 2006, accessed July 31, 2017, http://www.npr.org/templates/story/story.php?storyId=5624488, 2017.

65 Neda, an Iranian blogger who resided in the United States, was denied reentry when she visited Canada. Despite the fact that she was admitted to a prestigious university in the United States and held a valid student visa, she was stalled in Canada for months because of the lengthy background check by Homeland Security. Ultimately, she decided to stay in Canada and gave up the opportunity to pursue her education in the United States, which, as she put it, was imbued with *khaari* (humiliation). Another blogger, a refugee in Canada who was not yet a Canadian citizen, refused to travel with his Iranian passport and Canadian refugee travel document because he was worried about U.S. immigration laws. He told me that he was hesitant to accept an invitation to speak at a conference in the United States as he was not sure what would happen to him at the border. Simin, a doctoral student whose husband and teenage children had moved with her to the United States, was barred from reentry in 2005 after traveling to the United Kingdom to visit her parents. She was stuck there for five months, during which she missed a semester's worth of course work, not to mention being separated from her family. Frustrated by U.S. immigration policies, she asked me to help her start a blog in English, which she titled *Denied Entry* and in which she wrote about discriminatory U.S. immigration policies and her own experience of being denied reentry. Parastoo, a blogger whose husband was admitted to the United States with a work visa to work for Radio Farda, told me that she felt like a prisoner as she could not afford international-student tuition and could not legally work in the United States. She was not able to visit her family in Iran, for there was no guarantee that she would be able to get a reentry visa. For bloggers and blog readers such as Parastoo and Simin, the meaning of exile does not stem from a fear of persecution in the "homeland" but from the immigration laws that restrict movement and make border crossing risky.

66 For a gender analysis of the figures of the sun and the lion, see Najmabadi, *Women with Mustaches and Men without Beards* (2005).

67 This is not to say that prerevolutionary Iranian nationalism embraced queers. Modern nationalist discourses before and after the revolution have produced a heteronormative image of Iran and Iranianness. See Najmabadi's *Women without Mustaches and Men without Beards* for a historical study of the formation of a heteronormative modern national culture in Iran.

68 For the Google bomb error message see, "The Gulf You Are Looking For Does Not Exist," accessed July 31, 2017, http://arabian-gulf.info.

69 See *National Geographic*'s press release, accessed July 31, 2017, http://press.nationalgeographic.com/2004/11/23/statement-on-persian-gulfarabian-gulf.

70 For a discussion of this Google bombing and cybernationalism, see Niki Akhavan, *Electronic Iran: The Cultural Politics of an Online Evolution* (2013). As Akhavan argues, internet-enabled nationalist mobilizations by the Iranian diaspora go back to the 1990s.

71 See Megan Stack, "Iran's Anger over a New Map Magnifies a Perception Gulf," *Los Angeles Times*, December 2, 2004, accessed June 18, 2018, http://articles.latimes.com/2004/dec/02/world/fg-gulfwar2.

72 See Abtahi's blog post, accessed June 18, 2018, http://www.webneveshteha.com/weblog/?id=1100608704.

73 Historically referred to as the "Persian Gulf," some Arab states have used "Arabian Gulf" to refer to this body of water, especially since the 1960s and the rise of pan-Arabism. The conflict over the three islands of Abu Musa, the Greater Tunb, and the Lesser Tunb, which since 1971 has become a matter of discord between the UAE and Iran, was initially a dispute started by British colonizers. In the mid nineteenth century, Iran refused to grant the British a military base in the islands to protect the British trade routes in the Persian Gulf. In retaliation, the British attempted to produce evidence of the inheritance rights of Oman to some of the islands. In 1903 Iran's attempt to establish customs offices in Abu Musa and the Tunbs was stopped by the British, who claimed that the Qawasim sheikhs of Sharjah and Ras al-Khaimah had "inherited rights" in the islands. Since 1971, when the British left the gulf and the UAE was formed, the matter has been handled by the rules of international law. Currently, Iran rejects the jurisdiction of the international court, while the United Arab Emirates prefers to submit the issue to this court. The islands were declared by the Iranian Foreign Ministry to be "inseparable parts of Iran." In 2001 the Gulf Cooperation Council announced UAE's sovereignty over the islands.

74 Blog games function like a snowball effect: A blogger invites a few bloggers to write about a concept. The invited bloggers, in turn, invite others, and thus a large number of bloggers write on the same subject.

75 See Kowsar's post, accessed July 31, 2017, http://nikahang.blogspot.com/2007/09/blog-post_4084.html.

76 As Najmabadi (2005) argues, the nationalist imaginations of Iranianness have consistently denied the existence of homosexuality, relegating it to "foreign" influence.

77 See http://noqte.com/blogs/blog.php?code=172, accessed February 27, 2006. (Khaledian has since deleted his blog.) Kamvari and I responded separately to Khaledian's offensive post with satire and received a large number of extremely hostile comments directed not only at us but also our mothers and sisters.

78 Interestingly, some of the responses to Khaledian included examples of homosexuality in seventh-century Iranian poetry. While this response was meant to counter Khaledian's historical amnesia, it often fell into ahistorical traps. That is, in the earnest attempts to excavate homosexuals in Iranian history, transhistorical identities were assigned to those who may have practiced homosexual acts or homoerotic *shahid baazi* (the Sufi practice of contemplating the beauty of God by looking at and describing the beauty of beardless youth) as rites of passage in Sufism.

79 See Steve Duin, 2010, "Mana Neyestani Honored for Courage in Cartooning," *The Oregonian*, June 19, accessed July 19, 2018, https://www.oregonlive.com/news/oregonian/steve_duin/index.ssf/2010/06/mana_neyestani_honored_for_cou.html.

80 William Beeman, "Will the U.S. Support the Terrorists to Destabilize Iran?" New America Media, http://news.newamericamedia.org/news/view_article.html?article_id=0a3f42cca536140506e6a708be367b98.

81 For the U.S. secretary of energy statement about the Baku-Tbilisi-Ceyhan pipeline, see http://turkey.usembassy.gov/news_05252005.html.

82 Jokes that portray Azeri people, the largest "minority" ethnic group in Iran, as gullible and stupid "asses" are prevalent among Persians.
83 See http://alpr.30morgh.org/archives/004471.php.
84 See "The Obama Record on Deportations: Deporter-in-Chief or Not?" Migration Policy Institute, January 26, 2017, accessed July 1, 2018, https://www.migrationpolicy.org/article/obama-record-deportations-deporter-chief-or-not.
85 For a comparison of the Obama and Trump administrations' immigration policies, see https://www.vox.com/2018/6/21/17488458/obama-immigration-policy-family-separation-border, accessed July 1, 2018.
86 For the amendment to the original text of the lawsuit, see http://endthetravelban.com/blog/wp-content/uploads/2017/03/31-1-Amended-Complaint-for-Delcaratory-and-Injunctive-Relief-REDACTED-FOR-PUBLIC-RELEASE.pdf.
87 See the joint statement of Iranian-American Organizations on Detentions of Iranians at https://www.niacouncil.org/joint-statement-iranian-american-organizations-detentions-iranians.
88 Semira Nikou, "The Travel Ban and Iranian-Americans," MERIP, May 9, 2017, accessed April 9, 2019, https://merip.org/2017/05/the-travel-ban-and-iranian-americans/.
89 See "'Los Angeles Embodies Diversity': The City's New Sculpture Celebrating Freedom Is Unveiled," *Los Angeles Times*, July 4, 2017, accessed April 9, 2019, http://www.latimes.com/local/lanow/la-me-freedom-sculpture-20170704-story.html.
90 "'Los Angeles Embodies Diversity,'" July 4, 2017.
91 "'Los Angeles Embodies Diversity,'" July 4, 2017.

Chapter 2: Civil Society, Soccer, and Gendered Politics

1 In postrevolutionary Iran a large and diverse body of organizations that were involved in the Iranian polity created a complex and multicentered scene of exercising power. Despite the will of conservative factions, and against the erroneous assumptions by many opposition groups in exile, this fragmentation has prevented the government from containing the polyphony of politics, especially after the end of the war and the death of the unassailable leader, Khomeini. By 1981, when most political parties (including the Socialist and Communist Parties) that posed a threat to the *vilaayat-e faqeeh* (the rule of the faqeeh/source of emulation) had been suppressed, Khomeini's followers were divided into factions according to their views on political Islam and their interpretation of *fiqh* (Islamic jurisprudence). Those who believed in *fiqh-e sonnati* (traditional fiqh) claimed that the Islamic state should follow the pure Mohammadan Islam (*Islam-e naab-e Mohammadi*). They believed that primary ordinances based on the Qur'an and the Sunna were sufficient for governance and that secondary ordinances should be issued only in extraordinary circumstances. Others, who believed in a dynamic fiqh (*fiqh-e pouya*), argued that Sharia should produce new and changing decrees according to the needs of the time (Moslem 2002, 47–49). Although Iran's factions often overlap in their ideas, generally speaking, within the context of postrevolutionary Iranian politics,

the proponents of fiqh-e sonnati, who believe in the adaptation of the Islamic society and the state to orthodox Shia jurisprudence, formed the conservative camp. Those who believed that Islam should adapt to the needs of revolutionary Iran constituted the Left and later the "pragmatists." However, views on fiqh have not been the only dividing factor in Iranian politics. Different leftist and conservative factions have shifted alliances and diverge on sociopolitical issues, the economy, and foreign policy. As a matter of fact, it is not the question of "whose Islam is more authentic" that drives factional politics in Iran today. Contentions over democracy and civil society are the center of political debates.

2 It is beyond the scope of this chapter to provide a detailed account of the history of factional politics in prerevolutionary and postrevolutionary Iran. For a history of political parties before the revolution, see Ervand Abrahamian, *Iran between Two Revolutions* (1982). For a summary of factional politics in postrevolutionary Iran, see Mehdi Moslem, *Factional Politics in Post-Khomeini Iran* (2002).

3 See "Stay Out of It, Obama," *Daily Beast*, June 19, 2009, accessed July 31, 2017, http://www.thedailybeast.com/stay-out-of-it-obama. In a 2009 interview, Hillary Clinton, then secretary of state, claimed that the United States supported Iranian protesters behind the scenes. See the transcript of her interview with CNN's Fareed Zakaria, August 9, 2009, http://transcripts.cnn.com/TRANSCRIPTS/0908/09/fzgps.01.html.

4 Boroumand is the cofounder of the Abdorrahman Boroumand Foundation for the Promotion of Human Rights and Democracy in Iran.

5 In the first postrevolutionary period (1979–89), the conservatives (also known as "the traditional Right") held conservative views toward the economy and supported the *bazaar*. They defended the sanctity of private property and a free-market economy, opposed the taxation of the private sector, and countered the revolutionary redistributive tendencies of the Left. The conservative Right also advocated for strict implementation of Sharia and traditional fiqh and opposed the ideas of exporting revolution to other Muslim countries (Moslem 2002, 47–81). While Rafsanjani (the speaker of Majlis and his followers, later forming the "pragmatists") were inclined toward the dynamic fiqh and favored some statist measures and thus supported the Left on some issues, in the beginning of the revolution, after Khomeini's death, and up until the fifth Majlis (1996), they were more aligned with conservatives such as Khamene'i and certainly advocated a free-market economy. The Left (who called themselves *maktab-i*—followers of the school of Islam) had a more revolutionary stance and advocated state-controlled redistribution of wealth. They believed in the export of revolution, advocated dynamic fiqh, and had a less strict approach to sociopolitical freedoms. Just before his death, Imam Khomeini mediated between the two factions and encouraged the collaboration of the president (conservative Khamene'i), the prime minister (leftist Mousavi), and the speaker of Majlis (conservative ally and centrist Rafsanjani). After Khomeini's death in 1989, Khamene'i was appointed the supreme leader, and Rafsanjani became president. Rafsanjani had strategically formed alliances with conservatives, as his involvement with the "Irangate affair" had angered the Left. During the revisions to the Constitution, the Left and conservatives changed their positions on certain issues, according

to their future interests. Conservatives who backed Rafsanjani and expected his presidency started to advocate for a strong centralized state, something they had previously opposed, resenting the revolutionary redistributive tendencies of leftist prime minister Mir Hussein Mousavi. The Left (*maktabees*) who supported Khomeini's leadership were previously supportive of a strong *vali-ye faqeeh* (source of emulation). After Khomeini's death, they objected to the increased control of the faqeeh in the new Constitution, fearing that the conservative Khamene'i would not favor them (Moslem 2002, 82–84). Khamene'i and Rafsanjani formed a united front (up until 1994) to protect the vulnerable Islamic state after Khomeini's death.

6 In 1988 a group of leftist clergymen separated from the conservative Society of Militant Clergies (*jaamee'e-ye rouhaanyoun-e mobaariz*) and formed the Association of Militant Clergies (*majma'-e rouhaanyoun-e mobaariz*). Khatami (the minister of culture during Rafsanjani's presidency and the reformist president between 1997 and 2005), who was part of this new association, explained that majma'-e rouhaaniyoun-e mobaariz had no choice but to pronounce its opinions, and he condemned conservatives for their "American brand of Islam" (Moslem 2002, 70). Under Khatami's rule as minister of culture, films, books, and other artistic production proliferated. By 1992, however, a conservative backlash resulted in the removal of Khatami from the Ministry of Culture and culminated in his replacement by the conservative *mo'talefeh* (Islamic Coalition Party) members. Between 1992 and 1996, under Rafsanjani's presidency the conservatives who had succeeded in removing the Left from Parliament in the 1992 elections imposed strict sociocultural policies. The marginalization of the Left was mainly the result of the alliance among Rafsanjani, his supporters, and conservatives, who despised the revolutionary policies of the Left in economic and foreign policy matters. In 1990 the conservative Assembly of Experts changed the laws of election to the assembly, making it practically impossible for the Left to be appointed. This issue caused fierce clashes between the Left and the Right, pushing the country to the verge of civil war (Moslem 2002, 157). *Baazaaris* closed the bazaar, and conservatives demonstrated on the streets of Tehran and Qom, accusing the Left of being against the vilaayat-e faqeeh. Unlike the earlier years of revolution, it was the Left this time that was accused of advocating an "American Islam." In 1991 the Guardian Council made matters worse by announcing that its role was not merely supervisory but also included the approval of candidates for Parliament, even if the Ministry of Interior approved the candidates. Under the rhetoric of eliminating those who were against the vilaayat-e faqeeh, the Guardian Council disqualified many Left candidates who lacked the support of the deceased Imam Khomeini. Rafsanjani, who in his acceptance speech in the Majlis listed "freedom, democracy, and the individual and social rights of the people" as his priorities (after guarding Islam), was forced to replace the initial heads of his cabinet according to the demands of the conservatives. Under pressure from conservatives, on whom Rafsanjani relied for support, harsh "cultural purification" measures were taken in universities and with regard to women. Conservatives' threats to eliminate the "republic" in the Islamic Republic compelled Left scholars to produce philosophical and political scholarship on Islam and democracy. Fearing that the conservatives would betray the promise of the Islamic

revolution, the Left advocated for civil rights, rule of law, and economic transparency in governmental activities (something clearly missing in Rafsanjani's government).

7 In Islamic law, *ijtihad* refers to independent reasoning to arrive at solutions for problems that are not covered in the Qur'an. The concept of ijtihad in Shiite Islam, which entails the use of judgment to arrive at new rulings, has allowed for strategic maneuverability in *faqeeh*'s (the clergy who is a source of emulation) ruling according to the economic and political needs of the time. Ijtihad—which is based on the Qur'an, the Prophet Mohammad's tradition (*Sonna*), consensus among the clergy (*ijma'*), and reason (*aql*)—also created opportunities for changing restrictive laws and, in the case of the leadership of Khamene'i, opened the opportunity for other *foqaha* (plural of *faqih*/source of emulation) to question the legitimacy of the leader in 1997. For example, in 1997 Ayatollah Montazeri, a senior clergyman and powerful figure in the early years of the revolution who was marginalized by Khomeini in later years, questioned Khamene'i's qualifications as a source of emulation and critiqued him for his lack of support for Khatami (Moslem 2002, 41). But ijtihad has also allowed the conservative-dominated Guardian Council to veto bills proposed by leftist members of Parliament and has allowed the conservatives to override elections.

8 In 1996 almost 10,000 women were enrolled in religious seminaries (Kian-Thiebaut 2002).

9 In Rafsanjani's first term of presidency, his alliance with the conservative Right and *baazaaris* entailed a shift to a market economy and the curtailing of former prime minster Mousavi's statist policies. Rafsanjani's first Five Year Plan (1989/90–1993/94) included price decontrol, trade liberalization, deregulation, and attracting foreign capital and private-sector investments. The plan received strong support from conservatives who saw state intervention and the redistribution of wealth as un-Islamic. While the Left opposed Rafsanjani's economic plans, they supported his sociocultural views. Rafsanjani's emphasis on women's education and more freedom in the sphere of cultural life was reflected by the formation of the Women's Social-Cultural Council and the formation of a special Bureau for Women's Affairs. Rafsanjani also called upon Iranian expatriates to return and help with the reconstruction of Iran. In fact, most of Rafsanjani's cabinet was composed of technocrats who had received their education in Western universities. Ironically, despite their disagreement with Rafsanjani's sociopolitical issues and concern about the "un-Islamic" attitudes creeping into the Islamic culture, Khamene'i and the conservative Right tolerated and even at times defended these measures. In his second term, however, the alliance between Rafsanjani and the conservative Right weakened. Rafsanjani sought dynamic fiqh and advocated an industrial economy, foreign borrowing, taxation, IMF-induced structural-adjustment policies, and less strict social policies. Unlike in the past, the conservatives in the Majlis took on the plight of the poor and criticized the president for his structural adjustments. This opposition from conservatives came when Rafsanjani blamed the bazaar for the ills of the economy and for reaping the benefits of the free-market economy. Rafsanjani, whose economic policies in his first term were under attack, revisited his open-door policy, increasing government control by imposing import restrictions and increasing tariffs and quotas.

He changed the banking system to allow open foreign currency accounts inside and outside of Iran, and invited foreign capital for domestic projects. Rafsanjani's control of the bazaar's prices and his opening of the Refah chain stores, founded by government banks and the municipal government of Tehran in 1994, curtailed the autonomy of the bazaar. Rafsanjani's economic plan was based on a Thatcher–Reagan model of "share-owning democracy" and encouraged privatization. In a move toward the liberalization of economy, Tehran's stock market, which had been inactive since the revolution, resumed after 1989. Many economists have characterized Rafsanjani's development plans as the "rationalization" of the Iranian economy and the centralization of government. In his 1994 New Year message, Rafsanjani called upon educated Iranians abroad to return home, even if they "had previously committed wrongdoings" (Moslem 2002, 194). These measures were opposed by the conservatives, as they signaled Western cultural infiltrations and the return of the prerevolutionary industrialist bourgeoisie.

10 I will return to *javanmardi* and the gendered practices of self-making and citizenship in the next two chapters.

11 While Ahmadinejad's victory came as a surprise to pro-reform bloggers, the discontent with the reformist government set the ground for the conservative backlash that gave rise to Ahmadinejad's presidency. Khatami's second term was concomitant with the increased international pressure and concerns over stability in Iran, a factor that added to the conservatives' consolidation of power under the rhetoric of national security (Nasr 2005). Regime changes in Iran's neighboring Afghanistan and Iraq and the pressures over Iran's nuclear activities escalated tensions. The Iranian media reported mysterious chain murders of several writers and politicians, tracing them to the Ministry of Intelligence (*ettelaa'aat*) and the conservative networks of para-state foundations (*baseej*). Many reformist activists, including President Khatami's pragmatist allies, Abdollah Nuri and Tehran's mayor, Gholamhossein Karbaschi, were jailed for undermining Sharia and vilaayat-e faqeeh, and for corruption and embezzlement. Increasingly after 2000, hundreds of reformist newspapers were shut down, and many journalists were imprisoned. The rise of the private sector and foreign investment as a part of the reform movement in Khatami's period also helped the consolidation of conservative power. During Khatami's second term, the private sector, which had increasingly formed alliances with wealthy conservatives, was more concerned with stability than social reforms. In the 2004 elections for the seventh Majlis, almost one-third of all candidates were deemed unfit by the Council of Guardians. The disqualified candidates were mostly members of the Participation Front. Additionally, the Guardian Council vetoed almost half of the bills that were backed by President Khatami. The increasing discontent with the reformists led many supporters to question the political usefulness of the reformist agenda in Iran. Many of the bloggers in Toronto, mainly engineers or journalists, are among those who immigrated during this period. While they come from all different political positions, they are mostly reformists, disillusioned reformists, or pragmatists who were alienated during Khatami's presidency. The disillusionment of youth and women with the reformists culminated in a much lower voter turnout in the 2005 presidential elections.

12 While Khomeini's book, *Hokumat-e Islami* (Islamic Government), was clear on the reasons for an Islamic government and the qualifications of the *faqeeh*, the institution of the government and mechanisms of governance were not elucidated in this book. After the establishment of the Islamic Republic, this absence set the stage for the spontaneous emergence of revolutionary bodies such as the Guardian Council to ensure clerical rule, revolutionary courts to order summary executions, and a large number of revolutionary organizations to protect the revolutionary and religious doctrines of the state and to implement the redistributive promises of Imam Khomeini to *mostaz'afeen* (the disinherited). Because of the increasing conflict between the Left members of the Majlis and the conservative Guardian Council, in 1988 Khomeini established the Expediency Council. Headed by the president, this council acted as the final arbiter between the Guardian Council and the Majlis, thereby limiting the conservative Guardian Council's vetoing power.

13 Karrubi promised to pay a monthly allowance to every citizen over the age of eighteen. After his defeat in the 2005 election, Karrubi founded the National Trust Party (Hezb-e Etemaad-e Melli) and became increasingly critical of the Guardian Council. In 2009, when he ran for the presidency again, his campaign posters included the English word *change*, and his campaign slogans focused on human rights and freedom. In 2011, in the wake of the Arab Spring, Karrubi and Mousavi, who were deemed the leaders of the 2009 Green movement, were put under house arrest.

14 In the first round, Rafsanjani won 21 percent of the votes, Ahmadinejad 19.5 percent, Karrubi 17.3 percent, Moeen 13.93 percent, Qalibaf 13.89 percent, and Mehralizadeh 4.4 percent.

15 Khatami's reformist administration continued Rafsanjani's economic development plans, but at a slower pace. Privatization within various industrial sectors increased, and in 2002, for the first time after the revolution and the nationalization of banks, permits were issued to private banks. In 2004, 386 firms were listed on the market (Salehi-Isfahani 2004, 19). Despite liberalizing the foreign trade since Rafsanjani's reconstruction plans, the IMF kept pushing Iran to further liberalize and dissolve its protection of import-substitution sectors and labor-protection laws (IMF 2003). Despite certain economic reforms for which Khatami's government took pride, there did not exist sufficient employment opportunities for the growing number of job seekers, a factor that led to massive emigration of academics to Europe and North America.

16 See Nazila Fathi, "Blacksmith's Son Emphasized His Modest Roots," *New York Times*, June 26, 2005, accessed July 6, 2017, http://query.nytimes.com/gst/fullpage.html?res=9904E4DB173AF935A15755C0A9639C8B63&mcubz=2.

17 The tenth-century Persian poet Ferdowsi's *Shahnameh* (*The Epic of Kings*) is often used in modern nationalist discourses as a form of contestation to what is perceived as the Arab conquest of Iran in the seventh century. For instance, Qalibaf, a pilot and the former head of the Revolutionary Guard Corps, deployed nationalist sentiment shared by secularists by quoting Ferdowsi: "*cho Iran mabaashad tan-e man mabaad*" ("without Iran, may my body perish").

18 Nazila Fathi wrote that "one woman who introduced herself as Tahereh, 22, wore a narrow pink see-through material over her head and had a piercing in her nose. She said she received 300,000 rials, $33, per day to drive in her car around Tehran with Mr. Rafsanjani's poster on the rear window, though she is cynical about the result. 'I do it for the money,' she said. 'He is responsible for the situation. Why would he change it?'" See "Hundreds of Women Protest Sex Discrimination in Iran," *New York Times*, June 12, 2005, accessed July 3, 2017, http://www.nytimes.com/2005/06/12/international/middleeast/hundreds-of-women-protest-sex-discrimination-in.html?mcubz=2.

19 Many of the people whom she lists have since immigrated to Canada, the United States, and Europe. *Khorshid Khanoom*, June 20, 2005, http://www.khorshidkhanoom.com/archives/001390.php.

20 The Constitution of the Islamic Republic of Iran, Chapter IX (Executive Power), Section 1 (Presidency), article 115. See the translation of the Iranian Constitution here: http://www.iranonline.com/iran/iran-info/government/constitution-9-1.html, accessed July 31, 2017.

21 See Golnaz Esfandiari, "No Woman Has Ever Run for Iranian President. Will Azam Taleghani Be the First?" RadioFreeEurope/RadioLiberty, April 19, 2017, https://www.rferl.org/a/iran-taleghani-woman-president-election/28439661.html, accessed July 6, 2017.

22 The symbolic self-nomination of women in the Iranian presidential elections is documented in Shahla Haeri's 2002 film *Mrs. President: Women and Political Leadership in Iran*. Rakhshan Bani Etemad also directed a film about the demands of women from the presidential candidates in the 2009 film *We Are Half of Iran's Population*.

23 See "*Be Jaa-ye Dr. Moeen*" ("on Dr. Moeen's behalf"), *Webnevesht*, May 25, 2005, accessed July 31, 2017, http://www.webneveshteha.com/weblog/?id=1117021623.

24 Naseri is referring to the disillusionments with Khatami's administration. Khatami's period saw significant changes such as the increased emergence of independent press, augmented social freedoms (including decreased restrictions on internet cafés and satellite dishes), and the emergence of dissent. However, many of these achievements were later reversed and dissolved as a result of the vetoing power of the Guardian Council. Many reformist activists were jailed for undermining Sharia and vilaayat-e faqeeh. The tension between the revolutionary and populist promises of the Left and the neoliberal and conservative demands put reformers (especially Khatami) in a position of having to resort to "dual-containment" strategies. Even though Khatami's compromises with the conservatives on political matters disillusioned many who voted for him, he was reelected in 2001.

25 See "*daaran miterekoonan!*" ["They are exploding it!"] in *Azadiye shoma shabahi beesh neest* [Your Freedom Is Nothing but an Illusion], June 13, 2005, accessed July 20, 2005, http://naseria.blogspot.com/2005/06/blog-post_13.html. Naseri erased her old blog and started a new blog titled *Café Naseri*, accessed July 31, 2017, http://www.mimnoon.com/mana/archives/000022.html.

26 The activists who maintained Zanan-e Iran were forced to shut it down under Ahmadinejad's presidency. The link for the report was http://www.womeniniran.net/archives/FSR/002521.php.

27 See "Congratulations on Women's Entrance to the Stadium and the Victory of the National Team!" *Zan Nevesht* (*Woman's Writing*), June 9, 2005, http://www.parastood.com/archives/002032.php.

28 See "From Ganji to Azadi," *Iran-baan*, June 9, 2005, http://fereshteh.blogfa.com/post-20.aspx. Ghazi was imprisoned in 2004 for her women's-rights activism and articles in the *Etemad* newspaper. She has since immigrated to the United States.

29 See "The Freedom Game with Women's Presence" ("*Baaziyeh Azadi ba hozoor-e-e zanan*"), *Hanouz*, June 10, 2005, http://www.hanouz.com/archives/001719.html.

30 Mohammad Heydari, "About Iranian Feminism," in *Zemestan: Parakandeh neveshtehhaaye Mohammad Heydari* [Winter: Scattered Writings of Mohammad Heydari], June 9, 2005, http://heydary.blogspot.com/2005/06/blog-post_09.html.

31 *Jalaseh* literally translates into "meeting." Women's jalaseh is an informal gathering, often organized by a network of neighborhood women, where women recite the Qur'an, sometimes have food and tea, and listen to *mo'ezeh* (preaching) by either a clergyman or a woman *mo'ezegar* (preacher)/"*khanoom-e jalaseh*." The woman who hosts the jalaseh may do so as a personal *nazr* (religious due paid in monetary or nonmonetary fashion after making a wish to her God and promising to perform a pious act such as prayers, a charity act such as distributing food or money among the needy, or organizing a jalaseh).

32 The One-Million Signatures Campaign, which started in 2006, is a door-to-door and internet campaign that asks for changes in the Iranian constitution to eliminate discrimination against women. See http://we-change.org/english.

33 The lack of attention to economic concerns of rural and working-class women (and men) among many reformist intellectuals and activists may be one of the reasons for the victory of the populist candidate, Mahmoud Ahmadinejad, who focused his campaign on economic disparity and the plight of the poor. As I will discuss below, after the first round of the elections, Khorshid Khanoom noted in a defeated and self-critical tone that Karrubi's promise to give people 600,000 rials each month gained him some votes.

34 See *Zan Nevesht*, November 16, 2004, http://www.parastood.com/archives/001093.php.

35 See *Zan Nevesht*, November 25, 2004, http://notes.parastood.ir/archives/001119.php#more.

36 After women bloggers entered the stadium, many women bloggers posted "*bacheh-ha motshakereem!*" ["Thank you, gang!"], a slogan that fans of a sports team often shout after the game.

37 Some of these activists are Faezeh Hashemi (Rafsanjani's daughter) and Zahra Rahnavard (the scholar, politician, artist, and wife of the 2009 reformist candidate Mir Hussein Mousavi).

38 Seifi, who left Iran in 2007 and moved to Europe and later to the United States, was arrested by the Iranian Intelligence Ministry in January 2005 when she was traveling to India to attend a training workshop organized by *Shahrzad News*, a Persian-language news agency based in the Netherlands. Seifi also worked at Deutsche Welle Persian in Netherlands as a producer. Along with Radio Zamaneh, *Shahrzad News* received the bulk of the funding that was dispersed by the Dutch Parliament in 2006 (I discuss this in chapter 5). Out of fifteen women who were arrested at the airport on their way to the

workshop, twelve were released after being interrogated. However, Seifi and two other members of the Iranian Women's Cultural Center (which produced the website Zanestan), were kept in prison for a day on charges of "acting against the state security." She is unable to return to Iran.

39 See "Iran: Sit-in by Azam Taleghani in Front of Evin prison," http://www.payvand.com/news/03/aug/1071.html, accessed April 11, 2019.

40 On April 3, 2009, Taleghani told reporters: "The most important challenge confronting the elections is the *rejal* argument, which unfortunately, because of incorrect interpretations has blocked women's presence in the country's grand management arenas. For this reason, in order to break this taboo, I will participate in the elections." See *Entekhab News*, http://www.entekhabnews.com/portal/index.php?news=2110.

41 *Haj khanoom* translates into "Mrs. Haji": a woman who has performed *hajj*, the pilgrimage to Mecca. In colloquial Persian, *Haj khanoom* refers to an older woman who is religious.

42 Kamvari was referring to Mehrangiz Kar, the Iranian woman lawyer who was arrested after she returned from a conference in Berlin. Kar has since immigrated to the United States

43 Nooshin Ahmadi Khorasani is an Iranian secular feminist activist.

44 See *Sibil Tala* (blog), accessed July 31, 2017, http://sibiltala.blogspot.com/2005/06/blog-post_111779460797150361.html.

45 Khatami's cabinet, which included members of the Left and Kargozaaraan (Executives of Construction Party), relaxed policies in the sociopolitical realm. As a result, 1997 saw a proliferation of publications and press that fiercely criticized the conservatives. In 1997 and 1998 the Right attempted to curb the activities of the proponents of the *dovvom-e khordad* movement (a movement that refers to Khatami's victory on May 23, 1997). This movement's advocacy for democracy, civil society (*jaamee'e-ye madani*), and human rights received backlash from the right-wing conservatives, whose intimidation tactics included threats, shutting down of the press, physical attacks on some members of the cabinet and students, and chain murders during Khatami's two terms of presidency.

46 My translation. Amin is a former follower of the leftist group *Chereek haaye fadaayee-e khalgh aghaliyat* (Iranian People's Fedayee Guerrillas, Minority Branch). Her website is *shabakeh saraasari hamkaari-ye zanaan-e Iran* (the Iranian Women's Network). See her post on June 20, 2005, http://www.shabakeh.de/archives/individual/000290.html#more.

47 "An Intellectual without Action is Like a Bee without Honey" in the blog *Your Freedom Is Nothing but an Illusion*, June 23, 2005, http://naseria.blogspot.com/2005/06/blog-post_23.html.

48 An extremely conservative clergy and a member of the Assembly of Experts, Mesbah Yazdi was an avid critic of the reform movement and supported Ahmadinejad during the election. For the Persian text, see Foroogh's post on June 26, 2005, http://foroogh.malakut.org/2005/06//index.shtml.

49 See *Sibil Tala* (blog), http://sibiltala.blogspot.com/2005/06/blog-post_18.html.

50 See *Rooznameh* (blog), accessed July 31, 2017, http://rooznameh.blogfa.com/post-19.aspx.

51 See http://rooznameh.blogfa.com/post-28.aspx and http://rooznameh.blogfa.com/post-21.aspx, accessed July 31, 2017.

52 *Baazi-ye veblogi* is a blogging game wherein a blogger asks a question and invites other bloggers to answer to that question. Each invited blogger invites other bloggers by tagging them in their post. As a result, a large group of bloggers write about the same topic. Hamed Talebi, the author of the *Rooznameh negaar Mosalman* [Muslim Journalist], started this game. To read his post where he narrated his own memory and invited other bloggers to participate in writing their memoir, see http://hamedtalebi.blogfa.com/post-151.aspx. A list of memories of what Ahmadinejad's supporters have called "*Hemaaseyeh Sevom-e Tir*" can be seen here: http://hamedtalebi.blogfa.com/post-152.aspx.

53 For a list of discussions about this issue, see http://alpr.30morgh.org/archives/2005_08.php.

54 See "Who Are Boycotters?" *Alpr*, August 27, 2005, http://alpr.30morgh.org/archives/002866.php.

55 Ganji was a member of the Islamic Revolutionary Guard Corps but left the corps in the mid-1990s and became an investigative journalist and a critic of the conservative elements of the state. He was arrested in 2000 after returning from a conference in Berlin. Ganji wrote two manifestos while in prison and called for the boycott of the Iranian presidential elections. He left Iran in 2006.

56 *Alpr*, August 27, 2005, http://alpr.30morgh.org/archives/002866.php.

57 The coalition between the Left and conservative pragmatists was weakened as the Left held Rafsanjani responsible for prolonging the Iran–Iraq war against Khomeini's wishes and accused him of being related to murders and beatings inside and outside of Iran by a gang of right-wing forces in the Ministry of Information. The weakening of the former coalition became more pronounced as the Participation Front of Islamic Iran (*Jebhe-ye mosharekat-e Iran-e Islami*), a pro-Khatami coalition headed by the president's brother, outlined a manifesto that promised to undo the dominance of the conservative clerical elite over the political and economic spheres.

58 For Kowsar's post, see "Mosaadereh Eslaah Talabi?" [The Confiscation of Reform?] on his blog, *Yad-daasht-haaye yek Tab'eedee-ye asabaani* [Notes of an Angry Exile], August 27, 2005, accessed July 31, 2017, http://nikahang.blogspot.com/2005/08/blog-post_112512278226673494.html.

59 The Participation Front of Islamic Iran sought to recuperate the legacy of the revolution leader Ayatollah Khomeini. The reformist Participation Front advocated the strengthening of the rule of law, the expansion of civil society, freedom of the press, creating transparency in political and economic realms, and the dissolution of economic regulations and state monopolies that curbed private investment and development. For Seyyed Abadi's post, see "Eslaahaat beh manzeleye ravesh" [Reform as a Method], *Hanouz*, August 27, 2005, http://www.hanouz.com/archives/002179.html.

60 This could include a radio interview on BBC Persian, a link from the website of Radio Zamaneh, or an interview on Voice of America.
61 In the men's focus group in Toronto, one participant expressed that men are "naturally" more technologically capable and interested in politics than women.
62 Of course, this gendering is not specific to Weblogistan or Iranian public space. Feminist scholars have long argued that public space is often the arena of male subjects as political beings (Pateman 1988).
63 Habermas perceives the public sphere as a site of "pure speech," communication, and rational discussion, where self-interest, desire for power, and conflict do not appear. For Habermas, the salon has three characteristics: (1) disregard for status (opinion free of economy); (2) possibility of new critique, resulting from the commodification of culture; and (3) inclusiveness in principle (Dean 2001, 244). Seyla Benhabib's salon, which is based on Hannah Arendt's notion of public sphere in *The Human Condition*, focuses on the way that "self-revelation and self-concealment disrupt the public sphere's ideal of transparency" (245). The Habermasian public sphere as the mediator between the state and the citizen relies on this model, where the private/domestic is left out of the realm of politics.
64 As I discuss in chapters 3 and 4, this form of normative territorialization is characteristic of politics in Weblogistan, where discussions about sexuality and gender are charged with irrationality and traditionalism.
65 Soon after the establishment of the Islamic Republic, a number of para-state entities (*nihads*) were formed. Nihads such as the *sipah-e pasdaran-e inqilab-e Islami* (the Corps of the Islamic Revolutionary Guards) and *komiteh inqilab-e Islami* (the Committee of the Islamic Revolution) took on the task of suppressing the antirevolutionary forces, while those such as *bonyaad-e mostaz'afeen* (the Foundation of the Disinherited) and *komiteh imdad-e imam Khomeini* (Imam Khomeini Relief Committee) were responsible for the redistributive tasks (Moslem 2002, 14). Nihads were appointed by the leader and followed the line of the *vali-ye faqeeh*. These para-state organizations (e.g., Imam's Relief Committee, the Martyr Foundation, the Revolutionary Corps) were formalized in the Constitution, had legal status, were counted as a part of the government, and received government funding. However, because they were appointed by the leader, they were not accountable to the president and in fact at times turned against Parliament or the president for not adhering to "the line of Imam" and the leadership (*khatt-e imam va rahbariyat*).
66 Kamvari pointed out to me that none of the articles about Weblogistan mentioned her widely read blog, even though she generated controversial discussions. She attributed this elision to the fact that her posts were mainly about nonnormative sexuality and politics that were either labeled as radical (when it came to sexuality) or complicit with the "regime" when it came to discussing politics in Iran or critiquing the segments of the Iranian diaspora who work in U.S. think tanks (phone conversation, July 15, 2007).
67 Such binary narratives ignore the democratic political processes in the postrevolutionary Iranian state, conflate democracy with secularism, assume the incommensurabil-

ity of Islam and democracy, and legitimize imperialistic agendas under the cloak of democratization.
68 See "Open Letter to Farah Diba," *Peyvand News*, March 17, 2007, accessed July 1, 2018, http://www.payvand.com/news/07/mar/1231.html.
69 See "Open Letter to Farah Diba."
70 The lack of attention to Forghani's important statement was the reason that Niki Akhavan and I translated the open letter into English and circulated it online.
71 See Donald J. Trump, 2017, "Many Reports of Peaceful Protests by Iranian Citizens Fed up with Regime's Corruption & Its Squandering of the Nation's Wealth to Fund Terrorism Abroad. Iranian Govt Should Respect Their People's Rights, Including Right to Express Themselves. The World Is Watching! #IranProtests," Twitter, accessed July 10, 2018, https://twitter.com/realdonaldtrump/status/946949708915924994?lang=en.
72 Saeed Kamali Dehghan, 2018, "Tehran Hijab Protest: Iranian Police Arrest 29 Women," *Guardian*, February 2, 2018, accessed July 10, 2018, https://www.theguardian.com/world/2018/feb/02/tehran-hijab-protest-iranian-police-arrest-29-women.
73 See Hosseini's interview with Shahrzad Hemati, accessed July 4, 2018, https://iranianwomen.info/2018/02/15/i-acted-independently.
74 Sussan Tahmasebi's Facebook post, dated February 16, 2018. Quoted with author's permission.
75 Ben Affleck's 2012 film, *Argo*, is an example of the representations of Iranian women protesters.

Chapter 3: Whores, Homos, and Feminists

1 See Foucault (2007). For more on these techniques, see Miller and Rose (1992) and chapters by Gordon, Burchell, Ewald, Pasquino, Castel, and Donzelot in Burchell, Gordon, and Miller, eds. (1991).
2 In prerevolutionary Farsi films, *luti* often rescued prostitutes and made them into well-behaved housewives.
3 Kamvari wrote the Persian version of this story a few hours after the English one. See https://sibiltala.blogspot.com/2004/12/golden-mustache.html, December 17, 2004.
4 Even though chat and email are also sent through internet technologies, Persian bloggers considered interactions outside of Weblogistan to be "offline." By the time I was moving to Toronto for the offline part of my fieldwork, Nazli found me a sublet in another Iranian blogger's apartment. She also invited me to stay in her student-housing apartment for a couple of weeks until the sublet was available.
5 In order to protect the confidentiality of this blogger, I am not citing him here.
6 Ong (2006) focuses on self-management and the ethics of neoliberal citizenship in relation to freedom, including from the welfare state (445). I borrow from Ong to discuss the construction of ethical beings in cyberspace, where neoliberal notions of citizenship

in diaspora are articulated in relationship to the economic and political context of the "war on terror."

7 "You are such a Turk" is Persian slang for "You are so gullible!" Iranian Turks are an ethnic group from the province of Azerbaijan. Jokes about Iranian Turks are commonplace in Persian. This phenomenon may be related to the Persianization of Iran during the reign of Reza Shah Pahlavi, who overthrew the Azeri Qajar dynasty. Many Turks themselves (including Kamvari) repeat such jokes without malice. But in some instances these jokes have created ethnic tensions, such as in 2006, when the cartoonist Mana Neyestani depicted an Azeri-speaking cockroach in the children's section of a government-run newspaper; accessed July 31, 2017, https://www.vice.com/en_us/article/jmbnm7/persian-cartoonist-narrates-his-fall-from-grace-in-his-new-graphic-novel-116.

8 Phone conversation with Mitra (a blogger), June 2006.

9 Rostam al-tavarikh is a text written by Hashem Asef, also known as Rostam al Hokama, in the late eighteenth century. It describes the events of the era between the end of the Safavid period during Shah Hossein Safavid's time and the beginning of the Qajar period and Fath-ali Shah's time.

10 See Sibestaan (blog), accessed July 31, 2017, http://Sibestaan.malakut.org/archives/2006/01/post_442.shtml.

11 For the full post, accessed July 31, 2017, see http://sibiltala.blogspot.com/2006/01/blog-post_06.html.

12 See Sibestaan (blog). http://Sibestaan.malakut.org/archives/2006/01/post_444.shtml.

13 See the comments section in Jami's post, accessed July 31, 2017, http://Sibestaan.malakut.org/archives/2006/01/post_444.shtml.

14 See Sibestaan (blog), accessed June 7, 2017, http://sibestaan.malakut.org/3459.

15 I left a comment under Jami's post, pointing out that he was attributing agency solely to heterosexual revolutionary men. I questioned Jami's fetishization of women and critiqued his assumption that women become subjects only in relation to men. To my question of "What happens to women's participation in the revolution in your narration of history?" Jami responded that he wrote from "a man's point of view." He added that for him revolution was certainly feminine because it was a sign of dreaminess and the essence of conquering. See the comments under Jami's post here, accessed July 31, 2017, http://sibestaan.malakut.org/3459.

16 See Sibestaan (blog), accessed July 31, 2017, http://sibestaan.malakut.org/archives/2006/01/post_445.shtml#comments.

17 Although Khaledian has since deleted his blog, portions of his post can be found on Sanam Dolatshahi's blog, Khorshid Khanoom, accessed July 31, 2017, http://www.khorshidkhanoom.com/archives/001482.php#more.

18 See http://www.khorshidkhanoom.com/archives/001482.php#more, accessed July 31, 2017.

19 See http://farangeopolis.blogspot.com/2006/01/blog-post_11.html, accessed July 31, 2017,

20 See http://sibestaan.malakut.org/archives/2006/01/post_447.shtml, accessed July 31, 2017.

21 See http://farangopolis.blogspot.com/2006/01/blog-post_13.html, accessed July 31, 2017.

22 See http://sibestaan.malackut.org/archives/2006/01/post_452.shtml, accessed July 31, 2017.

23 See http://sibestaan.malackut.org/archives/2006/01/post_452.shtml, accessed July 31, 2017.

24 See http://sibiltala.blogspot.com/2006/01/blog-post_18.html, accessed July 31, 2017.
25 See the comments section of Kamvari's post, accessed July 31, 2017, http://sibiltala.blogspot.com/2006/01/blog-post_18.html.
26 Claiming that my critique of sexist language (informed by Iranian feminist scholars) was Western and did not apply to Persian, one male graduate student in the United Kingdom asked me to leave the Persian language alone.
27 See http://sibiltala.blogspot.com/2006/01/blog-post_18.html, accessed July 31, 2017.
28 In Louis Althusser's words (1971, 169), "the individual is interpellated as a (free) subject, i.e. in order that he shall submit freely to the commandments of the Subject, i.e. in order that he shall (freely) accept his subjection, i.e. in order that he shall make the gesturers and actions of his subjection 'all by himself.' There are no subjects except by and for their subjection. That is why they 'work all by themselves.'"
29 Aghdam's YouTube channels were removed after her death. Her videos are available on other YouTube users' pages. Her Instagram account (insta@nasimesabz1) and her website (nasimesabz.com) have also been erased.
30 See "Nasime Sabz/Nasim Aghdam 'Youtube Shooter' Re-Upload," accessed July 6, 2018, https://www.liveleak.com/view?t=Cm7EX_1522864851.
31 YouTube, April 12, 2018, accessed July 6, 2018, https://www.youtube.com/watch?v=N8BL3kkpx5M.
32 See See Radio Zamaneh (blog), accessed July 6, 2018, https://www.radiozamaneh.com/389149.
33 See "Additional Changes to the YouTube Partner Program (YPP) to Better Protect Creators," accessed July 9, 2018, https://youtube-creators.googleblog.com/2018/01/additional-changes-to-youtube-partner.html.
34 See Jason Koebler and Jillian York, "A Brief History of YouTube Censorship," *Motherboard* (blog), March 26, 2018, accessed July 9, 2018, https://motherboard.vice.com/en_us/article/59jgka/a-brief-history-of-youtube-censorship.
35 See Koebler and York, "A Brief History of YouTube Censorship."
36 See Koebler and York, "A Brief History of YouTube Censorship."
37 See "The Many Faces of Nasim Aghdam, Vegan Turned YouTube Shooter," accessed July 9, 2018, https://www.animals24-7.org/2018/04/05/the-many-faces-of-nasim-aghdam-vegan-turned-youtube-shooter.
38 See "Harf-e Raast o Hessab," YouTube, April 5, 2018, accessed July 6, 2018, https://www.youtube.com/watch?v=rGrb9ZbDEk8.
39 First introduced in Ayatollah Khomeini's 1971 book, *Hokumat-e Islami* [Islamic Government], vilaayat-e faqeeh would entail a system in which the Muslim community would willingly submit to the sovereignty of the vali-ye faqeeh, a source of emulation (*marja'-e taqleed*) clergyman who is just and has knowledge of the Sharia. Unlike his previous role in Shiite Iran as the custodian of the community and advisor on Sharia, the qualified clergyman would be the one to rule an Islamic state. Vali-ye faqeeh, as the ultimate authority, would carry the Islamic law during the absence (*gheybat-e kobra*, or the greater occultation) of the last of the twelve Shiite imams, Mahdi, whose messianic reappearance is believed to bring justice and peace to the world. However, the Islamic

state in Iran was announced as a republic, thereby basing its legitimacy not just in God but also in the people, who willingly submitted to the vali-ye faqeeh (Moslem 2002). Unlike the popular assumptions that all matters are decided by the vali-ye faqeeh in Iran, there is a system of checks and balances in the composition of the Iranian state. The drafting of the 1979 Constitution, which involved heated debates by seventy-three members of the Assembly of Experts for Constitution, generated factional disagreements over authority and legitimacy. Ultimately, the rule of the faqeeh was established, and religious institutions were granted supervisory roles. According to the 1979 Constitution, the president and three branches of government (executive, legislative, and judiciary) follow the religious leader, who is the source of emulation. The Guardian Council (*shoraa-ye negahbaan*) became responsible for reviewing all the laws passed by *Majlis* (Parliament) in order to safeguard Islamic values. The Assembly of Experts for Leadership (*majlis-e khobrigan*), whose members were elected under the supervision of the Guardian Council, was established three years later with the task of selecting the next faqeeh. The Expediency Council (*majma'-e tashkhees-e maslahat-e nizaam*) was established in 1988 to settle the disputes between Parliament and the Guardian Council and to make final decisions. A series of other religious supervisory bodies, such as Islamic Associations and the Association of Friday Prayer leaders, while not mentioned in the Constitution, represent the vali-ye faqeeh and ensure the observance of Islamic behavior in universities.

40 See "Aghdam's biography," YouTube, April 4, 2018, accessed July 6, 2018, https://www.youtube.com/watch?v=bGP_zgQeWwQ.

41 See "Meme Balonlu Kizin Sirri," YouTube, December 1, 2016, accessed July 6, 2018, https://www.youtube.com/watch?v=ZTr_ruwo8qo.

42 See "Nasimesabz on Instagram," YouTube, April 3, 2018, accessed July 6, 2018, https://www.youtube.com/watch?v=mU_5lc1wjm8.

43 See "Crazy YouTube Shooter videos Nasim Najafi Aghdam," YouTube, April 4, 2018, accessed April 23, 2019, https://www.youtube.com/watch?v=3kBNAV0Q8yM.

44 See Laura Loomer, Tweet, April 4, 2018, accessed July 6, 2018, https://web.archive.org/web/20180404225153/https://twitter.com/LauraLoomer/status/981549903016005634.

45 See Jacqueline Thomsen, 2018, "GOP Lawmaker Claims without Evidence That YouTube Shooter 'Could Be' an Illegal Immigrant," text, *The Hill*, April 3, 2018, accessed July 6, 2018, http://thehill.com/homenews/house/381522-gop-lawmaker-baselessly-claims-that-youtube-shooter-could-be-an-illegal.

46 See Laura Loomer, Tweet, April 5, 2018, accessed July 6, 2018, https://web.archive.org/web/20180410063530/https:/twitter.com/LauraLoomer/status/982052400168136704.

47 See "Anti-Trans Feminists Push 'Conspiracy Theory' That YouTube Shooter Was a Trans Woman," *PinkNews*, April 5, 2018, accessed July 6, 2018, https://www.pinknews.co.uk/2018/04/05/anti-trans-feminists-push-conspiracy-theory-that-youtube-shooter-was-a-trans-woman.

48 Bollinger, Alex, 2018, "Now Conspiracy Theorists Are Claiming the YouTube Shooter Was a Trans Woman," *LGBTQ Nation*, April 5, 2018, accessed July 6, 2018, https://www.lgbtqnation.com/2018/04/now-conspiracy-theorists-claiming-youtube-shooter-trans-woman.

49 See "Police Body Camera Footage Shows YouTube Shooter Nasim Aghdam Sleeping in Her Car in Walmart Parking," YouTube, April 13, 2018, accessed July 6, 2018, https://www.youtube.com/watch?v=_5aRnIIicYk.
50 Some conspiracy theories claimed that she was an artificial intelligence. See https://www.dailydot.com/upstream/nasim-aghdam-conspiracy-theories-youtube, accessed July 8, 2018.

Chapter 4: Weblogistan and Its Homosexual Problem

1 In 2007 Akbar Ganji (a famous Iranian dissident) published a series of online articles in Radio Zamaneh, arguing that Iranian *hamjinsgaraayaan* are a minority to be defended. In 2006, 171 diaspora academics, artists, and activists drafted and signed a statement condemning laws regarding homosexuality in Iran. The statement claimed that "in open and democratic societies, because enlightenment is possible, because it is possible for hamjinsgaraayaan and their supporters to gather, and because hamjinsgaraayaan enjoy rights and legal support, the violation of their rights is minimized" (my translation). In 2008 the Boroumand Foundation (a center documenting human rights violations in Iran) wrote a statement addressing homophobia and human rights violations of homosexuals in Iran. In June 2007, during an Iranian human rights conference in California, the violation of Iranian homosexuals' rights was the subject of several panels. In the past fifteen years, Persian, U.S., and Dutch government-funded diaspora media (e.g., VOA, Radio Farda, Radio Zamaneh) have produced programs about homosexuality. These are some of the examples of the sudden hypervisibility of queers among the Iranian diaspora. I discuss these examples later in this chapter.
2 Bloggers' responses to this campaign varied; some bloggers completely supported the campaign, while others rejected or critiqued it; some supported women's-rights movements in Iran, while critiquing the emphasis on the heteronormative nuclear family; others critiqued the June 12, 2006, women's-rights activists' street protests and considered them to be irrelevant to the majority of Iranian women, even if their requests for reforming patriarchal law were reasonable. For examples of these responses, see http://Sibiltala.blogspot.com/2006/06/blog-post_08.html; http://farnaaz.info/archives/001941.html; http://Sibiltala.blogspot.com/2006/06/blog-post_14.html; and http://nagoftaniha2.blogspot.com/2006/06/blog-post_12.html.
3 As Qolang (a blogger in New York) responded, this post established its author as one who is ethical, does not deviate from family values, is normal, and is fighting the enemies of such values. See http://qolang.blogspot.com/2006/06/blog-post_03.html.
4 This reference to Si-o-seh pol was a direct attack on Dara, a Toronto-based gay man from Isfahan.
5 See http://nikahang.blogspot.com/2006/06/blog-post_115121714600064367.html, accessed July 31, 2017.
6 See http://nikahang.blogspot.com/2006/06/blog-post_115164912850380549.html, accessed July 31, 2017.

7   See http://alimosleh.blogfa.com/post-79.aspx, accessed July 31, 2017.
8   See http://noqte.com/blogs/blog.php?code=201, accessed February 27, 2006.
9   Perhaps to prove his masculinity, Kowsar bragged about the way he had beaten up a few people at work. He established himself as a courageous man who often refused to obey his superiors when he did not agree with them.
10 Feminist bloggers who critiqued Kowsar's sexist posts often received extremely hostile and violent comments by anonymous readers.
11 Interestingly, Kowsar's blurring of public and private had limits. When I asked him why he barely mentioned his wife in his blog, he answered that his wife is his namoos (honor) and that his private family life is not a matter for public discussion.
12 See http://zamaaneh.com/kalaghestoon/2006/08/post_2.html, accessed July 31, 2017.
13 See http://zamaaneh.com/kalaghestoon/2006/08/post_3.html, accessed July 31, 2017.
14 See http://sibestaan.malakut.org/archives/2006/08/post_535.shtml#comments, accessed July 31, 2017.
15 Persian slang that means a worthless person, a nobody.
16 The Tudeh Party was one of the first Communist parties in Iran. "Seh kaaf" (three K's) refers to *keer*, *kos*, and *koon*, which translate to "cock," "pussy," and "ass."
17 See http://nikahang.blogspot.com/2006/08/blog-post_115549371458976995.html, accessed July 31, 2017.
18 See http://www.bbc.com/persian/iran/story/2006/08/060814_si-wmj-weblogs-namerica.shtml, accessed July 31, 2017.
19 During my fieldwork, the handful of LBGTQ blogs that existed at that time focused on queer bloggers' personal lives and daily activities, news about gay and lesbian celebrities in North America and Europe, or information and links to international gay and lesbian websites. More often than not, these blogs were read and linked to by a small circle of bloggers who were looking for an Iranian queer community. Of course, there were queer bloggers who wrote about Iranian electoral politics, women's issues, the war on terror, and other topics. But these bloggers were not "out" in Weblogistan, even if they were "out" offline.
20 See http://Sharh.com/archive/000565.html, accessed February 10, 2006.
21 The term *hamjinsgaraayee* was likely coined in the 1970s by the late Saviz Shafaii, an Iranian gay activist. It was later popularized by a diaspora Iranian gay/lesbian group, Homan, in its magazine in the early 1990s.
22 Mansour archived his post under the category "mo'zalaat-e jinsi," which roughly translates into "sexual problems" or "sexual disorders."
23 See "Blown Out of Proportion," an article I wrote about Ahmadinejad's comment, Iranian.com, January 10, 2007, accessed July 31, 2017, https://iranian.com/main/2007/blown-out-proportion.html.
24 See Global Research, September 25, 2007, accessed July 31, 2017, http://www.globalresearch.ca/index.php?context=va&aid=6889.
25 Promoting himself as the "first Iranian gay activist," Arsham Parsi, the then-executive director of the Iranian Queer Organization, appeared on several television programs, as living evidence of the existence of gays in Iran. For example, see the video "Arsham

Parsi Proves There Are Gays in Iran," accessed January 12, 2011, http://www.youtube.com/watch?v=tipSGYxK2yE.

26   See "Khatami and Homosexuals in Iran," accessed July 31, 2017, http://www.youtube.com/watch?v=H99du1-u2-0.

27   In *Desiring Arabs*, Joseph Massad (2007, 161) uses the term *the Gay International* to refer to gay and lesbian missionary tasks, "the discourses that produce them, and the organizations that represent them."

28   Examples include the three films *Out in Iran: Inside Iran's Secret Gay World*, *I Know That I Am*, and *Be Like Others*. The maker of *Out in Iran* was sued by a man who was filmed in a gay café in Tehran, without his consent. See Jillian Kester-D'Abours, "Gay Iranian Refugee Sues over Being 'Outed' in Documentary," https://www.alaraby.co.uk/english/society/2016/8/25/gay-iranian-refugee-sues-over-being-outed-in-documentary.

29   For Ganji's articles on homosexuality in Zamaneh, see http://zamaaneh.com/idea/2008/06/post_327.html, http://zamaaneh.com/idea/2008/06/post_328.html, and http://zamaaneh.com/idea/2008/06/post_332.html, accessed July 31, 2017. In 2006, not too long before publishing this series of articles, and soon after leaving Iran, Ganji delivered a talk to an English-speaking audience in Toronto about universal human rights in Iran. When a blogger asked him where queers fit in his vision of a democratic future for Iran, Ganji said that he would prefer not to answer. Assuming that the person who asked the question was not Iranian, he dismissed her question by saying, "even your own culture has issues with this issue." See Kamvari's account of her interaction with Ganji at http://sibiltala.blogspot.com/2006/08/blog-post_08.html, accessed July 31, 2017.

30   "Statement in Defense of Gay Rights and in Opposition to Homophobia and Pedophilia," accessed July 31, 2017, http://news.gooya.com/politics/archives/047290.php.

31   See http://www.akhbar-rooz.com/article.jsp?essayId=2721, accessed July 31, 2017.

32   As I discuss later in this chapter, Voice of America, Radio Farda, and Radio Zamaneh have produced several programs about homosexuality, while an Iranian blogger and at the time CBC (Canadian Broadcasting Company) producer has made documentary films about Iranian queer and transgender people.

33   I adopt Puar's definition of homonationalism as a form of normalization of homosexuality that serves the U.S. empire-building project. Puar defines this form of homosexuality "as a regulatory script not only of normative gayness, queerness, or homosexuality, but also of racial and national norms that reinforce these subjects" (2007, 2).

34   See Arsham Parsi's biography on his personal website at http://www.arshamparsi.net, accessed July 31, 2017.

35   This name change was an effort to be more inclusive of sexualities that PGLO had excluded. The use of the term *queer* by IRQO was merely shorthand for a list of identities and was not necessarily indicative of IRQO's anti-identitarian politics. *Degarbaash* was suggested as the equivalent for queer by IRQO.

36   An example of this omission is evident in Janet Afary's *Sexual Politics in Modern Iran* (2009).

37   For example, see "Arsham Parsi Proves There Are Gays In Iran," YouTube (video), May 7, 2008, accessed July 31, 2017, http://www.youtube.com/watch?v=tipSGYxK2yE.

38 Between 2004 and 2006, there were twenty-one regular issues and ten special issues of MAHA, the first online Iranian gay and lesbian magazine. *Cheraq* was the online publication of the Iranian Queer Organization. Between March 2005 and November 2008, IROQ published 46 issues of *Cheraq*. After disputes between Parsi and IROQ's Board of Directors, *Neda* replaced *Cheraq*. Between January 2009 and November 2011, IRQR published thirty-three online issues of *Neda*. Archives of *Cheraq* and *Neda* can be found at http://www.irqr.net/cheraq. *Neda* can be found at http://www.net/neda. *Cheraq*'s issues 26–60 (January 2009) are available at http://irqo.org/cheraq63-58.html.

39 See Voice of America Persian's program on homosexuality: http://www.youtube.com/watch?v=KOparg-Samk. See Parsi's interview with VOA at http://www.youtube.com/watch?v=9zUEreoVVQM. For Parsi's interview with BBC, see https://www.youtube.com/watch?v=WRIPGhRtB28, accessed July 31, 2017.

40 See Richard Kim's "Witnesses to an Execution: An International Furor over the Hanging of 'Two Gay Teenagers' in Iran," *Nation*, August 5, 2005, http://www.thenation.com/article/witnesses-execution.

41 MKO/MEK, a France-based organization, was listed as a terrorist organization by the U.S. State Department. However, it is quite active in lobbying in Washington, DC, against the Iranian state.

42 See Michael Petrelis, 2006, "Iran: Stop Killing Gays and Kids!" Petrelis Files (blog), June 26, 2008, accessed July 31, 2017, http://mpetrelis.blogspot.com/2006/06/iran-stop-killing-gays-apparently.html.

43 There were several conversations among Iranian queers in email lists and blogs about the complexity of this case and the geopolitical deployments of it. But the news reports featured only those who repeated the civilization narratives that fit the U.S. imperialistic agenda.

44 As I argued in chapter 1, Radio Farda and Voice of America Persian hire young, recent immigrants (some of whom are bloggers) in order to appeal to youths in Iran. Unlike the older cold war propaganda strategies, these programs do not send explicit political messages. Instead, they focus on pop culture, music videos, and other cultural productions that appeal to youths in order to represent a lifestyle that is characterized by "tolerance," freedom, and democracy in the United States. Ironically, these programs do not allow for any critique of American democracy. In fact, a member of the popular diasporic band Abjeez (Sisters) was fired by Voice of America after they produced a video called "Demokracy." In this video, Abjeez brilliantly exposed the hypocrisy of exporting democracy to the Middle East by showing images of war in Iraq. See the video here: https://www.youtube.com/watch?v=xC-q3hour14. See a report about the firing of a band member here: http://www.washingtonpost.com/wp-dyn/content/article/2011/03/01/AR2011030105451.html, accessed July 31, 2017.

45 This conference was held February 17–18, 1996, in New York City.

46 *Homan* nos. 10–11: 25. My translation. The word the organizers used is *kooni*, a derogatory term that literally translates to "of ass" or "one who likes ass."

47 *Homan* 16, 1999.

48 Elsewhere, I have argued that the exilic imaginations of Iranianness exclude queers by heterosexualizing the national culture (Shakhsari 2002).
49 See https://www.radiozamaneh.com/168999, accessed July 12, 2018.
50 See https://en.radiozamaneh.com/articles/out-of-iran-irans-unwanted-sons-and-daughters, accessed July 12, 2018.
51 See https://iranian.com/2007/05/28/staying-alive, accessed July 13, 2018.
52 For a promotional video of this film, see www.youtube.com/watch?v=wF_WOnSndgQ&feature=related.
53 Five years later, Haerinejad's 2013 film addresses Sayeh/Atrian's death, but with no reference to her hardship in Canada.
54 See this report for an example of the coverage of Sayeh's suicide: https://www.thestar.com/life/2010/11/19/refugees_sad_life_came_to_a_lonely_end.html, accessed July 12, 2018.
55 The film won the Melbourne Queer Film Festival Audience Choice Award for Best Documentary. The codirector's blog at the address www.baabakye.com is no longer active. See the film blog at http://iknowthatiam.blogspot.com, accessed July 13, 2018.

Chapter 5: The War Machine, Neoliberal *Homo Œconomicus*, and the Experts

1 In 2008 Omid left Canada for the United States and founded Iran & Its Future.org, a U.S.-based nonprofit organization that advocates for the "improvement of life in Iran." See https://www.linkedin.com/company/iran-&-its-future-org, accessed August 2, 2017.
2 As I have discussed in previous chapters, the particularities of politics and economic trends in Iran make any modular analyses futile and irrelevant. Scholars such as Aihwa Ong and Lisa Rofel have demonstrated that a universal or singular analysis of neoliberalism may fail to account for the particularities of neoliberalism in the "global South." However, it is important to acknowledge forms of economic domination, forms of cultural imperialism, and hegemonic forms of selfhood and nationhood that neoliberalisms espouse, even as they are rearticulated in the "global South."
3 See *Blogging Heroes: Interviews with 30 of the World's Top Bloggers* (Banks 2007); *ProBlogger: Secrets for Blogging Your Way to a Six-Figure Income* (Garrett and Rowse 2008); and *Start Your Own Blogging Business* (McDougall 2006).
4 Kowsar told me that his blog contained a counter that was invisible to his readers. He refused to tell me about the service he uses, explaining that he did not want other Iranian bloggers to take advantage of it.
5 Many of the bloggers in this documentary have since been hired by the Dutch, American, and British–funded media to produce and direct programs and reports about Iran.
6 His charges included insulting the sacred (*toheen beh moghaddasaat*) and publishing lies (*nashr-e akaazeeb*). Fortunately for him, Kowsar was protected by the Iranian press law that held the chief editor (and not the cartoonist) responsible for what was published in the paper. Knowing that he was protected, he refused to accept the charges.

However, Saeed Mortazavi, the former prosecutor general of Tehran, ordered his arrest: "I was arrested [and imprisoned] for six days, during which time I was sure nothing bad would happen to me . . . and it did not. I was more worried about them putting me in a car and beating me up when I was not in prison" (interview with Kowsar, February 27, 2006). I asked if Kowsar's connection to prominent statesmen was also the reason for him not to be summoned to the court for three years after his six-day imprisonment. He told me that the reason was a coincidence of sorts: "Zahra Kazemi's death and also the seventh parliament elections put a stop on the process." Kazemi was an Iranian journalist who lived in Canada and was arrested while taking photographs of the 2003 student protests in Tehran. She was brutally killed during the interrogations. Although President Khatami ordered an investigation and condemned her murder, the Canadian government issued a statement holding the Iranian state responsible for the death of a Canadian citizen.

7   Worried that receiving a monetary award would jeopardize his safety in Iran, he had asked the organizers for a plaque rather than money: "I told them that I did not want any monetary awards, because I did not want to be accused of receiving foreign money" (interview with Kowsar, February 27, 2006). Because his father-in-law was his cosigner when he left Iran, Kowsar told me, he did not stay in Canada in 2001.

8   There were five Toronto bloggers who were interviewed in *Blogger's War*, four of whom I interviewed.

9   Kowsar, a friend of Haerinejad, told me that he was supposed to get paid by the CBC for the animation work he did for the film: "I put in eighty hours of work and only got paid for twenty. I needed the money since I had stopped working in the dry cleaners" (Kowsar interview, February 27, 2006).

10 *Blogger's War* won the Bronze Plaque at the Christopher Columbus International Film and Video Festival Ohio. Shortly after making the film, Haerinejad was promoted by the CBC. In 2008, when Mehdi Jami, Zamaneh's first chief editor and director, was fired by the radio's Dutch managers, Haerinejad was hired on a six-month contract. Because of his films, Haerinejad, who, as he has admitted himself, had known very little about queer and transgender issues before he went to Iran for an assignment for the CBC, has been acting as an "expert" on Iranian queer issues in major international gay and lesbian organizations. The sentimentalization in Haerinejad's films borders on jeopardizing his films' subjects. For example, after his film *Out in Iran: Inside Iran's Secret Gay World* was aired in 2007, an Iranian gay man who claimed that Haerinejad filmed and outed him sued him, CBS, and the producer. See https://www.alaraby.co.uk/english/society/2016/8/25/gay-iranian-refugee-sues-over-being-outed-in-documentary, accessed June 29, 2017.

11 Interview, September 20, 2005.

12 Kowsar's wife and daughter have since moved to Toronto.

13 In the documentary, Kowsar tears up as he talks about leaving his daughter behind. The narrator tells him, in a patronizing tone, that Kowsar is safe in Canada. This moment in the film highlights tension between his vulnerability and his performances of hypermasculinity.

14 Mohsen Sazegara, a senior fellow at the Washington Institute, was the founder of the Revolutionary Guard Corps in Iran. After being disillusioned by the reform movement, he left Iran and launched a referendum to change the constitution. During the 2009 elections he posted YouTube videos about Gene Sharp's "nonviolent resistance" methods that had been used in the post-Soviet states in the form of velvet revolution.

15 *Estekhareh* is a practice in which Muslims open the Qur'an to a random page and decide (based on the interpretation of the text on that page) what course of action to take.

16 Press release posted on the Communication Initiative site, November, 7, 2006, accessed August 2, 2017, http://www.comminit.com/en/node/133950/2754.

17 According to Zamaneh's website, "The organization is supported by the Netherlands Ministry of Foreign Affairs, Free Press Unlimited, the European Commission, the Canadian Ministry of Foreign Affairs and many others. Radio Zamaneh is supervised by a board consisting of prominent members active in Dutch media, politics and business."

18 See Radio Zamaneh on Press Now's website: http://www.pressnow.nl/asp/programmes_new_details.asp?NewsID=63&ProgramID=4&offset=10, accessed August 2, 2017.

19 Although the Dutch Parliament had already planned, and received budget approval for, a Netherlands-based Persian television program to broadcast to Iran, the Parliament was not able to spend the money for a couple of years. Iraj Gorgin, the director of Iranian National Television during the Pahlavi era, was supposed to receive the funds to start a satellite television network. However, Gorgin did not reach an agreement with the board of directors of Press Now and withdrew from the project in March 2006. By summer of 2006, Parliament had a limited time to distribute the money. I was told by another blogger that because of trade agreements between Iran and the Netherlands, the funds to start a network were put on hold. However, the Dutch government–funded organizations conducted training in Iran for journalists.

20 Zamaneh wages were based on employees' age, which put a lot of young journalists who had recently migrated from Iran at a disadvantage compared to older staff such as Jami, Ebrahim Nabavi (a satirist who worked for the Ministry of Culture and Islamic Guidance and the Ministry of Interior before leaving Iran for Europe), and Nikahang Kowsar.

21 See http://www.roozonline.com/english/news3/newsitem/article/revelations-against-dutch-projects.html, accessed August 2, 2017. Rooz domain has been taken down and is not archived. For the controversy over Rooz, see the Wikipedia entry on Roozonline: https://en.wikipedia.org/wiki/Roozonline#cite_note-6, accessed April 24, 2019.

22 Phone interview, October 10, 2009.

23 Jami believed that the board retained and promoted his wife because they did not want to be accused of discrimination for firing her because of her association with Jami.

24 At the time of my interview with Jami in 2009, he was working as a consultant on a television network called Shoma (You). An acronym for "shabakeh-ye melli-ye Iran" (National Iranian Network), Shoma, he told me, would be funded exclusively by Iranian sources.

25 A critique of the internet presented in the packet was Cass Sunstein's warning of the risk of the "daily me syndrome," which entails the individual's walling off from the opinions they choose to avoid. This critique was repudiated in the briefing material by the Pew Internet and American Life Project's report in 2004, which claims that "wired" Americans

were more aware of "all kinds of arguments" during that year's campaign season. Disillusionment, government censorship, and surveillance were the other negative aspects of the internet mentioned in the conference packet. For the conference briefing material, see http://cyber.law.harvard.edu/is2k4/briefings.

26 See Iraq The Model (blog), http://iraqthemodel.blogspot.com, accessed August 2, 2017.

27 I discuss the Arabic Blogging Tool in the introduction. For information about the Spirit of America, see http://www.spiritofamerica.net/site, accessed August 2, 2017.

28 Omar and Mohammad went only by these first names (which may or may not have been pseudonyms) because of security concerns. Indeed, they were not mentioned on the conference brochure at all. The panel was presented as "Hoder et al." "Miliblogger" (military blogger) was not mentioned on the schedule either. The two Iraqi brothers had met with George Bush shortly before this conference. See Jeff Jarvis's post, "The Bloggers in the Oval Office," about their visit to the White House: http://www.buzzmachine.com/archives/2004_12_11.html#008654, accessed August 2, 2017.

29 Hoder, "How to Build a Blogosphere," conference presentation, December 11, 2004.

30 Citizenship panel, December 10, 2004.

31 Global Voices, question and answer period, December 10, 2004.

32 Editor Myself, August 4, 2004. Hoder erased his blog after being imprisoned in Iran. His new postprison release blog (with the same name) has a different address: http://hoder.ir/en, accessed August 2, 2017.

33 Interview, October 18, 2006.

34 When I emailed Hoder and asked him about his change of position, which had come as a sudden surprise to many, he replied that he had read Edward Said and Antonio Negri and had become aware of postcolonial studies.

35 I left a comment on Hoder's blog, critiquing his treatment of Sherkat. He wrote a post in which he defended his position in a defensive manner and expressed that Sherkat does not represent Iranian women.

36 For accounts of Iranian women's political participation, see Afary (1996), Kar (1996), Kian (1997), Mir-Hosseini (1996), Paidar (1995), and Tabari and Yeganeh (1982).

37 See "Boodjeh Amrika beh che martaakezi dadeh mishavad?" [To Which Centers Does the U.S. Funding Go?], accessed August 2, 2017, http://www.emadbaghi.com/archives/000897.php.

38 For more information on Hoder's arrest, see https://freehoder.wordpress.com/, accessed April 11, 2019.

39 The petition was later closed upon the request of Hoder's family.

40 The letter was translated into English by Niki Akhavan. See Akhavan's blog: http://benevis-dige.blogspot.com/.

41 For the text of this letter in Persian, see https://hosseinderakhshan.wordpress.com/muslimblogs/, accessed April 13, 2019.

42 See Paul D. Shinkman, "Obama: 'Global War on Terror' Is Over," *U.S. News & World Report*, accessed March 23, 2015, https://www.usnews.com/news/articles/2013/05/23/obama-global-war-on-terror-is-over.

43 For a critique of Iranian "native informants," see Hamid Dabashi, *Iran: A People Interrupted* (2007).
44 See DFI's website at http://www.dfi-intl.com/. For information about Detica (now BAE Systems), see http://www.baesystems.com/en-uk/home, accessed August 1, 2017.
45 See http://www.saic.com/news/saicmag/2006-winter/intelligencesupport.html. Also see SAIC's website: http://www.saic.com/markets/federal-government/federal-contract-vehicles, accessed August 2, 2017.
46 See "Three Groups Have Contracts for Pro-U.S. Propaganda," *USA Today*, December 13, 2005, accessed August 2, 2017, http://www.usatoday.com/news/washington/2005-12-13-propaganda-inside-usat_x.htm.
47 Conversation with Mahboubeh, July 17, 2006.
48 For a discussion of neoliberalism see the introduction in this book.
49 Neoliberalism actively creates a market through privatization and reorganizes social life from social solidarity to security, which is not provided by the state (social security) but through private purchase. This privatization does not make governmentality any less effective, as the autonomous, free individual becomes the active citizen/entrepreneur who desires self-advancement and can be governed through their "freedom to choose" (Miller and Rose 1992).
50 While Miller and Rose take similar positions to Brown when discussing neoliberalism and the (Western) state, Brown acknowledges the imperialistic practices of the United States. Furthermore, Brown's analysis departs from an evolutionary logic of institutional capitalism, put forth by Miller and Rose, and engages with political mobilizations in the formation of political subjectivities.

Coda

1 See *Washington Post*, November 3, 2018, accessed November 13, 2018, https://www.washingtonpost.com/arts-entertainment/2018/11/03/i-will-stand-against-you-trump-iran-crisis-is-literally-unfolding-through-game-thrones-dialogue/?utm_term=.21333078d545.
2 See Sune Engel Rasmussen, "Iran Responds to Trump Tweet with Warning against Military Action," *Wall Street Journal*, July 23, 2018, accessed July 23, 2018, https://www.wsj.com/articles/iran-responds-to-trump-tweet-with-warning-against-military-action-1532362011.
3 See Melissa Etehad and Sarah Parvini, "Blasting Iran's Regime as 'Not Normal,' Pompeo Calls on Iranian Americans for Support in California Visit," *Los Angeles Times*, July 22, 2018, accessed July 23, 2018, http://www.latimes.com/politics/la-na-pompeo-iran-talk-20180722-story.html.
4 For example, see Tim Kaine's article in the *Atlantic*: https://www.theatlantic.com/ideas/archive/2018/07/dont-let-trump-go-to-war-with-iran/565082/, accessed July 17, 2018.

5 The new laws make green card holders deportable. See https://www.miamiherald.com/news/local/immigration/article214844345.html, accessed July 16, 2018.

6 See "Iran's Khamenei Attacks Trump's Nuclear Deal Decision," *Al Jazeera*, May 11, 2018, accessed July 17, 2018, https://www.aljazeera.com/news/2018/05/iran-khamenei-trump-hell-180509115237052.html.

7 See Trita Parsi, "These Are the Real Causes of the Iran Protests," January 4, 2018, accessed July 18, 2018, https://www.thenation.com/article/these-are-the-real-causes-of-the-iran-protests/; Asa Fitch and Jared Malsin, "Behind Iran's Protests: A Struggling Economy Despite Sanctions Relief," *Wall Street Journal*, January 4, 2018, accessed July 18, 2018, https://www.wsj.com/articles/irans-economy-struggles-despite-sanctions-relief-fueling-unrest-1515007698; "Iran's Khamenei Attacks Trump's Nuclear Deal Decision."

8 For Trump's tweet, see http://www.latimes.com/politics/la-pol-updates-everything-president-1514606272-htmlstory.html. For Netanyahu's speech in support of the Iranian protests, see https://www.dw.com/en/israelis-watch-closely-as-iran-protests/a-42026288, accessed July 18, 2018. Netanyahu used the World Cup to support the protests in June. See https://www.timesofisrael.com/netanyahu-hails-iranian-peoples-courage-in-anti-regime-protests, accessed July 18, 2018.

9 For information about MEK's removal from the U.S. terrorist list, see https://www.nytimes.com/2012/09/22/world/middleeast/iranian-opposition-group-mek-wins-removal-from-us-terrorist-list.html.

10 See "Foreign Intervention behind Iran Protests. CIA Instigated Street Violence?," 2018, Global Research, January 2, 2018, accessed July 18, 2018, https://www.globalresearch.ca/foreign-intervention-behind-iran-protests-cia-instigated-street-violence/5624661.

11 See "Iran Blocks Instagram, Telegram after Protests," *Al Jazeera*, December 31, 2017, accessed July 18, 2018, https://www.aljazeera.com/news/2017/12/iran-blocks-Instagram-telegram-protests-171231133323939.html.

12 See Nazanin Soroush and Kaveh Madani, "Every Breath You Take: The Environmental Consequences of Iran Sanctions," *Guardian*, November 21, 2014, accessed July 18, 2018, https://www.theguardian.com/world/iran-blog/2014/nov/21/iran-environmental-consequences-of-sanctions.

13 See Soroush and Madani, "Every Breath You Take: The Environmental Consequences of Iran Sanctions."

14 See Sadegh Niazi Esfyani, Morteza Seifi, Samira Nabavi, Masud Yunesian, Hassan Amini, "Long-Term Air Pollution Exposure and Breast Cancer," in *Environmental Health Perspectives, ISEE Conference Abstracts*, accessed April 24, 2019, https://ehp.niehs.nih.gov/doi/10.1289/isee.2013.P-1-05-20.

15 See Bell Trew, "Iran Arrests Dozens in Crackdown on 'Immoral' Instagram Models," July 17, 2018, accessed July 18, 2018, https://www.independent.co.uk/news/world/iran-arrests-Instagram-models-immoral-crackdown-a8451631.html.

16 See Amnesty International, Tweet, July 9, 2018, accessed July 14, 2018, https://Twitter.com/amnesty/status/1016311680882692097?lang=en.

17 Ghasemi says that she was arrested for three days because her family was in Canada and was not able to post bail immediately. Ma'edeh and Shadab were released after a day. Ghasemi, who lives in Canada and was visiting Iran, returned to Canada and reactivated her account. See https://www.youtube.com/watch?v=iXO1TAX0_XI, accessed July 18, 2018.

18 The episode on social media can be seen here: http://tv1.ir/portal/ProgSections/%D9%85%D8%B3%D8%AA%D9%86%D8%AF%20%D8%A8%DB%8C%D8%B1%D8%A7%D9%87%D9%87. The complete film that features the "confession" of the "Instagram girls" is no longer available on IRIB's site but was posted on YouTube and can be accessed here: https://www.aparat.com/v/Yoc8w/%D9%81%DB%8C%D9%84%D9%85_%DA%A9%D8%A7%D9%85%D9%84_%D8%A7%D8%B9%D8%AA%D8%B1%D8%A7%D9%81%D8%A7%D8%AA_%D9%85%D8%A7%D8%A6%D8%AF%D9%87_%D9%87%DA%98%D8%A8%D8%B1%DB%8C_%D9%88_%DA%86%D9%86%D8%AF_%D8%AA%D9%86_%D8%A7%D8%B2_%D8%B4%D8%A7%D8%AE, accessed November 24, 2018.

19 See http://tv1.ir/portal/ProgramSection/587, accessed July 18, 2018.

20 The videos of the women who are interrogated in this video are unrecognizable to the point that several reports confuse Hojabri and Ghasemi's confessions. For example, in her YouTube video, Ghasemi clarifies that it was her (and not Hojabri) who was crying as she confessed to having received money for putting her dance music on music videos.

21 Sadeghi is referring to the allegations of sexual assault against Sa'eed Toosi, the Qur'an reciter in the supreme leader's court (*Beyt-e rahbari*). See https://www.youtube.com/watch?v=kwrHvCUdwIs.

22 See Maryam Zohdi, "The Controversy over Ma'edeh Hojabri's Confession Ended with a Warning to IRIB," BBC *Persian*, June 26, 2018, accessed July 18, 2018, http://www.bbc.com/persian/iran-44859887.

23 See Jason Rezaian, "What the Arrest of an 18-Year-Old Instagram Star Says about Iran's Backward Leaders," *National Post*, July 16, 2018, https://nationalpost.com/news/world/what-the-arrest-of-an-18-year-old-Instagram-star-says-about-irans-backward-leaders.

24 An example of this narrative is Karim Sadjadpour's "The Ayatollah under the Bed(sheets)," an anecdotal character study–like article in *Foreign Policy* that seeks to understand the perverse mentality of the Iranian mullahs and the practicing Muslims who emulate them. Sadjadpour tells his readers that "for those in the West who seek to better understand what makes Tehran tick, the regime's curious fixation on sex cannot be ignored." See https://foreignpolicy.com/2012/04/23/the-ayatollah-under-the-bedsheets, accessed July 19, 2018.

25 See my response to Sadjadpour at http://www.jadaliyya.com/Details/25882/War-of-Position-and-War-of-Maneuver-Sexperts,-Sex-Pervs,-and-Sex-Revolutionaries, accessed July 19, 2018.

26 This is not to say that dance or sex do not have political significance or transgressive potential. On the contrary, sex is political, not least because of its centrality in the binaries

of freedom/oppression. As many scholars have pointed out, women (and increasingly queers) are markers of freedom or oppression within colonial discourses. Ironically, sexual freedom, a shared obsession of the conservative Iranian politicians and regime-change enthusiasts, is deployed to save the Iranian population either from the objectifying gaze of the "West" or the oppressive restrictions of the "Islamic regime."

27 See "U.S. Senator John McCain on Iran and Tribute to Neda Agha-Soltan," YouTube, June 22, 2009, accessed July 14, 2018, http://www.youtube.com/watch?v=biAlyEa6l9E.

28 See "Neda Agha Soltan's Fiancé, Caspian Makan, visits Israel," YouTube, August 8, 2010, accessed July 14, 2018, https://www.youtube.com/watch?v=5l8jNrd7SrQ.

29 See "Iran and the Twitter Revolution," June 25, 2009, accessed June 7, 2018, http://www.journalism.org/2009/06/25/iran-and-Twitter-revolution.

30 See "A Look at Twitter in Iran," *Sysomos* blog, accessed June 7, 2018, https://sysomos.com/2009/06/21/a-look-at-Twitter-in-iran.

31 See the "cyberwar" guide at https://boingboing.net/2009/06/16/cyberwar-guide-for-i.html, accessed June 7, 2018.

32 See Maximilian Forte, "America's Iranian Twitter Revolution," *Zero Anthropology* (blog), June 17, 2009, accessed June 7, 2018, https://zeroanthropology.net/2009/06/17/americas-iranian-Twitter-revolution.

33 See Mike Musgrove, "Twitter Is a Player in Iran's Drama," *Washington Post*, June 17, 2009, http://www.washingtonpost.com/wp-dyn/content/article/2009/06/16/AR2009061603391.html?noredirect=on; and Golnaz Esfandiari, "The Twitter Revolution," *Foreign Policy*, June 8, 2010, accessed June 7, 2018, http://foreignpolicy.com/2010/06/08/the-Twitter-devolution.

34 See *The Daily Dish*, "The Revolution Will Be Twittered," *Atlantic*, June 13, 2009, accessed June 7, 2018, https://www.theatlantic.com/daily-dish/archive/2009/06/the-revolution-will-be-Twittered/200478.

35 See Mark Pfeifel, "A Nobel Peace Prize for Twitter?," *Christian Science Monitor*, July 6, 2009, accessed June 7, 2018, https://www.csmonitor.com/Commentary/Opinion/2009/0706/p09s02-coop.html.

36 The cyber-enthusiasts of the early 1990s included scholars, journalists, and politicians who celebrated the new democratic "electronic frontier." If prior to the mid-nineties (before the popularization of the World Wide Web), enthusiastic studies of cyberspace focused on text-based internet communications and were mainly concerned with Multi User Domains (MUDs), user groups, and lists, the more recent studies have celebrated empowerment via new forms of computer-based communications enabled by the social media.

37 While Morozov discusses the failure of the Google Doctrine and the false assumptions about the liberalizing potentials of the internet, he is not necessarily critical of the imperialist liberalizing projects, but more concerned about the failure of these projects. Morozov attributed this failure to the U.S. politicians' transparency in funding the propaganda and social media trainings, and the use of social media by "authoritarian states" such as the Iranian state against the protesters.

38 After overthrowing the last Qajar king (Ahmad Shah) through a coup d'etat in 1921, Reza Shah consolidated power as the first shah of the Pahlavi dynasty. On August 19,

1953, the democratically elected prime minister, Mohammad Mossadegh, was captured in a CIA-backed coup. Muhammad Reza Shah (Reza Pahlavi's son) was reinstalled as the monarch. The 1979 Iranian revolution, which toppled Pahlavi's dictatorship, ended the monarchical rule in Iran.

39 I am thankful to Hae Seo Kim for their insightful comment about pessimism and cruel optimism in my Empire of Insecurity seminar at UMN. My use of pessimism here, while having some similarities to Afro-pessimism, particularly the literature that discusses resilience, renunciation, and dreaded life (Sexton 2009; Weheliye 2014), departs from it in that it doesn't limit the analysis of race and racism to the U.S. understandings of blackness. Rather than the wholesale rejection of biopolitics and bare life, and instead of finding the promise of liberation in the flesh, I am more interested in the kind of life that is cultivated in liberal democracy.

[References]

Abrahamian, Ervand. 1982. *Iran between Two Revolutions*. Princeton, NJ: Princeton University Press.

Abu-Lughod, Lila. 1991. "Writing against Culture." In *Recapturing Anthropology: Working in the Present*, edited by Richard G. Fox, 137-62. Santa Fe, NM: School of American Research Press.

Abu-Lughod, Lila. 2013. *Do Muslim Women Need Saving?* Cambridge, MA: Harvard University Press.

Adelkhah, Fariba. 2000. *Being Modern in Iran*. Translated by Jonathan Derrick. New York: Columbia University Press.

Adibi, Hossein. 2003. "How Iranians View Their Return Migration to Iran." In *Iran Encountering Globalization: Problems and Prospects*, edited by Ali Mohammadi, 199-211. London: Routledge Curzon.

Afary, Janet. 1996. *The Iranian Constitutional Revolution 1906-1911: Grassroots Democracy, Social Democracy, and the Origins of Feminism*. New York: Columbia University Press.

Afary, Janet. 2009. *Sexual Politics in Modern Iran*. Cambridge: Cambridge University Press.

Agamben, Giorgio. 1998. *Homo Sacer: Sovereign Power and Bare Life*. Stanford, CA: Stanford University Press.

Agamben, Giorgio. 2005. *State of Exception*. Translated by Kevin Attell. Chicago: University of Chicago Press.

Ahmadi, Nader. 2003. "Migration Challenges Views on Sexuality." *Ethnic and Racial Studies* 26 (4): 685-707.

Ahmed, Sara. 2004. *The Cultural Politics of Emotion*. New York: Routledge.

Akhavan, Niki. 2013. *Electronic Iran: The Cultural Politics of an Online Evolution*. New Brunswick, NJ: Rutgers University Press.

Akhavan, Niki, Golbarg Bashi, Mana Kia, and Sima Shakhsari. 2007. "A Genre in the Service of Empire: An Iranian Feminist Critique of Diasporic Memoirs." ZNet. http://www.zmag.org/znet/viewArticle/2141.

Alavi, Nasrin. 2004. "Freedom in Farsi Blogs." *Guardian*, December 20. http://www.guardian.co.uk/technology/2004/dec/20/iran.blogging.

Alavi, Nasrin. 2005. *We Are Iran: The Persian Blogs*. Brooklyn, NY: Soft Skull Press.

Alexander, Annie, and Miryam Aouragh. 2011. "The Egyptian Experience: Sense and Nonsense of the Internet Revolution." *International Journal of Communication* 5: 1344-58.

Alexander, Annie, and Miryam Aouragh. 2014. "Egypt's Unfinished Revolution: The Role of Media Revisited." *International Journal of Communication* 8: 890–915.

Althusser, Louis. 1971. "Ideology and Ideological State Apparatus (Notes toward an Investigation)." In *Lenin and Philosophy and Other Essays*, translated by Ben Brewster, 127-86. New York: Monthly Review Press.

Amar, Paul. 2013. *The Security Archipelago: Human-Security States, Sexuality Politics, and the End of Neoliberalism*. Durham, NC: Duke University Press.

Amini, Hassan, et al. 2013. "Long-Term Air Pollution Exposure and Breast Cancer." *Environmental Health Perspectives, ISEE Conference Abstracts*. Accessed April 24, 2019. https://ehp.niehs.nih.gov/doi/10.1289/isee.2013.P-1-05-20.

Amir-Ebrahimi, Masserat. 2004. "Performance in Everyday Life and the Rediscovery of the 'Self' in Iranian Weblogs." *Bad Jens: Iranian Feminist Newsletter*, September. http://www.badjens.com/rediscovery.html.

Amuzegar, Jahangir. 2000. "Iran's 'Virtual Democracy' at a Turning Point." *SAIS Review* 20 (2): 93-109.

Anderson, Benedict. 1983. *Imagined Communities: Reflections on the Origin and Spread of Nationalism*. London: Verso.

Ansari, Abdolmaboud. 1988. *Iranian Immigrants in the United States: A Case Study of Dual Marginality*. Millwood, NY: Associated Faculty Press.

Ansari, Abdolmaboud. 1992. *The Making of the Iranian Community in America*. New York: Pardis Press.

Ansari, Ali M. 2003a. "Continuous Regime Change from Within." *Washington Quarterly* 26 (4): 53-67.

Ansari, Ali M. 2003b. *Modern Iran since 1921: The Pahlavis and After*. London: Pearson.

Appadurai, Arjun. 1996. *Modernity at Large: Cultural Dimensions of Globalization*. Minneapolis: University of Minnesota Press.

Appadurai, Arjun. 2002. "Deep Democracy: Urban Governmentality and the Horizon of Politics." *Public Culture* 14 (1): 21-47.

Arjomand, Said Amir. 2002. "The Reform Movement and the Debate on Modernity and Tradition in Contemporary Iran." *International Journal of Middle East Studies* 34 (4): 719-31.

Askari, Hossein, John T. Cummings, and Mehmet Izbudak. 1977. "Iran's Migration of Skilled Labor to the United States." *Iranian Studies* 10 (1/2): 3–35.

Axel, Brian Keith. 2002. "The Diasporic Imaginary." *Public Culture* 14 (2): 411–28.

Babayan, Kathryn. 1998. "The 'Aqa'Id Al-Nisa': A Glimpse at Safavi Women in Local Isfahani Culture." In *Women in the Medieval Islamic World: Power, Patronage, and Piety*, edited by Gavin Hambly. The New Middle Ages, vol. 6. New York: St. Martin's Press.

Babayan, Kathryn. 2008. "'In Spirit We Are Each Other's Sorrow': Female Companionship in Seventeenth-Century Safavi Iran." In *Islamicate Sexualities: Translations across Temporal*

Geographies of Desire. Edited by Kathryn Babayan and Afsaneh Najmabadi. Harvard University and Radcliffe Institute for Advanced Study. Harvard Middle Eastern Monographs 39. Cambridge, MA: Center for Middle Eastern Studies, Harvard University Press.

Bacchetta, Paola, Tina Campt, Inderpal Grewal, Caren Kaplan, Minoo Moallem, and Jennifer Terry. 2003. "Transnational Feminist Practices against War." In *Terror, Counter-Terror: Women Speak Out*, edited by Ammu Joseph and Kalpana Sharma, 266-72. New Delhi: Kali for Women.

Badr, Hanan. 2018. "Social Movements and Social Media in a Post-revolutionary Political Culture: Constitutional Debates in Egypt." In *Digital Media and the Politics of Transformation in the Arab World and Asia*, edited by C. Richter, A. Antonakis, and C. Harders, 161-86. Studies in International, Transnational and Global Communications. Wiesbaden: Springer.

Banks, Michael. 2007. *Blogging Heroes: Interviews with 30 of the World's Top Bloggers*. Indianapolis: Wiley.

Bardhan, S., and R. Wood. 2015. "The Role of Culture in Civil Society Promotion in the Middle East: A Case Study Approach with Technology for Social Networking." *Digest of Middle East Studies* 24 (1): 111-38.

Barlow, John Perry. 1996. "A Declaration of the Independence of Cyberspace." http://w2.eff.org/Censorship/Internet_censorship_bills/barlow_0296.declaration.

Barnett, Clive. 2004. "Neither Poison nor Cure: Space, Scale, and Public Life in Media Theory." In *MediaSpace: Place, Scale, and Culture in a Media Age*, edited by Nick Couldry and Anna McCarthy, 58–74. London: Routledge.

Baudrillard, Jean. 1981. *Simulacres et Simulation*. Débats. Paris: Galilée.

Bauer, Janet L. 2000. "Desiring Place: Iranian 'Refugee' Women and the Cultural Politics of Self and Community in the Diaspora." *Comparative Studies of South Asia, Africa, and Middle East* 20 (1-2): 180-99.

Beauchamp, Toby. 2009. "Artful Concealment and Strategic Visibility: Transgender Bodies and U.S. State Surveillance after 9/11." *Surveillance and Society* 6 (4): 356–66. https://doi.org/10.24908/ss.v6i4.3267.

Bell, David. 2001. *An Introduction to Cyberculture*. New York: Routledge.

Benhabib, Seyla. 1990. "Models of Public Space: Hannah Arendt, the Liberal Tradition, and Jürgen Habermas." In *Habermas and the Public Sphere*, edited by Craig Calhoun, 73-98. Cambridge, MA: MIT Press.

Benhabib, Seyla. 1994. "Deliberative Rationality and Models of Democratic Legitimacy." *Constellations* 1 (1): 25-53.

Berlant, Lauren. 1997. *The Queen of America Goes to Washington City: Essays on Sex and Citizenship*. Durham, NC: Duke University Press.

Bernal, Victoria. 2004. "Eritrea Goes Global: Reflections on Nationalism in Transnational Era." *Cultural Anthropology* 19 (3): 3-25.

Bernal, Victoria. 2005a. "Digital Diaspora: Conflict, Community, and Celebrity in Virtual Eritrea." *Eritrean Studies Review* 4 (2): 185-209.

Bernal, Victoria. 2005b. "Eritrea On-Line: Diaspora, Cyberspace, and the Public Sphere." *American Ethnologist* 32 (4): 660-75.

Bhandar, Davina. 2004. "Renormalizing Citizenship and Life in Fortress North America." *Citizenship Studies* 8 (3): 261–78.

BiParva, Ebrahim. 1994. "Ethnic Organizations: Integration and Assimilation vs. Segregation and Cultural Preservation with Specific Reference to the Iranians in the Washington, D.C. Metropolitan Area." *Journal of Third World Studies* 11 (1): 369.

Boal, Ian, and Brook James, eds. 1995. *Resisting the Virtual Life: The Culture and Politics of Information*. San Francisco: City Lights.

Boellstorff, Tom. 2008. *Coming of Age in Second Life: An Anthropologist Explores the Virtually Human*. Princeton, NJ: Princeton University Press.

Bollinger, Alex. 2018. "Now Conspiracy Theorists Are Claiming the YouTube Shooter Was a Trans Woman." *LGBTQ Nation*, April 5, 2018. Accessed July 6, 2018. https://www.lgbtqnation.com/2018/04/now-conspiracy-theorists-claiming-youtube-shooter-trans-woman/.

Boroumand, L. 2007. "The Untold Story of the Fight for Human Rights." *Journal of Democracy* 18 (4): 64–79.

Bourdieu, Pierre, and Loïc Wacquant. 2001. "New Liberal Speak: Notes on the New Planetary Vulgate." *Radical Philosophy* 105 (January–February): 1–7.

Bozorgmehr, Mehdi. 1997. "Internal Ethnicity: Iranians in Los Angeles." *Sociological Perspectives* 40 (3): 387–408.

Bozorgmehr, Mehdi. 1998. "From Iranian Studies to the Study of Iranians in the United States." *Iranian Studies* 31 (1): 5–30.

Bozorgmehr, Mehdi, and Georges Sabbagh. 1987. "Are the Characteristics of Exiles Different from Immigrants? The Case of Iranians in Los Angeles." *Sociology and Social Research* 71: 77–84.

Bozorgmehr, Mehdi, and Georges Sabbagh. 1988. "High Status Immigrants: A Statistical Profile of Iranians in the United States." *Iranian Studies* 21: 5–36.

Bozorgmehr, Mehdi, and Georges Sabbagh. 1989. "Survey Research among Middle Eastern Immigrant Groups in the United States: Iranians in Los Angeles." *Middle East Studies Association Bulletin* 23 (1): 23–34. https://doi.org/10.1017/S0026318400021015.

Brah, Avtar. 1996. *Cartographies of Diaspora: Contesting Identities*. New York: Routledge.

Brown, Wendy. 2003. "Neo-liberalism and the End of Liberal Democracy." *Theory and Event* 7 (1). http://muse.jhu.edu/login?uri=/journals/theory_and_event/v007/7.1brown.html.

Brown, Wendy. 2005. *Edgework: Critical Essays in Knowledge and Politics*. Princeton, NJ: Princeton University Press.

Brown, Wendy. 2006. *Regulating Aversion: Tolerance in the Age of Identity and Empire*. Princeton, NJ: Princeton University Press.

Bruno, Giuliana. 2002. *Atlas of Emotion: Journeys in Art, Architecture, and Film*. London: Verso.

Buchanan, Ruth, and Sundhya Pahuja. 2004. "Legal Imperialism: *Empire*'s Invisible Hand?" In *Empire's New Clothes: Reading Hardt and Negri*, edited by Paul A. Passavant and Jodi Dean, 23-94. New York: Routledge.

Bull, Malcolm. 2004. "Smooth Polities." In *Empire's New Clothes: Reading Hardt and Negri*, edited by Paul A. Passavant and Jodi Dean. New York: Routledge.

Burchell, Graham, Colin Gordon, and Peter Miller, eds. 1991. *The Foucault Effect: Studies in Governmentality*. Chicago: University of Chicago Press.

Butler, Judith. 1990. *Gender Trouble: Feminism and Subversion of Identity*. New York: Routledge.

Butler, Judith. 1993. *Bodies That Matter: On the Discursive Limits of "Sex."* New York: Routledge.

Carr, Robert. 1994. "Crossing the First World/Third World Divides." In *Scattered Hegemonies*, ed. Inderpal Grewal and Caren Kaplan, 153-72. Minneapolis: University of Minnesota Press.

Carsten, Paul. 2012. "Barack Obama Condemns Iran for Creating 'Electronic Curtain,'" March 20, 2012, *The Telegraph*. https://www.telegraph.co.uk/news/worldnews/barackobama/9155783/Barack-Obama-condemns-Iran-for-creating-electronic-curtain.html.

Castel, Robert. 1991. "From Dangerousness to Risk." In *The Foucault Effect: Studies in Governmentality*, edited by Graham Burchell, Colin Gordon, and Peter Miller, 281-99. Chicago: University of Chicago Press.

Castells, Manuel. 2009. *Communication Power*. Oxford: Oxford University Press.

Castells, Manuel. 2015. *Networks of Outrage and Hope: Social Movements in the Internet Age*. 2nd ed. Cambridge: Polity Press.

Center for Constitutional Rights. 2009. "Restore. Protect. Expand: Stop Warrantless Wiretapping." Accessed July 31, 2017. https://ccrjustice.org/sites/default/files/assets/files/CCR_100days_Wiretapping.pdf.

Chaichian, Mohammad A. 1997. "First Generation Iranian Immigrants and the Question of Cultural Identity: The Case of Iowa." *International Migration Review* 31 (3): 612-27.

Clifford, James. 1997. *Routes, Travel and Translation in the Late Twentieth Century*. Cambridge, MA: Harvard University Press.

Cohen, Jean L., and Andrew Arato. 1992. *Civil Society and Political Theory*. Cambridge, MA: MIT Press.

Comaroff, Jean, and John L. Comaroff. 2000. "Millennial Capitalism: First Thoughts on a Second Coming." *Public Culture* 12 (2): 291-343.

The Committee on the Present Danger. 2007. "Committee on the Present Danger: About Us," October 9. Accessed July 31, 2017. https://web.archive.org/web/20071009234735/http:/www.committeeonthepresentdanger.org/AboutUs/tabid/363/Default.aspx.

The Committee on the Present Danger. 2007. "Committee on the Present Danger: Iran Update," October 21. Accessed July 31, 2017. https://web.archive.org/web/20071021153814/http://www.committeeonthepresentdanger.org/IranUpdate/tabid/668/Default.aspx.

Dabashi, Hamid. 2006. "Native Informers and the Making of the American Empire." *Al Ahram Weekly Online*. Special Issue 797, June 1-6. http://weekly.ahram.org.eg/2006/797/special.htm.

Dabashi, Hamid. 2007. *Iran: A People Interrupted*. New York: New Press.

The Daily Dish. 2009. "The Revolution Will Be Twittered." *The Atlantic*, June 13. Accessed June 7, 2018. https://www.theatlantic.com/daily-dish/archive/2009/06/the-revolution-will-be-twittered/200478/.

Dallalfar, Arlene. 1994. "Iranian Women as Immigrant Entrepreneurs." *Gender and Society* 8 (4): 541–61.

Dallalfar, Arlene. 1996. "The Iranian Ethnic Economy in Los Angeles: Gender and Entrepreneurship." In *Family and Gender among American Muslims: Issues Facing Middle Eastern Immigrants and Their Descendants*, edited by Barbara C. Aswad and Barbara Bilgé. Philadelphia: Temple University Press.

Dean, Jodi. 2001. "Cybersalons and Civil Society: Rethinking the Public Sphere in Transnational Technoculture." *Public Culture* 13 (2): 243–65.

Dean, Jodi. 2004. "The Networked Empire: Communicative Capitalism and the Hope for Polities." In *Empire's New Clothes: Reading Hardt and Negri*, edited by Paul A. Passavant and Jodi Dean, 267–90. New York: Routledge.

Dean, Jodi. 2005. "Communicative Capitalism: Circulation and the Foreclosure of Politics." *Cultural Politics: An International Journal* 1 (1): 51–74. https://doi.org/10.2752/174321905778054845.

Dean, Jodi. 2009. *Democracy and Other Neoliberal Fantasies: Communicative Capitalism and Left Politics*. Durham, NC: Duke University Press.

Delany, Samuel R. 1999. *Shorter Views: Queer Thoughts and the Politics of the Paraliterary*. Hanover, NH: University Press of New England.

Deleuze, Gilles. 1992. "Postscript on the Societies of Control." *October* 59: 3–7.

Deleuze, Gilles. 1995. *Negotiations, 1972–1990*. Translated by M. Joughin. New York: Columbia University Press.

Deleuze, Gilles. 2005. *Pure Immanence: Essays on A Life*. 2nd ed. New York: Urzone.

Deleuze, Gilles, and Félix Guattari. 1986. *Nomadology: The War Machine*. Translated by Brian Massumi. New York: Semiotext(e).

Deleuze, Gilles, and Félix Guattari. 1987. *A Thousand Plateaus: Capitalism and Schizophrenia*. Translated by Brian Massumi. Minneapolis: University of Minnesota Press.

Doostdar, Alireza. 2004. "The Vulgar Spirit of Blogging: On Language, Culture, and Power in Persian Weblogistan." *American Anthropologist* 106 (4): 651–62.

Drezner, Daniel W., and Henry Farrell. 2008. "The Power and Politics of Blogs." *Public Choice* 134 (1–2): 15–30.

Duggan, Lisa. 2003. *The Twilight of Equality? Neoliberalism, Cultural Politics, and the Attack on Democracy*. Boston: Beacon.

Dunn, Kevin. 2004. "Africa's Ambiguous Relation to Empire and *Empire*." In *Empire's New Clothes: Reading Hardt and Negri*, edited by Paul A. Passavant and Jodi Dean. New York: Routledge.

Duin, Steve. 2010. "Mana Neyestani Honored for Courage in Cartooning." Oregonlive.com. June 19. Accessed July 19, 2018. https://www.oregonlive.com/news/oregonian/steve_duin/2010/06/mana_neyestani_honored_for_cou.html.

Ehteshami, Anoushiravan. 1995. *The Politics of Economic Restructuring in Post-Khomeini Iran*. Durham, UK: Center for Middle Eastern and Islamic Studies, University of Durham.

Eichhorn, Kate. 2001. "Sites Unseen: Ethnographic Research in a Textual Community." *Qualitative Studies in Education* 14 (4): 565–78.

Electronic Civil Disobedience and Other Unpopular Ideas: Critical Art Ensemble. 1996. Autonomedia New Autonomy Series. Brooklyn, NY: Autonomedia.

The Electronic Disturbance: Critical Art Ensemble. 1994. Autonomedia New Autonomy Series. Brooklyn, NY: Autonomedia.

Erdbrink, Thomas. 2012. "Iran Sanctions Take Toll on Medical Imports." *New York Times*, November 2, sec. Middle East.

Escobar, Arturo. 1996. "Welcome to Cyberia: Notes on the Anthropology of Cyberculture." In *Cyberfutures: Culture and Politics on the Information Superhighway*, edited by Ziauddin Sardar and Jerome R. Ravetz, 111-37. New York: New York University Press.

Esfandiari, Golnaz. 2017. "No Woman Has Ever Run for Iranian President. Will Azam Taleghani Be the First?" RadioFreeEurope/RadioLiberty. April 19. Accessed July 6, 2017. https://www.rferl.org/a/iran-taleghani-woman-president-election/28439661.html.

Etehad, Melissa, and Sarah Parvini. 2018. "Blasting Iran's Regime as 'Not Normal,' Pompeo Calls on Iranian Americans for Support in California Visit." *Los Angeles Times*, July 22.

Etling, Bruce, and John Kelly. 2008. "Mapping Iran's Online Public: Politics and Culture in the Persian Blogosphere." Berkman Klein Center for Internet and Society at Harvard University. Berkman Center Research Publication no. 2008-01. April. http://cyber.law.harvard.edu/publications/2008/Mapping_Irans_Online_Public.

Ewald, François. 1991. "Insurance and Risk." In *The Foucault Effect: Studies in Governmentality*, edited by Graham Burchell, Colin Gordon, and Peter Miller, 197-210. Chicago: University of Chicago Press.

Fadaak, Talha H., and Ken Roberts. 2018. "Young Adults, New Media, Leisure and Change in Saudi Arabia." *World Leisure Journal* 60 (2): 127-39.

Fay, Michaela. 2007. "Mobile Subjects, Mobile Methods: Doing Virtual Ethnography in a Feminist Online Network." *Forum Qualitative Sozialforschung/Forum: Qualitative Social Research* 8 (3). https://doi.org/10.17169/fqs-8.3.278.

Feher, Shoshanah. 1998. "From the Rivers of Babylon to the Valleys of Los Angeles: The Exodus and Adaptation of Iranian Jews." In *Gatherings in Diaspora: Religious Communities and the New Immigration*, edited by R. Stephen Warner and Judith G. Wittner, 71-94. Philadelphia: Temple University Press.

Femia, Joseph. 2001. "Civil Society and the Marxist Tradition." In *Civil Society: History and Possibilities*, edited by Sudipta Kaviraj and Sunil Khilnani, 131-46. Cambridge: Cambridge University Press.

Ferguson, James. 2006a. *Global Shadows: Africa in the Neoliberal World Order*. Durham, NC: Duke University Press.

Ferguson, James. 2006b. "Transnational Topographies of Power: Beyond the State and Civil Society in the Study of African Politics." In *Accelerating Possession: Global Futures of Property and Personhood*, edited by Bill Maurer and Gabriele Schwab, 76-98. Critical Theory Institute Books. New York: Columbia University Press.

Ferguson, James, and Akhil Gupta. 1997. "Discipline and Practice: 'The Field' as Site, Method and Location in Anthropology." In *Anthropological Locations: Boundaries and Grounds of a Field Science*, edited by Ferguson and Gupta, 1-46. Berkeley: University of California Press.

Ferguson, James, and Akhil Gupta. 1999. "Introduction." In *Culture, Power, Place: Explorations in Critical Anthropology*, edited by Ferguson and Gupta. Durham, NC: Duke University Press.

Ferguson, James, and Akhil Gupta. 2002. "Spatializing States: Toward an Ethnography of Neo-liberal Governmentality." *American Ethnologist* 29 (4): 981–1002.

Fitch, Asa, and Jared Malsin. 2018. "Behind Iran's Protests: A Struggling Economy Despite Sanctions Relief." *Wall Street Journal*, January 4. Accessed July 18, 2018. https://www.wsj.com/articles/irans-economy-struggles-despite-sanctions-relief-fueling-unrest-1515007698.

Fontana, Benedetto, 2006. "Liberty and Domination: Civil Society in Gramsci." *boundary 2* 33 (2): 51–74.

Forte, Maximilian. 2009. "America's Iranian *Twitter* Revolution." *Zero Anthropology*. June 17. https://zeroanthropology.net/2009/06/17/americas-iranian-Twitter-revolution.

Fortier, Ann-Marie. 2000a. "Coming Home: Intersections of Queer Memories and Diasporic Spaces." Paper presented in the "Queer Theory" seminar series of the Institute of Women's Studies, Lancaster University. http://www.comp.lancs.ac.uk/sociology/soc062af.html.

Fortier, Ann-Marie. 2000b. *Migrant Belongings: Memory, Space, Identity*. Oxford: Berg.

Fortier, Anne-Marie. 2001. "'Coming Home': Queer Migrations and Multiple Evocations of Home." *European Journal of Cultural Studies* 4 (4): 405–24. https://doi.org/10.1177/136754940100400403.

Foucault, Michel. 1983. "The Subject and Power." In *Beyond Structuralism and Hermeneutics*, edited by Hubert L. Dreyfus and Paul Rabinow, 2nd ed. Chicago: University of Chicago Press.

Foucault, Michel. 1984. "What Is Enlightenment?" In *The Foucault Reader*, edited by Paul Rabinow, 32–50. New York: Pantheon Books.

Foucault, Michel. 1986. "Governmentality." *Ideology and Consciousness* 6 (summer): 5–21.

Foucault, Michel. 1988. "Technologies of the Self." In *Technologies of the Self: A Seminar with Michel Foucault*, edited by Luther H. Martin, Huck Gutman, and Patrick H. Hutton, 16–49. Amherst: University of Massachusetts Press.

Foucault, Michel. 1990. *The History of Sexuality: An Introduction, Vol. I*. Translated by Robert Hurley. New York: Vintage.

Foucault, Michel. 2003. *Society Must Be Defended: Lectures at the Collège de France 1975-1976*. Edited by Mauro Bertani and Alessandro Fontana. Translated by David Macey. New York: Picador.

Foucault, Michel. 2007. *Security, Territory, Population: Lectures at the Collège de France 1977-1978*. Edited by Michel Senellart. Translated by Graham Burchell. New York: Palgrave Macmillan.

Foucault, Michel. 2010. *The Birth of Biopolitics: Lectures at the Collège de France 1978-1979*. Edited by Michel Senellart. Translated by Graham Burchell. New York: Palgrave Macmillan.

Franklin, Seb. 2012. "Virality, Informatics, and Critique; or, Can There Be Such a Thing as Radical Computation?" WSQ: Women's Studies Quarterly 40 (1–2): 153–70. https://doi.org/10.1353/wsq.2012.0007.

Gajjala, Radhika. 2001. "Studying Feminist E-Spaces: Introducing Transnational/Postcolonial Concerns." In Technospaces: Inside the New Media, edited by Sally Munt, 113–26. London: Continuum International.

Gajjala, Radhika. 2002. "An Interrupted Postcolonial/Feminist Cyberethnography: Complicity and Resistance in the 'Cyberfield.'" Feminist Media Studies 2 (2): 177–93.

Garrett, Chris, and Darren Rowse. 2008. ProBlogger: Secrets for Blogging Your Way to a Six-Figure Income. Indianapolis: Wiley.

Gauntlett, David, and Ross Horsley, eds. 2004. Web.Studies, 2nd ed. London: Arnold Publications.

Gerbaudo, Paolo. 2012. Tweets and Streets: Social Media and Contemporary Activism. London: Pluto.

Ghaffarian, Shireen. 1987. "The Acculturation of Iranians in the United States." Journal of Psychology 127: 565–71.

Gilanshah, Farah. 1990. "The Formation of Iranian Community in the Twin Cities from 1983–1989." Wisconsin Sociologist 27 (4): 11–17.

Gilroy, Paul. 1993. The Black Atlantic: Modernity and Double Consciousness. Cambridge, MA: Harvard University Press.

Gilroy, Paul. 1997. "Diaspora and the Detours of Identity." In Identity and Difference, edited by Kathryn Woodward, 299–346. London: SAGE.

Gilroy, Paul. 1999. "Diaspora." In Migration, Diasporas and Transnationalism, edited by Steven Vertovec and Robin Cohen. Cheltenham, UK: Edward Elgar.

Gordon, Colin. 1991. "Governmental Rationality: An Introduction." In The Foucault Effect: Studies in Governmentality: With Two Lectures by and an Interview with Michel Foucault, edited by Graham Burchell, Colin Gordon, and Peter Miller. Chicago: University of Chicago Press.

Graham, Mark, and Shahram Khosravi. 2002. "Reordering Public and Private in Iranian Cyberspace: Identity, Politics, and Mobilization." Identities: Global Studies in Culture and Power 9 (2): 219–46.

Grewal, Inderpal. 2005. Transnational America: Feminisms, Diasporas, Neoliberalisms. Durham, NC: Duke University Press.

Grewal, Inderpal. 2017. Saving the Security State: Exceptional Citizens in Twenty-First-Century America. Durham, NC: Duke University Press.

Grewal, Inderpal, and Caren Kaplan. 1994. "Transnational Feminist Practices and Questions of Postmodernity." In Scattered Hegemonies: Postmodernity and Transnational Feminist Practices, edited by Grewal and Kaplan, 1–34. Minneapolis: University of Minnesota Press.

Grewal, Inderpal, and Caren Kaplan. 2001. "Global Identities: Theorizing Transnational Studies of Sexuality." GLQ 7 (4): 663–79.

Gupta, Akhil, and Arandhana Sharma, eds. 2006. *The Anthropology of the State*. Malden, MA: Blackwell.
Habermas, Jürgen. 1989. *The Structural Transformation of the Public Sphere: An Inquiry into a Category of Bourgeois Society*. Translated by Thomas Burger. Cambridge, MA: MIT Press.
Habermas, Jürgen. 1992. "Further Reflections on the Public Sphere." In *Habermas and the Public Sphere*, edited by Craig Calhoun, 421-61. Cambridge, MA: MIT Press.
Haeri, Shahla. 2002. *Mrs. President: Women and Political Leadership in Iran*. Film.
Haerinejad, Farid. 2005. *Blogger's War*. Canadian Broadcasting Company.
Haerinejad, Farid. 2007. *Out in Iran: Inside Iran's Secret Gay World*. Canadian Broadcasting Company.
Hale, Henry E. 2013. "Regime Change Cascades: What We Have Learned from the 1848 Revolutions to the 2011 Arab Uprisings." *Annual Review of Political Science* 16: 331-53.
Hamman, Robin B. 1996. "Rhizome@Internet. Using the Internet as an Example of Deleuze and Guattari's 'Rhizome.'" http://www.socio.demon.co.uk/rhizome.html.
Hanassab, Shideh. 1998. "Sexuality, Dating, and Double Standards: Young Iranian Immigrants in Los Angeles." *Iranian Studies* 31 (1): 65-76.
Hanassab, Shideh, and Romeria Tidwell. 1989. "Cross-Cultural Perspective on Dating Relationships of Young Iranian Women: A Pilot Study." *Counselling Psychology Quarterly* 2 (2): 113-21.
Hardt, Michael, and Antonio Negri. 2000. *Empire*. Cambridge, MA: Harvard University Press.
Hardt, Michael, and Antonio Negri. 2004. *Multitude: War and Democracy in the Age of Empire*. New York: Penguin Press.
Harvey, David. 1990. *The Condition of Postmodernity: An Enquiry into the Origins of Cultural Change*. Cambridge, MA: Blackwell.
Hassanpour, Amir. 2001. "Homeland and Hostland: Iranian Press in Canada." *International Institute for the Study of Islam in the Modern World (ISIM) Newsletter* 8. http://www.isim.nl/files/newsl_8.pdf.
Hendelman-Baavur, Liora. 2007. "Promises and Perils of Weblogistan: Online Personal Journals and the Islamic Republic of Iran." *Middle East Review of International Affairs* 11 (2). http://meria.idc.ac.il/journal/2007/issue2/jv11no2a6.html.
Hill, Kevin A., and John E. Hughes. 1998. *Cyberpolitics: Citizen Activism in the Age of the Internet*. Lanham, MD: Rowman and Littlefield.
Hindman, Matthew Scott. 2009. *The Myth of Digital Democracy*. Princeton, NJ: Princeton University Press.
Hine, Christine. 2000. *Virtual Ethnography*. London: SAGE.
Hivos. 2011. "United States Policy on Democratizing Iran: Effects and Consequences," January 26. Accessed April 6, 2019. https://www.hivos.nl/united-states-policy-on-democratizing-iran-effects-and-consequences/.
Hofheinz, Albrecht. 2008. "The Internet in the Arab World: Playground for Political Liberalization." *Uluslararası İlişkiler* 16 (4): 79-96. https://www.researchgate.net/publication/289256667_The_internet_in_the_Arab_World_Playground_for_political_liberalization.

Howard, Philip N., et al. 2011. "Opening Closed Regimes: What Was the Role of Social Media during the Arab Spring?" Working paper. Project on Information Technology and Political Islam. https://deepblue.lib.umich.edu/bitstream/handle/2027.42/117568/2011_Howard-Duffy-Freelon-Hussain-Mari-Mazaid_PITPI.pdf?sequence=1&isAllowed=y.

Howard, Philip N., and Muzammil M. Hussain. 2013. *Democracy's Fourth Wave? Digital Media and the Arab Spring*. Oxford: Oxford University Press.

International Monetary Fund. 2003. *Islamic Republic of Iran: 2003 Article IV Consultation—Staff Report; Staff Statement; Public Information Notice on the Executive Board Discussion; and Statement by the Executive Director for the Islamic Republic of Iran*. IMF Country Report no. 03/279. Washington, DC: IMF.

Iran Human Rights Documentation Center. 2009. "Ctrl+Alt+Delete: Iran's Response to the Internet." *IDHRC Report* (May). http://iranhrdc.org/httpdocs/English/pdfs/Reports/Ctr+Alt+Delete%20-%20Iran's%20Response%20to%20the%20Internet.pdf.

Iskander, Elizabeth. 2011. "Connecting the National and the Virtual: Can Facebook Activism Remain Relevant after Egypt's January 25 Uprising?" *International Journal of Communication* 5: 13–15.

Jahanbakhsh, Forough. 2001. *Islam, Democracy and Religious Modernism in Iran (1953-2000): From Bazargan to Soroush*. Boston: Brill.

Jarvis, Jeff. 2011. *Public Parts: How Sharing in the Digital Age Improves the Way We Work and Live*. New York: Simon and Schuster.

Kamali Dehghan, Saeed. 2018. "Tehran Hijab Protest: Iranian Police Arrest 29 Women." *The Guardian*, February 2. Accessed July 10, 2018. https://www.theguardian.com/world/2018/feb/02/tehran-hijab-protest-iranian-police-arrest-29-women.

Kamarack, Elaine Ciulla, and Joseph S. Nye, eds. 1999. *Democracy.com: Governance in a Networked World*. Hollis, NH: Hollis Publishing.

Kaplan, Caren. 1996. *Questions of Travel: Postmodern Discourses of Displacement*. Durham, NC: Duke University Press.

Kaplan, Caren. 2008. "'Everything Is Connected': Aerial Perspectives, the 'Revolution in Military Affairs,' and Digital Culture." Proceedings of the Electronic Techtonics: Thinking at the Interface Conference. HASTAC Lulu Press. http://www.hastac.org/informationyear/ET/BreakoutSessions/7/Kaplan.

Kaplan, Caren, Norma Alarcón, and Minoo Moallem. 1999. *Between Woman and Nation: Nationalisms, Transnational Feminisms, and the State*. Durham, NC: Duke University Press.

Kar, Mahranguiz. 1996. "Women on Their Way: A Report on the Presence of Women in the Election." *Zanan* 28 (in Persian).

Karatzogianni, Athina. 2016. "Beyond Hashtags: How a New Wave of Digital Activists Is Changing Society." *Conversation*. https://theconversation.com/beyond-hashtags-how-a-new-wave-of-digital-activists-is-changing-society-57502.

Karim, M. Persis, and Mohammad Mehdi Khorrami. 1999. *A World Between: Poems, Short Stories, and Essays by Iranian-Americans*. New York: George Braziller.

Kashani-Sabet, Firoozeh. 2000. *Frontier Fictions: Shaping the Iranian Nation, 1804-1946*. https://doi.org/10.1515/97814008650.

Kaviraj, Sudipta, and Sunil Khilnani, eds. 2001. *Civil Society: History and Possibilities.* Cambridge: Cambridge University Press.

Kendall, Lori. 1999. "Recontextualizing 'Cyberspace': Methodological Considerations for On-Line Research." In *Doing Internet Research: Critical Issues and Methods for Examining the Net*, edited by Steve Jones, 57–74. London: SAGE.

Kenny, Sean. 2006. "The Revolution Will Be Blogged." *Salon.* March 6. Accessed July 31, 2017. https://www.salon.com/2006/03/06/iranian_bloggers.

Khalili, Laleh. 2013. *Time in the Shadows: Confinement in Counterinsurgencies.* Stanford, CA: Stanford University Press.

Khiabany, Gholam, and Annabelle Sreberny. 2007. "The Politics of/in Blogging in Iran." *Comparative Studies of South Asia, Africa and the Middle East* 27 (3): 563–79.

Khilnani, Sunil. 2001. "The Development of Civil Society." In *Civil Society: History and Possibilities*, edited by Sudipta Kaviraj and Sunil Khilnani, 11–32. Cambridge: Cambridge University Press.

Khodamhosseini, Ali, and Ali Mostashari. 2004. "An Overview of Socio-economic Characteristics of the Iranian-American Community Based on the 2000 U.S. Census." Iranian Studies Group at MIT. http://www.isgmit.org/projects-storage/census/socioeconomic.pdf.

Kia, Mana, Afsaneh Najmabadi, and Sima Shakhsari. 2009. "Women, Gender, and Sexuality in Historiography of Modern Iran." In *Iran in the 20th Century: Historiography and Political Culture*, edited by Touraj Atabaki, 177–98. London: I. B. Tauris.

Kian, Azadeh. 1997. "Women and Politics in Post-Islamist Iran: The Gender Conscious Drive to Change." *British Journal of Middle Eastern Studies* 24 (1): 75–96.

Kian-Thiebaut, Azadeh. 2002. "Women and the Making of Civil Society in Post-Islamist Iran." In *Twenty Years of Islamic Revolution: Political and Social Transition in Iran since 1979*, edited by Eric Hooglund, 56–73. Syracuse, NY: Syracuse University Press.

Koebler, Jason, and Jillian York. 2018. "A Brief History of YouTube Censorship." *Motherboard* (blog). March 26. Accessed July 9, 2018. https://motherboard.vice.com/en_us/article/59jgka/a-brief-history-of-youtube-censorship.

Kolko, Beth E., Lisa Nakamura, and Gilbert B. Rodman, eds. 2000. *Race in Cyberspace.* New York: Routledge.

Kuntsman, Adi. 2004. "Cyberethnography as Home-Work." *Anthropology Matters* 6 (2). http://www.anthropologymatters.com/index.php?journal=anth_matters&page=article&op=view&path%5B%5D=97&path%5B%5D=191.

Kuntsman, Adi. 2009. *Figurations of Violence and Belonging: Queerness, Migranthood and Nationalism in Cyberspace and Beyond.* Bern: Peter Lang.

Laffey, Mark, and Jutta Weldes. 2004. "Representing the International: Sovereignty after Modernity?" In *Empire's New Clothes: Reading Hardt and Negri*, edited by Paul A. Passavant and Jodi Dean, 121–42. New York: Routledge.

Landow, George P., ed. 1994. *Hyper/Text/Theory.* Baltimore: Johns Hopkins University Press.

Landow, George P., ed. 1997. *Hypertext 2.0.* Rev. and amplified ed. Parallax. Baltimore: Johns Hopkins University Press.

Long, Scott. 2009. "Unbearable Witness: How Western Activists (Mis)recognize Sexuality in Iran." *Contemporary Politics* 15 (1): 119–36.

Lynch, Marc. 2007. "Blogging the New Arab Public." In *Arab Media and Society*, March 12. https://www.arabmediasociety.com/blogging-the-new-arab-public/#_ftn2.

Macintyre, Ben. 2005. "Mullahs versus the Bloggers." *The Times*, December 23. Accessed July 31, 2017. https://www.thetimes.co.uk/article/mullahs-versus-the-bloggers-k23nk7z7n0k.

Mahdi, Ali Akbar. 1998. "Ethnic Identity among Second-generation Iranians in the United States." *Iranian Studies* 31 (1): 77–95. https://doi.org/10.1080/00210869808701897.

Mahdi, Ali Akbar. 2002. "Perceptions of Gender Roles among Female Iranian Immigrants in the United States." In *Women, Religion and Culture in Iran*, edited by Sarah Ansari and Vanessa Martin, 185–210. London: Curzon Press.

Mahmood, Saba. 2001. "Feminist Theory, Embodiment, and the Docile Agent: Some Reflections on the Egyptian Islamic Revival." *Cultural Anthropology* 16 (2): 202–36.

Mahmood, Saba. 2005. *Politics of Piety: The Islamic Revival and the Feminist Subject*. Princeton, NJ: Princeton University Press.

Maljoo, Mohammad. 2006. "Worker Protest in the Age of Ahmadinejad." *Middle East Report* 241 (winter). http://www.merip.org/mer/mer241/maljoo.html.

Malkki, Liisa. 1997. "News and Culture: Transitory Phenomena and the Fieldwork Tradition." In *Anthropological Locations: Boundaries and Grounds of a Field Science*, edited by Akhil Gupta and James Ferguson, 86–101. Berkeley: University of California Press.

Margolis, Michael, and David Resnick. 2000. *Politics as Usual: The Cyberspace "Revolution."* Thousand Oaks, CA: SAGE.

Markham, Annette. 2004. "Reconsidering Self and Other: The Methods, Politics, and Ethics of Representation in Online Ethnography." In *Handbook of Qualitative Research*, edited by Norman K. Denzin and Yvonna S. Lincoln, 793–820. Thousand Oaks, CA: SAGE.

Martin, Biddy, and Chandra Mohanty. 1986. "Feminist Politics: What's Home Got to Do with It?" In *Feminist Studies/Critical Studies*, edited by Teresa De Lauretis, 191–212. Bloomington: Indiana University Press.

Martin, Emily. 1996. "Citadels, Rhizomes, and String Figures." In *Technoscience and Cyberculture: A Cultural Study*, edited by Stanley Aronowitz, Barbara R. Martinsons, and Michael Menser. New York: Routledge.

Massad, J. 2002. "Re-Orienting Desire: The Gay International and the Arab World." *Public Culture* 14 (2): 361–86. https://doi.org/10.1215/08992363-14-2-361.

Massad, Joseph. 2007. *Desiring Arabs*. Chicago: University of Chicago Press.

Mattelart, Armand. 2000. "The Mythology of Progress: Communication Breeds Democracy." Translated by Ed Emery. *Le Monde Diplomatique* (December).

Mbembe, Achille. 2003. "Necropolitics." Translated by Libby Meintjes. *Public Culture* 15 (1): 11–40.

McDougall, J. S. 2006. *Start Your Own Blogging Business*. Newburgh, NY: Entrepreneur Media.

McInerney, Stephen. 2012. "The Federal Budget and Appropriations for Fiscal Year 2013: Democracy, Governance, and Human Rights in the Middle East and North Africa." Washington, DC: Project on Middle East Democracy.

Milani, Abbas. 2005. "U.S. Foreign Policy and the Future of Democracy in Iran." *Washington Quarterly* 28 (3): 41–56. https://doi.org/10.1162/0163660054026533.

Miller, Daniel, and Don Slater. 2000. *The Internet: An Ethnographic Approach*. Oxford: Berg.

Miller, Peter, and Nicholas Rose. 1992. "Political Power beyond the State: Problematics of Government." *British Journal of Sociology* 43 (2): 172–205.

Mir-Hosseini, Ziba. 1996. "Women and Politics in Post-Khomeini Iran: Divorce, Veiling, and Emerging Feminist Voices." In *Women and Politics in the Third World*, edited by Haleh Afshar, 142–70. London: Routledge.

Moallem, Minoo. 1991. "Ethnic Entrepreneurship and Gender Relations among Iranians in Montreal, Quebec, Canada." In *Iranian Refugees and Exiles since Khomeini*, edited by Asghar Fathi, 180–204. Costa Mesa, CA: Mazda.

Moallem, Minoo. 1999. "Universalization of Particulars: The Civic Body and Gendered Citizenship in Iran." *Citizenship Studies* 3 (3): 319–35.

Moallem, Minoo. 2000. "'Foreignness' and Be/longing: Transnationalism and Immigrant Entrepreneurial Spaces." *Comparative Studies of South Asia, Africa, and Middle East* 20 (1-2): 200–216.

Moallem, Minoo. 2002. "Whose Fundamentalism?" *Meridian* 2 (2): 298–301.

Moallem, Minoo. 2005a. "Am I a Muslim Woman? Nationalist Reactions and Postcolonial Transactions." In *Shattering the Stereotypes: Muslim American Women Speak Out*, edited by Fawzia Afzal-Khan, 51–55. New York: Feminist Press.

Moallem, Minoo. 2005b. *Between Warrior Brother and Veiled Sister: Islamic Fundamentalism and the Politics of Patriarchy in Iran*. Berkeley: University of California Press.

Mobasher, Mohsen Mostafavi. 1996. "Class, Ethnicity, Gender, and the Ethnic Economy: The Case of Iranian Immigrants in Dallas." PhD diss., Southern Methodist University.

Modarres, Ali. 1998. "Settlement Patterns of Iranians in the United States." *Iranian Studies* 31 (1): 31–49. https://doi.org/10.1080/00210869808701894.

Mohammadi, Ali. 2003. "Iran and Modern Media in the Age of Globalization." In *Iran Encountering Globalization*, edited by Mohammadi, 24–45. New York: Routledge.

Momeni, Jamshid. 1984. "Size and distribution of Iranian ethnic group in the United States: 1980." *Iran Nameh* (2): 17–21.

Morgan, Jamie. 2003. "Words of Warning: Global Networks, Asian Local Resistance, and the Planetary Vulgate of Neoliberalism." *Positions: East Asia Cultures Critique* 11 (3): 541–54.

Morley, David. 2000. *Home Territories: Media, Mobility and Identity*. Comedia. London: Routledge.

Morley, David, and Kevin Robins. 1995. *Spaces of Identity: Global Media, Electronic Landscapes, and Cultural Boundaries*. New York: Routledge.

Morozov, Evgeny. 2012. *The Net Delusion: The Dark Side of Internet Freedom*. New York: Public Affairs.

Moslem, Mehdi. 2002. *Factional Politics in Post-Khomeini Iran*. Syracuse, NY: Syracuse University Press.

Mostashari, Ali, and Ali Khodamhosseini. 2004. "An Overview of Socioeconomic Characteristics of the Iranian-American Community Based on the 2000 U.S. Census."

Iranian Studies Group at MIT. http://www.isgmit.org/projects-storage/census/socioeconomic.pdf.

Mostofi, Nilou. 2003. "Who We Are: The Perplexity of Iranian-American Identity." *Sociological Quarterly* 44: 681–703.

Moulthrop, Stuart. 1995. "Rhizome and Resistance: Hypertext and the Dreams of a New Culture." In *Hyper/Text/Theory*, edited by George P. Landow, 299–320. Baltimore: Johns Hopkins University Press.

Moulthrop, Stuart. 1998. "Rhizome and Resistance: Hypertext and the Dreams of a New Culture." In *Contemporary Literary Criticism: Literary and Cultural Studies*, edited by Robert Con Davis and Ronald Schleifer, 4th ed. New York: Longman.

Murphy, Brian. 2004. "Iran's Blogging Boom Defies Media Control." *USA Today*, February 19.

Naber, Nadine. 2006. "The Rules of Forced Engagement: Race, Gender, and the Culture of Fear among Arab Immigrants in San Francisco Post-9/11." *Cultural Dynamics* 18, no. 3 (November).

Naficy, Hamid. 1991. "The Poetics and Practice of Iranian Nostalgia in Exile." *Diaspora* 1 (3): 285–302.

Naficy, Hamid. 1993. *The Making of Exile Cultures: Iranian Television in Los Angeles*. Minneapolis: University of Minnesota Press.

Naficy, Hamid. 1998. "Identity Politics and Iranian Exile Music Videos." *Iranian Studies* 31 (1): 51–64. https://doi.org/10.1080/00210869808701895.

Najmabadi, Afsaneh. 1991. "Hazards of Modernity and Morality: Women, State and Ideology in Contemporary Iran." In *Women, Islam and the State*, edited by Deniz Kandiyoti, 48–76. London: Palgrave Macmillan UK.

Najmabadi, Afsaneh. 1992. *Nigarish va Negārish-i Zan: Ma'ayeb-al-rijal*. White Bear Lake, MN: Midland.

Najmabadi, Afsaneh. 1993. "Veiled Discourse—Unveiled Bodies." *Feminist Studies* 19 (3): 487–518.

Najmabadi, Afsaneh. 1998. "Crafting an Educated Housewife in Iran." In *Remaking Women: Feminism and Modernity in the Middle East*, ed. Lila Abu-Lughod, 91–125. Princeton, NJ: Princeton University Press.

Najmabadi, Afsaneh. 2000. "(Un)Veiling Feminism." *Social Text* 18 (3): 29–45. https://doi.org/10.1215/01642472-18-3_64-29.

Najmabadi, Afsaneh. 2005. *Women with Mustaches and Men without Beards: Gender and Sexual Anxieties of Iranian Modernity*. Berkeley: University of California Press.

Najmabadi, Afsaneh. 2014. *Professing Selves: Transsexuality and Same-Sex Desire in Contemporary Iran*. Durham, NC: Duke University Press.

Nakamura, Lisa. 2000. "Race in/for Cyberspace: Identity Tourism and Racial Passing on the Internet." In *Cybercultures Reader*, ed. David Bell and Barbara M. Kennedy, 712–20. New York: Routledge.

Nasr, Vali. 2005. "The Conservative Wave Rolls On." *Journal of Democracy* 16 (4): 9–22.

Nast, Heidi. 2003. "Queer Racisms, Queer Patriarchies, International." *Antipode* 34: 939–74.

Nazeri, Haleh. 1996. "Imagined Cyber Communities, Iranians and the Internet." *MESA Bulletin* 30 (2): 158–64.

NIAC Staff. 2005. "Iranian People Are Our Allies, Pressure on Regime Needed, Experts Testify at House Hearing." *NIAC* (blog), February 18. Accessed July 31, 2017. https://www.niacouncil.org/iranian-people-are-our-allies-pressure-on-regime-needed-experts-testify-at-house-hearing/.

Nicholson, Brian, and Sundeep Sahay. 2003. "Building Iran's Software Industry: An Assessment of Plans and Prospects Using the Software Export Success Model." University of Manchester, Institute for Development Policy and Management. Accessed July 31, 2017. http://unpan1.un.org/intradoc/groups/public/documents/NISPAcee/UNPAN015616.pdf.

Nikou, Semira. 2017. "The Travel Ban and Iranian-Americans." *MERIP*, 2017. https://merip.org/2017/05/the-travel-ban-and-iranian-americans/.

NITLE Blog Census. http://www.blogcensus.net.

Norris, Pippa. 2001. *Digital Divide: Civic Engagement, Information Poverty, and the Internet Worldwide*. Cambridge: Cambridge University Press.

Omid, Ghazal. 2004. *Living in Hell: A True Odyssey of a Woman's Struggle in Islamic Iran against Personal and Political Forces*. Oklahoma City: Park Avenue.

Ong, Aihwa. 1999. *Flexible Citizenship: The Cultural Logics of Transnationality*. Durham, NC: Duke University Press.

Ong, Aihwa. 2003. *Buddha in Hiding: Refugees, Citizenship, and the New America*. Berkeley: University of California Press.

Ong, Aihwa. 2006. *Neoliberalism as Exception: Mutations in Citizenship and Sovereignty*. Durham, NC: Duke University Press.

Paidar, Parvin. 1995. *Women and the Political Process in Twentieth-Century Iran*. Cambridge: Cambridge University Press.

Palmer, Mark. 2005. *Breaking the Real Axis of Evil: How to Oust the World's Last Dictators by 2025*. Lanham, MD: Rowman and Littlefield.

Palumbo-Liu, D. 2002. "Multiculturalism Now: Civilization, National Identity, and Difference Before and After September 11th." *Boundary 2* 29 (2): 109–27. https://doi.org/10.1215/01903659-29-2-109.

Parsa, Sepideh. 2008. "Weblogistan Key to Democratization in Iran." October 20. Accessed July 31, 2017. http://archive.atlantic-community.org/app/index.php/Open_Think_Tank_Article/%22Weblogistan%22_Key_to_Democratization_in_Iran.

Parsi, Trita. 2018. "These Are the Real Causes of the Iran Protests," January 4. Accessed July 18, 2018. https://www.thenation.com/article/these-are-the-real-causes-of-the-iran-protests.

Passavant, Paul A., and Jodi Dean. 2004. "Representation and the Event." In *Empire's New Clothes: Reading Hardt and Negri*, edited by Passavant and Dean. New York: Routledge.

Patel, Geeta. 2006. "Risky Subjects: Insurance, Sexuality, and Capital." *Social Text* 24 (4): 25–65. https://doi.org/10.1215/01642472-2006-010.

Pateman, Carol. 1988. *Sexual Contract*. Stanford, CA: Stanford University Press.

Pervushyn, Mikhail. 2018. "Liberalization of the Internet and Regime Survival in the Middle East." https://www.researchgate.net/publication/324274278_LIBERALIZATION_OF_THE_INTERNET_AND_REGIME_SURVIVAL_IN_THE_MIDDLE_EAST.

Petrelis, Michael. 2006. "Iran: Stop Killing Gays & Kids!" *Petrelis Files* (blog). June 26. Accessed July 31, 2017. http://mpetrelis.blogspot.com/2006/06/iran-stop-killing-gays-apparently.html.

Pew Research Center, New Media Index. 2009. "Iran and the 'Twitter Revolution,'" June 15-19. http://www.journalism.org/2009/06/25/iran-and-Twitter-revolution.

Puar, Jasbir. 2007. *Terrorist Assemblages: Homonationalism in Queer Times*. Durham, NC: Duke University Press.

Puar, Jasbir K. 2017. *The Right to Maim: Debility, Capacity, Disability*. Durham, NC: Duke University Press.

Puar, Jasbir K., and Amit S. Rai. 2002. "Monster, Terrorist, Fag: The War on Terrorism and the Production of Docile Patriots." *Social Text* 20 (3): 117–48. https://doi.org/10.1215/01642472-20-3_72-117.

Rahimi, Babak. 2003. "Cyberdissent: The Internet in Revolutionary Iran." *Middle East Review of International Affairs* 7 (3). http://www.gloria-center.org/meria/2003/09/rahimi.html.

Rajaee, Bahram. 2004. "Deciphering Iran: The Political Evolution of the Islamic Republic and U.S. Foreign Policy after September 11." *Comparative Studies of South Asia, Africa and the Middle East* 24 (1): 159-72.

Rasmussen, Sune Engel. 2018. "Iran Responds to Trump Tweet with Warning against Military Action." *Wall Street Journal*, July 23. Accessed July 23, 2018. https://www.wsj.com/articles/iran-responds-to-trump-tweet-with-warning-against-military-action-1532362011.

Razack, Sherene. 1998. *Looking White People in the Eye: Gender, Race, and Culture in Courtrooms and Classrooms*. Toronto: University of Toronto Press.

Razack, Sherene. 1999. "Making Canada White: Law and the Policing of Bodies of Colour in the 1990s." *Canadian Journal of Law and Society* 14 (1): 159–84.

Rezaian, Jason. 2018. "What the Arrest of an 18-Year-Old Instagram Star Says about Iran's Backward Leaders." *National Post*, July 16. Accessed July 18, 2018. https://nationalpost.com/news/world/what-the-arrest-of-an-18-year-old-instagram-star-says-about-irans-backward-leaders.

Rofel, Lisa. 2007. *Desiring China: Experiments in Neoliberalism, Sexuality, and Public Culture*. Durham, NC: Duke University Press.

Rosenberg, Martin. 1994. "Physics and Hypertext: Liberation and Complicity in Art and Pedagogy." In *Hyper/Text/Theory*, edited by George P. Landow, 268–98. Baltimore: Johns Hopkins University Press.

Safran, William. 1991. "Diasporas in Modern Societies: Myths of Homeland and Return." *Diaspora* 1 (1): 83-99.

Salehi-Isfahani, Djavad. 2002. "Population, Human Capital, and Economic Growth in Iran." In *Human Capital: Population Economics in the Middle East*, edited by Ismail Sirageldin, 141-60. London: I. B. Tauris.

Salehi-Isfahani, Djavad. 2004. "Turning Wealth into Economic Growth: An Evaluation of Iran's Performance and Potential." Paper presented at the Conference on Politics, Society, and Economy in a Changing Iran at Hoover Institution.

Salehi-Isfahani, Djavad. 2010. "Iran's Contested Election: Populism and Youth Power." *Virginia Tech Research Magazine* (winter). http://www.research.vt.edu/resmag/2010winter/iran.html.

Sardar, Ziauddin. 1996. "alt.civilization.faq: Cyberspace as the Darker Side of the West." In *Cyberfutures: Culture and Politics on the Information Superhighway*, edited by Jerome Ravetz and Ziauddin Sardar, 14-41. New York: New York University Press.

Schiller, Dan. 1999. *Digital Capitalism: Networking the Global Market System*. Cambridge, MA: MIT Press.

Sexton, Jared. 2011. "The Social Life of Social Death: On Afro-Pessimism and Black Optimism." *InTensions* 5: n.p.

Shakhsari, Sima. 2002. "Diasporic Sexualities: Discursive Formation of Iranian Queer Subjects in Diaspora." MA thesis, San Francisco State University.

Shakhsari, Sima. 2005. "No War on Iran!: Insurance Brokers." *No War on Iran!* (blog). February 20. Accessed July 31, 2017. http://no-war-on-iran.blogspot.com/2005/02/insurance-brokers.html.

Shakhsari, Sima. 2012. "From Homoerotics of Exile to Homopolitics of Diaspora: Cyberspace, the War on Terror, and the Hypervisible Iranian Queer." *Journal of Middle East Women's Studies* 8 (3): 14–40. https://doi.org/10.2979/jmiddeastwomstud.8.3.14.

Shams, Alex. 2012. "The Shahs of Sunset . . . and the Rest of Us: 'Persian Money' in an Era of FBI Surveillance." Ajam Media Collective. February 9. Accessed July 17, 2018. https://ajammc.com/2012/02/08/the-shahs-of-sunset-and-the-rest-of-us-2/.

Shirky, Clay. 2011. "The Political Power of Social Media: Technology, the Public Sphere, and Political Change." *Political Affairs* 90 (1): 28–41.

Shohat, Ella, and Robert Stam. 1994. *Unthinking Eurocentrism: Multiculturalism and the Media*. London: Routledge.

Sohrabi, Naghmeh. 2006. "Conservatives, Neoconservatives and Reformists: Iran after the Election of Mahmud Ahmadinejad." Brandeis University Crown Center for Middle East Studies. *Middle East Brief* 4 (April).

Sokolski, Henry. 2005. "Getting Ready for a Nuclear-Ready Iran." NPEC, February 16. Accessed July 31, 2017. http://www.npolicy.org/article.php?aid=305&rtid=8.

Soroush, Nazanin, and Kaveh Madani. 2014. "Every Breath You Take: The Environmental Consequences of Iran Sanctions." *The Guardian*, November 21. Accessed July 18, 2018. https://www.theguardian.com/world/iran-blog/2014/nov/21/iran-environmental-consequences-of-sanctions.

Snyder, Ilana. 1997. *Hypertext: The Electronic Labyrinth*. New York: New York University Press.

Spivak, Gayatri C. 1988. "Can the Subaltern Speak?" In *Marxism and the Interpretation of Culture*, edited by Lawrence Grossberg and Cary Nelson, 271-316. Chicago: University of Illinois Press.

Spivak, Gayatri C. 1997. "Diasporas, Old and New: Women in the Transnational World." In *Class Issues, Pedagogy, Cultural Studies, and the Public Sphere*, edited by Amitava Kumar, 87–116. New York: New York University Press.

Spivak, Gayatri C. 2004. "Terror: A Speech after 9-11." *boundary 2* 31 (2): 81–111.

Sreberny, Annabelle. 2007. "Becoming Intellectual: The Blogestan and Public Political Space in the Islamic Republic." *British Journal of Middle Eastern Studies* 34 (3): 267–86.

Sullivan, Zohreh T. 2001. *Exiled Memories: Stories of Iranian Diaspora*. Philadelphia: Temple University Press.

Stoler, Ann L. 1995. *Race and the Education of Desire: Foucault's History of Sexuality and the Colonial Order of Things*. Durham, NC: Duke University Press.

Tabari, Azar, and Nahid Yeganeh, eds. 1982. *In the Shadow of Islam: The Women's Movement in Iran*. London: Zed.

Tavakoli-Targhi, Mohamad. 2001. *Refashioning Iran: Orientalism, Occidentalism, and Historiography*. New York: Palgrave Macmillan.

Taylor, Charles. 1990. "Modes of Civil Society." *Public Culture* 3 (1): 95–118.

Terry, Jennifer, and Raegan Kelly. 2007. "Killer Entertainments." *Vectors* 3 (1). http://www.vectorsjournal.org/index.php?page=7&projectId=86.

Terry, Jennifer. 2017. *Attachments to War: Biomedical Logics and Violence in Twenty-First-Century America*. Durham, NC: Duke University Press.

Thomsen, Jacqueline. 2018. "GOP Lawmaker Claims without Evidence That YouTube Shooter 'Could Be' an Illegal Immigrant." *The Hill*, April 3. Accessed July 6, 2018. https://thehill.com/homenews/house/381522-gop-lawmaker-baselessly-claims-that-youtube-shooter-could-be-an-illegal.

Tohidi, Nayereh. 1993. "Immigrant Iranians and Gender Relations in Los Angeles." In *Irangeles: Iranians in Los Angeles*, edited by Ron Kelley, Jonathan Friedlander, and Anita Y. Colby. Berkeley: University of California Press.

Tölölyan, Khachig. 1991. "The Nation-State and Its Others: In Lieu of a Preface." *Diaspora* 1 (1): 3–7.

Ulrich, Brian. 2009. "Historicizing Arab Blogs: Reflections on the Transmission of Ideas and Information in Middle Eastern History." *Arab Media and Society*, May 6. https://www.arabmediasociety.com/historicizing-arab-blogs-reflections-on-the-transmission-of-ideas-and-information-in-middle-eastern-history.

Ungar, Sanford J. 1995. *Fresh Blood: The New American Immigrants*. New York: Simon and Schuster.

Visweswaran, Kamala. 1997. *Fictions of Feminist Ethnography*. Minneapolis: University of Minnesota Press.

Warner, Michael. 1992. "The Mass Public and the Mass Subject." In *Habermas and the Public Sphere*, edited by Craig Calhoun, 377–401. Cambridge, MA: MIT Press.

Watney, Simon. 1995. "AIDS and the Politics of Queer Diaspora." In *Negotiating Lesbian and Gay Subjects*, edited by Monica Dorenkamp and Richard Henke, 53–70. New York: Routledge.

Weheliye, Alexander G. 2014. *Habeas Viscus: Racializing Assemblages, Biopolitics, and Black Feminist Theories of the Human*. Durham, NC: Duke University Press.

Weston, Kath. 1997. "The Virtual Anthropologist." In *Anthropological Locations: Boundaries and Grounds of a Field Science*, edited by Akhil Gupta and James Ferguson, 163-84. Berkeley: University of California Press.

Wheeler, Wendy. 1994. "Nostalgia Isn't Nasty: The Postmodernising of Parliamentary Democracy." In *Altered States: Postmodernism, Politics, Culture*, edited by Mark Perryman, 94-107. London: Lawrence and Wishart in association with Signs of the Times.

Wilson, Samuel M., and Leighton C. Peterson. 2002. "The Anthropology of Online Communities." *Annual Review of Anthropology* 31 (1): 449-67.

Wynter, Sylvia. 1989. "Beyond the World of Man: Glissant and the New Discourse of the Antilles." *World Literature Today* 63 (4): 637-48.

Yaghmaian, Behzad. 2002. *Social Change in Iran: An Eyewitness Account of Dissent, Defiance, and New Movements for Rights*. New York: State University of New York Press.

Zubaida, Sami. 2001. "Civil Society, Community, and Democracy in the Middle East." In *Civil Society: History and Possibilities*, edited by Sudpita Kaviraj and Sunil Khilnani, 232-49. Cambridge: Cambridge University Press.

[Index]

Abtahi, Mohammad Ali, xxi, 43, 59, 83
activism, 1, 13, 20, 29, 39, 48, 73, 78–79, 81, 85–87, 97, 99, 105, 108, 169, 185, 188, 193, 200, 203; cyber-activism, 38–39; and women's rights, 1, 39, 78, 87–91, 169, 187
Adelkhah, Fariba, 78–79, 117
affect, 1–2, 16, 19, 24, 57, 65, 71, 143–44
Agamben, Giorgio, 21–22, 167
Agha Soltan, Neda, 18, 111, 139, 201–3
Aghdam, Nasim Najafi, 136–44
Ahmadinejad, Mahmoud, 43, 63, 74, 79–81, 92, 94–96, 153–54, 163, 186
Ahmed, Sara, 12, 71
Alinejad, Massoumeh (Masih), 108–9, 198–99
Amar, Paul, 28–29, 109–10
America (desire for), 52–54, 66–67, 70–71, 166, 193
Anti-Arab sentiments, 12, 24–25, 60–62, 65–66, 69–71
Arabian Gulf, 58–60. *See also* Persian Gulf
Arab Spring, 138
arrests, 31, 106–8, 199; blogger arrests, 173, 183; cartoonist/journalist arrests, 62–63, 188–89; Instagram arrests, 198–203; women's rights activists arrests, 106–9
Aryan past, 65–66, 70, 197
Azadi Stadium, 79–80, 82, 85, 87–88

Babayan, Kathryn, 122
Balatarin (blog tool), 40, 202
biopolitics, 2, 12, 20–22, 26–28, 69, 71, 91, 113, 136, 165–67, 192. *See also* necropolitics
bisexual, 150
blogs, 1, 24–25, 40–43, 52, 80–83, 85, 88, 92–101, 104–5, 113–16, 118–19, 122, 124–27, 131–35, 138, 146, 148–49, 151, 153–54, 157, 159, 165, 170–77, 181–89, 202; *Blogger's War*, 163, 172–76, 181; blogging revolution, 7, 25; diaspora bloggers, 42, 45, 59, 92, 155, 170, 177; Iranian bloggers, 2–6, 12, 29–31, 33–43, 45–49, 51–61, 63–66, 97–98, 104–5, 113–20, 122–26, 128–38, 145–51, 153, 159, 163, 170–78, 181, 183–86, 188–90, 192–94; Persian-language (Farsi) blogging, 1, 4–5, 7, 13–14, 16, 23, 29, 32–34, 43, 45–47, 54–56, 63, 65, 93, 115, 116, 118–21, 127–28, 128, 131–34, 137–39, 159, 170–71, 173, 181–84, 189, 191; Persian-speaking bloggers, 4, 7, 29, 32–33, 45–47, 54–55, 119, 137–38, 191; sexist language in blogs, 35, 109, 118, 132, 148–49; women bloggers, 37, 42, 79, 81–82, 84, 92, 100–101, 105, 125–26, 133–35, 149, 175. *See also* Weblogistan
borders, 54–55, 64–65, 155, 190
Butler, Judith, 55, 89, 151

Castel, Robert, 14, 16–17
censorship, 23, 35–38, 132, 134, 137–39, 144
chic of queer, 30, 145, 153, 155
citizenship, 11, 13, 30, 78–79, 85, 89, 91, 99, 101, 131–32, 152, 182, 189–90; digital citizenship, 7–8, 12, 23, 28, 65, 103, 113–14, 135, 142; exceptional citizenship, 2, 8, 11–12, 16, 29–30, 70–71, 129, 134–35, 142; gendered citizenship, 30, 79, 85, 89, 104, 124; risky citizenship, 12–13, 70, 135–44
civilization, discourses of, 7, 21, 66–67, 93, 109–10, 141, 155, 157, 162–63, 167, 173, 196
civilizational thinking, 66–67
Committee on the Present Danger (CPD), 13–17, 214
conflict, 8, 41, 57, 73, 79, 98–99, 101–2, 104–5, 192–93
consensus, 29, 76–77, 79, 96, 99, 101, 104
consumerism, 19, 49, 52–53, 70
contagion, 12, 29, 143
cosmopolitanism, of Iranians, 33, 49, 68–70, 114, 165, 176, 181, 185, 201
counter-public, 99–100, 102, 105
cyber civil society, 8, 12, 19, 28, 101, 104, 111, 150, 196, 200; cyber-citizen, 12
cyber-enthusiasm, 10, 24, 26–28, 38, 53, 92, 102, 108, 110, 119, 170–71, 175, 181–84, 201, 203
cybergovernmentality, 8, 11, 29, 113
cyberspace, 1–2, 7, 19, 23–24, 29, 32–33, 38–39, 55, 60, 65, 99–102, 109, 147, 155–57, 162, 199–200
Cyrus Cylinder, 68–70

danger (discourse), 13–16, 23, 63, 71, 110, 118, 128–29, 137, 143, 151–52, 166, 173, 186, 199
Dean, Jodi, 27, 101–3, 219
Delany, Samuel, 130
Deleuze, Gilles, 2, 26, 39, 191–92, 205
democracy (rhetoric of), 2–3, 5, 7–13, 15–16, 19–20, 22–31, 53, 55, 66, 74–75, 77–78, 101–3, 105, 113–14, 116–18, 124, 131, 135–36, 138, 148, 150–53, 155–56, 182, 186; democratization, 2, 5, 7–9, 11–14, 16, 22–25, 27–28, 30–31, 91, 111, 155, 162, 181, 201–2; practicing democracy, 11, 30, 75, 113–14, 118, 135
Derakhshan, Hossein (Hoder), 32, 181, 189, 207–8
desire, 2, 8, 12–13, 19–20, 27, 29–30, 52–53, 124, 194; desiring subjects, 8, 30, 52, 136, 153
de-territorialized, 58, 65
diaspora, 1, 4–5, 7, 11–13, 16, 28–29, 32–33, 35, 42, 44–45, 47, 49–51, 53, 55, 58–61, 65–66, 68, 70–74, 79, 85, 88, 92, 98–99, 104, 109, 127, 148, 152–58, 162–63, 165, 168, 170, 176–77, 180, 186, 190–92, 196–97; Canada, Iranians in, 32, 41, 45–48, 51, 54, 56, 61, 65, 90, 130–31, 153, 156, 164–65, 172–73, 175–76, 184, 199; diaspora Iranians, 5, 7, 13, 29, 32, 42, 44, 46–47, 51, 60–61, 66–68, 70–71, 79, 117, 143–46, 153–55, 157, 162–63, 170, 186, 192, 197–98; Los Angeles Iranians (see fieldwork: Los Angeles)
dictatorship, 52, 81, 139
digital citizenship, 2, 7–8, 23, 28, 65, 103, 113–15, 117–18, 134–36
discipline (discourse), 8, 10–11, 21–22, 30–31, 35, 64, 73, 76, 78, 103–4, 112–14, 117–18, 122–23, 126–27, 133–36, 138, 190, 199
disposability, 19, 22, 28, 194
dissident, 8, 13, 15–16, 31, 64, 78, 99, 105–6, 111, 154–55, 191, 195, 198
Dokouhaki, Parastoo, 84, 86–88
Dolatshahi, Sanam, 81, 125–26

Ebadi, Shirin, 186–87
Editor Myself (blog), 181–89
electronic curtain, 19, 38, 215
embodiment, 30, 144
empire, 8, 13, 26–27, 31, 38, 68, 113, 121, 189, 193
entrepreneurship, 7–8, 13, 28, 30–31, 39, 47, 113, 168, 170–71, 174, 177, 181, 189–90, 192–94
ethicopolitics, 12, 30, 71, 76, 91, 113–15, 117, 122, 133, 135–36, 141, 152, 164, 169, 188, 190, 199, 205

ethnic conflict, 62–64
ethnography, 23, 28
Eurocentrism, 91, 129
exceptional citizenship. *See* citizenship
exile, 48–51, 61, 73, 133, 155–56, 159, 161–62, 176
experts, 13–18, 190–91

Facebook, 7, 18, 25, 37, 40, 109, 203
Faghfoori, Geesoo, 84–86
family values, 117, 145, 199
FATA, 38, 199
feminism, 29, 37, 50, 67, 72, 81–84, 86–88, 90–93, 101, 112, 115, 125, 127–29, 132–33, 135, 142, 146–51, 174, 187
Ferguson, James, 9–11, 113
fieldwork, 18, 36, 39, 41–42, 45, 118, 133, 159, 164, 166, 169, 175, 178, 184–85, 191; Los Angeles, 45–48, 52; Toronto, general, 32, 41, 45–47, 55–58, 60, 72, 92, 97, 100, 116–18, 123, 125, 130, 133–34, 146, 156, 159, 163–64, 172, 174, 184–85; Toronto, North York neighborhood of, 55–56; Washington, DC, 49, 159–60, 169, 174, 176, 192–93
filtering, 35–37, 39, 101, 134–35, 137, 139–40
Flickr, 40, 130
Forghani, Azadeh, 106–8, 110
Fortier, Anne-Marie, 50, 55, 165
Foucault, Michel, 10, 13, 16, 18, 20–22, 26, 50, 73, 111–14, 132, 136, 166, 194
freedom (discourse), 2–5, 8–13, 16, 18–20, 23–25, 27, 30–31, 37, 51–53, 55, 62, 64, 74, 76–77, 82, 84, 86, 88, 92, 101–6, 108–9, 112–14, 116–18, 129, 133–37, 139–40, 144, 148, 150, 152, 156, 159, 161, 163, 165–66, 170–72, 174–76, 182–86, 188–90, 193–94, 198, 201, 203–5
Friends Feed (Ferfer), 40
fundamentalism, 75, 91, 127, 165, 187, 190
futurity, 7–8, 11, 30, 135, 144, 204

Ganji, Akbar, 75, 97–98, 155
gay, 37, 55, 62, 67, 127–29, 145–46, 151–66, 175, 202, 243–48, 265, 259, 272, 274–75

gender politics, 1–2, 7, 10–11, 29–31, 35, 41–43, 48–49, 51, 53, 55, 57–58, 62, 66, 72, 75, 77, 79, 81, 83, 85, 87–89, 91, 93, 95, 97, 99–101, 103–5, 109, 111–14, 116–19, 122–24, 126–28, 133–34, 136–37, 143, 145, 148, 163, 165–67, 173–76
geopolitics, 2, 13–14, 24, 28, 38, 53, 167, 172
global capitalism, 13, 17, 19, 27, 70, 153, 190
Google bombing, 58–60
Google Doctrine, 203
Google Reader (Goder), 40
governmentality, 8, 10–11, 17, 20, 23, 28, 39, 91, 103–5, 112–13, 136, 167, 190, 193
Green Movement, 7, 74, 109, 139, 180, 202–4
Grewal, Inderpal, 11, 28, 50, 53, 155
Gupta, Akhil, 10–11, 113

Habermas, Jürgen, 99, 101, 103
hacking, 26, 38–39
Haerinejad, Farid, 163–64, 172, 181
hamjinsbaaz/hamjinsbaazee, 151–53
hamjinsgara/hamjinsgaraayaan/hamjinsgaraayee, 145–55
Hardt, Michael, and Antonio Negri, 26–27
hashtags, 31, 199
Haystack (software), 38
hegemonic ideals, 12, 42, 49–50, 61, 65–66, 75, 103, 124, 126, 157, 167
heteronormativity, 8, 29–30, 55, 61–62, 69, 117–18, 122, 124, 128, 131, 134–36, 144, 147, 150, 152, 161, 163, 166, 171, 201
heterosexuality, 50, 116–17, 124, 127–28, 130, 151, 153, 161, 166, 175; heteropatriarchy, 131; heterosexualization, 62, 161; heterosocial, 122, 147
hijab, 72, 80, 108–9, 139
Hoder. *See* Derakhshan, Hossein
hojb o haya, 125–28, 130–32
homeland, politics, 7, 36, 45–47, 50–51, 55, 58–62, 73, 81, 89, 92, 147, 161–62, 171, 176
homoeroticism, 62, 152–53, 156, 161–62
homoerotics of exile, 156–62

homonationalism, 113, 129, 156, 164, 167
homonormative, 30, 69, 129, 201
homo œconomicus, 18, 30, 169–70, 173, 175, 177, 179, 181, 183, 185, 187, 189, 191, 193–94
homophobia, 30, 42, 57, 145–48, 150, 153, 155, 157, 159, 161–62, 164, 166–67
homopolitics of diaspora, 156, 162–63
homo politicus, 194
homo sacer, 23, 167
homosexuality, 13, 30, 57, 61–62, 116, 128–29, 131, 142, 145–47, 150–55, 157–59, 161–63
homosociality, 123, 147
hostage crisis, 66, 111
humor, 57, 119, 140, 163
hybridity, 27, 49–51
hypermasculinity, 166, 176, 196
hypervisibility, 4, 12–13, 105, 110–11, 145, 154, 157, 162, 164–67

immigration, 8, 28, 32, 42, 46, 49–54, 56–57, 66–70, 108, 117, 143–44, 159, 162, 190–92
imperialism, 29, 50, 53, 108, 170, 186–87, 193
individualism, 12, 35, 69, 76–78, 113–14, 136, 144, 162, 190, 194
influencers, 198
Instagram, 31, 136, 139, 197–201; Instagram girls, 199–200
international civil society, 13, 16, 20, 22–23, 28, 110–11, 190, 194
internet, 1–5, 7–11, 14, 16–19, 23–29, 31, 33, 35–39, 41, 43–45, 47–48, 52, 58–59, 65, 68, 71, 74–75, 78–79, 102, 154–58, 163, 172, 180–83, 185–86, 200–201; internet democracy, 2, 26, 28, 31, 186; internet freedom, 16, 18, 23, 25, 38, 201
Iran, 1–4, 7, 9, 11, 21, 24–25, 28–29, 32–51, 53, 55, 60–65, 67–70, 73–75, 77–80, 83–85, 92–93, 96–98, 108, 127–28, 132–33, 147, 152–59, 161–62, 195, 197–204; bloggers, Iranian, 1–2, 4, 7, 12, 14, 32–35, 38, 40, 42–43, 45, 51, 54–55, 57–59, 65, 94, 113, 133, 170, 172, 177, 183–84, 189; Iranian-American, 70; Iranian culture (discourse), 131–32, 146, 164; Iranian exile (discourse), 49–50, 161–62, 176; Iranian feminism, 86, 88, 90–92, 132, 187; Iranian intellectuals, 64, 75, 77, 119–21, 132, 135, 145, 150, 153–54; Iranian nationalism, 12, 55, 58, 60; Iranianness (representation), 7, 11–12, 29–30, 35, 47, 51, 55, 61–62, 64–66, 71, 86, 113–14, 116, 118, 124, 126–27, 131, 134–36, 142–43, 150–51, 162–63, 169; Iranian opposition groups, 45, 59, 72–73, 97, 104, 155, 158–59, 161, 163, 177, 179, 187, 202; Iranian Revolution, 9, 46–47, 66, 78, 104, 140, 157, 162, 202–4; Iranian state, 18, 36–38, 41, 43–44, 48, 51–53, 58–59, 63, 73–75, 83, 89, 91–93, 104–6, 108, 110, 135, 140, 162, 173, 177–78, 180, 185–89, 198–204; Iranian womanhood, 114, 122; Iranian women, 3–4, 30, 59, 61, 75, 79, 82–83, 85, 87, 89–91, 104–6, 108–11, 116, 122–23, 125, 134, 141, 143, 147, 169, 175, 186–87; Iranian women's movement, 9, 36, 74–75, 82, 86–88, 90–91, 106; Iranian youth, 52–53; un-Iranian, 62, 147, 152
Iran-Iraq war, 1, 7, 48, 104, 198
Iraq, 8, 24–25, 44, 67–68, 86, 162, 173, 182, 204
Islam, 60, 65, 67–68, 77–78, 91, 132; Islamic feminism, 90–91, 93, 148, 187; Islamic sexuality, 201; Islamic state, 48, 51, 56, 61, 63, 72–73, 77, 81, 88–89, 153, 161; Islamic terrorism, 15, 143, 202; Islamophobia, 2, 61, 67, 109, 143, 149, 202

jaame'e-ye madani, 29, 75–78
Jami, Mehdi, 118–32, 149, 178–81
javanmardi, 78, 115–17

Kamvari, Nazli, 90–92, 95, 101, 115–20, 122–28, 130–34, 136–38, 146, 149, 174–75
Karimi, Farah, 177, 180
Khaledian, Nasser, 61–62, 125–26, 147
Khamene'i, Seyyed Ali, 63, 97, 188
Khatami, Seyyed Mohammad, 9, 74–75, 77, 79–80, 83–84, 92, 97–98, 154, 176
Khilnani, Sunil, 10, 75–77

Khomeini, Ruhollah, 9, 140
Khorshid Khanoom (blog), 81–83
killing (discourse), 2, 5, 8, 18–19, 21–24, 28–29, 31, 39, 106, 111, 120, 136–37, 144, 160, 164–65, 167, 192, 194, 205; politics of rightful killing, 2, 5, 8, 18, 21–22, 29, 31, 39, 136, 165, 205
knowledge production, politics of, 10, 13, 53, 99–100, 113, 119, 158, 162, 192, 194
Kowsar, Nikahang, 60–61, 97–98, 125, 146–50, 170–74, 176–77
kulthum naneh, 118, 121–30

lesbian, 62, 66, 127–30, 133, 146–47, 156–58, 161, 163, 166
LGBTQ (representation), 62, 66, 127–30, 133, 142, 146–47, 156–58, 161, 163, 166
liberal democracy, 3, 9, 11–12, 15–16, 18, 20, 23, 69, 113, 181, 185–86
liberalism, 13, 17, 73, 153, 193–94
liberalizing regimes, 2, 9, 23–24, 29, 155, 181, 211
liberation, discourses of, 18–19, 24, 26, 28–29, 73, 85, 109–11, 157, 162, 167, 170, 173, 175, 182, 192, 201, 205
living dead, 22
loaned life, 22–23, 29, 138, 165, 205

market virility, 12, 29, 70, 142
masculinity, 2, 57, 115, 176, 210, 244, 247
Mbembe, Achille. *See* necropolitics
military, 1, 10–11, 19–21, 24, 26, 28, 41, 43, 65, 170, 174, 181–82, 186, 192, 196
misogyny, 64, 106, 149–50
Moallem, Minoo, 7, 47, 55, 60, 91, 104, 114, 121, 127, 132, 157, 162, 166, 190
modernity, 7, 30, 113–14, 120, 122–23, 126–27, 132, 135, 167
multiplicity, 26, 43, 49–50, 98
Muslim (representation), 15, 24, 56, 60, 66–70, 108, 110–11, 140–43, 166, 168, 189–91, 196
Muslim ban, 66–70, 108, 196

Najmabadi, Afsaneh, 58, 62, 64, 91, 114, 122, 132
Nasim Sabz. *See* Aghdam, Nasim Najafi
National Geographic, 57–59
nationalism, 2, 29–30, 42, 50–51, 54–55, 57–62, 64–66, 88–89, 113, 152, 163, 166
national security, 1, 17, 25, 28–30, 36, 38, 66–67, 105, 110, 187, 191, 197–98, 203–4
necropolitics, 2, 20–22, 28, 164–65, 167, 192. *See also* biopolitics
Negri, Antonio. *See* Hardt, Michael, and Antonio Negri
neocolonial, 5, 10, 24–25
neoconservative, 10, 15, 19, 63, 109, 174, 187, 191
neoliberalism (discourse), 2, 9, 12, 19, 30, 38–39, 43, 53, 67, 103, 105–6, 113–14, 152, 169–71, 175, 181, 190, 194, 201; neoliberal citizenship, 11; neoliberal economies, 10–11, 38, 41, 113, 167, 190; neoliberal entrepreneurship, 8, 30–31, 117, 162, 192; neoliberal governmentality, 23, 28, 103; neoliberal market, 16, 162, 171; neoliberal self-care, 136, 193
Netanyahu, Benjamin, 12, 109, 197
networks, 10–11, 26–27, 36, 43–44, 46, 78–79, 87, 98, 112, 154, 157, 163, 184, 197, 199
Neyestani, Mana, 62–64
nonviolence (rhetoric), 9, 16, 40, 74, 99
normalization, techniques of, 2, 8, 11–12, 18, 22, 24, 30, 35, 91, 113–14, 117–18, 128, 133, 135–36, 138, 141, 163–64, 166, 186, 199

Obama, Barack, 18–19, 67, 190, 198
occupation, military, 21, 24–25, 28, 86, 144, 204
offline (internet), 2, 5, 8, 11, 25, 29, 34–36, 41, 43, 54, 57–58, 100, 104–5, 113, 116, 118, 142, 150, 159, 196
Ong, Aihwa, 30, 190
online (internet), 3, 8, 11, 14, 19, 25, 27–29, 41–43, 54, 57–58, 67, 92, 96, 100–101, 104–5, 108, 113–14, 116, 118, 138, 150–51, 155, 158–59, 171, 177–78, 196, 199–200

opposition groups, 29, 45, 59, 63, 72–74, 86, 89, 92, 97, 104, 106, 108–10, 145, 154–55, 158–59, 161–63, 177, 179, 187–88, 197–98, 202
Orientalist, 12, 62, 71, 121, 132, 161, 201

Pahlavi, Mohammad Reza, 55, 60, 63, 85, 90, 106, 108, 197
Pahlavi, Reza Khan, 65, 211, 240
Palmer, Mark, 13, 15–17
Palumbo-Liu, David, 66
panopticism, 13
para-human, 29, 109–10, 144, 167
Parsi, Arsham, 156–59, 161–62
patriarchy, 122–23, 135, 155, 169, 179
performativity, 43, 55, 104, 131
Persian Gulf, 41–42, 58–59, 65
Persianization, 63, 65
pink-washing, 154
political participation, 7–8, 78, 81, 101–2, 110, 123, 169, 175–76, 187
political subjectivity, 27, 48, 163, 194
post-1989 Iran, 7–9, 44, 211, 231–32
postrevolutionary Iran, 8, 40, 44, 47, 52, 55–57, 73–75, 78–79, 85, 89, 104, 140, 153, 157, 185
prerevolutionary Iran, 52, 55–57, 115
presidential election, 2005 Iranian, 18, 29, 40–41, 43, 72–73, 79, 82, 84, 90, 92–94, 101, 104, 172, 174–75, 201
protests (in Iran), 16, 18, 26, 37–38, 65, 67, 74–75, 105–6, 108, 111, 159, 197–98, 201–2, 204
proxies, 36–37, 191–92
Puar, Jasbir, 2, 12, 22, 69–71, 122, 142, 144, 156, 164, 166–67
public spaces, 78–79, 85, 98, 101, 117, 127
public sphere, 78, 99–104, 117

queer, 8, 20, 30, 56, 120, 127–30, 142–48, 150–59, 161–68, 174–75; queer death, 30, 164–65; queer refugees, 156, 166; queers, Iranian, 30, 145, 154–57, 159, 161, 164–65, 168, 174; queer subjects, 56, 166

racism, 11, 18, 21, 23, 30, 51, 53–54, 62, 111, 142–43, 164, 166, 173; anti-Arab racism, 12, 24–25, 60–62, 65–66, 69–71; anti-Iranian racism, 12, 41, 46, 48, 66
radio, 31, 52, 148, 157
Radio Farda, 25, 37, 52, 177, 180
Radio Zamaneh, 137, 148–49, 164, 172, 177–79
Rafsanjani, Akbar Hashemi, 9, 44, 75, 78–81, 92–98, 133, 148
reformists, Iranian, 7, 9, 41, 43, 48, 52, 57, 73–81, 83–84, 86–88, 92–98, 154–55, 162, 172, 174–75, 178, 185, 204
representability, 108, 162, 165; hyper-representability, 110–11, 145, 154, 157, 162–67; un-representability, 13, 108, 145, 184
representation (discourse), 12, 19, 29–30, 41, 46, 48, 71, 98–99, 108, 113, 158, 174–75
re-territorializations, 26, 29, 32, 114, 124, 163
revolution, Iranian, 7–9, 44, 46–47, 60–61, 66, 90, 104, 140, 154, 157–58, 162, 204
revolution, sexual, 200–201
revolutions, Internet, 5, 7, 19, 24–26, 28, 201–2
risk, 15–18, 23, 110–11, 138
risky citizens, 12–13, 70, 167, 214n15
Rofel, Lisa, 52–53, 66, 152–53
Rooz Online (website), 177–78
roshanfekr, 77, 120, 147
Rouhani, Hassan, 195–97

sanctions, economic, 1, 12, 15, 18–23, 29, 31, 38–39, 44, 52, 66, 108, 110–11, 195–98, 201, 203–5
secularism (discourse), 41, 73, 75–77, 80, 87, 90–92, 105, 184, 187
security, rhetoric of, 1–2, 8, 10–11, 13, 16–17, 19–21, 23, 25, 28–30, 36–39, 54, 65–67, 76–77, 83, 88, 94, 105, 109–10, 113, 139, 167, 170–71, 185, 187–88, 190–92, 194, 197–99, 203–4
Seifi, Farnaz, 90
self-censorship, 35, 133–34
self-entrepreneurship, 8, 12, 31, 117, 162, 170–71, 190–92, 194

sexual freedom (discourse), 13, 62, 176, 201
sexuality (discourse), 41–43, 62, 66, 69, 92, 109, 116–18, 122, 126–29, 133, 137, 144–45, 148, 158, 163, 167, 175, 200–201
Sharp, Gene, 16, 40
Sibestaan (blog), 118–21
Sibil Tala (blog), 90, 115–16, 118, 121, 134
soccer, 55, 57, 80, 82–85
social capital, 117, 171, 174
social freedom, 9, 52, 75, 80–82, 94, 183
social networks, 8, 18, 25, 27–28, 31, 40, 47, 52, 83, 105, 109–10, 137, 140, 142, 163, 196–202, 204
Soroush, Abdolkareem, 75, 77, 198
sovereignty, 18, 20–23, 27, 50, 54, 64, 76, 112–13, 166
Spivak, Gayatri Chakravorty, 3, 143–44
subjectivity, 1, 7, 11, 21, 43, 48, 50, 55, 89, 102, 114, 156, 175
suicide, 136, 143–44, 164–65
surveillance, 1–2, 16–17, 23–24, 26, 35, 38–39, 63, 65, 102–3, 116, 135, 151, 185–86, 203
symbolic capital, 49, 70

Taleghani, Azam, 75, 82, 90
technologies of the self, 8, 30, 113–14, 166
technology, 4, 7, 11, 14–16, 24, 26–29, 39, 44, 47, 50–51, 65, 79, 99, 102, 120–22, 133, 135, 139, 155, 162, 182–83, 186, 191, 198, 203; communication technologies, 27, 44, 47, 162; technologies of digital citizenship, 114
Tehran, 64, 188, 202
Telegram (application), 136, 197
territorialization, 102, 135
Terror, Global War on, 1, 5, 7, 9, 11, 15, 21, 23, 28, 31, 53, 65–67, 113, 154–57, 161–62, 167, 170–71, 182, 190–92, 194, 203; terrorism, 13, 15–18, 22–23, 38, 69, 143, 202; terrorists, 12, 15, 17, 20, 23, 70–71, 111, 122, 140, 142–43, 166, 168
Toronto bloggers. *See* fieldwork: Toronto
transgender, 141–42, 154, 163–65, 167–68, 174; transphobia, 142, 164

transnational, 2, 7–11, 13, 20, 24, 26–29, 33, 41–44, 47, 49–50, 52–53, 55, 60, 75, 78–79, 91–92, 98–99, 104–5, 110, 112–14, 136, 154–55, 163, 189–90; transnational civil society, 8, 10–11, 47, 75, 79, 98, 105, 112, 136; transnational governmentality, 10–11, 113, 136; transnational nationalism, 55, 60; transnational networks, 10, 26–27, 112
Trump, Donald, 67–68, 70, 108–9, 143, 195–97
Twitter, 18, 37, 75, 108, 137, 141, 144, 195–96, 198, 200–203; Twitter Revolution, 7, 25, 31, 37–38, 201–4

utopianism, 26, 99, 101

vatan, 58–61
velvet revolution, 174
victimhood, discourses of, 15, 29–30, 61, 105, 108–10, 130, 143–44, 148, 162, 164–69, 175, 199–200
viral democracy, 24–26, 39
virality, 18, 24, 39, 111, 195–96, 198–99
violence, 12, 21, 24, 29, 66, 71, 73, 99, 101, 104, 137–39, 142
visas, 45, 48, 51, 54, 56, 111, 170, 178, 185, 196
visibility (representation), 40, 108, 164, 167
Voice of America (VOA), 16, 25, 52, 108, 159, 177–78, 192, 198
voting, 29, 40, 72–73, 80–82, 85–86, 92–98, 172, 175, 177, 181, 184, 186
vulgarity, 35, 57, 118–20, 122–25, 128–33, 135, 146, 149
vulnerability, 14, 29, 61–62, 101, 109–11, 134, 176

war machine, 26, 30–31, 39, 171–75, 191–93
war on terror. *See* Terror, Global War on
Weblogistan, 1–3, 5, 7–8, 10–11, 13–14, 18–19, 23, 25, 28–36, 39–43, 54–55, 60–61, 63, 65–66, 72, 74–75, 78–79, 93–101, 103–5, 112–21, 124–25, 129–38, 145–48, 150–51, 162–63, 170, 172, 174–77, 181, 184–85, 188, 191–92, 194–95, 200–201

Western modernity, 53, 62, 77, 113, 126, 132, 146–47, 179
women bloggers. *See* blogs: women bloggers
working-class, 19, 24, 38, 45, 51, 59, 87, 93–94, 109, 149, 158, 164, 173, 176–79, 182, 195, 198, 200

YouTube, 24, 40, 136–44, 154, 157, 164, 199, 201; YouTube shooter, 136, 141–43; YouTube users, 138–39, 143; YouTube videos, 24, 40, 154, 199

Zanan-e Iran (website), 83
Zan Nevesht (blog), 83

www.ingramcontent.com/pod-product-compliance
Lightning Source LLC
Chambersburg PA
CBHW051049230426
43666CB00012B/2619